STAR TURNS AND CAMEO APPEARANCES

BERNARD JACOBSON

STAR TURNS AND CAMEO APPEARANCES

MEMOIRS OF A LIFE AMONG MUSICIANS

UNIVERSITY OF ROCHESTER PRESS

First published 2015

University of Rochester Press
668 Mt. Hope Avenue, Rochester, NY 14620, USA
www.urpress.com
and Boydell & Brewer Limited
PO Box 9, Woodbridge, Suffolk IP12 3DF, UK
www.boydellandbrewer.com

ISBN-13: 978-1-58046-541-0

Library of Congress Cataloging-in-Publication Data

Jacobson, Bernard, author.
Star turns and cameo appearances : memoirs of a life among musicians / Bernard Jacobson.
pages cm
Includes index.
ISBN 978-1-58046-541-0 (hardcover : alkaline paper) 1. Jacobson, Bernard. 2. Music journalists—Biography. 3. Musicians—Anecdotes. I. Title.
ML423.J115A3 2015
780.92—dc23
[B]

2015024762

A catalogue record for this title is available from the British Library.

This publication is printed on acid-free paper.
Printed in the United States of America.

for Laura

CONTENTS

Preface ix
Acknowledgments xi

1 "Till Ready," to 1960 1

2 Inside the Record Industry, 1960–64 25

3 Freelance in London and New York, 1964–67 48

4 Chicago Years, 1967–73 78

5 Exchanging Criticizing for Supporting, 1973–76 124

6 The Pastoral Dream, 1976–79 139

7 Inside Music Publishing, 1979–84 146

8 Philadelphia, First Installment, 1984–91 178

9 Back to Holland, 1992–95 210

10 Philadelphia, Second Installment, 1996–2005 233

11 West Coast Years, 2005–14 247

12 Philadelphia, Yet Again, 2014–? 264

Afterword 267
Index 279

Photographs follow page 148.

PREFACE

"My memoirs? My memoirs . . . !" No one who has seen that delightful film *Kind Hearts and Coronets* will need to be told that to write such a volume is a dangerous indulgence. Danger aside, autobiography has always seemed to me an excessively self-absorbed field of activity. Every man, leaving the devoutly religious for the moment out of account, is the center of his own life, and by the same token is not the center of anyone else's. But when friends and acquaintances have urged me, as many have, to put together a memoir, they have done so not because I am so interesting, but because I have had the privilege and pleasure of knowing and working with an extraordinary collection of interesting other people. The stories emerging from those activities are in many cases so illuminating about the character of such people that I think it would be a pity if they were not to be widely disseminated. And so, after much thought, I have decided to write an "allobiography" instead of an autobiography—"allo" from the Greek "allos," meaning "other," instead of "auto" from the Greek "autos," meaning "self."

What follows is an account of the life I have been lucky enough to lead in and around the world of music. If it reads, Will Cuppy style, rather like "The Wit and Wisdom of Practically Everybody," that is because I have been the happy enjoyer of much wit and the recipient of much wisdom at the hands of many wonderful men and women, and I want to share that good fortune with you. My "Star Turns"—the people whose effect on my professional life has been most substantial and long-term—may be identified by the use of Small Capitals for the initial appearance of their names in the body of the book, and in the index. And if the word "I" is found rather frequently in my text, that is simply because my own part in all these proceedings constitutes the connective tissue necessary to hold all these diverse experiences together.

Blessed or cursed as I am with nearly total recall (unfortunately for my wife, who has to hear every one of my stories in exactly the same words every time I tell it), I can vouch for the fact that practically every conversation recounted in these pages is given in its original words, or as close to them as makes no substantial difference. And to preserve the flavor of many such conversations, I think it will be best to keep to their original language also, offering a translation in a footnote in cases where that seems necessary.

On a few occasions, I have found some phrases or sentences in one of my published reviews that I have here taken over wholesale, since they provide "eyewitness" (and, more to the point, "earwitness") details about a given performance or flesh out some more general point I want to make.

ACKNOWLEDGMENTS

Given the somewhat idiosyncratic nature of *Star Turns and Cameo Appearances*, any adequate list of acknowledgments would have to be virtually coterminous with the book itself. All of the persons featured in it have contributed in varying degrees to the development and rewards of my musical life, and to all my thanks are due. Perhaps I should also apologize to the many unmentioned others who have influenced me in a more personal way: they make no appearance in the book only because they do not fit into a context deliberately restricted to the professional sphere.

Singling some of the featured persons out to the exclusion of others would be inappropriate. The substantial exception I make is of Laura, my wife, without whose unstinting enthusiasm and encouragement this book would never have come into being.

Besides all those persons mentioned in the course of my narrative, another indispensable group has emerged since the University of Rochester Press first became interested in the project, back in spring 2013. Megan Milan, an editor at the British publisher Boydell & Brewer, had suggested I should send my proposal for the book to Sonia Kane, editorial director at Boydell's "sister press" in the United States. Responding positively to my submission, Sonia put me in touch with Ralph Locke, professor of musicology in the University of Rochester's Eastman School of Music.

This proved to be the crucial step. I find it hard to believe that Ralph and I have still never met, because for nearly two years he has filled the role of *fidus Achates* to me and to the project. By way of e-mails—often several in a single day—he has responded with the utmost sensitivity to my ideas, unerringly identifying any potential problems they contained, and frequently offering creative suggestions of his own. Without his part in this collaboration, the book could not have taken anything like its present form, and might well never have been completed at all.

More recently, Mark A. Radice, professor of music theory, history, and composition at Ithaca College, having read the burgeoning manuscript, generously offered to work with me on its further refinement. He too has spotted important omissions in some of the stories I have told, and given me many suggestions for improvements, most of which I have adopted with alacrity.

As we have come closer to actual publication, several other staff members at URP have joined the list of my collaborators, including Julia Cook, Tracey Engel, and managing editor Ryan Peterson. They have all, like Sonia and Ralph, been a pleasure to work with, and Emily Kilpatrick's skillful and sensitive copyediting has been like the best kind of surgical procedure: minimally invasive, and productive of immediate improvement.

I am deeply grateful to all of these talented people, and hope the result of their help and encouragement lives up to their hopes and expectations.

CHAPTER ONE

"TILL READY"

To 1960

I was about eleven years old, living in London, and my musical tastes, formed through constant listening to the BBC, were primitive to say the least. They mainly embraced regimental marches played by the Black Dyke Mills Band (associated with an industrial company in West Yorkshire), along with songs sung by a robust English bass named Norman Allin and vocal duets by the wife-and-husband team of Anne Ziegler and Webster Booth. Occasionally I would give ear-time to a "classical" selection like the overture to Offenbach's *Orpheus in the Underworld*—the one that ends with the famous cancan—which I first heard played by Sir Dan Godfrey and what was still called the Bournemouth Municipal Orchestra (today's Bournemouth Symphony).

Then I fell in love with the Trumpet Voluntary by Jeremiah Clarke, attributed at that time to Purcell. Years later, at a Manhattan School concert in New York, I heard the conductor Walter Susskind cut the Gordian knot of attribution by outlining the various theories and then summarizing his conclusion as "Purcell's Trumpet Voluntary, by Jeremiah Clarke." Anyway, back then in 1947, I had to find a record of it. I saved my pennies, went along to the HMV shop on Oxford Street, and bought a 78 that had the Voluntary on one side, played by a leading trumpeter of the day, Harry Mortimer, with an organist of equal fame and equally middlebrow style, Reginald Foort. I didn't even notice what was on the other side. Then one evening, after playing the Voluntary on the old wind-up gramophone in my bedroom, I turned the record over, and found something called the finale of the Trumpet Concerto in E-flat Major by Haydn, again played by Mortimer, but this time, mercifully, with an orchestra. I put it on the turntable, wound the machine up, inserted a brand-new steel needle—and the rest is history. This was the record that projected me headlong into my lifelong love-affair with music. Within about three weeks, by playing "side two" about five times every night before going to bed ("side one" remained thereafter unheard), I and my steel needles had completely worn out the Haydn recording. But to this day, whenever I hear that wonderful work, I am transported instantly back to the pristine enchantment that is as hard to forget as any legendary first kiss.

Two other important things followed. My parents took me to two orchestral concerts in the East London neighborhood we lived in. One was in Hackney Town Hall, the other in Hackney Empire. I think the London Philharmonic Orchestra was conducted at both by Basil Cameron. The piano soloists were Lance Dossor and Noel Mewton-Wood respectively. I was particularly impressed by the poetry and clarity of Mewton-Wood's playing. An Australian whose teachers had included Artur Schnabel, he was soon to be mourned as a tragic figure: blaming himself for the death of a friend, who, the critic John Amis told me, was his partner in a gay relationship, he committed suicide at the age of thirty-one. I fell instantly in love with the Tchaikovsky symphonies on the two programs, though I was a little confused about which was No. 4 and which was the *Pathétique*, tending to conflate the two of them in my mind at the time.

The first of these concerts also included my first brush with contemporary music, in the shape of a piece for strings by the Romanian-born Francis Chagrin. (Years later, when I got to know this modest and charming man, I told him of that encounter. He asked whether I had liked the piece; by then, we were on good enough terms, and I had admired enough of his other works, for me to tell him that I'd hated it.)

The other big event of this period was that I was accepted as a pupil at the City of London School. My parents would certainly never have been able to afford the normal fees, but I got in, as it were, through the back door: being what was known as a "direct grant" public school (the English "public," in this context, being the equivalent of the Amerian "private"), CLS received some financial contributions from local government, and in return accepted about a dozen nonpaying pupils a year, selected through the results of the government-administered eleven-plus exam. I was interviewed by the headmaster, F. R. Dale, who was a distinguished classical scholar. As incredible as it seems in retrospect, when he asked me what

I wanted to do in life, I think I said I wanted to be an aircraft designer. A later enthusiasm was for architecture: I took the *Architectural Review* every month for about a year, and spent all my spare time planning new towns, in which pursuit I was considerably ahead of my time: all the houses I designed were equipped with large-screen projection television sets—quite an imaginative idea back in the 1940s!—and with whole-house heating supplied by ducts from the living-room fireplace. But then, one day, the thought suddenly struck me, "My goodness, if I'm going to be an architect, I'm going to have to know about drains"—and that was another possible future abandoned.

My good fortune in attending CLS was a life-changer for me. The education I received there from 1947 to 1954 was, if somewhat overspecialized in separating humanities from science at too early an age, superlative in quality and nurturingly human in tone and feeling. Mathematics was never my strong suit, and one year, when we were taught by C. G. Nobbs, my scores came out twenty-ninth in a class of thirty boys. Yet, on my end of year report form, he wrote: "Has worked hard and improved greatly. He thinks, and I have enjoyed teaching him."

My only formal music study was confined to my first year, and it was the least satisfactory aspect of my lessons. At that time, Leslie Taylor taught music in a purely mathematical manner: for the weekly eight-bar harmony exercise, you simply noted the figures that defined the intervals between the various lines, and woe betide the unfortunate pupil who had allowed a parallel fifth or octave to infiltrate his texture. Then, however, Taylor was succeeded by John Wray, whose approach was far more humanistic, and focused strongly on actual performance.

There was now an orchestra, in which, having had a few lessons, I played the violin for a couple of terms. I was on the second desk of second violins—not an especially impressive achievement, since there were only two desks of second violins. I had taken some lessons at school from André Mangeot, who had formed and led several successful string quartets, and who was said to have taught Yehudi Menuhin briefly at a time when Menuhin's teacher, George Enescu, was ill. Unfortunately, at this late stage of his life Mangeot was not a helpful teacher. Slovenly though he seemed to be, slouching in a chair at lessons with a cigarette dangling precariously from slack lips, he was a martinet in enforcing unwavering physical rigidity on a pupil's wrist. As a result, within ten minutes of starting to play, I always found myself with a painfully stiff neck. So I never became a violinist. But, more importantly, I started on the road to a journalistic career by writing reviews of the orchestra's concerts in the school magazine.

Besides the orchestra, there was a very active choir, in which I sang for several years. I found this to be an ideal, painless way to learn to read music fluently: you start by listening to the singers next to you, and gradually become able to take your pitches straight from the score. The term after I left school, Dr. Wray insisted on my coming back to sing in Bach's Cantata no. 65 at the December concert, since, being emphatically a second bass, I was almost the only one of his present and recent choristers who could sing a bottom C. The baritone soloist in that performance was a student at the Guildhall School of Music, next door to our school. His name was John Shirley-Quirk, and we established friendly relations a few years later, when he had become a prominent figure in British musical life and we finally met face to face. His contribution to Colin Davis's first recording of Handel's *Messiah* in 1966 had a stylistic and technical authority that I was to write about with enthusiasm.

Apart from music, my most important teachers were Roy Bentham and Cecil Ellingham. Mr. Bentham taught me English when I was eleven and, crucially, instilled a sense of the value of making words rather than punctuation do the work of expression. We had to write an English essay for him each week; he marked each one out of twenty—and docked us one mark for each appearance of an exclamation mark in our texts. The assignment I remember best was to write our obituaries for the *Times*, an ingenious way of focusing our minds on what we wanted to do with our lives. When he handed our marked essays back, Mr. Bentham remarked that, in a class of about thirty boys, one other and I were the only two who had not become either "Sir" or "Lord" by the time of our predicted deaths. My own first sentence, while innocent of aristocratic aspirations, evinced a certain burgeoning flair for the melodramatic: "Mr. Bernard Jacobson, who died yesterday in a space-ship explosion at the age of forty-two, is a grievous loss to British astronautics."

The Reverend Cecil Ellingham, with whom I studied both English and classics a few years later, was an inspired and inspiring teacher. He used games between teams with titles like "The Boneheads" and "The Numbskulls" to dramatize points he wanted to teach, and invented wonderfully wacky sentences for us to translate into Latin or Greek, such as "I bought a very sharp knife to cut my beloved brother's throat with, did I not?" He stressed at all times the central importance of pleasure in our reaction to literature. When my fellow-student (and lifelong-friend) John Simpson confessed to having enjoyed reading some poems by Shelley, whose work Mr. Ellingham disliked, his response was, "Good heavens, don't apologize—the more things you can enjoy, the better off you are."

This was a healthy principle that I have never lost sight of. During one term, he told us that, since we'd already covered the syllabus sufficiently, he was going to spend a few weeks taking us to the National Gallery and teaching us how to look at pictures; the main principle he emphasized in this pursuit was to think about color and composition, rather than saying to ourselves, "Wow—those grapes look absolutely real!"

One of my activities at CLS was to start an Architecture Society. A number of my fellow-students and I enjoyed attending its meetings for a year or so, and I managed to bring in, as guest speakers, such distinguished architects as Sir Hugh Casson, who had been much involved in designing the site and buildings for the 1951 Festival of Britain on London's South Bank, celebrating the nation's creativity, and Maxwell Fry. When Mr. Ellingham discovered my enthusiasm for architecture, he asked me whether I knew a book about English parish churches by J. Charles Cox and Charles Bradley Ford. When I said I didn't, he said, "When's your birthday? I'd like to give it to you if I may—it's so rarely you encounter someone who's interested in something worthwhile, may as well encourage them." The next summer, taking my cues from the book, I spent a couple of weeks cycling around East Anglia photographing the most beautiful of that region's superb Gothic churches. When the next term began I presented Mr. Ellingham with a portfolio of the results.

Through the enterprise of Dennis Moore, a classics master who was also an excellent violinist, and of Dr. Wray, we were treated to visiting lecture-demonstrations by performers including the clarinetist Ronald Moore (Dennis's brother, and a member of the London Symphony Orchestra), the oboist Janet Craxton, and Bernard Shore, who had studied viola with Lionel Tertis and whose book *Sixteen Symphonies* is a highly informative account of rehearsing those works with sixteen different conductors when he was principal violist of the BBC Symphony Orchestra in the 1930s.

Besides school music, I also enjoyed a good deal of success in various forms of declamation and acting. The middle term of each year was devoted, under Mr. Ellingham's tutelage, to the study of a Shakespeare play, and the annual competition in recitations from the text was my reliable passport to a winning berth at prize-day. Mr. Dale had trained me up as a reader of Latin, and I won the London Schools Latin Reading Competition two years running. On the second occasion, Dale, as judge (no thought of recusing yourself in those days!), remarked: "When Jacobson started reading, I thought he wasn't reading very well—for him. But anyway he was better than anyone else." In the wake of that questionable success, I was invited to read one of Virgil's *Georgics* at a meeting of the Virgil Society in the Senate House of London University, in the presence of the Society's president, T. S. Eliot.

Mr. Dale's somewhat left-handed compliment was echoed at the second of the two school plays in which I appeared. Having one year played the Messenger in Sophocles's *Antigone*, I was cast as the Duke of Venice in the following year's production of Shakespeare's *Othello*. A day or so before the performance I developed a sore throat, which lowered my speaking voice by about half an octave—and when Mr. Clark, the excellent director of the plays, came backstage at intermission, he enthused to me, "Just the voice I was waiting for last year!"

Throughout my schooldays, there were also important influences outside school. My parents, Cecil and Paula Jacobson, were unfailingly supportive, though they had little direct help to offer in the musical field that was becoming central to my interests. The closest they came was to give me, as a thirteenth-birthday present, a delightful book by the London music critic Eric Blom entitled *A Musical Postbag*, to which I have had frequent recourse as a source of opinions and pithy quotations for more than sixty years.

I also owe them gratitude for indulging my apparent childhood aspiration to be a kind of pseudo-impresario. From 1949 on, long-playing records were becoming available in England in increasing numbers and variety. The first four I bought included Brahms's Fourth Symphony conducted by Toscanini, Vaughan Williams's *London* Symphony conducted by Adrian Boult, and Schubert's "Great" C Major Symphony conducted by Josef Krips. I was fortunate indeed to make my first acquaintance with the "Great" C Major in Krips's interpretation. I have since encountered several readings of the work—among others, those of Boult, Giulini, Muti, and more recently Franz Welser-Möst—that have paid more respect to its structural qualities, but for sheer *Gemütlichkeit* (and this is perhaps the most *gemütlich* of all symphonies) Krips, both on record and in the concert hall, surely took the cake, especially for the *Schwung* he brought to the scherzo. My fourth choice among those first LPs was prophetic of interests to come—Mozart's Piano Concerto no. 17 in G (K. 453), coupled with his Violin Concerto no. 4 (K. 218), and played by Ralph Kirkpatrick on a John Challis reproduction of a period instrument.

So, armed with these and others that soon joined them on our shelves, I set up what we grandly called "Jacobson Concerts": record recitals to which we invited as many family members and friends as could fit into our modest living room. We served coffee and sandwiches during the intermission, and handed out my program notes, neatly typed by my mother, which remain in my files as the earliest surviving examples of my musicological efforts. Nielsen and Prokofiev soon made appearances on our programs, which continued for a year or two, and I also had the effrontery to include a song of my own composition. Having woken up one morning with a complete setting of "Sabrina Fair," from Milton's *Comus*, in my head, I had written it down and then recorded it at a studio in London, with me at the piano accompanying a young fellow-pupil, Peter Hudson, who had a fine treble voice. We played the ten-inch acetate disc to his mother, and she, wanting to be encouraging but clearly not aware that there was a distinction to be made between Milton and me, commented amiably, "Nice words!"

My mother, who worked part-time as a shorthand-typist, did play the piano—by ear: she couldn't read music. I asked her once to play for me the first eight bars of the finale of Brahms's Fourth Symphony, because I wanted to get a clearer idea of the highly individual harmony I had heard in an orchestral performance, and I remember how frustrating it was that she could only come up with a version with totally conventional harmony. My father, a tailor like every other member of his generation on both sides of the family, had no musical or indeed any outside interests at all; he was a lovely man who, while radiating inexhaustible benevolence, simply ate, drank, worked, and slept, and was deservedly loved by everybody that knew him.

One of the other tailors, on my mother's side of the family, was cousin Reuben, whom I knew honorifically as "Uncle Rue," since he was a generation older than I. He should never have been a tailor. As a child, he had cherished the dream of becoming a doctor, but his parents were disinclined to let him continue studies after the minimum school-leaving age of fourteen. Persuaded by his head teacher that he was exceptionally intelligent, they agreed to let him be interviewed by a visiting inspector of schools, and in principle to allow him to stay on if the inspector recommended that. Sadly, just in the week before the interview, Rue had suddenly conceived an interest in horses. When he was asked what he wanted to be when he grew up, he answered, "a doctor or a blacksmith"—and the inspector's conclusion was that he was not a serious enough boy to warrant a positive recommendation. But Rue never lost his appetite for intellectual and artistic pursuits. We had vigorous, indeed often quite fierce, discussions about all manner of subjects whenever we met at family gatherings. He was a constant attender at the Covent Garden opera, and he took me on one unforgettable occasion to a recital by Jussi Björling at the Royal Albert Hall. We sat in the cheaper but perfectly good seats at the back of the stage, and were thrilled when, for one of several encores, Björling turned round and sang directly to us. Rue, incidentally, had an excellent singing voice of his own, and enjoyed using it around his house on a variety of operatic arias.

One of my many cousins, Bernard Marcus, a few years my senior, who went on to become a successful psychologist, was an early mentor in both music and atheism. We used to improvise vocally together: on one occasion we indulged our imagination with an extemporized version of what a symphony by Grieg might sound like, and when his suppressed 1864 essay in the genre was finally resuscitated in the 1970s we were amused to find that it was not very different from our early imaginings. More seriously, Bernard gave me vital moral support in the first big rebellion of my life. My refusal to be bar-mitzvah'ed entailed battles with my parents, often ending in tears, every night for several months, on the grounds that I wasn't willing to stand up and say things I didn't believe in. It ended with my victory. It was not until some years later that, coming to the conclusion that atheism was just as dogmatic a position as convinced belief in a deity, I became instead a convinced agnostic (if that is not an oxymoron).

I'm not sure whether winning such a fight with my parents was more or less traumatic than losing it would have been. I like to think that, if they had been deeply religious, I might have acquiesced for their sake. But they were very far from being strictly observant, and only went to synagogue once or at most twice a year, on the most important of the high holidays. The nub of their argument was "What will the neighbors say?" and neither that nor a foolish uncle's comment—"But Bernard, think of all the lovely presents you'll get!"—was calculated to convince an idealistic thirteen-year-old.

The uncle in question was Morrie, Bernard Marcus's father, whose wife was one of my least personable aunts. Though a piano teacher, Fanny was somewhat ignorant of her craft. When Bernard asked her one year what her favorite pupil was going to play at her annual pupils' recital, she replied, "Beethoven—the 'Drair' Sonata." Bernard, puzzled, asked if he could look at the score, and found "Beethoven: Drei Sonaten" (Three Sonatas) printed on the cover. At the age of sixteen, I had one lesson with her—it was the same day as my first violin lesson—but I instantly concluded that I could do better studying by myself. And so again, rather as with Mangeot and the violin, I can credit or blame a teacher for the fact that I never became a pianist. I did gradually develop the ability to study a score at the piano, but not to play well enough for anyone else to enjoy listening. My highest achievement in the field was to play the whole of Beethoven's Sonata in C Minor, op. 111, with all the simultaneous trills in several parts. To get to the end of this roughly twenty-five-minute work took me two hours and twenty minutes—but believe me, I know the piece cold.

Bernard died some years ago, but another cousin, Bella, remains not only a relative but also a dear friend. It was she who took me, when I was still in my teens, to several plays at the Old Vic, where we saw such memorable performances as Richard Burton's Hamlet and Coriolanus and Michael Hordern's King John.

Equally vital was the contribution of my sister. Ten years older than I, Betty, as she was originally named, and Anne, as she later chose to be called, shared her musical enthusiasms with me in a variety of ways. She took me on many weekends to the South Place chamber music concerts in Conway Hall, near the British Museum. Founded in 1878, and thus the longest-running classical concert series in Europe, they were incredibly cheap (tickets sold for two shillings—one-tenth of a pound in that day's currency) and incredibly good. The programs followed a well-established pattern, often beginning with a Mozart or Haydn string quartet and ending with Beethoven, Schubert, or Brahms, usually with something like a clarinet quintet sandwiched between, and the performers were leading ensembles from the international music world. The Haydn quartets were something Anne and I particularly enjoyed: we would sit chuckling silently to ourselves over the witty touches in the music, and puzzled by the air of solemn rectitude that seemed to envelop most of our fellow audience members.

One episode was amusing for entirely nonmusical reasons. The members of the Netherlands String Quartet were staying in various private accommodations, and one of their violinists, Nap de Klijn, had locked himself out of his room and couldn't retrieve his violin. The management asked whether anyone in the audience had access to a violin, and a doctor who lived just round the corner promptly provided his, with which unfamiliar instrument de Klijn promptly and bravely played the concert.

Anne ruined my receptivity to German Lieder for some time by asking me once, "Have you noticed how the only word you can ever actually hear is 'Herz'?" Try it—all too often, it's true. It was Anne, too, who introduced me to opera. The first attempt didn't work: we went to see *Die Fledermaus* at Sadler's Wells Theatre, and I found it boring. (Loving the opera as I do now, I am convinced that it's exactly the wrong kind of piece to attract an inexperienced young person to opera, because its enjoyment requires in its listeners both an acquaintance with the kinds of works it satirizes and a decidedly adult sophistication.) But I agreed to try again—and *Don Giovanni* worked its irresistible magic: I was hooked. In 1951 it was through Anne that I was presented with the chance of a very special operatic experience. She had a friend, Ralph Schwiller, who played the violin in the orchestra of the Royal Opera House, Covent Garden, and who was named for his godfather, Ralph Vaughan Williams. (The composer paid tribute to the younger Ralph's violinist father, Isidore, for teaching him how, as a conductor, to start an orchestra on an upbeat.)

It was Ralph who arranged a ticket for me to the dress rehearsal of that year's run of *Der Rosenkavalier*. When I asked at the box office for a ticket in the name of Jacobson, the official looked through his box of tickets and asked, "Is it Maurice Jacobson?" I was rather excited to be mistaken, at the age of fiften, for a composer of some distinction who was fifty years my senior. Anyway, when the right ticket was duly found, I had the privilege of sitting in the theater just a few seats away from the director's desk, and experiencing Richard Strauss's most popular opera with a cast headed by Sylvia Fisher, Constance Shacklock, Howell Glynne (not to be confused with Gwynne Howell), and Ruth Guldbæk. What is more, though I didn't realize it at the time, the conductor was one of Strauss's greatest interpreters, Erich Kleiber, whose 1954 recording of the work still stands as perhaps the finest ever made (even if the quality of an ensemble of singers including Sena Jurinac, Ludwig Weber, and Hilde Gueden is somewhat let down by Maria Reining's rather prosaic Marschallin).

In my last year of school, to earn some pocket money, I took a vacation job as a sort of clerk or general office-boy at the Hackney Electric Company in east London. At the time, my parents and I were living in South Woodford, a little farther out beyond London's eastern edge. And for the summer vacation, impelled by my ever-increasing enthusiasm for music, I bought a half-season ticket for the BBC's Henry Wood Promenade Concerts in the Royal Albert Hall. So for four weeks I cycled five miles from home to Hackney in the morning of every weekday, another eight miles to Kensington in the afternoon, and perhaps a dozen miles back home after the concert. My fellow "Prommers" and I would line up for an hour or two outside the hall, often chanting rather scurrilous songs about Sir Malcolm Sargent, chief conductor of the Proms from 1948 to 1967. ("They've locked up Flash Harry in Kensington jail—the Duchess of Kent said she wouldn't go bail" was a typical example.) When the doors opened, we would run to our standing positions at the front of the promenade, often having asked our queue neighbors "Are you going fiddles or cellos tonight?" (house-left or house-right). That was in the days long before orchestras had started to revert to the old layout with the violin sections split, the firsts on house-left, and the seconds on house-right, with immeasurable benefit to performances of the classical repertoire, and even more in the music of such composers as Bruckner, Elgar, and Mahler; think of the opening of Mahler's Ninth Symphony, where the seconds carry the initial melodic burden, and the firsts don't even enter for a minute or more.

The atmosphere of those concerts was electric, enhanced as it was by the spontaneous chants that would greet the musicians as they came onstage: my impression, watching some of the concerts on television in recent years, is that the demonstrations of enthusiasm have latterly taken on a depressingly regimented quality. However that may be, my four weeks of regular attendance, supplementing much devoted listening to the BBC Third Programme, enabled me to get to know a huge swath of the repertoire in short order.

So far as ordinary concert life was concerned, the Albert Hall was superseded in 1951 by the Royal Festival Hall. Concert-going became a much easier business for me, since the new hall was just a short distance down-river from CLS. I started saving my pennies, and managed to afford a concert roughly once every six weeks.

My first visit to the hall was for a recital of French piano music by Walter Gieseking, who was especially masterful as an interpreter of Debussy and Ravel. When the official program was over, he gave us almost a dozen encores, but then the staff, obviously eager to go home, turned the house light fully up, and the pianist cheerily waved goodbye. The first orchestral concerts I went to were by Harry Blech's London Mozart Players, with the soprano Irmgard Seefried and her violinist husband, Wolfgang Schneiderhan, as remarkable soloists, and by Hans Schmidt-Isserstedt with the NWDR Symphony Orchestra. The conductor had created a fascinating program: between Mozart's "Haffner" Symphony and Strauss's *Ein Heldenleben* (which with ninety-eight players, as the press gleefully reported, brought the largest number of musicians to the stage since the hall had opened), he led a performance of Michael Tippett's Concerto for Double String Orchestra. This marked for me the beginning of what was to be a long and cordial relationship both with Tippett's music and, after I met him a few years later, with the man himself.

My Festival Hall tickets were almost always for the cheapest seats, but this was actually an advantage because, being placed on the platform behind the orchestra, they enabled me to watch conductors closely, often with a score in my hand. Josef Krips was a frequent RFH guest, and I heard my first live performance of Schubert's "Great" C Major Symphony under his direction. Other regular visitors to the podium included Adrian Boult, John Barbirolli, Otto Klemperer, and Thomas Beecham, who could always be relied on for an entertaining end-of-concert speech, telling us on one occasion, “I will now play for you Lollipop No. 1 of the Royal Philharmonic Orchestra: you will find it sweet, soothing, succulent, and soporific!” (The piece in question was the Entr’acte from act 3 of Massenet’s *Manon*, a saccharine morsel of which “soporific” is a highly appropriate description.) Beecham’s programming was, to say the least, unpredictable: the criterion for works to be included on the programs he gave with his “Thomas Beecham Popular Concerts” seemed to consist solely of their popularity with Thomas Beecham—I would hardly call Benjamin Godard, whose *Concerto romantique* for violin and orchestra was heard at one of them, a household name. He was also inveterately cavalier with the texts of the music he conducted. A performance of that same “Great” C Major Symphony featured a horn section beefed up from Schubert’s two players to Beecham’s preferred six, and he cut perhaps half-a-dozen measures from the ritornello in the first movement of Mozart’s *Sinfonia concertante* for violin and viola, a work whose score ought surely to be sacrosanct.

Two pianists trained me in listening to their instrument’s most important repertoire. One was Solomon Cutner, known simply as Solomon, whose performances of such works as Beethoven’s Piano Concerto no. 4 were a miracle of limpidity and grace. The other was Clifford Curzon, who taught me about Mozart and Schubert. I hasten to add that I didn’t meet either of them at the time, but years later I came to know Curzon, who was not only a musician of rare poetic sensibility, but a perfect example of the old-fashioned English gentleman, modest and gracious, yet with an unshakable inner vein of integrity.

I met Curzon several times after performances in which he was the soloist with Daniel Barenboim conducting. On one occasion, I had a seat at the Royal Festival Hall next to the spot at which stage-right abutted the audience’s part of the hall, and I was able to see, practically over Curzon’s shoulder, that he was playing Mozart’s Concerto no. 23 in A (K. 488), with not a piano part or a two-piano reduction but a full score in front of him (turning pages only occasionally). It was a valuable lesson to see that he would still keep in front of him the text of a work that he must have played dozens, if not hundreds, of times, and in which he was still keenly interested in keeping the various aspects of solo-tutti relations firmly in view.

In 1954, my concert life was destined to come to a temporary end. I was awarded a scholarship to Corpus Christi College, Oxford, and the college authorities wanted me to do my two years of National [military] Service before coming up. The Royal Air Force officials at my initial assessment and medical examination asked me, rather charmingly, at what date I should like to be called up. I requested that it should be after mid-August, because I had a ticket for a performance of *Don Giovanni* then, but before the beginning of September, so that I would be discharged in time to start the academic year in Oxford. The suggestion was honored, a courtesy I somehow doubt would have been bestowed by the military organizations of many countries, and so I headed off to the induction center in Bedfordshire at the end of August.

Though it was staged—and fully staged—on the rather cramped platform of the Royal Festival Hall, the *Don Giovanni* I had held out for was a dazzling experience in musical respects. The cast comprised George London as a dangerously sexy Giovanni, Erich Kunz as Leporello, Elisabeth Grümmer as Donna Anna, Léopold Simoneau—the great Canadian rival of Anton Dermota in the role—as Don Ottavio, Walter Berry as Masetto, Rita Streich as Zerlina, Paul Schöffler as the Commendatore, and, most memorably of all, Sena Jurinac as Donna Elvira. Having previously regarded the last of these as a somewhat colorless role, I told that wonderful soprano years later, after a recital she gave in Wigmore Hall that included a ravishing performance of the Marschallin's monologue from *Der Rosenkavalier*, that I had been in love with her ever since seeing her as Elvira.

I served my military time in four stages: a week or so of induction, several weeks of "square-bashing" (drill training under the supervision of a set of sadistic noncommissioned officers) in Staffordshire, two months of trade training in Herefordshire, and, for the last year and a half, working as the Equipment Officer's clerk at RAF Old Sarum, outside Salisbury in Wiltshire. Several of my fellow-sufferers in "square-bashing" were to become also my friends. Keith Holloway was scheduled to go to Corpus at the same time I would, and, like me, would be studying classics. John Marlow Rhys, also headed for Oxford, was a composer; over the years, we would occasionally attend concerts together, and I followed his career with interest and considerable admiration. I lost touch with another budding composer, Roger Wilton, but kept in touch with Tim Robinson, who went on to study physical sciences at Cambridge: he commissioned some writing from me when he was serving as an editor of *Cambridge Opinion*, and I ran a cartoon by him when I was in charge of the opposite number magazine at Oxford.

I made good use of my time at Old Sarum, thanks to several excellent cultural institutions in the city of Salisbury. I acted in a couple of productions by a local theater group—the Studio Players, I think it was called—playing several small roles in *Macbeth* and portraying the butler, Lane, in *The Importance of Being Earnest*, for which I also served as stage manager.

Our Algernon, Derek Warner, was a fine actor, but during rehearsals he persistently forgot the crucial line at the end of the play, stopping short after "On the contrary, Aunt Augusta, I've now realised for the first time in my life the vital Importance . . . Importance . . . ," and the rest of us would chime in with "of Being Earnest." He had a similar problem with "Yes. The . . . the . . . ," leaving "The Brighton line" for us to fill in—but happily he managed both passages perfectly in the actual performances. We played in a tiny theater with only sixty seats, and, in my *Macbeth* role as Macduff's son, Fleance, I had to jump over the feet of the people in the first row to escape from the murderers.

We also planned a production of Sophocles's *Women of Trachis*. The production never happened, because Ezra Pound's estate refused us permission to use his translation, but while it was in preparation I got to know the scheduled director. An English teacher at a Salisbury grammar school, he was a genial, seemingly relaxed man. Over drinks together at a local pub, however, I suddenly realized from something he said that the person I knew as "Bill Golding" was none other than William Golding, whose first novel, *Lord of the Flies*, I had recently enjoyed reading. The apparent disconnect between the amiable chap I was sipping sherry with and the writer of that violently dyspeptic book gave me a useful lesson in distinguishing between an artist's work and his personal character.

Besides my activity in the theater, I also joined the Salisbury Musical Society, an amateur choir of about 140 voices directed by Douglas Guest, organist and master of the choristers at Salisbury Cathedral. (The audition required me to sight-read a passage written in five flats from a Mass by Kodály.) Accompanied by the Bournemouth Symphony Orchestra, we gave our concerts in the cathedral. The program at one of them, conducted by Guest, consisted of the first three parts of Bach's *Christmas Oratorio* and Fauré's Requiem. In the final movement of the latter, "In paradisum," the voices of a dozen of the cathedral's boy choristers came floating down from a gallery above the platform like an intervention of angels. The cathedral was so cold, however, that for his solos in the Bach, the BSO's principal trumpet had to lip almost every note individually, as it was impossible for him to set the tuning firmly. My other performance with the choir was of Beethoven's Missa Solemnis in D Major, under the baton of the orchestra's principal conductor, Charles Groves.

For all the rehearsals entailed by my activities with the theater group and the choir, the education officer at RAF Old Sarum gave me a monthly note excusing me, on the relevant evenings, from being placed on such duties as guarding the airfield from the Irish Republican Army. This was a chore for which we were armed with nothing more than a stick, which I think any IRA man who might ever have showed up would have found reasonably easy to cope with.

When I wasn't either rehearsing or on guard duty, I spent most evenings in Salisbury, writing letters or reading under the shade of the magnificent trees in the Cathedral Close. Strolling there one evening, I noticed a man wearing an old-school tie that identified him as a former pupil at the City of London School. We got into conversation. He was Stephen Lock, a doctor who was doing his National Service as medical officer at another RAF station in the area, and would later become editor of the *British Medical Journal.* I enjoyed several delicious dinners with Stephen and his wife, Shirley—he was an excellent cook, and we have remained friends ever since. Shirley was a professional singer, and the family often spent time in the summers at Benjamin Britten's Aldeburgh Festival. Britten and Peter Pears were godparents to the Locks' son, who once, they told me, spotting one of his godparents on the sea-front, excitedly remarked, "Look—it's Uncle Ben-Peter."

Quite apart from my choral singing, Salisbury was the scene of a most enlightening musical encounter. At a concert of relatively early chamber and vocal music in the cathedral's beautiful octagonal Chapter House I heard some Elizabethan lute songs, including Rosseter's *What then is love but mourning*. I fell instantly in love with music in this genre by Rosseter, Campion, Dowland, and others, and some years later it was one of the areas I specialized in as a record critic for *High Fidelity* and *Stereo Review* magazines.

In retrospect, another cathedral episode makes me abashed at my own temerity. Walking past one of the houses that border the Close, I heard some extraordinarily fine piano-playing emerging from an open window. Having rung the doorbell and been admitted, I expressed my admiration. The pianist, who had been playing the piano part of a Beethoven cello sonata, turned out to be a sixteen-year-old named Hamish Milne. I asked if I could come back with a tape recorder. The result was a stunning tape of part of Schumann's *Kreisleriana*, which I still have.

Hamish went on to a distinguished career as a musician of fastidious taste, successful with composers as disparate as Mozart and Medtner. My encounter with him proved productive in a different way, because I met his father, John Milne, who was the conductor of an amateur orchestra. I became involved in its activities as an occasional assistant to the librarian, Eileen Merry, and was allowed to sit in and enjoy chamber-music evenings at her house, where string quartets by Haydn and others would be played. The orchestra, incidentally—as a zestful performance of Beethoven's Second Symphony conducted by John Milne bore out—boasted among its personnel at least two outstanding players, both of woodwind instruments, whose careers soon took them to considerable heights. One was Celia Nicklin, who played with the London Mozart Players, and served for many years as principal oboe with the Academy of St Martin in the Fields and head of oboe at the Royal Academy of Music. Her flutist colleague in Salisbury was David Butt, later principal flute of the BBC Symphony Orchestra.

Two years in the RAF duly completed, Oxford finally beckoned. One thing I am quite clear about is that having been forced to do my National Service first did me more good than harm. If I had been allowed to go straight up to the university from school I think I should have escaped military service altogether, because conscription was phased out in Britain around this time. But with no disrespect to the superb teaching I was to receive at Corpus, I would judge that the interaction with fellow students of all social and intellectual varieties, and from all over the world, played at least as large a part as formal education did in my own personal development. If I had become an undergraduate at the age of eighteen, without those two years spent in the outside world's vastly different milieu, I should undoubtedly have neglected the social side of Oxford and hunkered down unwaveringly over the books.

As it was, when I took the Classical Moderations examination during the second year of my four-year course and earned Second Class Honours (out of the four classes possible at that time), my Greek tutor, Hugh Lloyd-Jones, remarked, "I'm sure if you'd worked all the time you'd have got a First, but there are other things in life." Two years later I earned Third Class Honours in the final examination of Literae Humaniores, colloquially known as "Greats." As a lunch guest in college a few months after graduation, I said to Frank Lepper, the distinguished Roman historian who had been my history tutor, "You were very understanding when I hadn't finished an essay on time." His reply—"Well, you see, I always knew you had another line, so there seemed little point in making a fuss"—has always seemed to me a perfect embodiment of the principle of a liberal education. It was Frank that had encouraged me to become a candidate for my first job, and we were to remain on terms of warm friendship for more than forty years until he died in his nineties.

My main formal tutors at Corpus, besides the two already named, included the philosopher David Pears. A brilliant teacher, he would never, in discussing an essay, tell me anything I hadn't yet thought of, instead asking questions that would lead me to think of it myself. With him, too, I had great difficulty finishing an essay, finding it impossible (for example) to reach a conclusion on the question of free will versus determinism. But one day David said: "Bernard, you seem to think your essay has to solve the problems of philosophy. Let me just remind you that we've been wrestling with these problems for more than two thousand years and we still haven't solved them. So I think it might be helpful if you were to regard your essay more as work in progress." After that, I had no difficulty in finishing my essays.

As I have already suggested, however, it was from my fellow-students as much as from my teachers that I did my most important learning. I had originally thought, when applying for admission to Oxford, of studying music when I got there, but the excellent senior classics master at CLS, Horace Oakley, urged me very strongly to keep music as a vocation rather than a profession. I therefore continued instead with my previously established academic concentration on classical languages and ancient history, branching out also in the course of the Literae Humaniores curriculum into philosophy both ancient and modern. In the event, my purely amateur musical activities during my student years were to equip me very adequately for a life not necessarily as a musician but in the world of music. I believe, in any case, that the study of philosophy is an excellent preparation for the profession of music critic. Criticism is a branch of aesthetics, which may be regarded as a branch of ethics, which is a branch of philosophy, and I think my philosophy studies were crucial in helping me to make the vital distinction between factual statement and value judgment. (This distinction, which I feel is not made with sufficient clarity or consistency by some of my colleagues in the field, is discussed further in the afterword.)

It was, however, the activities I engaged in outside my official studies that related most directly to a future in music. With my friend Brian Ponsford, whom I had known at CLS, I joined the Oxford Bach Choir. We attended weekly practices together, and sang in several concerts in the course of our student years. The programs ranged from Bach's B-minor Mass (with a choral complement of several hundred voices, which today would certainly be greeted with critical derision), by way of the Verdi and Brahms Requiems to Vaughan Williams's *Sea Symphony*. This last was probably the most difficult piece I've ever sung in, not because the writing is taxing in any specifically technical way, but because the long lines demand enormous reserves of breath if they are to be sung coherently. During the summer term, the choir shrank down to a mere fifty (!) voices known as the Motet Choir: we sang repertoire including Palestrina, Bach, and the Vaughan Williams unaccompanied Mass in G Minor, in such congenial locations as St George's Chapel in Windsor Castle. Before one engagement, in Tewkesbury Abbey, the Motet Choir's dinner was served in a deconsecrated church that had been turned into a corset factory—an example, perhaps, of descent from the sublime, if not to the ridiculous, at least to the unexpectedly banal.

Just as important a musical training stemmed from my friendship with another fellow student, John Moffat. Even in his student days John was a true renaissance man. He went on to take First Class Honours in Literae Humaniores and then in Law, besides serving as secretary of the university's entomological society, and it was with him at the piano that I spent several terms in an intensive study of the German Lieder repertoire, concentrating in turn on Schubert, Schumann, and Brahms, and more cursorily on Wolf (whom I confess I have never come to love) and Richard Strauss. John's piano-playing, if not unfailingly accurate, revealed the musicality of his mind—any wrong notes he perpetrated, instead of creating horrible dissonances, always fitted naturally into the harmonic context. Brian, John, and I formed a close-knit triumvirate throughout our student years, enjoying many pursuits together besides studying in each other's rooms. Brian went on to be a senior civil servant, and John to be professor of constitutional law at Edinburgh. I lost both of these dear friends too early, John when he was run over and killed by a bus in Karlsruhe, Brian when he took his own life.

Peter Delin was another friend who had much to teach me. He was studying (or, in Oxford terminology, "reading") "PPP" (Psychology, Philosophy, and Physiology), an elite course to which only a small handful of exceptional students were admitted each year. It was in an area of thought related to that composite subject that I learned something from Peter that I had never previously imagined. When I think of a thing or a word—say, "elephant" or "pagoda," I immediately *see*, in my mind's eye, a visual image of the thing in question. But Peter's thinking, he told me, was totally devoid of visual images: he thought exclusively in words. This was to me a difficult, even an inconceivable, notion, but it was salutary to be presented with the suggestion that there could be radical differences in the way people think. I still wonder whether there might be something again, neither images nor words, that forms the environment of other people's mental life?

Words, in any case, were something Peter and I could never get enough of. On many evenings, separating to go respectively to his lodgings and my room in college, we would often walk halfway, then a quarter of the way back, then an eighth . . . and so on, so hard was it to bring a conversation to an end. Then there was the occasion when one of us dictated an entire new poem to the other in a dream. It was good enough to be published, under the title *When this day's earth is ended*, in the *Pelican Record*, the college magazine of which I was one of the editors for a term or two. However disparate our mental processes may have been, I am completely unable to remember whether it was my dream in which Peter dictated the poem to me, or the other way around.

I seem anyway to have been dreaming quite productively in those days. I woke up one morning with the beginning of the slow movement of a previously undiscovered Haydn string quartet in my head. Unfortunately, however, my imagination had only reached as far as the fourth measure, and all attempts to take it further failed.

Peter was a talented guitarist, and I enjoyed hearing him sing folk songs to his own accompaniment. He also had a strong interest in paranormal phenomena, which I did not share. He continued to explore all these pursuits when, after graduating, he moved to Australia, where he became a lecture at the University of Adelaide. Some years later, when I was reviewing in Chicago, I met the Israeli conductor Elyakum Shapirra, and discovered that his young wife, Svetlana, was a graduate of that university. I asked Svetlana if she knew Peter Delin—and she said, "I certainly do. He was my professor, and he was the best teacher I ever had."

In line with Peter's psychological interests, he and I decided at one point to see how long we could stay awake and continue working. We armed ourselves with an outsize coffee maker and camped out in one of our rooms for two successive nights, getting on—as we were also doing during the day—with our respective studies. We made a point of drinking coffee every two hours or so, and made notes of our mental processes, which in retrospect seemed, to me at least, unenlightening.

One result of this exercise was to make us preternaturally outgoing and talkative at college breakfast. Our obtrusive brightness annoyed William Prosser, a fellow-student one year senior to me, who treasured his peace and quiet at the breakfast table. I didn't know William well, but I was always impressed by his air of calm self-assurance. When I confessed to John Moffat, a fellow-Scot of his, that I found William intimidating, he told me that *William* was equally intimated by *me*, whereupon I made overtures of friendship, so successfully that fully fifty-five years later I still counted him as one of my most valued friends. Known informally as Willie, and formally, having served as a judge in the Scottish courts, as Lord Prosser, he lived with his wife, Vanessa, in Edinburgh, on the same handsome crescent where he was born. Our contact, after a long and regrettable gap, was resumed when they came to dinner with Laura and me in The Hague on the first day of 1994, bringing a bottle of delectable Knockando single-malt Scotch with them, and right up until his death early in 2015 our visits to them have been revelations both of their warm hospitality and of Edinburgh's charm and beauty, already known to me, but a fresh discovery for Laura.

Another long friendship begun at Oxford that was just as central for the development of my own powers of thought was with Tony Brown, a fellow Corpuscle a year junior to me who was reading "PPE" (Philosophy, Politics, and Economics), and who remained perhaps my single closest friend until his death. Tony had suffered an attack of rheumatic fever when he was thirteen, which left him with damage to the cardiac valves. The physical consequences included a series of related illnesses over the years; he had valve replacement surgery in 1979, and it was during an operation in June 1996 to replace the valves again that he died. Tony had a much narrower choice of career than most of his contemporaries, as many companies in the late 1950s would not employ a person with a history of rheumatic fever (for reasons having to do with pension plans). Insurance was one of the few fields open to him, and Tony joined the Provincial Insurance company, serving in a number of locations and eventually as the firm's City Manager in London before his health led him to take early retirement at the end of 1992.

Tony had too acute and inquiring an intellect to limit himself to just his professional field. For much of his life he was a devoted student of Jungian analysis. He was also a voracious reader and looker at pictures, and himself commissioned works from an outstanding English artist in stained glass. Nothing, though, was more important to him than his home life. Tony married in 1964, and he and his wife, Kate, raised a family of seven children—four boys and three girls—that could stand as a paradigm of what a family can and should be. The combined respect and freedom with which the younger Browns would dispute Roman Catholic doctrine with their parents were matched by their intensely supportive interest in each other's talents. And when my first marriage broke down and I told Tony of my intention to marry Laura, he wrote her a surpassingly kind letter welcoming her to the prospect of future acquaintance with his family. When I told him how surprised I was by this, given Catholic doctrine on the indissolubility of marriage, he replied: "Bernard, I would have thought you knew us well enough to realize that we have strong beliefs of our own but that we don't impose them on other people. It's obvious that you're doing the right thing *for you*, and that's all that concerns us." (If only all Christians could be as Christian as that, the world would be a much better place.)

Having said all this about Tony, I am conscious of having quite failed to convey the essence of the man. To approach it more closely, I would add something that may on superficial consideration sound negative, but is actually intended as the highest praise. Being with Tony sometimes demanded patience. This was not because he was boring. Quite the contrary: his conversation was full of arresting insights, and his humor was as sparkling as it was devoid of malice. It is rather that when you asked his advice or opinion about something—and I valued both enormously—you did it knowing that the response would be measured and thorough, and would go to the root of the question. Tony never skimped on thought. If the question was a weighty one, then so would be the answer. Nevertheless, I do not think my time was ever better spent than in listening to him, and the repeated experience administered a powerful corrective to my penchant for jumping to instant conclusions.

Among the many musical pleasures on offer at Oxford, I attended performances of remarkable quality in several genres. The Oxford University Opera Club, conducted by Professor Sir Jack Westrup, put on a fully-staged production of Ravel's *L'Enfant et les sortilèges* in Town Hall; in all my experiences of the work since then, I have never seen one that realized the scenic transition from the naughty boy's room to the garden so magically. The harpsichordist Thurston Dart gave a performance of Bach's "Goldberg Variations" in a college chapel, which drew so large an audience that, along with many others, I had to stand throughout. Peter Pears and Benjamin Britten gave a Lieder recital in Town Hall at which I found their performances of Schubert's *Die Sterne* and *Nacht und Träume* revelatory. Pears's platform manner was both charming and unusual: he held a small piece of paper in his hands, presumably as an *aide-mémoire* for the song texts, but he never unfolded or looked at it.

It wasn't just music that constituted my cultural education at Oxford: there was an abundance of theatrical and cinematic offerings to absorb. The Oxford Playhouse presented an excellent variety of plays, among which I particularly remember seeing Jean Giraudoux's *Amphitryon 38* and Elias Canetti's chilling *The Numbered*. For much of my four years I was seeing anything up to five films a week. As a member of the Oxford University Film Society, I was able to see such classics as D. W. Griffith's *Intolerance* projected at the correct speed—that is, more slowly than usual and much less jerkily—with piano accompaniment extemporized by David Harvey, a friend and fellow Greats student at Oriel College next door. The Scala Cinema (since renamed the Phoenix Picturehouse) on Walton Street presented such unlikely double bills as *The Importance of Being Earnest* together with *The Seventh Seal*. It changed its program twice a week, thus giving me an early opportunity to get to know and love the work of such directors as Ingmar Bergman and Satyajit Ray. Some of my friends found Ray's *Pather Panchali* "terribly slow," but I loved every lingering minute of it.

Christopher McCulloch, who occupied the room next to mine in our first year at Corpus, had a problem with tempo in a context other than that of film projection. The first man in our circle to own a recording of Beethoven's Ninth Symphony, he played it for me one day, but when we reached the third movement he said, "Oh, let's skip this bit—it's so slow!"

In addition to music and theater, I followed a natural progression from school-magazine reviewing by becoming involved with *Oxford Opinion*, a newer and somewhat more serious (or should I say pompous?) counterpart to the popular *Cherwell*. After serving in turn as music editor and assistant editor, I eventually succeeded my contemporary and friend John Field as editor and spent several terms producing the magazine, which was regularly pasted up on the floor of my room to be sent to the printers in a format that seems, as I look back from these computer-facilitated days, charmingly picturesque. One of our most notable small coups was to include a previously unpublished English translation of a poem by Boris Pasternak, which came into my hands when his sister, Lydia, who lived in Oxford, called out of the blue and offered it to me.

Another activity closer to my academic commitments was serving as secretary of the Socratic Club. C. S. Lewis had been the club's first president, and he was succeeded shortly before my arrival in Oxford by Basil Mitchell. The society held meetings at which the relations between religion and science were discussed, usually with a pair of invited speakers representing those two fields; my cousin Bernard Marcus was one of those I invited to bat for the ungodly team. I was also involved with a Corpus Christi dining club known as the Sundial. When I invited Isaiah Berlin, a former Corpus undergraduate, to come and give a speech to us, he demurred on the highly unconvincing plea that he was "a miserable after-dinner speaker." His letter is one of three such communications from great men that hang on the wall of my office—the others are from Eubie Blake and Oliver Sacks—to remind me of my good fortune. (Eubie's letter, written to thank me for my review of a superb ragtime concert he and Bill Bolcom gave in Chicago, is on paper with the touching printed letterhead, "Eubie Blake – Arranger – Composer of 'I'm Just Wild About Harry.'") Berlin graciously invited me to come and drink a glass of sherry with him in his rooms at All Souls College. He was generous with his time, and our half-hour chat, focused on his crucial opinion that there are important and conflicting positive values that cannot be reconciled, was one of my most memorable Oxford experiences.

Another Oxford luminary of comparable eminence was W. H. Auden, Professor of Poetry at the university from 1956 to 1961. Auden's obligations in the post were light, amounting to a requirement to give three lectures a year. His inaugural lecture gained wide circulation in a printed version, which included a charming cartoon about two examiners in the English course. Their dialogue ran as follows:

> 1st English Examiner:
> O, cuckoo, shall I call thee bird,
> Or but a wandering voice?
>
> 2nd English Examiner:
> State the alternative preferred,
> With reasons for your choice.

In addition to formal lecturing, during the periods he was in Oxford Auden also hosted a weekly gathering, too informal to be called a seminar, at a coffee shop in the middle of the city. I attended once, found the atmosphere congenial, and had the feeling that this was the closest thing Oxford had to offer to the intellectual coffee house society of old Vienna.

During our last long summer vacation, my colleagues and I spent a couple of weeks at a reading party in the French Alps near Chamounix, with Frank Lepper in the role of Monsieur le Directeur. Although Frank read improving literature to us in the evenings after dinner, careful research established that the only book on the chalet shelves that every member of our group read while we were there was a bodice-ripper entitled *Vera at Mystery Manor*.

On the way back to England, I stopped for a few days in Paris, where I was impressed by Alain Vanzo as Don Ottavio and Gérard Souzay in the title role in a Paris Opera production of *Don Giovanni*. Marivaux's *Le Jeu de l'amour et du hasard*, at the Comédie-Française, was a stimulating test of my French comprehension. Fortunately, however, Marcel Carné's hilarious film *Drôle de drame* (1937) was shown in a print with English subtitles.

Back in Oxford, in addition to preparing for final exams, I had to start thinking about what I was going to do with my life. When I told David Pears, three years into my course, that I had decided to leave Oxford without waiting to complete the fourth year, because I had realized that I had to work in music, I was convinced by his wise response: "Bernard, why don't you wait another year? You'll have a degree, which won't do you any harm, and music will probably still be there." Then, in the spring of 1960, an advertisement appeared in the *New Statesman* magazine calling, as one could do in those days, for "a young man, preferably under 35 and unmarried," to work for Philips Phonographic Industries in the Netherlands as sleeve-note writer. Going to Frank Lepper for advice, I said I supposed there would be little point in my applying, since there would obviously be candidates much more experienced than I. "Well," he said, "if you don't try, you'll never know, will you?"

So I responded to the advertisement, fulfilled the various test writing assignments I was sent, and was invited to Baarn for an interview. This was in fact not the only possibility I had in mind. My "road not taken" had just come in the form of a job offer from an antiquarian bookshop near the venerable Cheshire Cheese pub off Fleet Street. The owners, Justin and Adelaide Clark Hall, were beginning to feel their age. They proposed that I should join them as an employee, move on in a year or so to a partnership, and then take full control when they retired. Justin was particularly excited when I told him of my musical interests, saying that I should certainly be able to make this a specialty, there being only one antiquarian music bookshop in London at the time.

They were charming people, it was a fine shop, and I was attracted. But when I told them that I was waiting for the result of my application for a job even better fitted to my main interests, they kindly agreed to give me a couple of weeks to come to a decision. My friend Brian Ponsford had asked me what I would do if I were not allowed that breathing space before making up my mind. "Well," I said, "I'd obviously have to turn the bookshop job down." "But how can you do that," Brian asked, "if you have nothing else definite arranged?" The answer was obvious to me—I've always lived my life on the basis of going out on any limb that presented itself—and the question merely illustrated the fundamental difference of attitude that separated Brian and me.

The upshot, at my interview in Holland, was that the portly man who thrust a hand in my direction and rapped out "Zalsman" (the Dutch style of introducing oneself) promptly offered me the job. I have never regretted taking that path, but I have often wondered who I would be now if I had taken the other one.

CHAPTER TWO

INSIDE THE RECORD INDUSTRY

1960–64

It was a month after I left Oxford that I arrived in Baarn, about twenty-two miles south-east of Amsterdam, to start my first job. I rented a room in a lodging-house about five minutes by bicycle from Hoog Wolde, the rather palatial building that housed PPI—Philips Phonografische Industrie. My office, however, was in the Koetshuis, or Coach House, an outbuilding in the grounds. I've always had a physique that is somehow immune to cold: I usually kept my window open, even in the depths of the Dutch winter, so my office rapidly came to be known as the Icebox, and colleagues who planned to come across from the main building to discuss a project would call an hour in advance and ask me to warm the place up for their arrival.

My immediate predecessor was Conrad Wilson, who served subsequently for many years as music critic of the *Scotsman*. He helped to ease me into the linguistic demands of a first job abroad by taking me around the various shops he frequented in Baarn and insisting to their staff members that they should speak only Dutch with me. This deep-end approach to the language served me well: after only two or three weeks I managed to order a complete meal in an Amsterdam restaurant without speaking—or forcing the waiter to speak—a single word of English.

Through Conrad I got to know Carli van Emde Boas, a graphic designer, formerly with Philips, who had left to go into the world of public relations. Carli was a multitalented man who played drums in a jazz band but was also a lover of early music, and especially of the English lute-song school of composers. In the following years, on our way to meals in and around Amsterdam in his car, we would often pass the time singing Dowland or Campion, or sometimes English folk song, he in a cultivated countertenor and I in my low bass. Carli is another of the friends from those days with whom I have stayed in touch. I still receive his New-Year's greeting cards every year, and never cease to marvel at the way he can devise, every time, a creative and often amusing graphic treatment of the numbers in question.

My sister had told me that, in the time when she first left the family home, she had had a friend who worked for Philips, though she didn't know exactly what his job was or where he was located. Well, of course, it turned out that his office was next door to mine. So I was able to astonish him by saying, at our first meeting, "Ah, yes, your wife is called Maria, and you have three children, named Paulette, Marlies, and Philip." That first meeting was indeed life-changing for me, because I owe the start of my professional career as a critic to GASTON RICHTER.

An Austrian Jew who had survived the war hidden on a Dutch farm and had married a Dutch woman, Gaston was a graphic designer and a gifted photographer. While I wrote the notes for the backs of record sleeves, he designed the fronts. When we got to know each other, he suggested that we should do some interviews for the *Times* of London, with his photographs accompanying my text. I was twenty-four and fresh out of college, and I had a very exalted idea of that newspaper's status, so I said, "Don't be ridiculous—you can't write for the *Times* just like that." When he nagged me on the subject, I said, "All right, we'll have a go, just to show that it can't be done," and we visited a former next-door neighbor of Gaston's in Amsterdam, who happened to be the famous harpsichordist Gustav Leonhardt. Gaston took pictures of Leonhardt's remarkable collection of old instruments, and I sent them to the *Times* along with a three-thousand-word text. For about two months we heard nothing—"You see," I said, "I told you so!"—and then suddenly a latter arrived apologizing for the delay, expressing the wish to publish the interview, and suggesting that I become the *Times*'s Amsterdam music correspondent. This was a dream assignment, since I could review anything I liked and did not have to write about anything I didn't like, and over the rest of my two years at Philips I contributed about a dozen pieces to the paper, including interviews with the composer Frank Martin and the conductor Bernard Haitink, as well as a variety of concert reviews.

Gaston's wife, Maria, is a beautiful, warm, and highly intelligent woman. Once, having driven me back to Baarn after a concert in Amsterdam, Gaston stopped the car, turned to me, and said, "Bernard, do you love my wife?" "How," I retorted, "can you question my taste so far as even to doubt it?" "Good, good," he said. The two were an inexhaustible social and intellectual resource for me during my time at Philips. We soon established Tuesday as the day for my weekly dinner at their house, because Tuesday evening was when the week's English film was shown on television, and reading the subtitles while listening to the dialogue was an ideal way of expanding my Dutch vocabulary. It was a pleasantly convivial way to pick up such useful phrases as the Dutch equivalent of "I need a room."

I kept up a close friendship with Gaston and his family long after leaving Baarn. But it is only fifty-two years later, as I write this memoir, that I have learned that my small world might have been even smaller. In a short memoir of her own that my sister sent me, I found that her friendship with Gaston had been close enough that they even contemplated marriage. It didn't happen, but if it had, sister and brother might have ended up living in the same small Dutch town.

A friendship ensued with Bernard Haitink that lasted for some years. During the times when I was working in London I saw him fairly often after concerts, and on one occasion he invited me to his West End apartment to share a dinner cooked by his daughter, a professional caterer. In spring 1974, when I was happily ensconced in a recently acquired job running the Southern Arts Association, he got in touch to ask whether I might be interested in the post of artistic director for the Concertgebouw Orchestra. I had no wish to leave Southern Arts but the thought was tempting. I told Bernard that I'd be happy to come to Amsterdam for an interview but that I preferred to pay my own fare, so that if I were offered the job and decided to turn it down I should not have to feel guilty.

The interview took place in a smoky room of the kind common in Holland at that time. I thought it went well, but subsequently received a very polite letter from the Concertgebouw Orchestra thanking me for my visit but explaining that the management had decided to appoint a Dutch musicologist, Hein van Rooyen (who held the post until his death in 1991). Haitink telephoned to apologize, saying, "If they knew they wanted a Dutch musicologist, they should never have bothered you to come for an interview." I assured him that, in view of my own expressed doubts whether the job was right for me, he had no need to apologize. He then said, "Please do stay in touch, wherever you happen to be and whatever you're doing, because there's no telling when we might be able to work together." I valued the suggestion, and called him on a few occasions. But in the end I decided, purely for his sake, not to continue doing so. Bernard is a deeply sensitive and introverted person: if Leonard Bernstein was always somehow able, postconcert, to externalize the emotions that conducting a Mahler or Shostakovich symphony would arouse in him, Bernard, by contrast, internalized those feelings. After hearing him several times on the phone saying, in tortured tones, "Oh, I'd so much love to see you, but I don't know when I'm going to have time . . . ," I concluded that the considerate thing to do was to take him off a hook that was really not important to him.

A mere few weeks after arriving in Baarn, I had an encounter that could well have derailed my whole purpose in working for Philips. A charismatic and very handsome Indian named Deben Bhattacharya was visiting the office in connection with his plan to make authentic recordings of folk song in his native country. We had coffee together, he described the project, and invited me to join him on his forthcoming trip.

I had already developed an interest in Indian classical music through my sister, who had married an Indian a few years before. (I was so gastronomically inexperienced that at their wedding meal at an Indian restaurant, I ordered an omelet. It was a gaffe that I have made up for very emphatically since!) Through that family connection I had attended a number of presentations of Indian music and theater, including Rabindranath Tagore's enchanting dance-drama *The Kingdom of Cards*, and had actually heard Ravi Shankar play in the intimate confines of Wigmore Hall, in the days before he became a star of the first magnitude. So I was strongly tempted by Deben's invitation, but I was sufficiently focused on the satisfactions of what I was already doing in Baarn that I turned down his proposal.

My responsibilities at Philips were not limited to writing sleeve notes. I also served as consultant on all matters connected with the English language, and thus was frequently in contact not only with the sleeve department but also with the public relations staff. I had the benefit of tickets to the concerts of the Concertgebouw Orchestra in Amsterdam, as well as performances by the Netherlands Opera and the various presentations of the Holland Festival.

At one of the latter I experienced a moment of high—and slightly embarrassing—drama. On the day I was planning to attend a performance of Mozart's *Le nozze di Figaro* conducted by Carlo Maria Giulini, a rumor started circulating that Elisabeth Schwarzkopf, the scheduled Countess Almaviva, had been taken ill and would not be able to appear. By the time

I took my seat in the Municipal Theater, however, no announcement had been made. Just before the performance was to begin, the curtain parted and the festival's director, Peter Diamand, emerged to the sound of a nervous intake of breath around the house. But what he told us was that the Holland Festival regretted to announce that, owing to indisposition, Miss Graziella Sciutti would not be able to appear in the role of Susanna. The general sigh of relief from the audience at the cancellation by that fine artist was the embarrassing part. It seemed, furthermore, that a young American soprano by the name of Marilyn Tyler had happened to be seen in the theater that afternoon, and had agreed to step in as Susanna at a few hours' notice, and without benefit of rehearsal, though she had not sung the role for several years.

It was a pleasure to watch Madame Schwarzkopf gently shepherding her young colleague through all the requisite stage movements. Ms. Tyler sang beautifully and acted better than one had any right to expect in the circumstances. She had apparently been on the point of giving up on her attempted European career, but this performance revived her fortunes: she went on to enjoy a good deal of success on European stages, before eventually returning to the United States and becoming director of opera studies at the University of New Mexico in Albuquerque.

In connection with another opera production I made the acquaintance of H. C. Robbins Landon, the editor of much of Haydn's oeuvre and a specialist also in Mozart's music and life. We had lunch together at the Richters' house in Baarn, and then traveled to Rotterdam to attend a production of *Don Giovanni*. Staying in touch after I had left Philips, we met again in 1965 at the Holland Festival's modern premiere of Haydn's *Le pescatrici*, for which Robbie had reconstructed the long-neglected score.

Some of the most memorable performances at the Concertgebouw were conducted by Bernard Haitink, who after Eduard van Beinum's sudden death on the podium had taken over as the orchestra's principal conductor, initially in partnership with Eugen Jochum. A Mahler Fifth Symphony under Haitink and a Bruckner Fifth under Jochum stay most vividly in my mind, along with guest performances by Giulini, Pierre Monteux, and that gifted maverick Hans Rosbaud, who preferred exploring unfamiliar repertoire rather than limiting himself to the core classics, and who, when I met him, insisted on not talking about himself but praising the talent of the then thirty-five-year-old Pierre Boulez.

Aside from the opera and the Concertgebouw Orchestra, Dutch musical life offered a wide variety of events in all corners of the country. Under the auspices of the Holland Festival, Hermann Prey gave a stunning performance of *Die Winterreise*. The Netherlands Chamber Orchestra (Nederlands Kamerorkest, or NKO) was another source of delight. The great former concertmaster of the Berlin Philharmonic under Furtwängler, Szymon Goldberg, at that time the NKO's principal conductor, led stylish performances of a variety of repertoire, including some crisply articulated Haydn. Years later, when Laura and I were living in Philadelphia, I was delighted to run into Goldberg (by that time teaching at the Curtis Institute) in the lobby of our apartment building, and to hear that he lived there too. Szymon and his wife, Miyoko, were cat-lovers, but couldn't have a cat of their own because they traveled so much. They came for tea with us several times, not so much because they wanted to see us, but because of the opportunity of socializing with our two cats.

David Zinman, then Monteux's assistant and shortly to become "second conductor" of the NKO under Goldberg, made a strong impression as a conductor still in his midtwenties who would certainly go on to a big career. There was also a guest appearance with the orchestra by Benjamin Britten and Peter Pears. I was impressed by the way Britten laid out his program: it consisted of two of his own works (with Pears as soloist in the Nocturne), a group of Mozart concert arias, and Mozart's Symphony no. 40 in G Minor. He ended each half with the Mozart works, choosing not to give his own pieces that limelight.

On the day after that concert, Britten and Pears met me for coffee on the companionable terrace of the American Hotel, surely one of the least American-looking buildings in all of Amsterdam. (I learned to play billiards in the splendid room it then devoted to the game.) I took the liberty of asking Britten why he hadn't observed the second repeat in the finale of the Mozart symphony, which he had observed in his English Chamber Orchestra recording. The program, he explained, had been so taxing for the players that he had decided it would simply be too much to ask of them to take that repeat—a practical consideration that I didn't feel any sensible person could argue with.

Many of these events I duly reviewed for the London *Times*. One concert conducted by Otto Klemperer, however, I refrained from writing about: Bruckner's Sixth Symphony was done well enough, but Klemperer's own Second Symphony struck me as ineptly constructed and even, surprisingly for so experienced a conductor, ineffectively scored, and I saw no need to beat a gifted musician figuratively on the head.

One aspect of Dutch musical life that I found refreshing was the willingness of performers to include in their programs music of less than towering greatness. Of course one wants to hear masterpieces, but it seems to me illuminating to hear such great works in the company of lesser ones, so long as a certain standard of quality is always maintained. So, for example, a stimulating program can include not only composers of the caliber of Johann Sebastian Bach, but also his son Johann Christian, a musician of unfailing charm who moreover had a considerable influence on the shaping of the young Mozart's style. Again, it's good to hear not only the Joseph Haydns of this world but also the Luigi Boccherinis—or for that matter why not an occasional dip into the work of Michael Haydn? I suppose this could be called programming pluralism, and it seems to me just as desirable a method as the stylistic pluralism in composition that helped in the last years of the twentieth century to extricate contemporary music from the tyranny of serial and other doctrinaire modernist methods.

I was about to make the acquaintance of a composer who had begun that process of emancipation in his own music. Back in England for a few days' vacation, I was invited by a young English pianist, Norma Fisher, to a private concert she was to play in the strikingly modern Hampstead house of the playwright/politician Benn Levy and his celebrated actress wife, Constance Cummings. Norma played some solo pieces and Constance read poetry in between them. Here I found myself sitting next to the composer Wilfred Josephs, who told me that his Concerto da Camera was to have its premiere later in the year in Maastricht. In view of my *Times* connection, I told him I would travel down to the province of Limburg for the concert. I loved the piece and wrote my review, and a friendship was born that opened many doors for me and lasted until Wilf's death in 1997.

At that time Wilf and his wife, Valerie (usually known as Val), were living with their young daughter, Philippa (their second daughter, Claudia, was born around the same time), in a pleasant Victorian house on Maida Avenue, on the bank of the Grand Union Canal in Maida Vale. From then on, no visit to London passed without my spending some time with them, and when I moved back to London in March 1962 we became very close.

It would be hard to exaggerate the role my friendship with Wilf played in my own musical education. There are those who believe that a music critic should remain aloof from any close association with those categories of person—composers and performers—it is his task to review. I have always felt, however, that an intimate acquaintance with the stresses and struggles that such people undergo can only help in arriving at a critical view that is not only fair but also humane. As to the supposed influence of personal prejudice on critical judgment—well, integrity is a quality a critic cannot do without; either he has it or he doesn't. If he does, he will judge fairly, regardless of personal ties (and indeed, if he believes in someone's artistic gifts, he will be all the more unwilling to allow lapses from that person's standards to go unremarked); if he doesn't, regardless of the absence of personal ties, he is unlikely to judge other than unfairly and arbitrarily.

Over the years, I was able to attend many Josephs premieres. Most of the works of his that I heard, including especially some finely crafted symphonies, the Second Piano Sonata, and such choral works as his highly individual *Mortales*, pleased me greatly. On the other hand, there were one or two pieces, the Third Symphony and the Second Piano Concerto among them, that I disliked intensely, and by the time they appeared we were good enough friends that I had no need to hesitate in telling him so. Fortunately, none of the pieces that Wilf dedicated to me fell into the latter category. The first of them was announced on a postcard: he had just finished his Second Symphony and asked permission to dedicate it to me. The work had its premiere at the Cheltenham Festival in 1965, sharing a program with *Le Sacre du printemps* (no less!).

In the same year, when I was freelancing in New York, Irving Kolodin commissioned me to write an article about Wilf Josephs's Requiem in the *Saturday Review*. Max Rudolf, who was music director of the Cincinnati Symphony Orchestra at the time, read the article and immediately decided to present the first American performances of the work in January 1967, first in Cincinnati and then at Carnegie Hall in New York. The bass-baritone soloist in these performances was Norman Treigle, who around this time was costarring with Beverly Sills in the City Opera production of Handel's *Giulio Cesare*. Along with such other members of the profession as Morton Gould, Beverly attended the Carnegie Hall performance of the Requiem, and we all stepped next door after the performance for a convivial supper at the Russian Tea Room, popular in those days as a gathering place for after-concert festivities, though reportedly now, after several closures and reopenings, no more than a shadow of its former self.

The American premiere of Wilf's Second Symphony was given in 1968, again by the Cincinnati Symphony under Rudolf's direction. My first wife, Bonnie, and I traveled to Cincinnati to hear "my" symphony, and our visit turned into quite a drama. Between movements, I had leaned forward to ask the man in the seat in front of me, as politely as I could, please not to talk during the music. He bided his time, and when the work ended turned around and placed his hands violently around my neck. It was intermission, and the attack was so traumatic that Bonnie and I made our excuses to Lloyd Haldeman, the orchestra's executive director, and went straight back to our hotel at that point. Lloyd told me later that my attacker was the husband of the *Cincinnati Enquirer*'s restaurant critic—perhaps he had accompanied her on one of her assignments and imbibed too liberally. In any case, Mary Nic Shenk, who was also reviewing the concert for the *St. Petersburg Times* in Florida, heard the story of the attempted strangling and published a piece about it under the title "Music Critics Live Dangerously Too."

My two marriages led to two further Josephs dedications: *Nightmusic* for voice and orchestra, inscribed in 1974 "for Bonnie and Bernard Jacobson as a belated wedding present," and the solo piano Arabesques "For Laura and Bernard Jacobson," which was similarly belated but no less welcome.

I spoke of the opening of doors. The educational effect of our friendship for me, however, consisted not only in the many musicians and musical works Wilf introduced me to, but also in the opportunity it gave me to observe the creative process at close quarters. During the time we were both living in London, Wilf would often call me to say, "Bernard, can you come over? I'm stuck!" When that happened, we would sit together at the piano or at his desk and thrash out what was troubling him in the piece he was working on. Very often, after perhaps an hour, he would then say, "Okay, go away—I think I see what I have to do." I have no desire to claim too much credit for the results—certainly I would have been quite unable myself to create what he went on to create—but I *was* sometimes able to pinpoint for him where the problem lay. One particularly dramatic instance came when he was working on his Daphne du Maurier opera, *Rebecca*. About half an hour into the first draft of his score, he found himself up against a brick wall, and this time, when we had finished looking at it together, he simply scrapped everything he had written of the piece and started again. What emerged was, I think, an extremely attractive, musically compelling, and theater-worthy work, which was successfully premiered in due course by Opera North in Leeds under the baton of David Lloyd-Jones (who had written an article on Russian music for me when I was the editor of *Oxford Opinion*).

The most substantial product of my association with Wilf was the antiwar piece we created together, *Death of a Young Man*. Meeting in New York at the time of the Vietnam War, we sketched a scenario in close collaboration. I then wrote sixteen poems, and Wilf set them to music in two versions, one for baritone and piano, the other with accompaniment for chamber orchestra. The latter has never to my knowledge been performed, but Thomas Hemsley and Paul Hamburger gave a superb premiere of the piano version in 1971 at the Harrogate Festival in northern England. Tom Hemsley was also the baritone soloist when Wilf's Requiem had its London premiere. He was one of those baritones whose sheer clarity of tone meant that one always knew exactly what pitch he was singing—but that very quality proved at one brief moment in this performance to be something of a liability. Tom sang all his solos beautifully except one, where for just a few seconds he could be clearly heard to be singing a perfect fourth away from the correct pitch. After the concert he told us, in deep embarrassment: "Just as I was getting up to sing that passage, I had a sudden thought—had I forgotten to make an important call to Zurich? [where he was principal lyric baritone of the opera company]—and that completely threw my entry off."

For much of Wilf's later life we met relatively rarely, since we were living in widely separated places. But I saw him as often as I could, and it was poignant to witness what I can only call his sad decline in prosperity and health. He had been a highly successful and popular composer of scores for numerous films and for such substantial television series as *The Great War* and *I, Claudius*, but by the 1980s most of the directors he had worked with had retired or died. Commissions in those commercial fields all but dried up, and he had to move into progressively smaller apartments to make ends meet. His marriage to Val, moreover, had broken up around 1970, his sexual orientation (or his perception of it) had changed, and his failure to find a male partner of any permanence led to a dispiriting round of overeating that eventually made him so obese that, if we walked from his last residence in London's Camden Town to eat lunch at a Chinese restaurant barely two hundred yards down the road, he would have to stop at least twice on the way to take breath. When he died in 1997 at the relatively early age of seventy, sorrow was leavened by a degree of relief at his release from what had clearly become a burdensome and depressing life.

Aside from performances, I was also able during my time at Philips to attend a number of recording sessions, with performers including the French baritone Gérard Souzay with the American pianist Dalton Baldwin, and the Italian baroque ensemble I Musici. I was also sent to London to watch Sviatoslav Richter recording the Liszt piano concertos in the Walthamstow Town Hall, with the intention that I would include an account of the sessions in the liner notes. During the breaks between sessions, Richter and Mstislav Rostropovich spent their time practicing, mostly separately, for their upcoming recording of the Beethoven cello sonatas: at one point Richter, the inveterate perfectionist, practiced a pair of trills continuously for an hour and a half, while Rostropovich several times mischievously tried to distract him by playing one or two passages an octave too high. Rostropovich's wife, the soprano Galina Vishnevskaya, also came to the hall once or twice to rehearse for a song recital she was about to give with her husband at the piano.

Partnered in the concertos by the London Symphony under Kirill Kondrashin, Richter achieved prodigies of virtuosity coupled with a philosophical profundity not often encountered in performances of these works. When both the concertos were complete on tape, the producer, Alex Saron, declared that everything was satisfactorily "in the can," and suggested canceling the one remaining scheduled session. Richter, however, the inveterate perfectionist, wanted to play the end of the Second Concerto one more time, and also the whole of the First Concerto. Saron joked that the record could be released with a label saying, "Sviatoslav Richter, grosse Künstler, kann dieses Konzert noch besser spielen" (The great artist Sviatoslav Richter can play this concerto even better). Richter smiled for a moment, but then turned serious, and said, "Nicht kann—*muss*!" (Not "can"—*must*!) Who was right? Well, when the record eventually came out, both of those last-session versions had displaced the previous efforts.

The sessions, incidentally, provided me personally with one episode of somewhat alarming drama. One morning I happened to be the only representative of the Philips management in the hall, and so, Walthamstow in those days being a desert as far as decent restaurants were concerned, I was entrusted with distributing packed lunches to all the musicians. These, I might say, were no down-market lunches: they came from the famous West End store Fortnum and Mason, and contained such sophisticated treats as roast pheasant. When the time came to reassemble for the afternoon session, I inquired, through Kondrashin's KGB handler, whether the Maestro had enjoyed his lunch. The question translated, Kondrashin, with brow furrowed and in ominously serious tones, launched into a response that must have gone on for at least two or three minutes. I thought I had an international incident on my hands—and I was greatly relieved to hear the summary translation: "Mr. Kondrashin says he has had lunches which were better and lunches which were worse, but in the circumstances it was quite acceptable."

The I Musici sessions in Amsterdam yielded some amusing memories. When we all left the studio, one of the group's coconcertmasters, Felix Ayo, used to enjoy walking along the side of the neighboring canal and testing the bells of all the bicycles parked there, and would punish the owner of any bike without a functioning bell by letting the air out of its tires. More serious, and more long-lasting for me, was the friendship that developed with the producer of most of these sessions, Milanese-born VITTORIO NEGRI. Vittorio was not only a producer: I learned later to appreciate him as a musicologist and as a talented conductor, who was responsible in the succeeding years for many fine performances in the Philips Vivaldi

Edition. During my Philips days, he was the one person on the staff that I felt I could really learn from in musical matters. But Vittorio spent most of his time traveling to recording sessions in other countries, and was in Baarn for only a few weeks of the year. My own position in the company left me feeling intellectually isolated and deprived of good musical influences. There was, moreover, no one on the staff qualified to offer salutary criticism of my work on either musical or linguistic grounds. As someone with a natural tendency to think of myself as God, I felt the danger of this situation, and it was for this reason that, after two years, I resigned without having any clear idea of where I was going to go next.

The only criticism that my writings for Philips were subjected to (one or two negative reviews aside) came from the company's London office. Quita Chavez, who was my editorial opposite number there, invited me to come for an exploratory meeting to discuss her misgivings. This turned out to be thoroughly amicable, and furthermore led to a most cherished contact: DERYCK COOKE, the distinguished musicologist who was to be the resuscitator of Mahler's unfinished Tenth Symphony, was invited to read some of my liner notes and offer his opinion about them. This was so positive that we became firm friends. Some years later, after a conversation we had about the sheer scale of certain musical ideas, I played Deryck an Archiv Produktion recording of a piece he didn't know and that I particularly admired, *Machet die Tore weit*, by Sebastian Knüpfer, one of Bach's predecessors as cantor of the Thomanerchor in Leipzig. Deryck was as vividly impressed as I already was by the long-breathed size of its main idea.

Despite my departure from Philips, my association with Vittorio lasted to the end of his life. I took the opportunity in 1993, when I was serving as artistic director of the Residentie Orkest in The Hague, to invite him as a guest conductor, with excellent results, especially in a graceful performance of Schubert's Fifth Symphony. Later, a few years before his death, my wife and I visited him in the Swiss town of Blonay, where he lived with his French wife, Georgette. Our reunion was as cordial as ever, and it was characteristic of this generous man that, when I went to pay the bill at the hotel where he had booked a room for us, I was told that of course Signor Negri had already paid it.

The musical world, like the recording world within it, is a notoriously small place. Long after I left Philips, I learned that Costa Pilavachi, whom I knew later when he was a leading figure with the company, had served as artistic administrator at the Boston Symphony Orchestra from 1985 to 1989. He was succeeded in the post by another acquaintance of mine, Evans

Mirageas, who had worked for Chicago's radio station WFMT. As the first Greek-American on the BSO staff, Costa used to write his file notes about guest conductors and soloists in Greek with the intention of keeping them confidential. But then another man with the same background came on the scene, and Costa's notes were no longer confidential.

In the course of my editorial work at Philips, I had developed an excellent relationship with the Public Relations Department, working most closely with Jacqueline Lamers, a delightful lady now in her nineties, with whom my wife and I are still in touch. When I announced my resignation, the department's head, Piet Beishuizen, invited me to work for him, but just at this time an opening came up at EMI International in London for a classical promotion executive, and that was the direction I decided to take.

In addition to Jacqueline, I was on terms of cordial friendship with Margreet Korsman, who was in editorial charge of sleeve design in my own department. Margreet lived in a spacious apartment on the edge of Baarn, looking out across the street into woods, where we sometimes went to gather chanterelles for dinner. On one occasion, Vittorio was a fellow guest. At that time his English was much more rudimentary than it later became, but he knew enough to be able to say to me in strongly accented tones as the evening wore on, "Bernard, you need more wine." That was the evening also when I heard for the first time (in a Philips recording from the Casals Festival) Brahms's Sextet no. 1, falling instantly in love with it and especially with the slow movement variations.

It was at a dinner at Margreet's that I discovered quite how problematic and even embarrassing the French distinction between "vous" and "tu" (the formal and informal second person) could be. The guests that evening included the Italian baritone Renato Capecchi. On his earlier visits to Baarn, we were accustomed to converse with him in French, because it was the best language for our particular combination of nationalities and fluencies. Italian being much more relaxed about making the transition from "voi" or "lei" to "tu" than French was about switching from "vous" to "tu" (which latter form really did in those days imply an intimate relationship), we took this as warrant for readily using the French equivalents "tu" and "toi" in speaking with him. This time, however, he was accompanied by his new French wife, so Margreet and Jacqueline felt reluctant to "tutoyer" Renato, because, after all—what was his wife going to think? So for the first half-hour of that evening, until everybody felt more relaxed, they found themselves practically unable to talk to him at all.

I moved back to London in spring 1962, living at first in a flat near Paddington Station belonging to my cousin Bella, who had moved to the

United States, and later sharing a flat just off Edgware Road with John Emanuel. Though John and I had both attended the City of London School, and indeed were supposed to be related in some way (when someone asked him how we were related, he answered, "Our fathers meet at funerals"), we didn't really know each other until he approached me about the possibility of my replacing his flatmate, who was moving out and getting married. We very quickly enjoyed the amalgamation of our two sets of friends into one wider group, and John has remained another of my dearest lifelong friends.

At EMI, I reported most directly to Peter Andry, a former orchestral flutist who had moved from his native Australia to England and was one of the heads of the company's classical operations. Much of the decision-making was done in meetings of the ICRC, or International Classical Repertoire Committee, which met fairly often in London to work out what recordings should be made and which territories they should be marketed in. One committee member was the suavely elegant John Coveney, who represented EMI's US operation, Angel Records. I would get to know John better when I moved to New York, and he invited me to dinner in his Murray Hill apartment, which had a waist-high display cabinet full of beautiful jade that ran all round the hallway. I already found him both impressively cultivated and quite amusing: at one meeting, when the soprano Anneliese Rothenberger's impressive musical and dramatic gifts were being discussed, he remarked to the committee member from Germany, "She is also, saving your presence, Frau Berthe, a very nice shape." I knew the expression "saving your presence" from the work of long-dead authors, but had never heard anyone actually say it.

My own responsibilities at EMI included providing press information on recording sessions and arranging photographic coverage; Godfrey McDomnic and Axel Poignant were our excellent sources for the latter. Over the next two years I got to know many front-rank performers, both at actual sessions and in informal contact. One set of sessions that McDomnic photographed took place in the Temple Church just off Fleet Street, and produced one the finest recordings of music by Elgar and Vaughan Williams for string orchestra. The conductor was Sir John Barbirolli, and at one session he had an unexpected visitor. Bernard Herrmann was a composer celebrated for the scores he wrote for such Alfred Hitchcock classics as *North by Northwest*, *The Man Who Knew Too Much*, *Vertigo*, and, most famously, *Psycho*, but he also created a more-than-respectable output of concert and stage works, including the opera *Wuthering Heights*. Barbirolli was a great fan of his, and was delighted during a break in recording to share a few sips from his hip flask with his guest.

One particularly stimulating conductor was Josef Krips, whom it was a pleasure to meet after all the concerts I had heard him conduct in my first years of attendance at the Royal Festival Hall. Though born in Austria, from the late 1940s to 1970 he conducted most actively in the United Kingdom and the United States. Generally regarded as a fairly relaxed and not especially intellectual musician of predominantly classical interests, he was nevertheless possessed of a sharp curiosity and an equally sharp tongue. Over lunch once, when he expressed admiration for the music of Pierre Boulez (which, so far as I know, he never conducted), I asked him what he thought of Karlheinz Stockhausen: his instant retort was, "That is not the music of a gentleman!" At a recording session for a record coupling Stravinsky's *Firebird* Suite with a suite from Richard Strauss's *Der Rosenkavalier*, he became incensed with some slovenly orchestral playing, and rapped out: "And now, for the special effect, all the second violins will play *together*." Clearly, this was not a man much concerned with making friends and influencing people, and yet, over the years, he was able to produce many persuasive, charming, and technically adroit performances and recordings, including a supremely relaxed and idiomatic reading of Schubert's "Great" C Major Symphony.

My closest connection with a conductor in those days was with Colin Davis. He was the first conductor with whom I established ties of warm friendship, and reading of his death in April 2013 saddened me deeply, especially because I had neglected in his last years to stay in touch with him.

Back in my first years at Oxford, the Chelsea Opera Group used to mount three concert performances of each of three operas, one in London, one in Cambridge, and one in Oxford. An amateur organization that nevertheless maintained professional standards, it was founded in 1950 and is still active more than half a century later. Davis, who later became president of the group, conducted most of its performances during the 1950s, and it was in Oxford Town Hall that I first heard him at work. I remember in particular a 1957 performance of *Die Zauberflöte* in which his seemingly effortless way of drawing thrilling sonorities from the chorus provoked me to go to the hall's telephone booth at the end of the evening to tell a friend, "I've just heard the greatest English conductor, and I don't just mean 'since Beecham' or 'since Boult' or since anybody else—I mean *the greatest*." in 1959, there was a concert that included a Beethoven Second Symphony where the sudden *sforzando* in the trio section of the third movement had me practically jumping out of my seat. I have still never heard another performance of the work that made this moment so effective.

It was around 1963, during my time at EMI, that Davis and I finally met, first at a recording session in which he conducted Berlioz's *Harold en Italie* with Yehudi Menuhin as viola soloist. At that time he was chief conductor of the Sadler's Wells Opera and I attended several outstanding performances that he conducted there, including an *Idomeneo* in which the opening storm scene gained in dramatic aptness from the old-fashioned London fog that seeped into the theater off the streets and rendered the stage only intermittently visible. We agreed to have lunch together, at an unfancy pub just around the corner from the theater, where I think we ate the standard pub fare of that era—Scotch eggs and ploughman's lunch. With characteristic directness, Colin said to me: "I've been offered contracts by Philips and by EMI, and I've refused to sign with either. Am I a fool?" My reaction was to say that in the short term he had done the right thing, because with links to both companies he would have a fairly free choice of the repertoire he wanted to record; that in the medium term he had done the wrong thing, because in those circumstances neither firm would have a strong reason to promote him; but that in the long term, again, he had done the right thing, because he was so talented that he was going to make a successful career anyway. Nothing that came later proved me wrong.

One of the things I loved most about Colin was his lack of pomposity. In the course of an interview one day, mentioning how much I liked his recording of Mendelssohn's "Italian" Symphony with the Boston Symphony Orchestra, I asked whether his unbroken continuation of a series of timpani strokes near the end, a series that was discontinued for several bars in my score, came from an edition that I was unfamiliar with. His response, in his dark brown velvet voice, along with a slow smile and a crinkling around the eyes, was: "Oh, dear. Have I been naughty?"

We continued to meet frequently in the 1960s. One especially revelatory recording session, in 1966, was of the first of Davis's three recordings of Handel's *Messiah*: in it, he went further than any conductor before him in observing baroque rhythmic conventions, and encouraging vocal embellishment by his soloists. Soon afterward, now living in New York, I told him in the course of a telephone call that I had just been listening to Charles Mackerras's recording of *Messiah*, but assured him that it wasn't better than his own version. "Oh," he replied, "I'd be delighted if he got it more right than I did."

It was in 1967 that Colin called one day and asked if I would be free on the following Friday. I told him I would, and he asked if I would mind taking his wife to the opening night of the production of *Peter Grimes* in which he was about to make his US debut. I said, "Well, I'm not actually allowed in at the Met"—one of my proudest achievements as a critic (discussed in chapter 3) had been to be banned by that organization. Colin said, "Of course, you won't be there as a critic—you'll be there as my guest." So Shamsi and I attended the performance together. Heading backstage at the intermission, we encountered Leonard Bernstein, who said to me, "After you—critics before artists," and when I explained my noncritical status with the Met, he said, "Oh, did you tell the truth about this place? Did you say what a load of shit it is?" But it was what happened when we went back again at the end of the performance that totally endeared Colin to me. Rudolph Bing came bustling into the dressing room, saying, "You must come now, Mr. Davis—the reception is just about to start," to which Colin replied, "Mr. Bing, there are a lot of people in the corridor out there who want to shake my hand, and they have every right to do so. I'll join you when I've said hello to all of them." Exit Bing, muttering angrily.

Most of our later encounters, apart from a few pleasant days at the music festival in Daytona Beach, Florida, when he was there with the London Symphony Orchestra, were to take place in New York. Colin was a warmly welcomed guest conductor with the Philharmonic during the time I was living in Philadelphia, and thus within easy reach of renewing acquaintance with him and with his inspired music-making.

Three composers were most central to Colin's early repertoire and to establishing his reputation: Mozart, Stravinsky, and Berlioz. The first two were apparently also the favorite composers of Bertrand Russell, and so they made up the program when Davis led the London Symphony Orchestra in a concert to celebrate the philosopher's ninetieth birthday. In addition to two works by Stravinsky and Mozart's Piano Concerto no. 21 in D Minor (K. 466), the evening's music included Mozart's Symphony no. 39, whose finale Davis had a way of pacing in such a way that it seemed liable at any moment to run out of control and yet never did, keeping the listener's ears constantly alert: it was excitingly different from the "business as usual" manner of conducting. Informal by nature, after the concert Davis sat companionably with the evening's soloist, Lili Kraus, on the edge of the Royal Festival Hall stage, legs dangling, while a series of distinguished guests stepped up to greet Russell. The philosopher's American-born secretary, Ralph Schoenman, also read greetings from a long list of well-wishers who could not be present. Given the controversial political views that had landed Russell in hot water with the British establishment—and indeed on two occasions in prison—we were not surprised when the list of messages proceeded for a long time with no greeting from the Queen. Then Schoenman read out congratulations and good wishes from "Queen Elisabeth [. . . dramatic pause . . .] of the Belgians." It brought the house down.

Berlioz, like Mozart and Stravinsky, was well represented in the many programs Davis led in New York in the late 1980s and beyond. There was some sprightly Haydn too, and a sprinkling of Elgar, including, in 2002, a particularly memorable First Symphony. But perhaps the most prominent name of all was Sibelius, with whose music Davis developed a rapport over the years that made his recorded cycles the versions of choice for many collectors. The New York performances I heard were certainly memorable in the way they combined lucid presentation of the classical symphonic elements underlying the composer's style with no less convincing realizations of the often violently dramatic elements subversive of that traditional stability.

It was during my time at EMI that I finally heard the explanation of a story whose first act had played out long before. In the 1950s Otto Klemperer gave a series of Beethoven cycles with the Philharmonia Orchestra at the Royal Festival Hall. One year I saved my pennies, joined the queue, and bought a ticket for the final concert, comprising the First and Ninth Symphonies. I was mortified when it was announced that Klemperer had fallen ill. The program was conducted instead by Paul Hindemith, and I was even more mortified by the concert itself, which was a disaster. The third movement of the First Symphony lumbered along at a lugubrious three beats to the bar, instead of the dynamic one-to-a-bar that we usually, and surely more appropriately, hear, while the Ninth was performed with a complete lack of purposeful forward motion and dramatic force.

Fast forward to 1963, when I was working at EMI and heard act 2 of the story. It seems that Walter Legge, founder and for a long time manager of the Philharmonia Orchestra, had visited Klemperer in the hospital and asked, "Who do you want me to get to conduct the Ninth? I'll get anybody you want." "Anybody?" said Klemperer. "Anybody!" "Get Hindemith." "Hindemith?" "Yes, you said you'd get anybody—get Hindemith."

So the invitation went to Hindemith. After the concert, Legge went back to the hospital, and Klemperer asked him, "How was the Ninth?" "It was a disaster," said Legge. Whereupon Klemperer observed, "Yes, I thought it would be." "You thought it would be!," Legge exclaimed—"But then why did you tell me to get Hindemith?" "I wanted to see how far you would go to please me."

Hindemith was not the only colleague for whom Klemperer felt contempt. After Bruno Walter's death, Klemperer prefaced a Mahler Second Symphony he was conducting at the Royal Festival Hall with a performance of Mozart's *Masonic Funeral Music* in Walter's memory—but his attitude in conversation was anything but respectful. He never accepted Walter's dropping his family name, Schlesinger, and is said to have told friends after a Walter concert: "I went to this concert that Schlesinger conducted. I went to see him afterward, and I told him, 'Schlesinger, I heard you conduct Mozart's Fortieth Symphony twenty years ago, and you conducted it again tonight, and the two performances were identical. [Dramatic pause] And you know, he took it as a *compliment?!*'"

The music-making at most of the Klemperer sessions I attended was of a riveting intensity, but the extra-musical aspects were often distasteful. The maestro had a talent for bullying that he indulged without restraint, and if you were an attractive young soprano, like Ingeborg Hallstein (the Marzelline in his perhaps unsurpassed recording of Beethoven's *Fidelio* with the Philharmonia Orchestra), you had to be very fast on your feet around the listening room to evade his predatory grasp.

Working at EMI in my junior position under Walter Legge was a fascinating but similarly mixed pleasure. It was said that Legge would step on anyone in his efforts to get ahead. The stepping on people was undeniable, but I soon came to realize that it was done out of dedication to making records of the highest possible artistic standard. Like Klemperer, Legge was not one to govern his tongue. Sessions conducted by Lovro von Matačić, with Legge's wife, Elisabeth Schwarzkopf, in the title role, produced a magical recording of Lehár's *The Merry Widow*; but at one point Walter snatched up the listening-room telephone and barked at the conductor, "In der Partitur steht es geschrieben, 'Allegro vivace'; es klingt wie ein Elephantenballett" (In the score it says "Allegro vivace"; it sounds like a ballet of elephants).

It was in connection with this recording that I distinguished myself by smashing Madame Schwarzkopf's cheese knife. Having broken his arm, Walter felt unable to come to work in the office, where he and I were preparing the booklet that would accompany the release, so he invited me to lunch at their house. At the appropriate moment, Schwarzkopf handed me a sizeable hunk of Parmigiano cheese and a very delicate-looking cheese knife—perhaps predictably, the only result when I tried to cut the cheese was that the blade broke off the mother-of-pearl handle and flew across the room. I must say that Madame was very gracious about it.

In his pursuit of audio perfection Walter was often frustrated. The last straw came when, having rejected a whole series of test pressings of Karl Böhm's *Così fan tutte* recording and refused to authorize its release, he was told by management that they intended, with or without his approval, to base the release on the latest set, which was perhaps the eighth or ninth attempt the studio had made. Walter invited me to join him in one of the Abbey Road listening rooms, where he had Edward Fowler, the studio manager, put the original tape on one machine and the latest test pressing on another. We listened to several passages, first in one version and then in the other. The loss of quality from tape to test pressing was drastic, but Fowler said, "I can't hear any difference." "You see what I'm up against, my boy?" Walter said to me. So it was no surprise when, a short time afterward, he resigned his position with EMI.

During his sessions, Walter would routinely work his way through an entire carton of two hundred cigarettes, dumping the butts in an outsized ashtray after taking only one or two puffs at each. He would also go through several large bottles of San Pellegrino mineral water. This prompted his less sophisticated fellow producer for EMI, Victor Olof, to comment after spending a few minutes at a Legge session, "This chap Pellegrino must be makin' a fortune out of Walter!"

Though at EMI I was not a member of the sleeve department (as I had been at Philips), I enjoyed a close relationship with the people responsible for creating the fronts and backs of the record jackets. Along with many well-conceived and stylishly executed jackets, they had their share of potential disasters. Having selected for Sir Thomas Beecham's recording of Handel's *Solomon* a seemingly suitable illustration of "The Judgment of Solomon," they had to search hurriedly for a replacement when it emerged that this was one of the several scenes in the oratorio that Beecham had cut. (Memorably, the conductor's recorded spoken introduction to the performance ended with the resounding proclamation: "The entire work has been reorchestrated by me.")

Then there was a jacket that went as far as the proof stage but no further. We were about to issue a record of piano-duet music with one pianist superimposing the second part on the first by overdubbing: it was among the first attempts at this technology. Then someone walked through the sleeve department one morning, looked at the proof in question and said, "You can't put that out!" "Why not?" the editor asked him. "You can't put out a record titled *Leonard Pennario Plays with Himself*!" I have kicked myself ever since for not having purloined a copy of that proof as a memento.

Even when the record jacket presented no such fundamental problems, one of my colleagues, Nick Boyle, could always be relied on to come up with an irreverent comment on a design. A cover for a recording of Strauss's *Tod und Verklärung* that featured an extensive detail from the ceiling of the Sistine Chapel provoked the observation "Ah, yes—'Friday night is bath night.'" There were in any case few topics immune from Nick's brand of humor. He remarked to me about a man we had both had dealings with, "The trouble with John is that he thinks the sun shines out of his bottom . . . and really it doesn't, you know."

Having experienced the polyglot culture of Holland, where at that time it was impossible to get even a modest job as a secretary if you didn't speak at least four languages, I suggested in the course of discussions that it might be sensible to use a Dutch printer for our multilingual opera librettos. My colleague John Bush and I took a ferry trip and paid an exploratory visit to one of the oldest firms in the business, Johannes Enschedé in Haarlem, founded in 1703. We were warmly received by two charming gentlemen, one of whom drily remarked that he understood England was "in the throes of a prostitutional crisis"—this was at the time of the scandalous Profumo affair. Our hosts took us around the company's museum, where one of the exhibits under glass was, they told us, "a little job we did for Mozart when he was here in 1765." It was all enormously impressive, and it was clear that the firm could have done a wonderful job for us, but their prices proved to be beyond our budget. In the end we had to content ourselves with English printers, who after all had their own high standards and served us well.

Another trip abroad for EMI took me to Paris, to attend sessions in the Salle Gaveau at which Sviatoslav Richter was to record Schubert's "Wanderer" Fantasy and his Sonata in A Major, D664. In order not to be interrupted by such mundane concerns as breaks for meals, Richter chose to record at night, so I developed a routine of arriving at the hall around 10 p.m. for the start of a session, which would last until about 4 or 5 a.m., walking back to my hotel through largely deserted streets, ordering a cup of hot chocolate, going to bed for a few hours' sleep, going to the firm's Paris office around 2 or 3 p.m. to look after administrative chores, eating dinner at about 8 p.m., and then beginning the sequence again.

At these sessions, there being no orchestra involved, I had much more opportunity to chat with Richter than there had been at the London Liszt sessions. The pianist was making one of the first recordings of the Fantasy to incorporate Paul Badura-Skoda's numerous editorial corrections. When I asked him what kind of differences there were, and why, he explained that the copyists in Schubert's time must have found it hard to believe some of the composer's highly original harmonies, so they had inserted more conventional harmonies—several hundred of them—into the text. "It's just like what Rimsky-Korsakov did to *Boris Godunov*," he said, going to the piano: "For instance, this [he played an extended passage entirely from memory] is what Musorgsky wrote, and this [playing again] is what Rimsky turned it into."

Such erudition was impressive enough, but I was perhaps even more surprised when Richter told me that his greatest musical ambition—as far as I know never realized—was to conduct a production of Britten's *Peter Grimes*. There was indeed no end to the lessons to be learned from this supreme musician. I was to continue his devoted admirer until very near the end of his life, and one of the most enthralling recitals I ever heard from him was given in the Amsterdam Concertgebouw when Laura and I were living in The Hague in the early 1990s. By this time fairly frail, he told the hall staff not to let anyone backstage to greet him after the performance. This was given with the entire hall darkened except for one small lamp on the piano, and in the resulting tiny pool of light he gave performances of five Beethoven sonatas—culminating in a riveting, even terrifying, account of the "Appassionata"—that in no way fell short of the standards he had set himself in his prime.

With the move back to London my Dutch connection with the *Times* had been severed, but I soon developed a relationship with the *Guardian*, formerly known as the *Manchester Guardian* but now firmly established as a leading London newspaper, for which I wrote frequent concert reviews. I reviewed concerts also for *Music and Musicians*, one of the Seven Arts group of magazines, and started reviewing records in the sister publication *Records and Recording*. To avoid any danger of impropriety arising out of my record company job, I reviewed only recordings that were not competitive with anything in the EMI catalogues. And to avoid even the possible *appearance* of impropriety, I wrote as "Robert Carlyle," choosing that simply because it was the most euphonious name I could think of.

By the beginning of 1964 it was becoming hard to find the time for all my freelance reviewing, on top of a very full schedule in my job at EMI. Then my friend the musicologist Alan Walker, who was preparing a symposium on the music of Chopin, asked me to contribute a chapter on the songs. If ever I was going to freelance full-time again, this seemed like the right moment to cut loose from EMI, where I was already feeling frustrated by such matters as the heavily cut recording of Monteverdi's *L'incoronazione di Poppea* that the management had released. So at the end of January I decided to take the plunge.

It was a decision, incidentally, that flummoxed my father. He had spent his entire working life as a hired hand in other people's tailoring shops. When I told him I was leaving my job at EMI and going completely freelance he said, "But who will be your boss?" I explained that I wouldn't have one. All he could do was shake his head in total incomprehension.

Walter Legge had resigned from EMI a few weeks earlier, and the day after announcing my own resignation I was both touched and amused to find a memo on my desk headed "To Bernard Jacobson, from WL, Artists' Department," with just three words typed in the middle of the page: "Et tu, Brute?" My decision made, I launched myself on the exhilarating if dangerous waves of the freelance sea.

CHAPTER THREE

FREELANCE IN LONDON AND NEW YORK

1964–67

The first few months after EMI saw me busier than ever. In preparing my chapter on Chopin's songs I consulted Doris Kaye, my cousin Rue's wife, who was Polish by birth. Having come to England as a student in the 1930s, she was the only survivor of a family whose other members had remained in Warsaw and were all murdered in the early days of the Holocaust. Doris was of indispensable assistance in translating the song texts from a language of which I knew nothing. We simply sat down together, she told me what every single word in each poem meant, and I then transformed the result into reasonably graceful but still literal English.

One does not enter the profession of music critic in order to make a fortune. By way of illustration, my first batch of records for review in London included seven or eight releases, and I was paid ten shillings (fifty pence in modern British currency, if not in present-day value) for each of the reviews—but one of the recordings was of Messiaen's *Turangalîla-Symphonie*, and the score of that work, which I felt obliged to buy in order to write a properly responsible and well-informed review, cost twenty pounds, or five times what that entire month's work for *Records and Recording* earned me. Busy though I was, besides working on the Chopin songs, with my various reviewing assignments for the *Guardian* and two of the Seven Arts magazines, it was getting so hard to pay my bills that I was beginning to think I needed to crawl back into some kind of paid job. What rescued me, just a day before I planned to take that step, was the kindness of my friend Joan de Smith, my flatmate John's cousin, who was a frequent visitor to our flat. She handed me one hundred pounds: "Maybe that will tide you over," she said, and it did.

The flat was within about fifteen minutes' drive from the Royal Festival Hall, where many of my evenings were spent, though the summer shifted the focus of reviewing to the Royal Albert Hall for the BBC's Henry Wood Promenade Concerts. While Sir Malcolm Sargent was chief conductor at the Proms until 1966, Beecham, Boult, Klemperer, and Barbirolli were by now among the conductors I heard most frequently. I remember a Strauss program at the Proms conducted by Norman Del Mar (author of an indispensable three-volume study of the composer's music), which included a performance of the "Dance of the Seven Veils" from *Salome*. Del Mar being given to fairly active gyrations on the podium, I commented in my review that he had conducted it to his own choreography. The evening's soloist was the Dutch soprano Marijke van der Lugt, and so, since I have always felt that reviews should offer the reader some fun, the fact that "Norman of the Sea was joined on the platform by Little Mary of the Air" was too good not to be noted.

Barbirolli, like Beecham, was fond of making a short speech at the end of a concert, and on one occasion he congratulated the Festival Hall audience on having been present. There had been a new work on the program, a symphony by William Wordsworth (great-great-grandson of the poet's brother Christopher), which had actually sent a number of audience members heading for the exits between movements, so Barbirolli's remarks carried a certain edge of irony. For myself, I greatly enjoyed the new piece, and decided to write not just a review of it but a more extensive *Music and Musicians* article about the composer, who invited me to his home in Hindhead, Surrey, so that I could learn more about him.

Wordsworth's music seems to have fallen into near-total oblivion, perhaps partly because a distaste for his predominantly tonal idiom at the BBC—in the days when serialism was the doctrinaire "flavor of the month"—resulted in the proscription of broadcasts even of works of his that had won important prizes. His Second and Third Symphonies, however, are still available on a Lyrita CD conducted by Nicholas Braithwaite, and they are both strongly individual and genuinely beautiful works that would amply repay any open-minded listener's investigation. The Third, in particular, makes fascinating play with a major/minor oscillation rather like the finale of Schubert's Quartet in G Major, D887.

It was during this time that a friend drew my attention to an advertisement (as with the Philips job, in the *New Statesman*) calling for a musicologist to accompany a party of Americans on a tour of European music festivals. I applied, had an interview at a London hotel with a representative of an organization called Academic Travel Abroad, and in due course set off with the six people I was to shepherd around Europe. It turned out that ATA's organization was a total shambles. Only a few of the tickets promised for performances in France, Austria, Germany, and Italy had actually been secured, and after only two of the tour's fourteen days the modicum of money I had been given for use on the road was gone. I had had to use it to correct mistakes with reservations and to cheer my charges up with a couple of decent and inevitably expensive meals.

Our opening stay was in Paris, where, on Bastille Day, July 14, 1964, we witnessed a fireworks display of positively symphonic magnificence over the Seine. But I quickly realized the dire nature of my assignment, and took the group into my confidence. I told them that if they wanted to give up and return home, I would campaign with the organization for a return of their booking fees. But if they wanted to throw in their lot with me, I promised to make the trip as successful as I possibly could. My frankness won them over, and the rest of the tour proceeded with a good deal of satisfaction for everybody.

One especially rewarding encounter (though I regretted having to leave my charges to their own devices while I enjoyed it) was a meeting with Nadia Boulanger at The American School at Fontainebleau. The celebrated French organist André Marchal was her guest at the time, and I enjoyed a friendly and instructive lunch with these two luminaries of musical and intellectual life, Madame Boulanger reminiscing warmly about the composers, including the Americans Carter and Copland, who had studied with her back in the 1920s.

From my own point of view, the tour, chaotic though it was, changed the course of my life in no small degree. With one of the six members of the party, a young woman from Philadelphia named Diana Stambul, I very soon established the warmest possible personal relationship, and it was as a result of this that I decided to visit the States in November to see whether this was just a shipboard romance or something of more permanent nature.

I went for three weeks, but I had been wise enough to obtain a green immigration card—much easier in those days—in case I found occasion to work while I was in the United States. And though Diana and I soon realized that we were not meant for each other in perpetuity, I ended up staying nine years—and happily Diana (now Diana Burgwyn) has remained a good friend ever since, through the course of a couple of marriages on each side.

Not wanting to put too much pressure on our then-theoretical relationship, I didn't stay for those first weeks in Philadelphia, but in New York with my cousin Bella, who had herself moved to the States and married Bill Masters, a fellow social worker. They lived on Henry Street, on the Lower East Side, where they were employed at the Henry Street Settlement. My stay with these highly hospitable people lasted about two months, and taught me some small but illuminating first lessons about America. Their apartment was a walk-up on about the third floor. One day, Bill suggested we might go for a walk. "Let's see what the weather's like," he said, and walked across the living-room, I supposed in order to open the window—but instead he picked up the phone to find out what was going on outside. Whenever we did actually find ourselves on the street, any acquaintances he introduced me to wanted to talk to me about only two subjects, the Beatles and the royal family, concerning neither of which I could at that time claim either interest or enthusiasm. A more substantial and enjoyable experience of Americana came just a week after I arrived with the Thanksgiving holiday, which the three of us celebrated as guests at the Grand Street Settlement, another notable social-work agency just around the corner.

In the course of several visits to Philadelphia during those weeks, I attended both my first concert in the States and my first opera performance. The concert, given by the Philadelphia Orchestra with its former music director Leopold Stokowski returning as guest conductor, was a lesson in its own right. I had always snobbishly thought of Stokowski as a mere orchestral confectioner, all spectacular sound and no substance, but his direction of the Sibelius Second Symphony sparked a radical reassessment. Not only was his baton-less technique immaculate—he conducted the cross-rhythms just after the start of the slow movement with one hand, the other held firmly motionless by his side, and made it obvious that any kind of imprecision or accident was impossible—but the musical perceptions he conveyed were utterly convincing and idiomatic.

The Philadelphia Lyric Opera's production of *Tosca* was less impressive, though it was strongly sung, with a cast headed by Renata Tebaldi. Her "Vissi d'arte" was beautiful, but there were dramatic flaws that undermined the musical effect. When Giuseppe di Stefano, the Cavaradossi, was dragged across the stage after being tortured, Tosca, who is supposedly in love with him, coolly moved her skirt out of the way so that it shouldn't get bloodstained. Meanwhile, Spoletta made his entrance an embarrassing few seconds *before* Aldo Protti, the Scarpia, rang his bell to summon him into his office.

More persuasive was the company's production of *Die Walküre*, which I also saw during my first months in the States. The most memorable aspect was the superb Wotan of the Scottish bass-baritone David Ward, who had studied the role with the great Hans Hotter, and with whom I established a cordial friendship. That friendship even survived the time David telephoned Bella and Bill's number at one o'clock in the morning. They had a small baby at the time, and we had just gone to bed after finally getting the baby to sleep. Bill answered the phone, and when David asked to speak to me, said, "I think he's asleep." But David, who had clearly had a few drinks, apparently roared in full bass-baritonal splendor, "Well, wake him up, man, wake him up!" Fortunately, David was the sort of man it was impossible to be angry with for long; we agreed to meet soon for a meal at some more practical hour, and my cousins didn't seem to hold the episode against me.

I became increasingly focused on activities in New York once it became clearer that my relationship with Diana was not going to be a long-term one. Nor, unfortunately, was the exiguous amount of money I had brought with me going to last more than a few weeks. Early in January 1965, with about four-and-a-half dollars left and no job and no perceptible prospects, I made my typically rash decision: I went to the British Airways ("BOAC" in those days) office on Fifth Avenue and sold my return ticket back.

A day later I responded to an advertisement from a publishing firm in New York seeking someone to write a series of travel guides aimed at American students visiting Europe. The firm's editor, LLEWELLYN KING, invited me for an interview, at which I was hired and immediately thrown in at the deep end: the project was to consist of twelve paperbacks, of approximately one hundred pages each; I was to write three of them (on Holland, Belgium, and Luxembourg; on Great Britain; and on Israel—where I had never been); and I was required to have the first one, which would serve as pilot for the series, finished by the end of that weekend. So I buckled down on Saturday morning, wrote eighty-four pages of the book on the Low Countries by 6 o'clock that evening, and consigned the remaining space to be used by prospective readers "for notes." Llewellyn and I then spent several days at suitable sources in the city, such as the United Press International office, choosing pictorial material for the whole series.

Relatively low though the literary level of the series was, it did provide me with two new friends among the writers of the other books. One was Ken Platnick, who lived in New York and has written a variety of nonfiction, and with whom I am still in touch. The other was Bernard Rabb, who a few years later became the publisher of a more serious book of my own, *Conductors on Conducting*. Bernard lived in one of a linked pair of geodesic domes he had built in Frenchtown, New Jersey, and in the other one he ran his Columbia Publishing Company. He died a few years ago, but we enjoyed an excellent working relationship in the 1970s. I greatly admired his taste in words and images and the professionalism of his work as a publisher.

My collaboration with Llewellyn marked the beginning of drastic changes of fortune for us both. I now had an income, however meager, and he lent me some money to enable me to prolong my stay in New York. Then, through further contacts, I acquired some critical assignments. I had always wanted to meet Roland Gelatt, the editor of *High Fidelity*. I did so now through the good offices of a friend from EMI, Nick Boyle's former secretary Sheila Brown, who had moved to New York and was working for the magazine. When I told Roland that when he had been visiting EMI in London, I had asked Peter Andry several times to introduce me to him, without success, Roland said, "Oh, I used to ask him to introduce me to *you*—I know your writing very well." The upshot was that he engaged me to review records every month for the magazine; asked Shirley Fleming, who edited the *Musical America* live-music section, to give me access to her pages also; and offered me a monthly stipend of a generosity that, while leaving my freelance status intact, made my London-based expectations look quite paltry.

While I was thus prospering, Llewellyn's fortunes were going in the opposite direction. In short order, he lost his job and his apartment, and his wife left him. Repaying my debt to him, I now found myself in my turn lending *him* money. Some years later, when he had moved to Washington, DC, the decline in his fortunes was arrested by his foundation of a weekly news sheet devoted to covering the subject of energy. With the outbreak shortly afterward of the latest Israeli-Arab war the publication gained a large number of subscribers and moved from a weekly to a daily publication schedule. This was to be the beginning of a prosperous period for Llewellyn. We have known each other now for fifty years, meet whenever possible (though too rarely), and have continued our mutual borrowing-and-lending practice whenever one or the other was in need, determining only that repayments should always leave one of us in debt to the other to the tune of one dollar.

My collaboration with ROLAND GELATT was to open several doors for me and would ripen into a friendship that played out on both sides of the Atlantic and ended only with his death in 1986. Leaving his post at *High Fidelity* in 1968, Roland had served for a while as managing editor of the *Saturday Review*, and then moved with his second wife, Lois, to London, where he joined the editorial board of Thames & Hudson.

With my first wife, Bonnie, I actually saw more of Roland and Lois during their London residence than I had in New York. The four of us took several long weekend trips to Normandy, staying mostly in chateau hotels and indulging in some serious eating. Roland was a man of intense sensibility and strong gastronomic appetites. I was also much struck by his urbanity, which revealed itself in an amusing way when we were staying at a hotel in Bayeux. A few hours before dinner we had carefully reserved a particularly comfortable table, but when we came down we found that the restaurant was crammed with young people, apparently celebrating their First Communion, and the table had been given to some of them. The waitress took us to a much less desirable corner and asked whether this would be satisfactory. Quite simply, and without the slightest fuss or undue emphasis, Roland said "No." His combination of firmness, sang-froid, and courtesy set an example that I have subsequently tried, with mixed success, to follow—and it did result in our being escorted to a pleasanter spot for our dinner.

We also dined with the Gelatts several times in London, on one occasion having as our fellow-guest the actor René Auberjonois, whose grandfather, of the same name, had created the stage design for the 1918 world premiere of Stravinsky's *L'Histoire du soldat*. We learned from the younger René how miserly the composer had been. Royalties for the work were sent by the publisher to Stravinsky, who was supposed to divide them up and send the appropriate proportion to the Swiss librettist, Charles-Ferdinand Ramuz. The older René, however, discovered after several years that Ramuz had never received any money from Stravinsky. When Auberjonois upbraided Stravinsky for his failure to fulfill his obligation to Ramuz, who was in serious financial straits, the well-heeled composer apparently replied: "Oh, I didn't think he needed anything like that—he's just a peasant."

Eventually, suffering from cancer and seeking what he thought would be the best possible medical care, Roland moved with Lois to Philadelphia, where Laura and I were already living, but he did not survive the move for very long. At his death, he left a note for Lois asking her to organize in his memory no solemn services but just a party at which his friends could drink a few bottles of good wine, and suggesting that she should ask me to choose music for the occasion, "because Bernard knows my tastes better than anyone else."

In responding to this honor, I chose just three recordings. One of them Roland himself had requested: the terzetto "Soave sia il vento" from *Così fan tutte*, because it was, he said, "the most beautiful leave-taking music I know." To this I added an excerpt from Bach's "Goldberg" Variations, played by Wanda Landowska, whom Roland had interviewed and written about at some length. My final choice was Thomas Campion's song *My sweetest Lesbia, let us live and love*. If not particularly well known, this is one of the most gravely beautiful lute songs I am acquainted with, and the text of its last stanza—one of two that Campion himself added to his translation of the first six lines of Catullus's *Vivamus, mea Lesbia, atque amemus*—seemed to me to match Roland's own prescription for his memorial perfectly:

> When timely death my life and fortune ends,
> Let not my hearse be vexed with mourning friends,
> But let all lovers, rich in triumph, come
> And with sweet pastimes grace my happy tomb;
> And Lesbia, close up thou my little light,
> And crown with love my ever-during night.

The celebration went off well, and I met many friends of Roland's I had not previously known. One of them, as it happened (and as Roland, Lois told me, had hoped might happen), got in touch with me afterward with a professional proposal. Gerry Morse had retired from his job working for Bennett Cerf's Random House to become a freelance publisher. He was in the middle of planning a series of cassette tape recordings called "Talk a Walk," which were designed to be carried on walks around London as informative descriptions of the various buildings and other sites on their routes. They would have such titles as "The Inns and Outs of Court." Listening to the eulogy of Roland I had delivered, Gerry had thought that my voice and British accent suited me well to be the reader of the texts he had written. We did record a couple of them, but unfortunately for Gerry the Walkman itself was very soon to be superseded by newer technologies designed around the compact disc. He died before he could transfer the tapes to the new medium, and his creation disappeared virtually without trace.

The *High Fidelity* connection was a great source of satisfaction. In 1967, Ernest Ansermet took leave of the Orchestre de la Suisse Romande, which he had founded in 1918, with a pair of concerts in Philharmonic (renamed in 1973 Avery Fisher) Hall, and I reviewed both concerts for the *Musical America* section of the journal. It seemed to me characteristic of this firmly unsentimental man that he should be relinquishing his post after forty-nine—not fifty—years, and 3700 miles from home. One of the programs included a suite from Frank Martin's comedy-ballet after Molière, *Monsieur de Pourceaugnac*. It was a pleasure to renew personal acquaintance with the composer, whom I had interviewed at his home in Holland seven years earlier, and who was in the hall for the performance. There was a sprinkling of French music on the programs, played with all the refinement for which Ansermet's conducting of such repertoire was famous. But, perhaps more surprisingly, it was the performance of the Brahms Fourth Symphony, rhythmically pointed and at once rich and lucid in texture, that impressed me the most.

A few weeks later, Roland happened to be in touch with Ansermet on an unrelated subject, and sent me a copy of a letter he had received in which, after dealing with other business, the maestro thanked Roland for having sent him my review. "It is always a pleasure for an artist," he wrote, "when he feels he has been understood"; and he ended by saying he would be grateful if he could have a few copies for his friends.

Later that year, Ansermet was one of the guest conductors of the Chicago Symphony Orchestra in my first season in the city. His concert was one of only two during my six years in Chicago (the other was conducted by Stokowski) at the end of which the orchestra registered its enthusiasm for the conductor by saluting him with a *Tusch*—an impromptu flourish by brass and percussion. Never having met Ansermet before, I took the opportunity of greeting him backstage and introducing myself as the writer of the *Musical America* review. He embraced me warmly, and I was glad to think, when he died a few months later, that we had at least had one cordial meeting.

Another *Musical America* review was of the inaugural concert by the Chamber Symphony of Philadelphia. The new ensemble's conductor was Anshel Brusilow, the former concertmaster of the Philadelphia Orchestra. A batch of New York critics was bussed down to Philadelphia (and quaffed champagne during the drive through the Lincoln Tunnel) for the occasion, which was a notable artistic success. I particularly remember the beautifully pointed playing of the double basses in the "Pilgrims' March" second movement of Mendelssohn's "Italian" Symphony, and I was happy to encounter some of the players again when I joined the management staff of the Philadelphia Orchestra in 1984. I continued to follow the progress of the Chamber Symphony for the next year or so, and my enthusiasm for its work, especially in a performance of Brahms's Serenade no. 1 (op. 11), led to an invitation to serve as assistant producer to Howard Scott when he recorded that piece with the orchestra.

Anshel attended my first wedding, in Philadelphia in 1968, and in 1981, when I was in Dallas giving a series of lectures on Brahms and he was by then the ex-music director of the Dallas Symphony, he invited me to attend one of the classes in a conducting course he was teaching at the University of North Texas in Denton. His teaching method was unusual: the work being studied that day was *Le Sacre du printemps*, and for part of the class he assigned instrumental lines to all the students, whose task was to *sing* the music as well as they could. The resulting ensemble provided each student in turn, as he or she took the podium, with an ideal laboratory for the honing of conducting skills.

The professional and personal sides of life joined forces constructively for me in New York. Very early in my time in the city I met a young woman with whom I was to enjoy an intimate relationship for several years. Marilyn Dubow was a gifted violinist, with a successful record in competitions and in performance, though some reverses sustained in her studies diverted her from the soloist track, and she has now been for many years a member of the New York Philharmonic's violin section.

In about 1965, Marilyn gave a recital in one of the smaller Lincoln Center performance spaces and asked me to turn pages for her pianist, Marsha Cheraskin, with whom she was to play Charles Ives's Second Violin Sonata. At one point in the work, where both violin and piano parts are tumultuous in texture and speed, they needed me, after turning a page for the pianist, to dash around the piano within six measures of Presto, turn a page for the violinist, and then rush back in time for the next piano page turn. Having managed this without disaster, I was rewarded when the work ended with what must have been my first solo bow on a concert platform.

While she was still focused on freelancing, Marilyn also played in the American Symphony Orchestra, which Leopold Stokowski had founded in 1962 at the age of eighty. The young Uruguayan composer and conductor José Serebrier, some of whose works Stokowski himself premiered, had been appointed associate conductor. He led the orchestra several times in Carnegie Hall, and I remember encountering the music of the Mexican composer Revueltas for the first time when Serebrier conducted a brilliant performance of his *Redes*, in a program that also featured Schubert's Sixth Symphony, no less beautifully played. Serebrier also served alongside David Katz as assistant conductor for Charles Ives's Fourth Symphony when Stokowski gave the work its world premiere in 1965, eleven years after the composer's death, subsequently making its first recording.

Getting to know each other through these various activities, several of which I reviewed, José and I embarked on a friendship that has lasted half a century, enhanced a few years after its inception when he and the soprano CAROLE FARLEY were married and all three of us became close. I was to engage both of them for performances in The Hague when I was serving as artistic director of the Residentie Orkest there in the 1990s. In personal terms, José and Carole were wonderfully supportive friends during my uprooted months between marriages, when, with their daughter and my two children, we spent some relaxed and entertaining time together in London, including a visit to Madame Tussaud's.

Having won his Ivesian spurs assisting Stokowski in the Fourth Symphony's premiere, José made his own recording of the work with the London Philharmonic Orchestra twenty years later, convincingly demonstrating that, however complex its demands, the score can be more than adequately mastered by a single unaided conductor. It can also, I'm afraid, be thoroughly messed up by a single unaided conductor. Seiji Ozawa and the Boston Symphony Orchestra made a recording of it in 1976 in which, in the technically problematic second movement, the conductor gets his forces to the finishing-post together by the simple expedient of ignoring practically every one of Ives's frequent tempo changes.

In the mid-1970s, I was working on my book *Conductors on Conducting* and thinking of including a chapter on Ives. When it became clear that Stokowski, by then in his nineties, would not be available for a discussion, I invited José instead to be a part of the book, and profited from his experience with the composer both alongside his former mentor and in performances of his own. Our discussion about the Fourth Symphony made clear the cardinal importance of properly prepared orchestral parts in ensuring the successful realization of any potentially problematic score. Sitting up night after night marking parts was something that José was always ready to do. It is just one of the elements that have gone to make a career of extraordinary success in the recording studio, and his concerts in The Hague also benefitted from unusually meticulous preparation. It has always puzzled me that José is not a regular guest conductor, let alone music director, with the most important American orchestras, but it may well be that his busy peripatetic career of live and recorded performance and touring with excellent ensembles around the world has not left him with enough spare time to accept invitations from such sources.

My work for *High Fidelity* would also lead to a surprising and at the same time highly rewarding entry into the world of the Beatles. As I noted above, I was far from being a fan of the Beatles, even though, when I was working at EMI, I had chanced to go up in an elevator with them. The occasion for that elevator ride had been rather anticlimactic in outcome. They were visiting EMI's London headquarters in Manchester Square to receive their first platinum disc in recognition of healthy record sales. The management, fearing that we might be inundated by an army of fans, requested a police presence, which was duly granted. But it turned out that the time was not quite ripe for milling throngs of screaming teenagers: the Beatles were certainly already successful, but not yet sufficiently well known, and we had ended up looking at a group of about twenty-five policemen guarding us from about fifteen fans. Three months later, as the group's legend grew, it would have been a different story.

Marilyn was an enthusiastic fan of the Beatles. She persuaded me, much against my will, to accompany her to a double bill of *Help!* and *A Hard Day's Night*—and I capitulated instantly to the impact of their talent and lovability. So it was that, when my carton of LPs to be reviewed for *High Fidelity* arrived one month containing, among the more usual repertoire, a record titled "The Baroque Beatles Book," I was much readier than I would otherwise have been to listen to it with interest and sympathy. What the arranger and conductor of that recording, Joshua Rifkin, had achieved was musical satire on a much higher plane, I think, than that occupied by Peter Schickele's long-running P. D. Q. Bach industry. In comparison with Schickele's generally scatter-shot parodies, Rifkin, himself an impeccable baroque stylist, captured unerringly the character of both his selected Beatles songs and the baroque pieces he melded them with.

I like to do my homework, so, in preparing a suitably poker-faced pseudo-musicological feature review for the magazine, I paid several visits to the Greek coffee-shop where Llewellyn and I were in the habit of meeting for breakfast, and listened to all the relevant Beatles songs on the small juke box at my table. (I wondered whether the quarters and dimes I fed into the machine could be listed in my next tax return as "juke-box research expenses," but decided, when the time came, not to put the idea to the test.) When my review appeared, I was very soon contacted by Teresa Sterne at Elektra/Nonesuch Records, who had been responsible for the record's release, to ask whether I would be willing to write the program notes for a forthcoming Baroque Beatles Concert at Lincoln Center. This was a very agreeable assignment, which I promptly accepted, but the contact thus made also brought me into the Nonesuch ambit with much more serious and far-reaching consequences.

Along with his work on "The Baroque Beatles Book" and his recordings of piano rags by Scott Joplin, which would play a big role in the 1970s revival of interest in ragtime, Joshua Rifkin was and is a highly reputable musicologist and performer, whose argument that Bach's choral works were originally performed with one voice to a part has had a far-reaching effect in contemporary Baroque practice. In the 1960s he was closely associated with the Nonesuch record label in an advisory capacity, and as a result of our Beatles collaboration I soon found myself joining him and his colleague Jason Farrow in a kind of informal advisory committee for Nonesuch.

I soon found my Nonesuch involvement intensifying when Josh went off to Germany to continue his musicological studies with Alfred Dürr at the Johann-Sebastian-Bach-Institut in Göttingen. Jason and I did our best to take up the advisory slack, and in addition I was asked to write a number of liner notes for Nonesuch releases. One of these brought me into contact with the Claremont Quartet, and this in turn led to an invitation to record Schoenberg's *Ode to Napoleon Buonaparte* as speaker with the quartet and pianist Joanna Nickrenz for the label.

By way of preparation, we gave one or two public performances in Maryland and Virginia, and then made our recording in 1968 in Rutgers Presbyterian Church on West Seventy-Third Street in New York City. The acoustics in the church presented problems, so that even with an expert producer, Marc Aubort, at the controls, it took several hours to reach an acceptable setting of microphones and channels. The five instrumentalists then suggested that we go for something to eat before embarking on the actual recording, but I told them that while I was now feeling fully up to recording, if I once let the adrenalin ebb by going to dinner, I didn't think I would be able to raise the level again afterward. So we went right ahead and recorded. The session totaled something like eight hours, and when we did eventually go and eat, two of them had to support me, with one of my arms on each man's shoulder, so that we could make it to a nearby restaurant.

Neither when I listened to the replay, nor again when the record was released, could I tell whether we had succeeded in taping a good performance: I knew only that we had done the best we could. But, though I don't wish to sound vulgarly self-congratulatory, when I compared our version with another one that was released a year or so later, I concluded we had actually done very well, for the many changes of pulse and tempo in the score, which we had meticulously realized, were scarcely perceptible in our rivals' performance.

The recording was mostly well received, though Stephen Plaistow, reviewing it for the English magazine *The Gramophone*, commented that the narrator's strong American accent ruled it out of serious contention for collectors. I was amused rather than upset by this, but years later, when I was working for Boosey & Hawkes and had come to know Stephen as a congenial colleague, I felt it was time, at one of our after-concert parties, to ask him, "Do you remember reviewing a Nonesuch recording of Schoenberg's *Ode to Napoleon* for *The Gramophone*?" He said yes, whereupon I asked whether he remembered the narrator's strong American accent. By that point he was looking at me in a decidedly embarrassed manner. "You?" he asked, and we had a good laugh over the whole episode.

Another spin-off for me from my association with Nonesuch was the invitation to present my own radio program, with the title "Music Showcase," which ran weekly for thirteen weeks on half a dozen radio stations around the country, including the one—WFMT—for which I was to do so much broadcasting after moving to Chicago. We recorded the programs at WQXR, one of the principal New York classical music stations, where I sat across a desk from the station's own announcer: he made the basic routine announcements, and I added my commentary on the music from the Nonesuch catalogue that we had chosen to broadcast.

I have always had a fairly resonant voice, so it was amusing to find that, in order to obtain a proper balance of voices, we had to put the two-sided microphone much closer to my side of the table than to the WQXR man, who delivered his lines with positively titanic power. That was no problem. What *was* a problem was the number of takes we had to indulge in before I could get all the consonantal clusters and the umlauted vowel in the name of one choir, the Niedersächsischer Singkreis, to sound right.

Despite the positive effect that my association with Nonesuch Records had on my career, there is one aspect of the label's history about which I take a decidedly minority view. Teresa Sterne, or Tracy, as everyone called her, holds a position almost amounting to canonization in the recollection of many musicians, especially those active in the field of contemporary music, and it is true that she masterminded the evolution of the label into a force of extraordinary creative value. In fact, it was Jac Holzman, who founded Nonesuch in 1964 as a subsidiary of his already well-established Elektra Records, who played the key role in coming up with that new vision. Tracy's conversion of a budget label, releasing mainly recordings of baroque and chamber music licensed from small European record companies, into a trail-blazer of high-level contemporary innovation was an outcome wished on her much against her will.

Herself a talented pianist who had exchanged her performing career for an administrative role in the record industry, Tracy had well-informed enthusiasms of her own among the composers of the day. But when Jac decided on a radical change in the character of the label's releases, replacing the concentration on licensed baroque recordings with a high-profile emphasis on new music and new recordings, Tracy fought vigorously against the idea. Understandably, she liked Nonesuch the way it was, and that way certainly featured many high-quality recordings of baroque repertoire, including numerous works by Telemann, otherwise unavailable on record at the time. But Jac, as Tracy put it at the height of her resistance, "wants to turn it into some kind of avant-garde label." It was only when Jac made it clear to her that either she would bring the change he envisaged into reality, or he would find someone else to do so and she would no longer be in charge, that Tracy gave up the battle. To her, as a musician of elevated taste, and a woman gregarious enough—and sensible enough in the circumstances—to cultivate many valuable new contacts in addressing the new vision of Nonesuch, the credit for the skillful way she executed the task that had been forced on her is undoubtedly due. But I think it is high time for Jac's role in coming up with that new vision to be more widely recognized.

Another feature review I wrote for *High Fidelity* had consequences as important for me personally as professionally. The subject this time was a group of records devoted to baroque music by Albinoni and others with oboe soloists including Pierre Pierlot, André Lardrot, and Harold Gomberg. In my review I mildly criticized what I thought were some weaknesses in the liner notes for one of these records, which carried the byline of James Goodfriend. Within a few days, I received a letter from him, explaining that the record company in question had allowed him no control of the final version of his notes, and going on to say how much he admired my writing.

I was so impressed by the magnanimity of such a response to criticism that I took care to accept very quickly the suggestion in his letter that we might meet for lunch, and when we did, the warmest rapport was immediately established. Jim was at that time the music editor of *Stereo Review*, *High Fidelity*'s only serious rival publication. He asked me whether I was happy writing for *High Fidelity*, and told me that, if I was feeling any dissatisfaction with my role there, he would be delighted to have me on

Stereo Review's reviewing panel. I felt that Jim and I understood each other extremely well. His proposal presented me with less of a problem of loyalty to *High Fidelity* than it would have done a year or two earlier, because Roland had by now left the magazine. While I was on good terms with his very competent successor, Leonard Marcus, I didn't feel that I owed him anything, so I accepted Jim's invitation, and continued to write for *Stereo Review* for a considerable number of years, extending into the periods after my move from New York to Chicago in 1967 and then my return to England in 1973.

Besides the smoothness of our professional relationship, on a personal level Jim lived fully up to his surname, and became indeed so good a friend that he served in 1968 as best man at my first wedding. My friendship with Jim, and since his marriage also with his wife, Carol, has been rewarding on many levels. He is a man of remarkable breadth and depth of cultural interests. As an appreciator of music and a writer about it, he has few equals. I no longer possess the set of records of Debussy's complete piano music for which he wrote the accompanying booklet—but the booklet has a permanent place on my shelves. Clearly, his eye is as good as his ear, because a few years after we began our collaboration he left the field of music criticism and, with Carol, set up C.&J. Goodfriend, a highly successful dealership specializing in old master prints and drawings. He is also an enthusiastic *bon vivant* with a near-encyclopedic knowledge of wine, and I greatly regret that he has never found time for the book on the subject that he planned to write under the wonderful title *How to Read a Bottle*.

Jim and I agree about many musical matters. Our shared enthusiasm for the Czech pianist Ivan Moravec is one such, and in Jim's case has been pursued in a practical way through his joint foundation and leadership with Alan Silver of Connoisseur Society, the label that released many of Moravec's early recordings. But one of the many dinners we ate together while I was living in New York was instrumental in clarifying my own approach to the making of critical judgments. I happened to have just reviewed Colin Davis's first recording of Handel's *Messiah*. When I remarked to Jim that I thought it was superb, he registered emphatic dissent. And when I gave our disagreement some thought, I came to an important conclusion.

There is a terrible temptation for a critic, in such circumstances, to say to himself, "I loved it, but my colleague X, whom I respect, hated it. I must have missed something—I must have been snowed!" And yet, why should one succumb to what I have come to call the "fear of being caught with one's critical pants down" syndrome? Is it not equally likely that *X* missed something? I decided that there was no good reason for allowing Jim's negative judgment to call my own enthusiasm for Davis's *Messiah* in question: on the contrary, it was my duty as a critic to stick to my own perceptions and my own judgments. Having realized that there is no good reason to be more diffident in maintaining positive judgments than in entertaining negative ones, I have done my critical work since that time quite consciously on the basis of a principle borrowed from the field of jurisprudence. "Better that ten guilty persons escape than that one innocent suffer" is a dictum that first appeared in 1766, in Sir William Blackstone's *Commentaries on the Laws of England*. Surely still applicable to the administration of justice, and more emphatically so in countries that practice capital punishment, it is in my opinion equally valid in criticism of the arts, and I try to be faithful to it, even in the face of the outrage that the perception of unpunished vice can arouse in a critic's soul.

One reaction to my first record reviews in New York had come in the form of what I can only call a fan letter, from a man of whom I soon became a devoted fan myself. This was Henry Fogel. Writing to tell me how much he admired my work, he added that I might be interested to see the program sheet he enclosed from the FM station, WONO, that he ran in Syracuse, NY. It was indeed striking both for the volume of the music he was presenting there, and for the perceptive taste it revealed. Henry invented the concept of the fund-raising radio marathon, and hosted more than one hundred such "radiothons" in support of orchestras throughout the United States and Canada. He went on to an impressive career in orchestral management, in turn with the New York Philharmonic, the National Symphony Orchestra of Washington, and the Chicago Symphony, then became president and CEO of the American Symphony Orchestra League (now the League of American Orchestras), and has since served as Dean of the Chicago College of Performing Arts, a school of Roosevelt University.

During Henry's Chicago Symphony days around the year 2000, I enjoyed a particularly entertaining postconcert dinner at which the guests, besides him and his wife, Fran, included Bernard Haitink and Mr. and Mrs. Zarin Mehta. Zarin, a man of exceptional elegance and charm, held the post with the New York Philharmonic corresponding to Henry's in Chicago. His wife, the soprano Carmen Lasky, had previously been married to Zarin's brother Zubin. Asked about this in an interview, she explained, "I had everything monogrammed, and how many ZM's do you know?"

Patrick Smith was another contact I acquired through my record reviewing activities. The author of *The Tenth Muse*, an excellent historical study of the art of the opera libretto (which seems now to be out of print), Patrick also published an admirably unglossy magazine, the *Musical Newsletter*, from 1970 to 1977, and commissioned me to write some articles for it. One of them, titled "Once More with Feeling," expounded my view that the repeat marks classical composers put in their scores ought routinely, except in highly exceptional circumstances, to be respected, and it provided Alfred Brendel with ammunition in our disagreement on the subject, discussed in chapter 4.

At roughly the same time as my first contact with *High Fidelity* I had also met Martin Bernheimer, who was working as assistant critic to Irving Kolodin at *Saturday Review*. Martin welcomed me with warm generosity, inviting me to join him for performances when his wife couldn't be there. Our first opera attendance together, for Offenbach's *Tales of Hoffmann*, was also my first evening at the Metropolitan Opera. I arrived first, and when Martin took his seat he said to me, "Welcome to America's number one provincial opera house." That satirical judgment was to prove prophetic for my own future relations with the company, and Martin's friendship would also have a big effect on my career.

Opera, and specifically *Opera* magazine, became another string to my reviewing bow. At the start of my years in the States, and until he left in 1966 to become music critic of the *Dallas Morning News*, John Ardoin served as New York correspondent for the London-based *Opera* (an independent publication not to be confused with *Opera News*, which is a house publication of the Metropolitan Opera Guild). John invited me to be his assistant, which meant that he continued to review the Met's new productions, while I covered cast changes and also reviewed an occasional production by a smaller-scale company of lesser appeal to his essentially grand-opera interests. *Triple-Sec*, an uncharacteristically light-hearted and nonpolitical "opera-farce" in one act by Marc Blitzstein, made a hugely entertaining double-bill in the latter category when I saw it paired with Poulenc's *Les Mamelles de Tirésias*.

But it was my work at the Met that resulted in my being banned by the company. It wasn't an official out-and-out ban, but the assistant manager, Francis Robinson, called John and said, "We're not prepared to provide any further tickets for Mr. Jacobson's use." What occasioned this was my having dared, reviewing role debuts by young singers who had obviously been allowed no opportunity for rehearsal, to suggest that the Met was perhaps not a really serious artistic institution, and to suggest also that I didn't think I ought to have to ask not only audience members but ushers not to talk during the performance. The company was still in the old house at Thirty-Ninth Street, and I had seen some very fine performances there, most memorably two of Strauss's *Arabella*, with some new cast members, that both featured the dazzlingly beautiful Lisa Della Casa in the title role. But the lack of seriousness prevailing at that time both in the company's musical preparation and in its physical productions led me to say to myself, "Thank goodness I don't have to go to the Met any more!" I did expect that *Opera*'s editor, Harold Rosenthal, would protest on my behalf, but he—reprehensibly, I thought—kept quiet, perhaps because he was hoping to receive an official invitation to opening of the new house at Lincoln Center. I was rather gratified when he didn't.

In the middle of my first calendar year in America, there was an interval that took me back to London for a few months. I hadn't yet come to any firm conclusion about which side of the Atlantic my immediate future could be based on: I realized fairly soon that growing up, for someone in my line of work, consists in realizing that, whichever side of the ocean you are on, you are going to miss the other side badly. The specific occasion for my trip back in 1965 was the premiere at the Cheltenham Festival of what WILFRED JOSEPHS called my symphony—his Second, which he had dedicated to me. Just before the performance started, a door at the side of the hall opened to admit—looking very Byronic in an all-black outfit of a kind that was less often seen in those days—the celebrated English playwright Arnold Wesker (author of *Roots*, *Chips with Everything*, and *The Kitchen*). Arnold had collaborated with Wilf on a small-ensemble piece titled *The Nottingham Captain* that anticipated many features of the music-theater genre explored by other composers in the decades that followed. After the concert Arnold and I brought a celebratory evening to a close by taking Wilf and Val out to dinner.

At that Cheltenham Festival, I met for the first time the first contemporary composer whose music I had heard in a concert hall, Francis Chagrin. Francis had a close official connection with the festival, but he was so modest and retiring a man that he would patiently line up waiting to collect a ticket for a concert. At another concert I attended, dedicated like the festival as a whole to contemporary music, I happened to be sitting next to Frank Howes, who was approaching the conclusion of his tenure as chief music critic of the *Times*. After one monumentally uneventful new piece, he rumbled at me: "D'you know what the trouble with English music is? Andante, my boy—endemic Andante."

The Josephses and I were staying for several days at a comfortable country club just outside Cheltenham, and we had the company there of several other friends, musicians, and critics, including Vladimir Ashkenazy, Felix Aprahamian, Stanley Sadie, and Denby Richards. There was also an American couple staying there, and one morning I was astonished to hear them asking for fruit for their breakfast—quite an exoticism in England at that time. The gardens were extensive, and our group of friends and acquaintances developed a keen if short-lived passion for playing croquet on the lawn laid out for it. We enjoyed it so much that we couldn't bear to end our games when the sun went down, so play continued in the encroaching darkness by the feeble illumination of a couple of cigarette lighters.

Felix Aprahamian was one member of our group who enjoyed little success in the garden. At croquet, which for all its elegance can turn into a decidedly violent game, he often found himself vigorously croqueted into the rose bushes, extrication from which always took some time. And a young waiter in the club's dining room for whom he took a fancy (there was no secret about Felix's sexual orientation: John Amis, in an obituary notice in the *Guardian*, described him as "A lover of music; also of men and, occasionally, women") failed to show up for a nocturnal assignation Felix had made with him.

Felix was a distinguished musician and critic, and a man of striking elegance. He usually sported a dashing red-lined cape when he attended opera performances, and he once told the story of having for some reason been ushered into the ceremonial or royal box at an English Opera Group performance in Venice. The members of the orchestra spotted him, and mischievously offered an emphatic bow in his direction after playing the British national anthem. "What did you do?" we asked him. "Well," said Felix, "obviously, I stood up and bowed back." The film director John Schlesinger clearly thought Felix looked so much like a critic that he cast him in his 1965 film *Darling* for a walk-on role as an art critic attending a gallery opening.

Felix was especially focused on French music and on organ music. Years later, when Bonnie and I lived just around the corner from him in London's Muswell Hill, we discovered the two tastes conjoined, for his house contained the organ he had inherited from his friend André Marchal. As a teenaged music lover he visited Delius and sat beside Widor in the organ loft, and other close friends of his included Messiaen and Poulenc. A prominent member of the Delius Society, he also possessed keen enough insight to explain to me why I was not an admirer of the composer he loved so much: "Delius is all about harmony," he told me, "and you're a counterpoint man." It was a truth that had never occurred to me before.

Stanley Sadie, on the other hand, was a colleague with whom my relationship over the years became much less warm. I got to know him reasonably well after 1970, when he became the editor of the sixth edition of *Grove's Dictionary of Music and Musicians* (published in 1980 as *The New Grove Dictionary of Music and Musicians*). Bonnie worked for a time alongside Alison Latham, as one of the two editors reporting most closely to Stanley, and found it galling to observe how, if someone who was the subject of an article planned for publication called to complain to Stanley about some perceived slight or insult, he never supported his own staff but would always agree fulsomely with the caller. Talking with Stanley also had a curious effect on my own self-esteem. I don't know whether this was simply a characteristic of his, or whether it stemmed from some more complex flaw in our relationship, but I almost always felt that whatever I said to him was stupid. Fortunately, I haven't had that experience with anyone else, even if on occasion I perhaps should have.

I found Stanley's approach to criticism, when he was writing for the *Times*, radically different from my own. At a party he threw for *Grove*'s editorial staff and some outsiders, an American guest complimented him on the insight a recent review of his had shown, but went on to qualify his praise by saying that he felt the review could only have been understandable to a reader expert in music. "Well, of course," Stanley replied: "Who else am I writing for?" I am far from suggesting that a critic should lower his discourse to the level of the least knowledgeable or the least intelligent reader, nor do I rate the common standard of American music criticism higher in sheer expertise and perceptiveness than the British, but I have always preferred the typical American critics' desire to attract and involve readers from outside the pool of music-lovers to the in-group attitude too often found in their British colleagues.

The flat that John Emanuel and I still rented in London made a perfect *pied-à-terre* for my weeks back in the city. Aside from access to concert halls, it was also just a short walk away from the BBC Music Department on Clipstone Street, and I seized an opportunity that presented itself to work there for a while, reporting directly to Deryck Cooke and writing continuity for announcers on the music programs. My responsibilities also included reading and (when appropriate) replying to letters from listeners. Most of the letters were gratifying, and some were hostile, but the funniest was a highly appreciative tribute addressed to "Amadeus String and his Quartet." The celebrated Amadeus Quartet is said to have given a concert once in Texas at the end of which a gentleman in a ten-gallon hat came down to the front of the hall, told the players he had enjoyed their playing enormously, and hoped that they would come back in the future, and that by then, as he put it, "your little band will have grown."

Another European visit in 1965 took me, with Marilyn Dubow, to Milan, where WILFRED JOSEPHS's Requiem had its world premiere on October 28. A 55-minute work scored for solo baritone, solo string quintet, double chorus, and orchestra, it is a setting of the Hebrew Mourner's Kaddish. Dedicated "*pro defunctis iudaeis*," it incorporates the composer's slightly earlier string quintet, *Requiescant*, in its original chamber scoring, as three of its ten movements.

Wilf's career had been fairly low-key up to this time, but he was catapulted into international attention when, out of a well populated field of submissions from many countries, his Requiem won the First Composition Competition of La Scala and the City of Milan. The premiere, which the audience received with some enthusiasm, was conducted by Nino Sanzogno, who, under the chairmanship of Victor de Sabata, had been a fellow member of the jury with his conductor colleague Franco Ferrara and the composers Ghedini and Petrassi.

The end of the performance was followed by a few minutes of confusion, followed by widespread laughter: Sanzogno had turned to stage right to beckon Wilf onto the platform to share in the ovation, but Wilf, having asked an usher in his rudimentary Italian how to reach the door to the stage, had instead been shown out into the street through a door that wouldn't open to let him back in. So he ended up walking all the way around the outside of La Scala, somehow got back in, and appeared at the opposite side of the stage to the one the maestro was looking and gesticulating at.

Such adventures aside, the Requiem was for some years one of Wilf's most successful works. It had performances in London, New York, Chicago, Philadelphia, and elsewhere, and it is to be regretted that an excellent Unicorn-Kanchana recording on a now defunct LP label was never released on CD.

After our few days in Milan, Marilyn and I accepted an invitation from Robbins Landon and spent an idyllic week at his palatial villa in Buggiano Castello near Florence, where a harpsichord that had belonged to Handel stood in the hall. At the time, Robbie was in the early stage of planning what was to be the first complete recording of the Haydn symphonies. Leonard Bernstein, his first choice to conduct it, was unavailable, and I told Robbie about the sessions I had attended at which Antal Doráti had recorded exceptionally brilliant performances of the symphonies nos. 59 and 81. (During a session break, Doráti had asked me in his characteristically

Hungarian-inflected tones whether I knew the difference between a Greek and a Hungarian. I didn't, whereupon he said, "Both will offer to sell you their grandmother, but only the Hungarian will deliver." What I like most about that conclusion is that one doesn't know whether it is a good or a bad thing.) Robbie had not yet heard Doráti conduct Haydn but said he would investigate, and I like to think that the generally excellent set of Decca recordings that appeared not long after had its origin in our conversation.

Back in London, I had greatly enjoyed working under the wing of Deryck Cooke, who was both a great and a very kind man. Nevertheless, a phone conversation with Martin Bernheimer was to prompt my decision to return to New York. Martin had by this time become the music critic of the *New York Post*, but he had now been offered the more prestigious corresponding position at the *Los Angeles Times*. Ostensibly, the purpose of his call was to ask for my advice about whether he should make that transcontinental move (to a city where, to quote a line in Woody Allen's *Annie Hall*, "the only cultural advantage is you can make a right turn on a red light"). But I don't think Martin could have been much in doubt about what he should do—and when his decision to make the move became firm, he told me that he would give my name to all his freelance contacts in New York with the idea that I should inherit his various regular assignments. Martin was as good as his word, and on my return to New York I found myself, in addition to my continuing association with *High Fidelity/Musical America*, writing program notes for Thomas Scherman's Little Orchestra Society, for presentations arranged by Jay Hoffman's artists' management company, and for several other organizations.

Another contact that I had been given by my friend Malcolm Troup, a Canadian-born pianist resident for years in London, was with the editor—whose name I am ashamed to be unable to remember—of the New York-based *Musical Courier*, for which I reviewed a number of performances. The world premiere of Stravinsky's *Requiem Canticles* was one of these (or rather two, because the piece was played twice). It was performed in Princeton, at the McCarter Theater, and there during intermission I had a most unexpected encounter. As I reached the center aisle, heading for the lobby, my former Oxford philosophy tutor, David Pears, reached it from the other side of the theater. He made what struck me as the perfect philosopher's comment: "Good Lord, what are you doing here? What am I doing here? Exactly!" Years later, when we both attended the wedding of his colleague Hugh Lloyd-Jones, who had tutored me in classics, I twitted David with what he had said, but he denied all memory of having said it.

With regard to the work I was reviewing, I was somewhat embarrassed to find myself criticizing so technically adroit a master as Stravinsky for a technical failing, but on the basis of what I heard in the two performances I could not help finding one. There is a passage in the work where the solo voices have to sing in so low a register that there is no way they can make themselves heard through the texture. It is possible, of course, that this was a deliberate effect Stravinsky was aiming at, but I doubt it. Anyway, I found the passage muddy and ineffective, and felt I had to say so in my review.

Two trips farther afield took me to Florida. I accepted an invitation to attend and write about the opening of a new music building at Florida Atlantic University in Boca Raton, where I met JOHN CANARINA, a gifted conductor and writer who has remained a good friend. A few years later, when I was living in Chicago, he sent me a tape-recording of a performance he had given of Mahler's First Symphony with the Jacksonville Symphony Orchestra in Florida, of which he was the music director. I have to confess that I put off listening to it, thinking, how good can a Mahler symphony performance by such a provincial orchestra be? But then, one day, John called me from the airport, saying he had just arrived for a quick visit to Chicago. I naturally invited him to dinner, hastily found the tape, and discovered a genuinely magnificent realization of Mahler's far from easy score. Later experiences of John's Vaughan Williams performances, as well as his Mozart, have served to confirm that positive impression.

The other Florida trip, in 1966, was to cover the first of the London Symphony Orchestra's many visits to the Daytona Beach Festival. Colin Davis conducted, and John Ogdon was the soloist in a dazzling performance of Tchaikovsky's First Piano Concerto. I spent several days in the town, enjoying time spent talking with Colin, and one of the festival's board members invited me, together with several orchestra members, to a barbecue on the roof of the three- or four-story apartment building near the beach where he lived. There was a great deal of construction going on in the area, and I said to my host that, while he was beautifully situated, he must find the constant noise of the generators on the building sites annoying. But he explained that the noise was in fact produced by large numbers of cicadas. The noise being a natural one, I had to change my attitude in a hurry and approve of it.

Musical America provided many occasions for reviewing and often for meeting and interviewing performers and composers. Lili Kraus was the most charming of all the pianists I spoke with, while the US premiere of Krzysztof Penderecki's *St. Luke Passion*—conducted by Stanisław

Skrowaczewski in the vast space of the Northrop Auditorium where the Minnesota Orchestra used to play—took me to Minneapolis for the performance and for a long conversation with the composer. His *Threnody for the Victims of Hiroshima* had made a vivid impression when I heard it at a Holland Festival concert in the Amsterdam Concertgebouw. The audience response had occasioned an immediate repeat performance, though Frank Howes commented waspishly in the *Times* that Penderecki had required the members of the string orchestra "to do everything with their instruments short of actually playing them."

New York itself, however, was inevitably the richest source of musical stimulation and of new contacts. At the end of 1966, Michael Flanders and Donald Swann brought their second musical revue, *At the Drop of Another Hat*, premiered in London three years earlier, to New York. I saw the show and laughed a lot. Wilf Josephs was in the States to attend the performances of his Requiem that Max Rudolf was to conduct in Cincinnati and Carnegie Hall in the following month, and he introduced me to Michael, who two years earlier had narrated another work of his, an "entertainment" titled *Twelve Letters* set to a text from Hilaire Belloc's *A Moral Alphabet*.

Michael and his wife, Claudia, were staying for the several weeks of the revue's run at the Buckingham Hotel, and they invited me to a weekly salon they hosted there, attended by anyone from the British theater world who happened to be in New York. At these informal gatherings I had the pleasure of meeting Lynn Redgrave, in town for her Broadway debut, and Paul Scofield, who went on to play Salieri in the 1979 stage premiere of Peter Shaffer's *Amadeus* at the National Theatre in London.

At around this time I also had a visit from Annetta Hoffnung, widow of the celebrated cartoonist, humorist, and tuba player Gerard Hoffnung. I had never met Gerard, though I was a devoted admirer of his books of musical cartoons, loved his fake-musicological discussion and recording of *Punkt Contrapunkt* by the nonexistent but brilliantly named "Bruno Heinz Jaja," and greatly enjoyed the hilarious Hoffnung Musical Festivals he presented at the Royal Festival Hall in London. Annetta's visit was an indirect product of her acquaintance with Wilf, who had written several works for Gerard's festivals, and she wanted to talk about ways in which she could revive those events in American concert halls.

A few months further into 1967, Michael and Claudia invited me to visit them at their summer place in West Dennis, on Cape Cod. Another house-guest at the same time was Joanna Steichen, widow of Edward Steichen, creator of the famous *Family of Man* exhibition at New York's Museum of Modern Art. She had married him when he was eighty and she was twenty-seven. Asked how this had happened, she said simply that he had swept her off her feet with the violence of his sexual passion—he was, she told the *New York Times* some years later, "this vital, vibrant, sexy, charming, seductive character."

The several days I stayed on the Cape presented me with a number of new experiences. With Michael, whom we slid into my car from his wheelchair with the aid of a sturdy plank (he had contracted polio in 1943), I saw my first-ever drive-in movie, *Cool Hand Luke*. Claudia and I would also drive down to the beach with Michael, in his wheelchair, holding on to the door handle: as soon as we reached a suitable downward slope, he would let go and freewheel the rest of the way like a glider coming to earth. And with my hosts I ate lobster for the first time, on the deck of a suitably no-frills establishment where the food was served on several sheets of newspaper.

I had a professional commitment the following week to visit the Congregation of the Arts, an enterprising festival at Dartmouth College in Hanover, New Hampshire, to cover several concerts featuring composers in residence and to meet and interview one of them, HANS WERNER HENZE, so I set off early one day from West Dennis with the intention of arriving in ample time for that evening's concert. On the way, however, one of the tires blew out, and I was forced to leave the car I was driving and rent another one for the rest of the journey. With a great deal of time lost, I drove up a new highway that had just opened near the border between New Hampshire and Vermont at a speed considerably in excess of the limit. This led to an alarming moment just as I was passing through the area near Marlboro, Vermont, and suddenly caught sight of a bear stepping off the verge a few hundred feet in front of me. I wasn't sure whether I would be able to stop in time, but the bear looked in my direction, waited till I had passed, and then, as I saw in the rear-view mirror, calmly crossed the road when it was safe to do so. I concluded that Rudolf Serkin, the great pianist and the director of the music festival at Marlboro, must have bewitched the local wildlife through the magical power of music.

I made it to Dartmouth College just in time for the first concert on my agenda. The program reflected the conviction of the festival's director, Mario di Bonaventura, that contemporary works should not be isolated in some kind of musical ghetto: he believed that if a contemporary work was not strong enough to stand next to the classics of the repertoire, there was no point in playing it at all. So the two Henze pieces I heard that evening were stimulatingly juxtaposed with two by Ravel.

In the course of my first meeting with Henze the next day, I was much struck by a comment he made that clearly aligned his approach to the art of composition itself with that inclusive view of programming: "You have to remember your grandfathers. If you try to create art without a connection to your grandfathers—if you forget about Monteverdi, say, and Verdi—the art you create will be a sterile art, a fascist art." The precise meaning of that political allusion may not have been clear, but the notion that art, to be worthwhile, must exist in some kind of continuity with tradition was one that I fervently agreed with.

The rapport we established at Dartmouth established a friendly relationship, both personal and professional, that was to last for years. It would also lead to a commission to translate one of Hans's operas, the "vaudeville" *La Cubana*, for a London premiere production by the English Music Theatre Company that was to be sung in English at Sadler's Wells Theatre. The libretto, "after motifs by Miguel Barnet," was by the German poet Hans Magnus Enzensberger, and translating it was one of the most exacting tasks I had ever undertaken. This was because, in attempting to preserve as precisely as possible the rhyme scheme of the original, I was faced at various points by such passages as a trio in which the three voices sang a stanza of simultaneous superimposed lines with different words but ending on a common vowel-sound, which was followed by the next three lines, again on different words but ending with the same vowel-sound, which had to be incorporated in different words from the three that had ended the first stanza. If this sounds laborious in the explanation, it was no less so in the actual process of translation: that particular ensemble occupied me for two full weeks. I benefitted from helpful suggestions from Enzensberger, with whom I had a friendly meeting some time later at his home in Munich, and when my work was finished he sent me a thank-you gift: an appreciatively inscribed copy of his superb poem-cycle, or "comedy," *Der Untergang der Titanic* (*The Sinking of the Titanic*).

For purely geographical reasons, my subsequent contact with Hans was sporadic at best, but always cordial. We renewed acquaintance when he came to Chicago as a guest conductor. Later, in 1978, I took the opportunity to attend recording sessions at Rosslyn Hill Chapel in London at which one of my favorite Henze works, *Voices*, was recorded by Sarah Walker, Paul Sperry, and the London Sinfonietta conducted by the composer.

I have the feeling that Hans's output falls into two contrasted halves. There is the "straight line" Henze, metrically crisp, frequently diatonic, sometimes motoric music, descending stylistically from Stravinsky and including such works as *Moralities*, and the more chromatic and sensuous "curved" Henze, following in a tradition pioneered by Berg, featuring works like *Nachtstücke und Arien*, *Being Beauteous*, the Double Bass Concerto,

Die Bassariden, and the orchestral *Barcarola*—a more numerous representation of a manner I greatly prefer. My last meeting with Hans, in 2001, came when I was in New York to give a preconcert talk at a Philharmonic concert that included his Ninth Symphony. I asked him, "How are you?" "Old," was his terse reply.

Dartmouth's Congregation of the Arts presented literally hundreds of premieres and featured residencies by two dozen composers before it was regrettably closed down after the 1969 season. My association with Henze was not the only friendship I gained from my visits there: I also met Michael Steinberg, the American music critic that I most respected. Michael and I hardly ever agreed on a specific musical judgment—he once described Elliott Carter's Piano Concerto, which I disliked intensely, as unquestionably the greatest work by an American composer—yet our respect was mutual, and lasted until his death.

In 2009, when Laura and I, with our friends Dick and Bea Wernick, went to hear one of Muti's concerts with the New York Philharmonic, Dick said to me a few minutes before the concert began, "You should look at the program note, Bernard." (It has long been my habit, except in cases where I was in urgent need of information about the music to be performed, to defer program notes for a leisurely reading after the performance.) One of the works on the program that evening was Brahms's Serenade No. 1. In his notes, Michael observed that this was a work seriously underappreciated in the writings of commentators, but described the treatment of it in my book *The Music of Johannes Brahms* (Associated University Presses, 1977) as the "honorable exception." I was much touched that he should thus have gone out of his way to give credit to a fellow critic.

When we first met at Dartmouth, Michael also made a major contribution to my education in American gastronomy: he introduced me at dinner to the deliciousness of soft-shell crabs, which I had never heard of, and which I might well not have thought of ordering without his advocacy. Another encounter at the festival was with a very attractive young American woman I happened to sit next to at the bar before a meal and concert. We asked each other what we were doing there, and she answered that she was a member of the Hamburg State Opera, in the course of whose touring engagement in New York I had recently attended two productions. Perhaps stupidly, I asked her if she was a member of the chorus. No, she said, she was a soloist. "In what role?" I asked. "Baba the Turk, in *The Rake's Progress*," she replied. "Oh, well," I said, feeling less embarrassed over my gaffe, "given the makeup and beard you were wearing, you can hardly be offended that I didn't recognize you." Tatiana Troyanos and I agreed to go to the evening's concert together—it included a clarinet concerto by another composer in residence, Walter Piston, a modestly engaging piece that I liked a lot more than I usually like his music—and to the reception after that, and we stayed in touch until her death at the grievously early age of fifty-four.

Back in New York, I made the acquaintance of two superb record producers, Seymour Solomon of Vanguard Records and Bach Guild and Harold Lawrence of Mercury Records, who later became the general manager of the London Symphony Orchestra. I wrote liner notes for both of them, and with Harold I enjoyed turning pages for Käbi Laretei (Ingmar Bergman's wife at that time, and just recently deceased) when she recorded Hindemith's *Ludus Tonalis* for Mercury. At Harold's house I also heard Rafael Puyana play the harpsichord, at closer quarters than I had heard the instrument before, and discovered quite how challenging it is, with an instrument of such crisp sonority, to make all one's fingers come down on the keys simultaneously.

Through another record company, RCA, where Nancy Swift commissioned me to write some liner notes, I got to know Gustl Breuer, a former actor from Vienna who had lived in New York for years and did some management work for the company. He was one of the most generous people I have ever met, treating me to some excellent meals, and even, when my friend Carli van Emde Boas came over from Amsterdam with his first wife, Puck, for their honeymoon, immediately offering to lend them his comfortable apartment while he went off to stay with a friend. Gustl seems to have left little sign of his varied and distinguished career in the public record, but his little book about the brilliant Bulgarian-born pianist Alexis Weissenberg, whom I came to know and admire during my time in Chicago, was an excellent piece of work. (It is now apparently to be found only in a very expensive German edition.)

Buying records was a particularly pleasurable way of spending time in New York. I became an *habitué* of several downtown stores, and came to be on cordial terms with Egon Soika, who managed one near the corner of Forty-Second Street and Fifth Avenue. When I eventually told him I was leaving town, he reached into the shelves behind him and handed me a gift: a record of Lotte Lehmann's farewell recital in Town Hall, in which she broke down from sheer emotion one line before the end of Schubert's *An die Musik*, and the pianist, Paul Ulanowsky, had to jump in and play the rest of the melody. I learned later that the LP was being scalped on the street at the time for a full fifty dollars.

For a long time, leaving town seemed unlikely. All of my critical and social activities, together with the way friends from Europe seemed always to be turning up in New York, gave me the feeling that I was living in the center of the civilized world. (That was certainly the view of Jim Goodfriend, who for many years categorically refused to step beyond the confines of Manhattan.) But thanks to two of the friends I had made in New York, events far to the west were already presaging my next move. Chicago beckoned.

CHAPTER FOUR

CHICAGO YEARS

1967–73

In the course of 1967, Donal Henahan, the music critic of the *Chicago Daily News* (the *CDN*), left to join the reviewing staff of the *New York Times*, where he became chief music critic in 1980 and won the Pulitzer Prize for distinguished criticism six years later. The job he was vacating in Chicago was offered in turn to two excellent critics with whom I had become acquainted in New York. One was Martin Bernheimer, now at the *Los Angeles Times*; the other was Eric Salzman, a fellow record reviewer of mine at *High Fidelity*, and also a talented composer, whose entertaining *Nude Paper Sermon* recorded by Nonesuch had been something of a hit. Each of them, as they told me, had thanked the *CDN*'s features editor, Richard Christiansen, offered their regrets, and told him: "Get Jacobson." I suppose Richard began to suspect that he was fated to hire me, and that is what happened.

I knew next to nothing about the city of Chicago at the time, probably thinking of the place as some sort of primitive outpost miles from anywhere. (The journalist Jean Shepherd, who was born there, once wrote an article in the *New York Times* in which he said that Chicagoans thought of themselves as being in a state of constant rivalry with New York, whereas to a New Yorker Chicago was merely the place you ended up if you got lost going west on the New Jersey Turnpike.) But—an important "but"—I had reviewed a Chicago Symphony concert in Carnegie Hall in which Jean Martinon had led one of the finest performances of Brahms's *Tragic Overture* I had ever heard. It was the first time I had felt I was hearing an American orchestra play with a sonority that sounded authentically Brahmsian—and that, added to the attraction of a regular full-time post writing for an established public, was enough to convince me that a move to Chicago was a good idea.

The first thing that struck me as impressive about the *Chicago Daily News* was its integrity. At the time of my move—when I was still commuting weekly from New York and looking for a place to live—Jean Martinon was in his last season as music director of the Chicago Symphony Orchestra. A rumor began to circulate that Herbert von Karajan was likely to be his successor. I was writing a review late at night in the features department when someone from the city desk came and asked me whether I could get in touch with my contacts and find out if there was any substance to this. I didn't yet have more than a very few contacts locally, but I made a few phone calls, which yielded no information at all, so I went to the city desk and said, "I suppose you'll have to run it just as a rumor." The prompt reply was, "Oh, no—we're not going to run it at all if it's not confirmed." Given that there were four competing papers in town at the time, I found such restraint very praiseworthy. Aside from freelancing for the London *Times* and the *Guardian*, I had until that time written mostly for specialist magazines. Attracted by the experiences I'd had at CSO concerts in New York, I'd come to Chicago thinking that a year or two would probably be as long as I'd want to stay in my first newspaper-staff position. But after experiencing that piece of journalistic integrity I immediately began to feel differently, and I ended up staying for six exciting years.

After the Karajan episode, or rather non-episode, a different rumor started to circulate. The editor, Roy Fisher, called me into his office and said, "Don't you think you ought to go to London and talk to Georg Solti? I hear the Symphony is on the point of hiring him as music director." So I went, just for three or four days. When the appointment was announced, not only did my interview with Solti, accompanied by several photographs, fill the entire back page of the broadsheet, but the front-page banner headline was "Symphony Picks Solti," accompanied by a lead editorial. I couldn't imagine that a newspaper even in so music-focused a city as Vienna would have devoted so much premium space to such a story.

This, however, was still in the future. For the first few weeks, I commuted weekly from New York, each time reviewing one or two performances. Waiting for one of those flights at La Guardia Airport, I found myself serendipitously sitting next to Ravi Shankar—he was en route to giving a concert and I to reviewing it, and we chatted enjoyably for about half an hour.

My very first review for the paper, however, was of a concert Leonard Bernstein and the New York Philharmonic were giving on tour, with Tchaikovsky's Second Symphony, the so-called "Little Russian," as the main work. The performance, I was hardly surprised to find, was spectacular, but the experience of reviewing it taught me an important lesson. About to write my first review in the city I would be living and working in, I was feeling insecure, and caught myself, while the orchestra was playing, making phrases in my head to be used in my review. I quickly realized that it is not possible to be thinking about elegant phrases in the English language and at the same time listening to music, at least in the sense of "listening" that meets my own self-demanded level of attention and intensity.

Music is an art that subsists in time, and if you have taken yourself out of it to the extent of planning your words, you obviously cannot get back into it at the same point. Having once caught myself doing this, I think I have been immune to the temptation ever since. When, during my fifth season in Chicago, I came to teach a course on criticism as Visiting Professor of Music at Roosevelt University, I told my students that if they ever saw a critic writing notes to himself during a performance, they could disregard anything they might subsequently find him saying in his review. Even leaving aside that problem of divided attention, it should be remembered that a good memory is an essential tool for a critic—and if he cannot recall the details of a performance when he is writing about it maybe three or four hours later, how can we expect him to recall the details of a performance he heard ten years earlier with which he ought to be comparing it?

If note-taking during a performance was very definitely how I did not go about my reviewing, it may be useful here to offer some account of how I did. One aspect was preparation. I tried never to review a concert, even if the program consisted of works as familiar as, say, Beethoven's Fifth Symphony, without spending a couple of hours during the preceding afternoon reading the scores. I avoided listening to recordings during this process precisely because I wanted to get back to what the composer wrote, not what this or that interpreter, however eminent or gifted, had to say about it. Meanwhile, in the case of world or local premieres, I felt an obligation to get hold of the score of the new work, because you cannot fairly review a premiere performance without having come to some understanding, from the score, of the relation between what it sounded like and what it was *supposed* to sound like. So, for a Chicago Symphony premiere, I would go to the orchestra library and find almost always that there was one score on hand that I could borrow for a week or two in advance of the concert.

In the context of my score-reading practice, it was to prove interesting to discover, when I was later working for the Philadelphia Orchestra, what Riccardo Muti's scores looked like. I learned in the orchestra library that Muti's predecessor, Eugene Ormandy, had adorned his scores with all manner of arrows, triangles, and so forth in a veritable rainbow of inks. Muti, by contrast, did not mark his scores at all: he was determined, every time he approached a work he had conducted many times before, to start again from scratch, and develop the next performance from the unmediated notes on the page.

Very rarely, and only when there were technical matters of considerable complexity to be checked, would I follow the score during a performance: like writing notes to yourself, it takes you out of the essential listening experience, and is distracting for other members of the audience. I would liken the whole process to a kind of marinating: the music goes in at the ears, and gradually percolates through the organism until, back at the office a few hours later, the review emerges through the typing fingers. I never really knew how my review was going to come out—although I knew whether I felt good or bad about a concert—until I was actually writing it. Total strangers would often come up to Bonnie and ask her, "How did Bernie like the concert?" She soon learned to be evasive. When they asked the question directly of me, I would reply, "How would I know? I haven't read my review yet." I was not trying to be snide. It was just that, until I had organized my thoughts and put them on paper, I didn't want to run the risk that any differences of emphasis that might have developed during the marinating process would cause one of my questioners to think, on reading my review the next day, "Oh, he wasn't being straight with me."

When I reviewed my first Chicago Symphony concert for the *Daily News*, I was somewhat disturbed to find that, by way of publicizing my appointment, the paper had placed a full-page advertisement with my picture in the orchestra's program book. I was in any case sitting in the same seat my predecessor had occupied, but the photograph made recognition even easier for the people sitting in the same row, and it was alarming, at the end of each piece, to see heads craned all along the row as people looked at me to see whether or not they should applaud. I have never wanted to wield that sort of power, any more than did my friend Clive Barnes: in the first piece he wrote as theater critic of the *New York Times*, he announced that his first priority would be to destroy the power of the theater critic of the *New York Times*. For both of us, the purpose of criticism was not to force others to share our opinions, but to use our knowledge, experience, and judgment to illuminate our fellow audience members' experience.

For my second season I asked for different seats, and I sat from then on in the front row of the balcony, which had the advantages of better sound and the ability to see exactly which members of the orchestra were playing solos, thus avoiding the risk of misdirecting praise or blame. I enjoyed, too, the company of the man in the next seat to mine. Russian-born David Halperin, who was in his nineties, had been attending Chicago Symphony concerts every week for seventy years, and combined tremendous enthusiasm with certain strongly held prejudices. Whenever a score was placed on the desk for the conductor of the week to use during his performance, David would breathe the word "trouble!" I tried to explain that whether or not to conduct with a score was a purely personal choice on a conductor's part, but I never really succeeded in getting the message across.

From our vantage point at the front of the balcony, David and I used to see Rudolf Ganz, the Swiss-born pianist, conductor, composer, and former president of Chicago Musical College, being brought onto the main floor in his wheelchair. Ganz, like David, was in his nineties. (I once had dinner with him and his wife, Esther, but sadly it was after he had had a major stroke. This made it impossible for him to tell me anything much about his life, which was said to have included meeting Brahms and playing for Liszt.) David felt he was in competition with Ganz in the living-longer stakes: one Thursday evening when Ganz did not appear, and we learned that he had just died, David responded to the news, not with malice but in pure triumph, "I won!"

The tenure of Jean Martinon, who was to relinquish his post at the end of the 1967–68 season, was followed—while we waited for Solti's arrival—by a one-year interregnum in which the associate conductor, Irwin Hoffman, served as acting music director. There were meanwhile some impressive guest conductors and soloists, as well as some important premieres. One of the latter happened as early as November 2, 1967, when Gary Karr was the soloist, with Martinon conducting, in the world premiere of Hans Werner Henze's Double Bass Concerto. The work impressed me as a genuine masterpiece, perhaps the greatest ever created for the instrument, by virtue of the poetic quality and sheer beauty of both the solo and the orchestral writing. As for Karr, I had admired his playing ever since first hearing him in London's Wigmore Hall, and I was thrilled, in the days around this performance, to have the opportunity of getting to know him personally. The friendship that grew out of our contact was interrupted for some years by geographical separation, but after Laura and I moved to the Seattle area in 2005 we were able to enjoy frequent meetings with him and his partner and pianist, Harmon Lewis: they live in Victoria, British Columbia, where

I often had occasion to go as Pacific Northwest correspondent for *Opera* magazine.

Henze himself came to Chicago a year or two later as guest conductor in some of his own music. His program included his Second Piano Concerto, in which the soloist, the work's dedicatee Christoph Eschenbach, enjoyed something of a personal triumph. Even before the performance, I had witnessed with astonishment the pianist's ability to rehearse this massive work, which lasts about fifty minutes without any movement breaks, without so much as a solo part or a score in front of him.

Morton Gould was another composer-conductor who, though of less exalted repute internationally, proved on guest engagements with the CSO to be an interpreter of questing intellect and considerable interpretative depth. At the Popular Concerts he conducted, though there was nothing on the programs quite as *recherché* as the Shostakovich Second and Third Symphonies, of which he made world premiere recordings with the Royal Philharmonic Orchestra, he gave illuminating performances of a good deal of varied and out-of-the-usual-run repertoire, ranging from Schubert and Mendelssohn by way of Rimsky-Korsakov's *Antar* Symphony to the Vaughan Williams Tuba Concerto, and including some attractive pieces of his own.

I had first met Morton in New York, after a performance of the Josephs Requiem that he attended. Later, at a reception at the city's Alliance Française, he introduced me to Samuel Barber. I confess I found Barber's rather excessively smooth manner less agreeable than Morton's straightforward warmth, with which I enjoyed renewing acquaintance in Chicago. He was a man passionately devoted to the cause of peace, and indeed his invariable greeting and parting word, as I discovered when we had lunch together, was "Shalom." Pressed for an encore at the end of one concert, he gave us *John Brown's Body*, which, somewhat puzzlingly to a foreigner like me, but touchingly, he told the audience was being played in the cause of peace.

Martinon's last season proved, to my ears, just as impressive as that Carnegie Hall *Tragic Overture* had presaged, though in my admiration for the conductor I was clearly in a minority among the critics of the four newspapers in town. My three opposite numbers were Robert Marsh at our sister morning paper, the *Chicago Sun-Times*, Tom Willis at the *Chicago Tribune*, and Roger Dettmer at *Chicago's American* (later renamed *Chicago Today*, and subsequently scurrilously referred to by the rest of us in the trade as *Chicago Yesterday*). Marsh, who had studied philosophy with Bertrand Russell at Cambridge, had pretensions to being a sort of honorary

Englishman. Perhaps my arrival on the scene as a real one threatened to put his nose out of joint, which must have been why, when his colleagues on the other papers asked him who this Jacobson was, he told them I was "some English queer."

The opposition to Martinon existed not only among the current critics. An important factor leading to his departure had been the negative criticism he had received at the hands of Willis's predecessor at the *Tribune*, Claudia Cassidy, who had been instrumental also in prompting the removal of two earlier Chicago Symphony music directors, Rafael Kubelik and Désiré Defauw, from the post. Another problem for Martinon was his extremely public dispute with the orchestra's long-time principal oboist, Ray Still, whom he had fired over artistic disagreements, only to see him reinstated as the result of arbitration.

However the political maneuverings might have affected Martinon's tenure, I found him to be a technically and interpretatively impressive conductor with a much wider range of stylistic sympathy than he was generally given credit for. He was also a violinist who could join Chicago Symphony musicians in chamber concerts to excellent effect, and a composer of some talent—the program of that Carnegie Hall concert had included his attractive and poetic Cello Concerto.

With regard to his temporary successor I wish I could be as positive. But while Irwin Hoffman, solidly based as his technique was, had probably served the CSO well as associate conductor, I felt he was out of his league as acting music director. His artistic conscience, moreover, was not strong enough to dissuade him from some questionable interpretative choices. The episode I find hardest to forget or forgive was Hoffman's decision, as a guest conductor at the Grant Park Symphony Orchestra's open-air summer concerts on the Chicago lakefront, to engage in a wholesale rebarring (or perhaps I should say barring) of the score of Penderecki's *Threnody for the Victims of Hiroshima*. This is a score notated, not with the traditional metrical regularity represented by bar-lines, but purely in stretches of music indicated by durations in seconds. Hoffman rewrote it by inserting regular bar-lines, which he could beat in the traditional manner. Whether his motive was to make it easier for the players or for himself I do not know, but so far as the audience was concerned it totally disrupted the character of the piece, because if you are watching a conductor solemnly beating his regular way through a piece, you are bound to hear it that way also—and the incidence of the bar-lines very rarely coincided with the points of emphasis indicated by the composer's purely chronometric divisions of the score.

I was more impressed by Hoffman's young son, the cellist Gary Hoffman, a pupil of János Starker whom I had occasion to praise in one or two reviews. Years later, when I was visiting Chicago around the turn of the century, he made a point to seek me out in the intermission of a concert, and touched me greatly by telling me that my positive comments had helped materially in keeping him dedicated to the profession of music at a time when he had been afflicted with doubts about his ability and had seriously considered giving up.

Irwin Hoffman's recourse to inflicting bar-lines on an unbarred score raises some important points about conducting. During one particular week in Chicago, I heard two performances of Schubert's Fifth Symphony, one by the CSO conducted by Carlo Maria Giulini, the other by the Civic Orchestra (the CSO's training orchestra) conducted by Hoffman, and the two realizations of the slow movement taught me a fundamental lesson about music: pulse is a much more crucial factor than tempo in determining the success or otherwise of a performance. Giulini's reading of the *Andante con moto* proceeded at a distinctly slower pace than Hoffman's, but it also flowed much more persuasively, because it could be clearly felt as two large compound beats to the measure, whereas Hoffman's felt like six small beats.

Because of the fact—whose importance should not be forgotten—that what you see inevitably influences how you hear, I developed what was to be one of my basic tools in reviewing, and indeed in listening. Feeling that conductors' excessive visual subdivision of the beat was a cardinal reason why slow movements sometimes fall flat in performance, I started to close my eyes just before an Andante or an Adagio began. By the use of hearing uninfluenced by sight, I would then determine whether the beat was being chopped up too much, or whether it had the flow it needed. Then, after hearing a few phrases, I would open my eyes and see what the conductor was doing. If a 6/8 meter like that of the Schubert example, or a 3/4 like that of, say, the second movement of Brahms's First Symphony, had flowed convincingly, then there was little cause for complaint if, in visual terms, the conductor was subdividing—for what I heard quite properly, in that case, trumped what I saw.

When Georg Solti appeared on the scene, any misguided provincial contrivances such as I have laid to Hoffman's charge could safely be forgotten. This, clearly, was a performer of the utmost skill, underpinned by profound identification with musical traditions. He was also a human being with whom I was to enjoy the warmest of personal relations over my last four years in Chicago. The only exception to that came when I mis-spoke in congratulating him on the knighthood with which he was invested in 1971: I carelessly assumed that he would regard it in a similarly ironic light to my own republican (with a small "r"!) estimation of royalist honors, but his reaction made it clear that he valued the distinction highly. With that aside and suitably forgotten about, Sir Georg and his wife, Valerie, shared a few convivial evenings with Bonnie and me, and I was touched when, dining with us a few days before one of their periodic returns to London, Valerie asked me whether she might telephone my mother there and report on our health and happiness—and she actually did not neglect to do so.

The press conferences at which Solti briefed the press on the following season's programs were also straightforward and sometimes entertaining. When he announced the orchestra's plan for a concert performance of opera for the first time—the work he had chosen was *Fidelio*—he said to us, "You want to know why we are going to do concert opera? Well, when we have at the Chicago Symphony Orchestra two of the three best opera conductors in the world, it makes sense to make use of that. You want to know who I'm talking about? Karajan, Giulini, Solti . . . not necessarily in that order!"

I admired Solti in many ways, not least for his absolute professionalism, and for his honesty and directness when an orchestra member came to him with a suggestion. Where another man might have taken refuge in the familiar escape mechanism of, "Well, leave it with me—I'll think about it and get back to you," Solti would simply nod his head, think about the suggestion on the spot, and after perhaps thirty seconds respond with either "That's a very good thought—we'll do it" or "It's an interesting idea, but I don't think I want to do it because . . ." But though he was a brilliant performer and a superb communicator with a gift for inspiring orchestras and thrilling audiences, his interpretations very seldom told me anything about a work that I didn't already know—he rarely seemed to make a piece his own. Curiously enough, it was a performance of a Brahms symphony, the Second—not a work that I would have expected to arouse his strongest sympathies—that came closest to satisfying that criterion, and there were one or two Bruckner and Mahler performances that also approached doing so.

One concerto performance, too, stands out in my memories of Solti: the work was Bartók's Second Violin Concerto, and the soloist was György Pauk. I have always thought of Pauk as a paradigm of the kind of supremely gifted musician whose career never quite reaches the level of public acclaim his gifts warrant. But the result of this impeccably unified collaboration with Solti at his best was without question the greatest performance of the work I have ever heard, as subtle and lyrical as it was brilliant and passionate. György and I have been friends ever since my Philips days, when, having escaped from Hungary in 1956, he spent several years as concertmaster of the Brabants Orkest in Eindhoven. He is a very generous man, and after a lunch together in Chicago he insisted on picking up the check. I noticed he had not included a tip, so I said, "Let me do the tip." "Oh, no," he said, "it's included in the bill." When I explained that the figure he was looking at was not for service but for tax, he was mortified: "No wonder I've been getting black looks from waiters on this whole tour!"

In contrast with Solti's unfailing extrovert brilliance, it was for their richness in that sphere of interpretative depth that the performances I remembered and still remember most vividly from my Chicago days were those of Carlo Maria Giulini (Mozart, Brahms, and Mahler), Daniel Barenboim (especially Elgar), and James Levine (a wonderful Schubert "Great" C Major). These were musicians not only just as brilliant at communicating and inspiring, but also possessed of an interpretative depth that brought fresh insight even to works I thought I already knew inside out.

My first encounter with Carlo Maria Giulini had come in the Netherlands in the early 1960s, when I heard several concerts he conducted with the Concertgebouw Orchestra, as well as operas in the context of the Holland Festival. With the orchestra, I was impressed first by the richness of sound he elicited. The performances I particularly remember were of Mozart's Symphony no. 39 and Falla's *Three-Cornered Hat*, an odd pairing perhaps, but not so odd if you consider that those two composers share an ability to project melancholy emotions while never sacrificing euphony.

In the opera house, two performances of Mozart operas during my Philips years stand out in my memory. I have described the drama surrounding one of them in chapter 2. I saw the other on a visit back to Holland after I had left Philips, probably in 1963. On that trip I also went to Rotterdam for a production of *Don Giovanni* that turned out to be highly controversial. The director and the set and costume designers, whose names I seem to have successfully suppressed from recollection, were responsible for all sorts of ludicrous and ugly effects. There was what was obviously an outhouse dominating the scene. Donna Elvira seemed to be dressed as an old armchair, which was no favor to the beautiful Ilva Ligabue. She and the rest of the cast sang splendidly, but the dramatic aspect of the thing was so appalling that the director was actually pushed out before the first performance, and Giulini, who was conducting, gallantly assumed responsibility for keeping the performance on stage.

It was to be another six years before I got to know him personally. This happened when Solti brought him in as principal guest conductor of the Chicago Symphony Orchestra. I found the appointment a typical instance of Solti's magnanimity—a lesser man might have shrunk from challenging comparison with another conductor of such stature. As I commented in print, Solti's choice of Giulini meant that Chicago audiences would enjoy the regular presence in their concert hall of representatives of both the angelic and the diabolical temperaments—I didn't feel I needed to explain which was which.

An open house that the Chicago Symphony offered its subscribers at Orchestra Hall one year amusingly illustrated the difference between the two men's attitudes to their work. Giulini happened to be the conductor that week. There was a dinner in his honor, and the evening also included the first screening of a documentary about Solti and the orchestra. In his speech of thanks after the dinner, Giulini said, "I have always dreamed of making music with musicians." In the course of the documentary, we heard Solti declare, "I have always dreamed of having my own orchestra." The audience registered its amusement very clearly.

From 1969 until I left the *CDN* in 1973, Bonnie and I regularly had dinner once or twice a year with Giulini and his wife, Marcella. I was still somewhat ignorant of Italian eating habits. When Marcella cooked for us in their hotel suite, the lasagna was so delicious that I readily accepted a second helping, and then a third. Replete, I was astonished when she then produced large steaks as the main course. But ah, well, I did my best.

At the first of our dinners together, Giulini had said to me: "You know my style of music-making. You can also imagine how hard it is for me to find time to look at new scores. If ever you come across a work that you think I could perform well, don't hesitate to let me see it." I treated this invitation with restraint. But over the next two or three years I brought four pieces to his attention, and he programmed two of them with the Chicago Symphony. One was a Threnody for string orchestra written in memory of President Kennedy by the Chicago composer Robert Lombardo. The other was the Requiem by my old friend Wilfred Josephs. Nine of the work's ten movements are predominantly slow in tempo, and all the music is quiet, which might seem a bad prospect for viability in the concert hall. The Requiem is, however, a deeply felt and no less deeply moving composition. Giulini put it in a program together with Mozart's Symphony no. 40, and described it in an interview as "the most important work by a contemporary composer."

The Josephs Requiem performances, incidentally, occasioned an amusing episode. The Giulinis were staying at the Drake Hotel, and they invited a number of people to a small party in their suite. Wilfred and his wife, Valerie, were there, as were Bonnie and I, the members of the LaSalle Quartet, and the Bulgarian-born bass Raffaele Arié, the soloist in the performance. "I can read minds," Raffaele told us at one point. Well, then, tell us what we're thinking, the rest of us suggested. "First I have to look into your eyes and you must look into mine," he said. He proceeded to move round the circle, taking each of us in turn gently by the wrist while we gazed at him. This procedure completed, we said, "All right, then—what are we thinking?" "First," he said, "what time is it?" We looked at our wrists. All of them were bare—he had all our watches in his pocket.

On one occasion, I was able to stimulate Giulini's programming an important work without any direct personal attempt. I wrote an enthusiastic review of his performance of the Shostakovich Fourteenth Symphony, and mentioned my hope that he might be prevailed on to conduct the Eighth, which I described as perhaps the greatest of the composer's fifteen, and which had never been played in Chicago. The day after the review was printed, Giulini called me and asked where he could get the score. Two weeks later, he called again to say he was programming the work for the following season. The resulting Chicago premiere was superb. This whole episode was a happy confirmation of my view that performers and critics are not natural enemies, but can be on the same side—the side that is devoted to the benefit of musical life.

Over the years, I came to know Giulini as one of the greatest musicians of our time. One aspect of his integrity as a performer showed in his refusal to conduct any music that he didn't feel he completely understood and loved. Schubert's "Great" C Major Symphony, he once told me, was a work that he had long felt unable to conduct, because he couldn't solve what he felt was the problem inherent in the transition from the slow introduction into the main first-movement Allegro. Then, taking an opportunity to examine Schubert's autograph score in the library of the Vienna Philharmonic, he had discovered that the introduction was marked to be played *alla breve* (with two large beats to the bar, instead of the 4/4 time-signature indicated in some editions and even followed by Sir Donald Tovey in his *Studies in Musical Analysis*). This solved the problem for him, because it enabled him to move from *Andante* to *Allegro ma non troppo* seamlessly, and his subsequent performances and recording of the work were among the most convincing and satisfying accounts of it I have ever heard.

The man, moreover, was every bit as impressive as the musician. Giulini had a grace of expression that, if I may perpetrate an ethnic stereotype, struck me as peculiarly Italian. In 1971, on the Chicago Symphony's first-ever European tour, which I was covering for the *CDN*, we arranged one evening to dine together at one of those attractive subterranean restaurants in Stockholm's Old Town. Up till this time, he had always insisted on paying for every meal we had eaten together. "Now," I said, "we're on neutral ground, and I'm going to pay for dinner." "Oh, no," he said—"it gives me so much pleasure!" So there was no denying him.

Giulini had always called me "Bernard," and I had always addressed him, naturally enough, as "Maestro." But later in the 1970s I had a breakfast appointment with him on the morning after he conducted Beethoven's D-major Mass at the Edinburgh Festival. It was a performance of such inward intensity and concentration that I didn't want to break the spell by going backstage afterward, so, instead, I went to his hotel, asked the porter for a piece of paper, and wrote him a short note of appreciation, addressing it as usual "Dear Maestro." The next morning he began the conversation by remarking, "Before we say anything else, I have a bone to pick with you." Alarmed, I asked how I had offended him. "We have known each other all these years," he replied, "and still you forget my name." After which, of course, it had to be "Carlo."

Then came the day, in 1982, when I had to tell him that I was separating from Bonnie, my wife of nearly fourteen years, and planning to marry Laura, with whom I have been happily united ever since. I had already telephoned my sister, Anne, with the news, expecting a stern rebuke for splitting up with someone who was a brilliant woman and in many ways a fine one, albeit one with whom I had come to realize I was completely incompatible. Instead of yelling at me, however, Anne simply said, "Oh, Kumar and I always wondered how long you could put up with it." Telling Carlo, however, still awakened anxiety—he was, after all, a devout Italian Catholic, and moreover he and Marcella had always known Bonnie and me as a couple. When he came to London for a Verdi production at Covent Garden, I phoned him and said I had some important news I wanted to tell him, and he suggested I come to the flat he was staying in after a rehearsal. Having settled me in an armchair with a glass of sherry, he asked what this news was. I took a deep breath and told him.

"First of all," Carlo said, "let me ask you, are you happy?" I told him I was happier than I had been in years. "In that case," he went on, "of course I am a little sad for Bonnie, but I am not the least little bit surprised, because Marcella and I have always thought of you and Bonnie as two trains on parallel tracks that would never meet." I was astonished: it is always astonishing to discover how easily people see through what you thought was a convincing facade. But I was also enormously relieved and pleased, as well as touched at the thought that they had cared about us more than any merely professional relationship might have warranted. We talked for perhaps another half-hour, and when I got up to leave, he said, "Please give our love to Laura, because I know from everything you have told me that we will love her." The next time Laura came to London, we attended one of his concerts at the Royal Festival Hall, and went to greet him afterward. He kissed her hand. She didn't wash it for two weeks after that.

In later years I saw Carlo less often, largely because of the devastating misfortune that had blighted his life: Marcella, the warm and elegant other half of this supremely devoted couple, suffered a serious stroke, which left her impaired and literally speechless for the rest of her life. He curtailed his touring to a minimum thereafter so as not to leave her alone. In the 1980s, on two of our visits to Milan to attend Muti performances at La Scala, we visited Carlo at his house near the theater, and sat with him each time for an hour or so. He was, as ever, keenly interested in every topic we raised—he was mercifully different from those many musicians who can talk only about music—but I had the unmistakable impression that he had put on the cloak of tragedy: it had claimed him, and he needed it in order to come to terms with the loss of Marcella as she had been. On one of our visits, she came into the room for a few minutes, and looked at me with great intensity. After she left, Carlo said to me, "She recognized you—you could see that in her eyes. You can see how much she is feeling, but she cannot speak about it."

Some time later, I telephoned Carlo to tell him how greatly I had enjoyed his recording of the Brahms *German Requiem* (in which, his reputation in his last years for slow tempos notwithstanding, he actually comes much closer to the metronome markings the composer noted down for the work than any of the so-called "authentic" conductors). Surprised, when I asked after Marcella, that I was not aware she had died, he said simply, "She is in heaven!"

Solti and Giulini were both with the orchestra on its first-ever European tour, in 1971, a mammoth journey lasting six weeks, of which I covered the first three for the paper. Weather-wise, we had the most amazing good luck: in every city we visited, the sun came out on the day we arrived, and it started to rain on the day we left. The first actual concerts, after sessions to record Mahler's Eighth Symphony in Vienna's Sofiensaal, were given in

Edinburgh. The Usher Hall was in those days somewhat primitive in the matter of dressing rooms. The orchestra musicians had to change clothes in the open air, and I wrote, in one of my first dispatches back to Chicago, that the tour was shaping so well that the only complaint I had heard from an orchestra member was the purely theoretical comment I heard one player make to another, "It would be pretty unpleasant if it was raining!"

In those days, the only generally available technology for communicating written text over wide distances was the teleprinter. At Edinburgh's Caledonian Hotel, where we were staying, there was one in the lobby, which was what I had to use—adapting my fingers to a very differently arranged keyboard from a typewriter's—to write and send my reviews. I had been busily typing away about Solti's first concert for something like an hour when I suddenly became aware that Valerie Solti was standing behind me, reading over my shoulder every word I wrote. Fortunately, it was a highly favorable review.

On one Edinburgh evening when there was no concert for us, I walked back to our hotel after dinner in the company of Arrand Parsons, who was a professor at Northwestern University, and for thirty years the author of the voluminous program notes of the Chicago Symphony. As we came in sight of Edinburgh's famous castle, floodlit against the evening sky at the top of its rocky hill, I came out with some vapid touristic remark about its picturesqueness. Arrand, a profoundly cultivated man, was made of sterner stuff, and his response made me feel ashamed of my superficial comment: "Well," he said, "it certainly makes one wonder what it must have been like to live under it."

In the huge dining room at Edinburgh's splendid Caledonian Hotel, where a waiter suitably named Ian Stuart astonished me with his powers of observation by asking, "What can I bring you for breakfast? You had a kipper yesterday—you'd probably like something different today," I found myself one morning face to face with Sir Arthur Bliss. I had an assignment a few weeks later to write a program note on his *Morning Heroes* symphony for narrator, chorus, and orchestra, which I have always thought of as his masterpiece (and which I should dearly love to have the opportunity one day to narrate). Sir Arthur kindly made himself available over breakfast to brief me about the work, addressing me in avuncular tones as "my boy," and he subsequently sent me an autographed score of the work.

Accompanying the tour, as commonly happens with American orchestras, was a party of enthusiastic supporters from among the orchestra's subscribers, and, while I was not of their number, I enjoyed very pleasant contact with the man who, tour-guide fashion, was looking after them. He was a charming and musically sophisticated Greek Cypriot named Christopher Gerolemou, with whom I greatly regret having lost touch, and in spare moments between his official duties he introduced me to two impressive performers. One was Bruce Brewer, an American lyric tenor with a voice of superfine delicacy and a technique that enabled him to pass from the bottom of his range to stratospheric high notes without any perceptible break between registers. The other was a pianist of both French and American citizenship, François-Joël Thiollier, who possesses a formidable virtuoso technique and covers a vast range of repertoire, though the principal focus of his recordings has been on the music of Debussy and Ravel. We spent a stimulating hour or so talking about all kinds of musical subjects. The most surprising moment was when the subject of Mozart piano concertos came up. I asked him whether my favorite one was in his repertoire, and he said, "Oh, you mean K. 503." "How do you know that's my favorite?" I asked him. "Well," he said, "we've been talking about music all this time, and I've acquired a feeling for your taste in general, and from that it's just clear that K. 503 would be your favorite."

It was to be another twenty years before Solti resigned and DANIEL BARENBOIM succeeded him as music director of the Chicago Symphony Orchestra. Quite apart from his apparent ability to perform the entire orchestral and piano repertoire within a matter of hours—and not unconnected with that gift—is Barenboim's seemingly inexhaustible memory. The second time I met him was in 1970, when he and Jacqueline du Pré arrived in East Lansing, Michigan, for concerts in celebration of the Beethoven bicentenary. I was there to give a lecture and to review the concerts for the *Chicago Daily News*, and, knowing Jackie from London days, I went to their table in the university cafeteria to welcome them. I said to Daniel that he wouldn't know who I was, but he responded: "Oh, no, we met at Carnegie Hall," and even recalled when it had been. That meeting, at least a year earlier, had lasted perhaps two minutes, when Jackie had introduced me to him and to Zubin Mehta in the lobby before a performance in Mstislav Rostropovich's multiconcert survey of practically the entire cello concerto repertoire.

This was amazing enough; I also have a friend whose name the adult Barenboim clearly remembered, having met him only once, many years earlier, when he was still a child. It is important, however, to distinguish. Over breakfast some time later, when I alluded to the way in which what I supposed to be Barenboim's "photographic memory" must have helped him to build his huge repertoire, he demurred: "No, it isn't photographic. I have to learn scores just the way anyone has to." It was, incidentally, at this same breakfast that I asked him when, having recently recorded Bartók's first and third piano concertos, he was planning to record the second. "I can't play that," he told me—"my hands aren't big enough." It was the kind of surprising and illuminating fact that I, essentially a non-pianist, might not think of, like Alfred Brendel's explanation in his later years for no longer adding new works to his repertoire in terms of the diminishing power of his fingers to acquire and *remember* all the notes involved in such additions.

I have always, as a critic, loved going out on a limb, in preference to the safer method of hedging my bets. After my first encounter with Barenboim as a conductor, I declared in print that in perhaps fifty years' time we would be speaking of him in the kind of terms usually reserved for such figures as Nikisch, Weingartner, and Furtwängler, and I have to say that nothing in my subsequent experience has made me regret that prediction. Outside the hall on one of the first occasions he conducted the Chicago Symphony, I ran into one of the orchestra's coconcertmasters, Sidney Weiss, who had had the experience of performing with many of the leading maestros of the day, and who exclaimed, "Mr. Jacobson, that is absolutely the greatest conductor I have ever played with!"

Sidney, aside from being a most sensitive and technically adroit player, had himself made several violins. He told me that some of them had come out badly, but one or two were quite good. He actually played a test, concealed behind a curtain on the Orchestra Hall stage, in which, while Giulini sat listening, he played alternately on one of his own home-made instruments and on a Stradivarius. And Giulini was unable to tell which was which.

Some years later, another Sidney and Stradivarius story: in 1979, Giulini persuaded Sidney to leave the Chicago Symphony and become concertmaster of the Los Angeles Philharmonic. In 1980, after a concert they played on tour in London that included an absolutely stunning performance of Tchaikovsky's Sixth Symphony, Bonnie and I invited Sidney and his wife, Jeanne, to supper at our house in the Muswell Hill district. I suggested that we put his violin in a closed room for safety. After supper, they put their coats on and were standing by the front door about to leave, when I said: "Sid, I wonder if I could interest you in a violin." I had never seen anyone turn green before that moment. Sidney had completely forgotten about the instrument. He retrieved it, took it out of its case to show it to us, and explained that it was the Stradivarius that had formerly belonged to Fritz Kreisler, and was now owned by the Los Angeles Philharmonic for the exclusive use of the concertmaster.

While Barenboim's flexible and impassioned way of conducting has consistently delighted me, just as much as it has infuriated adherents of the doctrine of literalism associated with such conductors as Toscanini and Szell, he claimed in one of our conversations a certain influence on his interpretative style about whom I have a sharply dissenting view: Sergiu Celibidache. When I responded that this was a conductor whose work I had never been able to admire, Barenboim said: "One day, when we can find the time, we must sit down together and listen to some of Celibidache's recordings, and you must tell me what it is about them that makes you unhappy—because I respect you, and I want to understand your feeling about him." Sadly, but not surprisingly given Barenboim's unrelentingly hectic schedule, we have never found that time, but his remark showed how open he has always kept his mind to the ideas of others.

Among the signal virtues of Barenboim's tenure with the Chicago Symphony was the strong interest that, dedicated as he has always been to education, he took in the organization's training wing, the Civic Orchestra. In the 1990s, the Civic Orchestra's teenaged concertmaster, asked what it was like to play for Barenboim, responded: "He makes you remember why you wanted to be a musician in the first place."

It was in the intermission at a Civic Orchestra concert, after talking (as usual without written notes) about Tchaikovsky's Fifth Symphony in preparation for a complete performance in the second half, that Barenboim asked a group of us in the dressing room, "How long did I talk? Was it twenty minutes?" When we told him it had been fifty minutes, he said, "Oh, time is so subjective!," and proceeded to tell the story of two friends of whom one says to the other, "I know you don't like Wagner, but I've bought you a ticket for a wonderful production of *Parsifal*—you must go." Seeing his friend again a couple of weeks later, he asks him, "How was *Parsifal*?" "Well," his friend replies, "I'll tell you how it was. It started at 6 o'clock. Two hours later I looked at my watch, and it was 6:15." It was amusing to hear this from someone so devoted to conducting Wagner's music.

A highlight of Barenboim's years in Chicago was the 1997 reopening of the refurbished Orchestra Hall in the expanded setting of Symphony Center. The week-long festival that marked this event included a lavish array of performances in the Center's various performing spaces. There was also a press conference featuring the music director's appetizing account of the following season's plans, and marred only by one question from a reporter whose prurient curiosity outweighed any sense of the fitness of things. What did Barenboim think, he asked, of *Hilary and Jackie*, the supposedly scurrilous biographical film about his late wife and her family?

Barenboim's response was a characteristic model of dignified restraint: "I have not seen the film. I do not intend to see the film. I have no comment." (He is reported to have asked on another occasion when the film was mentioned, "Couldn't they have waited until I was dead?")

My last substantial involvement with Barenboim and his work came when I was commissioned to write the booklet accompanying his "Perspectives" season at Carnegie Hall in 2000. The project entailed interviewing many of his collaborators. I spoke at length with musicians and others including Pinchas Zukerman, Cecilia Bartoli, Pierre Boulez, and Edward Said, Barenboim's cofounder in 1999 of the West-Eastern Divan, their orchestra designed to bring together Israeli, Palestinian, and other Arab musicians in the interests of peace and international understanding. It was inspiring to listen to everyone's warm enthusiasm about Barenboim as both musician and man. Zukerman in particular, who had partnered Daniel and Jacqueline in many performances of the piano-trio literature, was passionate in rejecting any notion that Daniel had treated Jacqueline in the years of her mortal illness with anything but totally caring devotion.

Since that time, it has been at a distance that I have watched—and listened to—Barenboim's activities both musical and socio-political. There has been no decline in the quality of either his conducting or his piano-playing, while in the political sphere he has continued to work at initiatives dedicated to fostering ethnic and racial reconciliation. He is clearly under no illusion that projects like the West-Eastern Divan can solve the problems of the world at a stroke. But I think that, disparate though their general politics are, he might well empathize with a statement John Major made when he was Britain's Conservative Prime Minister in the 1990s. In the context of attempts to reach a solution of "the Troubles" in Northern Ireland, Major said that he might well end up with egg on his face for trying and failing, but that he would prefer having egg on his face to not trying.

One of the salient features of Daniel Barenboim's tenure as music director of the Chicago Symphony Orchestra was the close collaboration he fostered with Pierre Boulez. The seeds of this collaboration had been planted in the 1960s. The two performed together with the orchestra at least once in that period, Barenboim as soloist with Boulez conducting, and it was when Boulez was in town for a couple of weeks as guest conductor that I witnessed what I believe to have been a crucial moment in his career path.

James Hermes, who headed the Chicago chapter of the ISCM (the International Society for Contemporary Music), decided to take advantage of Boulez's presence to invite him to a meeting of the organization that was to be devoted to a discussion of electronic music, and he asked me, as someone already acquainted with Boulez, to chair the session. When Boulez was asked to speak about his own relationship with or attitude to electronic music, he surprised the assembled company by declaring in no uncertain terms that this was a field in which he had no interest. At the time, Chicago Musical College had an electronic music studio of considerable sophistication. Its director was a young composer named Ramon Zupko, who was, naturally enough, present at the meeting, and he, equally naturally, asked Boulez what electronic studios he had visited. None at all, said Boulez, whereupon Zupko graciously invited him to tour the CMC studio at his convenience. Somewhat embarrassed, Boulez felt he had to accept the invitation. I find it hard not to believe that the change of heart that led Boulez very soon after this to set up IRCAM, the Parisian Institut de Recherche et Coordination Acoustique/Musique, with its heavy concentration of interest in electronics, must have had its origin in those events in Chicago.

It was around this time, incidentally, that I received a review copy of a book by Boulez, *Relevés d'apprenti*, in an English translation titled *Notes of an Apprenticeship*. One chapter offers a metric analysis of the opening section of Stravinsky's *Le Sacre du printemps* that interprets it in terms of "al rovescio" or what might be loosely termed "reversible" form. Boulez's argument is that, after the midpoint of the section, its second half exactly reverses every rhythm from the first half. (A classic example of the "al rovescio" method can be found in the minuet of Haydn's Symphony no. 47, fascinatingly showcased in the twentieth-century English composer Robert Simpson's superb String Quartet no. 9, a homage to Haydn on his 250th birthday in which thirty-two variations on that minuet's theme preserve its forward-backward motion consistently.)

Boulez's analysis of the Stravinsky passage, however, ignores the fact that, to one side of the midpoint, or metric fulcrum, there are two fermatas—unmeasured pauses—that have no counterpart in the other half of the section, and that consequently render the reversal inexact to the listening ear, though not to the reading eye. It would of course be possible to suggest that these pauses do not invalidate the general conceptual accuracy of the argument—but I should have had more confidence in Boulez's thinking if he had at least mentioned the point, even if only to discount its relevance.

I think this illustrates a characteristic that aligns Boulez's unquestionably brilliant mind with a quality perhaps endemic to French intellectual thought: a lack of interest in any aspect of a subject or problem that is not literally quantifiable. This quality seems to me allied in turn with the dogmatic closed-mindedness that led Boulez (along with his admittedly non-French colleagues Stockhausen and Nono) to walk ostentatiously out of the hall during a Darmstadt performance of an early work by Hans Werner Henze because it did not meet his criterion of strict serial orthodoxy. (The episode is recounted in Henze's illuminating documentary DVD, *Memoirs of an Outsider*, with some charm, and a light touch that reinforces credibility.)

One afternoon in 1971, when I was sitting quietly at my desk in the *CDN* offices, the phone rang. "This is Carlos Basaldua, in the development office of the government of Puerto Rico. We are inviting three US critics to attend this year's Casals Festival in San Juan, one from the East Coast, one from the West Coast, and one from the Midwest, and I'm calling to ask whether you would like to be the Midwestern critic."

The invitation sounded too good to be true, and the paper had a very correct policy of not accepting transportation or hospitality from anyone we were going to be reviewing. In this instance, however, it was felt that there was a wide enough gap between the reviewees—Casals and his musicians—and the government of Puerto Rico to sanitize my acceptance, and so I went. I was accommodated for several days in a very pleasant hotel on the sea front, and provided with a car and driver that would take me wherever I needed—or wanted—to go. Frankie Pabón, the driver, served as my indispensable tourist guide to San Juan, introducing me to the beauty of the city and to such pleasures as tea in the gorgeous garden of the Hotel El Convento, while teaching me a good deal of useful conversational Spanish.

The language itself was something I found immediately seductive: Spanish usage seemed to facilitate a combination of informality and respect not available in other languages. As a member of the ordinary nonmusician public, Frankie referred to Casals not as Mr. or Maestro Casals, or the Maestro, nor on the other hand merely as Casals or Pablo, but as Don Pablo, which seemed just right.

I ate some excellent meals in San Juan, one of them at a Basque-style restaurant, and one afternoon I explored an equally good small art gallery. Browsing through a rack of lithographs, I found several, by the Uruguayan artist Luis Alberto Solari, that appealed greatly to my taste. They revealed a vein of what I would call *healthy* surrealism, as distinct from the grotesque manner of that style to which I am as unsympathetic as I am to the more aggressive manifestations of German Expressionism. I wanted at once to buy them, but the gallery's owner—Julián Domínguez, I think his name was—explained that they had only been delivered that day, and he did not yet have prices for them. "Why don't you come to dinner tomorrow after the concert," he said, "by when I should have the price-list?"

I accepted gladly, and over a delicious chicken dish the following evening discovered another agreeable thing about the Spanish or Spanish-derived life style: it goes on until all hours of the night. The streets were full of men and women enjoying themselves, and it must have been at least midnight when some of them, seeing that there was a dinner-party in progress, rang the doorbell and asked whether they might come in and look at the pictures. The lithographs now hang on the walls of my daughter's house in North Yorkshire.

Meanwhile the Casals Festival was in full swing. I attended several concerts, including the last, in which Don Pablo, seated for most of the time but rising to his feet for the big moments, led a dynamic performance of Mozart's 41st Symphony to end the festival. The concertmaster was Alexander Schneider, and when I ran into him at the airport on the way home and asked how much of the work's interpretation could be set down to his credit, he insisted that Casals had been in masterful command of all the rehearsals. At that concert, I stood just outside the spacious doors of the hall, blissfully breathing the fragrance spread by a beautiful woman standing in front of me and wielding a sandalwood fan.

There was also a reception in the governor's mansion, La Fortaleza, at which Casals was honored, and at which I was able to talk to him for several minutes. I was introduced to him as a critic from Chicago, whereupon the Maestro, all of ninety-five years old, unhesitatingly regaled me with an account of his most important appearances there, starting decades ago in the Auditorium Theater, with full recall of who the various conductors had been and what they had performed together.

My time at the festival was enjoyable enough by itself, but my conversation with Don Pablo was to lead to an experience that stands in my memory among the most remarkable I have ever had. In 1971, shortly after I had returned from San Juan, Business Executives Move for Vietnam Peace, or BEM, which had been in existence since 1967, decided to offer prizes to several individuals for their contributions to the cause of peace, and to have the prizes presented in the course of a gala evening in Orchestra Hall. One of the recipients was to be Casals, but in response to the invitation, he told the organizers that his doctor had forbidden him to travel. He added, however, that he had recently met a Mr. Jacobson from Chicago, and that it would please him greatly if that gentleman would be kind enough to accept the award on his behalf.

And so I found myself making the first quasi-political speech of my life, and hobnobbing backstage with the other award recipients, whose names make up a diverse and highly impressive list. There was Wayne Morse, who, as a Democratic senator, had in 1964 been one of only two senators (the other being Ernest Gruening of Alaska) to vote against the Gulf of Tonkin resolution. There was Ramsey Clark, who had served from 1967 to 1969 as United States Attorney General under President Lyndon B. Johnson, and subsequently lent his support to many campaigns in support of peace and civil rights. There was Frank Rosenblum, Secretary-Treasurer of the Amalgamated Clothing Workers Union in the 1940s. There was Dr. Benjamin Spock, whose books had been accused by Norman Vincent Peale of contributing to the alleged moral laxity of the time and thus (!) to the growth of the anti–Vietnam War movement (and who, piquantly enough in this company, had been prosecuted by Attorney General Clark for conspiracy to counsel, aid, and abet resistance to the draft). There was Daniel Ellsberg, the central figure in the Pentagon Papers affair. And there was the songwriter, folk singer, and activist Joan Baez, whose recordings had made her an iconic figure in the antiwar movement.

I put Ms. Baez last on this list because, when her turn to speak arrived, she very nearly derailed the whole progress of the evening. There were two American flags standing on the Orchestra Hall stage, one on each side. When Ms. Baez came on stage, she told that audience that there was something she had to do before making her speech: she went and laid each of the flags in turn on its side, explaining that she could not speak if the nation's shame were not thus symbolized. But the speaker who was to follow her to the podium was Senator Morse, and he explained to the organizers backstage that he could not possibly, as a former senator, step on stage if the flags were not returned to their proper upright position. Fortunately, this was done after Ms. Baez finished speaking, and the evening could thus continue to its appointed end. I suppose conflicting views could be advanced on the appropriateness of Ms. Baez's emotional gesture, but my own feeling was that it was an unnecessary and inappropriate provocation.

In the following year, 1972, I was invited to teach a course in criticism at Chicago Musical College (CMC) of Roosevelt University, where I was appointed Visiting Professor of Music. Teaching had always been an activity I enjoyed, whether in the form of preconcert and preopera or more general talks, at institutions ranging from Yale and Boston Universities and for orchestras and concert series around the world, but this was the only time I have taught a university course for official credit.

One benefit of teaching is the lessons one can learn from one's students: many an insight can illuminate or even correct a teacher's thinking. Students can also function as watchers over the clarity and good sense of what one writes. In that regard, it was not immaterial that my class was given on Fridays. Since I almost always attended the Thursday evening performance of the week's Chicago Symphony subscription program, it was on Friday that my review appeared in print. In writing it, I was always conscious of being reluctant to face my class the next day if I should have woken up with the awareness that something I had written the night before was silly, or even just infelicitously phrased. Depend upon it, as Samuel Johnson might have put it, when a man knows he is to face his pupils in a few hours, it concentrates his mind wonderfully.

It happened that Giulini's Chicago premiere of WILFRED JOSEPHS's Requiem was given in that same period, and in connection with the performance Wilf taught composition at CMC for a semester, so Wilf and I had the pleasure of serving on the Roosevelt faculty together. I certainly took great pleasure in the course I was giving, though it also provided both my students and me with shocks. For them, the shock came right at the start: they asked me for a reading list, and were astonished when, not being a theoretical kind of person, I gave them no musicology texts to study, but instead Henry Fielding's *Tom Jones* and Philip Roth's *Letting Go*, explaining that since they were presumably going to be writing in English, they would do well to read and learn from the two best-written books in the language I could think of at that time.

The British satirical magazine *Private Eye* supplied me with one very specific tool to aid the imparting of strict linguistic standards, in this case regarding the danger of leaving out the second in a pair of commas. The magazine used to publish, at the bottoms of pages, howlers taken from the newspapers of the day. One such, from the *Bournemouth Herald*, reported on a visit that Elizabeth Taylor and Richard Burton had paid to that south-coast town. "The couple," it said, "were accompanied by Lisa Todd, Miss Taylor's daughter by the late Mr. Mike Todd and several assistants."

Each week I assigned my students a different musical activity to attend and then write about, and *my* shock came in the week when the assignment was to join me at a Chicago Symphony concert I was reviewing. When the concert ended, they came back with me to the *CDN* office, I sat them down at typewriters, and told them to have their reviews ready by the time I finished mine. At that point we all repaired to the excellent pizzeria just down the road (Pizzeria Uno, or "Uno's" in Chicago-speak), and we discussed their work over a convivial late supper. The shock? Well, all nine of my students were music majors, and I think all of them were in their twenties, and yet on that evening seven of them heard the main work on the program, Beethoven's Seventh Symphony, for the first time. I found it hard to understand how anyone could reach that stage in a life that was presumably to be dedicated to music without having explored at least the core of the symphonic repertoire.

For all that, they were good students. I graded them with seven A's and two B's, and at least two of them went on to enjoy some success in and around music—though not, I have to admit, as critics. One of them was Becca Rubin, whose work has been mostly in the field of consulting, especially, I think, on educational subjects: I had occasion to draw on her expertise more than ten years later when I invited her to come and advise the Philadelphia Orchestra staff on the training of docents. The other was Frank Hudson, who surprised and moved me when, in the late 1990s, he suddenly got in touch to tell me that mine had been the best and most helpful course he had ever taken. We then met for the first time in a quarter of a century, and Frank, who was by then on the staff of the Fairfax Symphony in Virginia, arranged for me to give a series of preconcert talks for the orchestra, a series that continued for several seasons.

Besides Wilf and me, there was another teacher at CMC who was to become one of my dearest friends and most admired musicians: the great Czech pianist Ivan Moravec. I met him first when I went to Minnesota to review a concert in which he was the soloist with the Saint Paul Chamber Orchestra, as well as to investigate the innovative outreach programs that the orchestra's manager, Stephen Sell, had put in place. Ivan's immediate remark at that first meeting was, "I think Ashkenazy just played the Beethoven Third Concerto in Chicago. That must have been really wonderful!" This has proved, over the forty-plus years of our friendship, to be only typical of his generosity to his fellow performers. In Paris once, he was playing lunchtime recitals for perhaps a hundred listeners in the lobby of one of the theaters on the Place du Châtelet, while the theater on the other side of the square was displaying huge posters for a Schubert series with the German pianist Christian Zacharias. Much as I admired Zacharias, I remarked on what I thought was an unjust disparity in the scale and publicity of the two projects, but Ivan immediately replied, "Oh, he deserves it—he's a great artist." And I enjoyed telling Leif Ove Andsnes how much admiration Ivan had expressed for the recording the Norwegian pianist had made of music by Janáček—music that Ivan had himself recorded, and on the subject of which his praise may be characterized as coming "from the horse's mouth."

When Bonnie and I were getting to know Ivan in Chicago, he revealed another talent almost as impressive as his musical gifts: he commandeered our kitchen and turned out a delicious meal of potato pancakes, which actually consisted of an entire shredded head of garlic held together by a little egg and a few shreds of potato. Unfortunately, his days of turning out such treats are past, because a few years later his wife, Zuzana, developed an allergy to garlic.

Ivan's masterclasses at CMC soon became a model for my own lectures. They were not masterclasses in the usual understanding of the term: instead, he would choose three or four recordings of a work or a movement, play excerpts in sequence, have his students listen to them and declare and explain their preferences, and only then tell them who the performers were. I attended several of these sessions, and over the years I have found the method to be an excellent way of training the ears and minds of the participants.

One such class yielded a very surprising result. The music was Beethoven's last piano sonata, op. 111 in C minor, and we heard supberb recorded performances by Claudio Arrau and Daniel Barenboim. Yet the unanimous preference of all present fell on a recording by Shura Cherkassky, who—as he himself put it when I met him years later and expressed my enthusiasm for that performance—was "not even thought of as a Beethoven player."

In addition to my official students, there were perhaps half a dozen young people who during my six years in Chicago called me, told me they wanted to become music critics, and asked for advice. My response to this was to invite them to lunch and, when they asked (as they almost invariably did) whether they should take music courses or journalism courses, to reply "Neither!" I explained that music courses were a second-order method of study, whereas listening intensively to music and no less intensively studying scores, which had been my own way of studying, was a first-order method. And as for journalism courses, I assured them that, having seen the work of a number of graduates of such courses, I doubted whether I should ever care to hire one.

What should they do, then, they wanted to know. I told them that, if I were in their position, I would go to Europe and explore musical life there—not because I thought European music was better than American, but because it would give them a whole additional perspective; if we were having this conversation in Europe, I added, I should be advising them in the same way to go to America. I don't know what became of the others' critical ambitions, but one of them, Sedgwick Clark, went on to a very successful career as a contributor to a variety of publications such as the program books of Carnegie Hall and the New York Philharmonic, and as editor since 1993 of the *Musical America International Directory of the Performing Arts*. He has also, I have been told by people who have met him, graciously continued to name me as one of his mentors.

A natural companion activity to teaching and lecturing is broadcasting. I had already dipped my toe into that field both in London and in New York. My very first radio broadcast, for the BBC in 1964, had been an interview with Ernest Fleischmann, the general manager of the London Symphony Orchestra. The orchestra was about to leave on its first world tour, taking in Israel, Turkey, Iran, India, Hong Kong, Korea, Japan, and the United States. There had been reports in the press to the effect that the tour was expected to result in a financial loss of some £50,000. "If you're going to lose £50,000," I asked Fleischmann, "why are you going on the tour?" To look back on that question now, half a century later, is amusing: an orchestra today would probably be thrilled if a tour lost it such a small sum of money.

The "Music Showcase" series for Nonesuch that I had done in New York was my most ambitious effort thus far in the radio field. But then, in Chicago, I benefitted from the presence of an exceptionally enterprising FM station, WFMT, and NORMAN PELLEGRINI, its program director for forty-three years. Norm particularly appreciated the fact that I was the only person around willing to do unscripted live radio, a willingness that stemmed from not minding making a fool of myself, either in front of the microphone, or in foreign countries when attempting to speak languages with which I am only rudimentarily acquainted. I made many broadcasts for WFMT, some solo, others in conversation with Norm. I would call him; he would ask me what I wanted to talk about and how much time I would need; outrageously, I once responded, "Oh, about an hour and a half," and he, always unfazed, simply said, "Fine—why don't you come in on Wednesday at, say, 2:30?" (The ninety-minute session was devoted partly to an extended discussion of the Eric Salzman *Nude Paper Sermon* recording mentioned at the beginning of this chapter, and partly, if I remember rightly, to some blistering comments about a book by Harold Schonberg of the *New York Times* that I was reviewing in the paper.)

Part of the pleasure of working with Norm, quite apart from the *frisson* that always resulted from hearing his superbly warm and resonant voice, was the amiable way we could allow for and even enjoy our disagreement on a number of musical topics. One of his dislikes, at least in the singer's early days (I think he modified his view later), was the English tenor Ian

Bostridge, who for me is as great a singer as any now before the public—and not only, for that matter, among those now singing: a fairly recent seventeen-CD compilation on EMI of "Schubert Lieder on Record" features more than a few Bostridge performances that compare well with and in some cases handily surpass those of several "Golden Age" singers included in the same set.

My association with WFMT lasted well beyond my departure from the *Chicago Daily News*. Its last two episodes were an interview, taped in England, with Michael Tippett to herald Solti's 1977 world premiere of his Fourth Symphony, and a program in preparation for the same conductor's 1990 world premiere of Panufnik's Tenth Symphony, both of these being works commissioned by the Chicago Symphony Orchestra. Recording the interview with Tippett in his rural Wiltshire home turned out to be one of the easiest assignments I have ever had to fulfill. Norm wanted a broadcast lasting one hour, so I thought I should try to record perhaps seventy minutes of conversation, to allow for editorial trimming. What actually happened was that, after a delicious lunch, Michael stretched out full length on the couch and said, "All right, love: what do you want to know?" I asked a simple question, and in response he talked for fifty-eight minutes, so I reckoned that no extra talk was needed and sent the tape off to Chicago, where it was broadcast without any editorial intervention.

My friendship with Norm lasted until his death in 2009. I flew from Seattle to Chicago for the service in his memory, which revealed the Chicago community's admiration and indeed love for Norm by filling a spacious church to standing-room-only capacity half an hour before it began.

Of comparable importance with the CSO in the scheme of Chicago's musical life was Lyric Opera, where Bruno Bartoletti served from 1964 to 1999 as principal conductor, becoming artistic director in 1975. I thought him an excellent conductor, and with the company's practice, under general director Carol Fox, of engaging celebrated soloists in their prime for its productions, a high musical standard prevailed.

It seemed to me that the dramatic content of the operas presented was accorded less attention, and as a modest blow aimed against that imbalance I began, when preparing the listings of forthcoming productions for the paper, to place the stage director's name before that of the conductor. Looking back now, more than four decades later, on that quixotic notion, I find myself feeling retrospectively guilty. I think of the directorial missteps common in the 1960s and '70s, and how trivial such shortcomings were, compared to the pass to which we have now been brought by the excesses of operatic Regietheater, with its willful setting aside of librettists' and composers' specific intentions, its arrogant pretension to (as I once heard Jonathan Miller characterize it in a preproduction cast presentation) "moral superiority over the work in hand," and its wanton abandonment of such plot elements as social backgrounds, political implications, historical era, and even the sex of individual characters. And I am left regretting a silly editorial idea that could be seen in retrospect as a step in the direction of such derelictions of taste. (The present Afterword includes two reviews that bear on this matter.)

Nevertheless, there were indeed aspects of some of the productions that were no less silly than any modern extravagance. In act 2 of Rossini's *Barber of Seville*, for example, there is a traditional cut that makes nonsense of the plot: if Rosina has not been deceived by Bartolo into thinking that Almaviva is playing fast and loose with her, there is no conceivable reason why, having just hours earlier agreed to elope with him that evening, she should, when he appears at the top of a ladder to carry her off, change her tune and order him off the premises. The production I witnessed at Lyric Opera perpetrated that nonsense, directed by no less a luminary than Geraint Evans. When I interviewed him for a weekend piece in the *CDN* and asked him how he could have allowed such an absurd practice to be followed, his answer astonished me: "Well," he said, "I have never actually thought about it."

It must surely have been that kind of nonthinking, among other things, that provoked Samuel Johnson's gibe at opera as "an exotic and irrational entertainment." Happily, another celebrated baritone, Tito Gobbi, displayed a much surer theatrical as well as musical hand when he directed Verdi's *Falstaff* for Lyric, starring in the title role and investing it with as vivid a dramatic charge as achieved in any other production I have seen. His care for dramatic verisimilitude was borne out in a lecture I heard him give years later in which, sitting down, he demonstrated how he would vary his response to someone's tapping him on the shoulder: when he was playing a young character, he would effortlessly turn his head; but when the character he was playing was older, to respond took a slower swivelling of the whole upper body.

In 1971, when Gobbi was directing *Falstaff*, I happened to be presenting a series of talks about the season's repertoire at a downtown offshoot of the University of Chicago. Usually I did these talks by myself, but I was so impressed by Gobbi's dramatic and musical mastery of the opera and his role in it that I felt it would be wonderful for my students—all of them well above the age of the usual university student—if I could get him to come and speak to them. Not only did he readily accept my invitation, without asking for a fee: his contribution to the afternoon thrilled my students—and every year after that until he died in 1984 I received a Christmas card from him and his wife, who wrote me a touching letter after his death. I had always felt that his gifts shone at their brightest when he was seen as Falstaff and as Scarpia in *Tosca* (witness the unsurpassed recording of that opera conducted by Victor de Sabata that Gobbi made with Maria Callas and Giuseppe di Stefano), but he surprised me by telling me that his favorite role was Wozzeck.

Among Lyric's most notable nonartistic strengths was the company's dynamic press agent, Danny Newman. A few years after my time in Chicago, he wrote a seminal book, *Subscribe Now!*, which preached the gospel of subscription sales in ensuring financial health for performing arts organizations. Its influence resulted in the institution of subscription-sales campaigns in several countries where they had previously been uncommon. Even before the publication of the book, Danny had brought Lyric Opera's attendance record to a point that exceeded 100 percent of capacity, by impressing on subscribers the importance, whenever they might be unable to attend a performance they had booked for, of calling the box office and having their tickets released for resale. Quite aside from his dynamism, Danny was a delightful man to work with, endowed with an irrepressible sense of humor, and with keen interests in several fields unconnected with opera, most notably Yiddish theater, with which he had family connections.

At one point in my Chicago years, Northwestern University presented a public symposium on the subject of opera. The participants on the platform included Harold Schonberg and my friend Martin Bernheimer. I was not officially on the program, so I attended as a member of the public. But when Schonberg told us, "All this talk about production is all very well . . . I'll take production if it's there, but it's gravy. What I want is a tenor who can come down to the footlights, look me in the eye, and give me a good top C. All the rest is gravy," I felt the obligation to stand up and deliver from the floor an impassioned defense of opera as a dramatic art. When Martin and I met afterward, he told me that after my perhaps intemperate remarks Schonberg had asked him, "Who was the hostile unwashed Englishman?" and when Martin enlightened him said, "Hmm—that figures!" Could it be that he had seen my review of his book?

One tenor who, leaving the question of priorities aside, was certainly capable of a good top C was the intelligent and stylistically aware Frank Little, who sang at Lyric Opera for thirteen seasons and at the Met for five.

Coming to know and admire his work, I encountered in the same period another excellent Chicago tenor, Donald Doig, a long-time member of the city's Music of the Baroque ensemble. While such fine tenor singing was to be heard locally, in 1971 I was also smitten by the contribution of a then-unknown (to me) Spanish tenor on a Vanguard recording by Newell Jenkins and the New York Clarion orchestra and chorus of Rossini's *La pietra del paragone* (an unjustly neglected masterpiece). He was only twenty-four years old, and his name was José Carreras, later to star in "The Three Tenors" alongside Plácido Domingo and Luciano Pavarotti, both of whom he fully matched in artistry. Impressed by what seemed like a coincidental wealth of tenorial talent, I wrote a celebratory piece for the paper under the title "Tenors, Anyone?" and continued to watch the developing careers, on admittedly different levels, of all those three singers with steady satisfaction.

Lyric Opera also had on its roster a tall and handsome bass-baritone who, though he was born in Connecticut to Lithuanian immigrant parents and made his professional debut with New York City Opera, has lived for most of his life in Chicago with his wife, the model Nijolė, almost equally tall and, to my masculine eye, even more attractive. Arnold Voketaitis is a pillar of the city's long-established Lithuanian community, which is the largest in the world outside Lithuania. He appeared regularly at Lyric for more than two decades, and was equally impressive musically and in dramatic power.

It may well have been through Arnold's advocacy that I took the trouble to go out to one of the city's Lithuanian neighborhoods to review a production of *Fidelio* presented by the Lithuanian Opera Company of Chicago. I am, in consequence, probably the only person most readers have encountered that has heard *Fidelio* sung in Lithuanian—but I have to assure them, the experience certainly, as the Michelin guide might put it, merited a detour. The Florestan, singing and acting with riveting intensity, was Stasys Baras, who had studied singing extensively in Europe but at that time, having immigrated to the United States and settled in Chicago, was making his living as vice-president of a local bank. The production as a whole, enhanced by a thoroughly competent orchestral contribution, was memorably well-conceived, deeply moving, and ingeniously designed. Throughout the dungeon scene in act 2, a large black hook hung threateningly above the stage. With the transition from dungeon to courtyard and from darkness to light, it was raised smoothly out of sight in the flies—a touch of symbolism simplistic perhaps, but none the less arresting on that account.

Traveling around Chicago's widely spread neighborhoods on my critical or gastronomic rounds was easy, whether by car, bus, or taxi. My only problem arose for linguistic reasons when I wanted to visit a favorite Chinese restaurant on North Clark Street. Several Chicago streets have names that look familiar but are pronounced idiosyncratically. Mozart Street, for instance, comes out as "Moe's Art," and Devon as "Duh Vón." To native Chicagoans, Goethe Street is "Go Thee," the "th" unvoiced (as in "thin" rather than "than"). For that particular recurring taxi trip up North Clark Street, since I couldn't bring myself to call the street "Go Thee," I had to ask the driver to drop me off "one block south of Schiller"—a greater poet anyway than Goethe to my heterodox taste (just look at the text of his *Nänie*, of which Brahms made so aptly sublime a setting), if not perhaps as great an intellect.

Organizations with a prestige like that of the Chicago Symphony Orchestra and Lyric Opera were not the only ones whose performances I covered. There were many other performing groups and presenting organizations, large and small, that contributed to the diversity of options for the city's music-lovers.

Al Booth founded a splendid weekly series of Dame Myra Hess Memorial Concerts at the Chicago Cultural Center. With a somewhat higher profile, Harry Zelzer, whom Chicagoans tended to regard as the city's answer to New York's dominant impresario Sol Hurok, still ran the ambitious Allied Arts series of concerts and recitals that he had started in 1930. (Hurok was the man who was said to have remarked that, if people didn't want to go to a concert, there was nothing you could do to stop them.) One of the Sunday afternoon piano recitals Zelzer presented in Orchestra Hall was the cause of another of those unexpected phone calls, this time not from a Puerto Rican government official, but from one of the era's greatest pianists.

I was surprised when the voice at the other end of the line said, "Brendel here"—I had never met ALFRED BRENDEL, and I was intrigued to know why he was calling. "I expect," he said, "you will be reviewing my recital on Sunday, and that you will be preparing for the Schubert G-major Sonata with the Henle Urtext score. You know that in that edition there are some little turns in the theme of the slow movement, and you will notice on Sunday that I do not play them. The reason is that I happen to possess the manuscript, and they are not in it. I thought you might like to know this." It was extremely considerate of Brendel to save me in advance from making a fool of myself: I don't mind doing that, as I've said, on the radio or in foreign languages, but a review of a serious artist is another much weightier matter; and I felt much flattered also by his confident—and correct!—assumption that I would have done my homework.

The contact thus established was renewed on several subsequent occasions. On one of them, we had a lively disagreement on my old warhorse subject of repeats in the classical and romantic repertoire (there was one specific passage in a Schubert sonata on which our views differed sharply; see p. 234). I was amused some years later to find Alfred expressing, among the acknowledgments in a volume of his collected essays, his thanks to "Bernard Jacobson, whose views on repeats helped to clarify my own"—amused, but in this case by no means particularly flattered, because the phrase must surely have been his characteristically polite way of saying "Bernard Jacobson, whose views on repeats are idiotic."

As anyone acquainted with this extraordinary pianist, scholar, and writer would expect, meals with Alfred have yielded satisfactions ranging widely between instruction and entertainment. Over lunch once, he told me of his excitement at encountering the artistry of the young German baritone Matthias Goerne, who had impressed him so much that he had called the singer's management and volunteered to perform with him. Notable recordings of Beethoven's *An die ferne Geliebte* and Schubert's *Schwanengesang* were among the results.

Altogether lighter in tone, when I was working for the Philadelphia Orchestra, was a dinner at our house at which Alfred, in town for a concert with the orchestra the next evening, was the only guest. His spirits lubricated by the bottle of Calvados that we jointly finished, he drew from his wallet some of his "unintentional humor" clippings, including an advertisement for a recital by "die grosse lebendige Pianistin Elly Ney" ("the great living pianist," as distinct from all the dead ones that are in the habit of giving recitals). I was on concert duty the next night, and when he arrived at the hall Alfred urged me, with the utmost seriousness, to come and see him after the concert, "no matter," he said, "how badly I play." No such urging was needed; the performance—the first he had given of Brahms's Second Piano Concerto in a long time—was fully characteristic of his talent. But the point of the emphasis emerged when he handed to me a paper bag from his briefcase, which proved to contain a very good bottle of Calvados to replace the one he evidently felt guilty at having drained the night before.

Another performer who, like Brendel, supplied me with useful corrective information—only in this instance after the review rather than before—was that great and underrated conductor Charles Mackerras. In the context of the extremely positive review I wrote of a Chicago Symphony concert in which he conducted Shostakovich's Ninth Symphony, the one complaint I felt it fair to make concerned his treatment of a rhythmic detail: at each one of a considerable number of changes of meter, the score clearly and consistently specifies that, between one measure and the next, quarter-note should equal quarter-note in duration, whereas Mackerras had made the broader note-groups, not the individual notes, equal.

The day my review appeared, Mackerras phoned and thanked me for my positive comments, but then went on to tell me that he had studied the score in question with the composer. "No one," he said, "is clearer or more specific than Shostakovich about how he wants such passages to be played, and no one is more liable to change his mind." That, Mackerras said, was what had happened in this case: the way he had conducted the movement represented Shostakovich's latest thoughts on the metric changes, which had superseded what was shown in the printed score. I was delighted at the rare opportunity to publish a correction, just a day after my review had appeared, setting the record straight and exonerating Mackerras from any suspicion of infidelity to the composer's intentions.

Alongside the important chamber music series presented by the Milwaukee-based Fine Arts Quartet in the Goodman Theatre (and on WFMT radio), Zelzer's Allied Arts was the most prominent source of downtown musical sustenance outside the Chicago Symphony and Lyric Opera. The Fine Arts Quartet championed, often in world premieres, the works of such composers as Charles Wuorinen, Jean Martinon, Seymour Shifrin, Ruth Crawford Seeger, Ben Johnston, Karel Husa, and Milton Babbitt (whose String Quartet no. 3 proved to be a much more approachable and poetically lyrical work than his reputation as a forbiddingly intellectual composer had led me to expect). But while the group fulfilled its duty to contemporary music enthusiastically and skillfully, it was on Chicago's South Side, in the University of Chicago's Mandel Hall, that the most influential proponent of new music did his work.

To call Ralph Shapey a maverick would be to indulge in gross understatement. As the founder and director of the university's Contemporary Chamber Players, or CCP, he presented numerous premieres, but his own music often ran into roadblocks with performing groups and what might be called the critical establishment. When the jury chose his *Concerto Fantastique* as winner of the 1992 Pulitzer Prize for music, the Pulitzer Board unprecedentedly overruled that decision and awarded the prize instead to the jury's second choice, Wayne Peterson's *The Face of the Night, The Heart of the Dark*. Whatever the rights and wrongs of such matters, Ralph specialized in a vivid kind of prickly isolationism. This reached such a point that at one time anyone calling his number was greeted by a recorded announcement declaring "The music of Ralph Shapey is no longer available. Thank you for your interest." A while later, I happened to run into Annette Moreau, director of the Arts Council of Great Britain's Contemporary Music Network, on the street outside the BBC's music department, and she said: "Oh, I have a message for you from Ralph Shapey. He said I should tell you that he's composing again."

Ralph was certainly justified in thinking the news would interest me. Encountering him first in Chicago, I seemed to be the only one among the four chief music critics on the city's main newspapers that took him seriously as a major composer. In that capacity, he was delighted when the writer and philosopher Leonard Meyer and I both dubbed him "a radical traditionalist." But from the viewpoint of local musical life, his leadership of the CCP was perhaps even more vital.

On one occasion, when he had invited me to the rehearsal of a new work, I commented very negatively on its quality. He surprised me by agreeing, and went on to say that he felt it was his responsibility, as director of an important performing group, to program a wide variety of new works whether he happened to like them or not. This was an attitude diametrically opposed to Giulini's reluctance to perform Schubert's "Great" C Major Symphony until he had come to understand and value it fully. But Shapey's view is both comprehensible and admirable because, while Schubert's career was hardly likely to fade because of one twentieth-century conductor's neglect of one of his works, the conductor of a contemporary ensemble may justly feel that there are rising composers who do seriously depend on his advocacy to make their way in a competitive musical world.

Supporting the work of such organizations as the CCP was a devoted music-lover named Paul Fromm. Paul was a Jew who had fled Germany in 1938, settled in Chicago, and cofounded a wine-importing firm. It prospered so well that in 1952 he was able to establish the Fromm Music Foundation, which offered financial support to young composers. I was one of a group of people whose opinions Paul liked to canvass. Our discussions usually took place over lunch, which belied his status in the wine and gastronomic world by taking the austere form of sandwiches eaten at his office desk.

Chicago was not just a one-orchestra town. The summer featured a series of open-air concerts in the lakefront Grant Park, near Orchestra Hall, and when summer ended it was from the Grant Park Orchestra that Lyric Opera drew most of its orchestral personnel. When I first arrived in town, the Grant Park concerts were managed by Edward Gordon, but a year or so later he took charge of the Ravinia Festival, north of the city, the scene of the Chicago Symphony's summer activities. Ed, with whom I was on terms of warm friendship, directed both of those institutions with a rare combination of business acumen and keen musical understanding: he was a good enough pianist to appear at Ravinia in a fine performance of Schubert's "Trout" Quintet. Ed enjoyed a remarkable artistic partnership at Ravinia with James Levine, relatively unknown at this time, whom he had appointed the festival's music director in 1973. After retiring from his Ravinia post in 1989, Ed planned to resume his concert career as a pianist, but he died too young in 1996, the sixty-five-year-old victim of pancreatic cancer.

There was good orchestral playing to be heard also at Northwestern University in nearby Evanston, especially after the school engaged Bernard Rubenstein as its orchestral director. He demonstrated his readiness to live dangerously when, for his first concert a mere few weeks after taking up the post, he programmed Schoenberg's Five Pieces for Orchestra and Mahler's First Symphony, and prefaced those two demanding scores with the *Leonore* Overture no. 2, a much tougher nut for a student orchestra to crack than the more popular no. 3. Donald Tovey, from whose *Studies in Musical Analysis* I have learned more about music than from any other single source, vividly and illuminatingly described Beethoven's method in transforming the one piece into the other. In the process, the composer replaced instant with deferred gratification.

The field of composition, too, was far from one-dimensional. Besides Shapey, there were several figures of considerable talent on the scene, most of them associated with one or other of the universities. I particularly admired Alan Stout, a member of the faculty at Northwestern University, who wrote large-scale orchestral works in a modern but approachable idiom, and whose penchant for long note-values gave his scores a refreshingly uncluttered look and his music a welcome air of expansive dignity. But the local composer I came to know best was ROBERT LOMBARDO (not to be confused with the artists' manager of the same name). Bob, who was born in Hartford, Connecticut, of Sicilian immigrant parents and who had studied composition with Arnold Franchetti, Philip Bezanson, and Boris Blacher, had served since 1964 as professor of theory and composition and Composer-in-Residence at Chicago Musical College, and it was in the context of a temporary exchange—both of jobs and of Chicago and London homes—that WILFRED JOSEPHS found himself teaching in Bob's place in 1972.

I admired Bob's music enough to take a few composition lessons with him. (I did actually complete a few pieces both before and after that, and I have sketched several more: every few years I take an unfinished string quartet out of the drawer where it quietly reposes, and do a little work on it just to keep my hand in.) Bob likes to give his music fun titles. One of his pieces is called *Erogenous Zongs*. His catalog includes a *Fourplay*—no prizes for guessing how many musicians it is for—and his chamber opera *The Dodo*, equally predictably but amusingly, is based on a motto theme consisting of two Cs (thus, in tonic sol-fa notation, do-do). His sense of humor extends also to a gift for conceiving neatly original ideas of form. Even more arresting than the structure of Ned Rorem's cycle *Songs of Love and the Rain*, with its double settings of the poems included, is the design of Lombardo's cycle *Songs to Kandinsky*. It begins with the setting of a poem in English, and continues through a series of translations each time into a new language—Russian, Italian, and German—before returning to English for a final version that is inevitably quite different from the original form of the poem.

That cycle is one of many Lombardo works set to texts by his poet and playwright wife, Kathleen, whose death we mourned in 2013. Their house was always full of art in varied media, for Bob himself has developed in recent years into a painter of remarkable talent. Several of his works hold an honored place in our collection, as he himself continues to do in our circle of friends, even though the days when he and I would have breakfast together every week are long past.

Among Chicago's musical organizations there were some that were small by any standard, but that I did not want to neglect. A colleague told me one day that the features editor of our sister morning paper, the *Sun Times*, had called him into his office and asked whether he was planning to cover a certain concert, because, he said, "Jacobson will probably be reviewing it." I heard a similar line about a rehearsal by a local chamber group at which one player asked another, "Shall we take the repeat?" "We'd better," his colleague replied: "Jacobson may be there."

One of my excursions outside the usual run of major concert venues took me to the Bernard Horwich Jewish Community Center, on West Touhy Avenue in the northern part of the city. From the concert of contemporary chamber music that was being played there I gained the acquaintance of a really outstanding pianist. Born in Israel and long resident in the Chicago area, Abraham Stokman was an ex-pupil of Eduard Steuermann, who had studied piano with Busoni and composition with Humperdinck and Schoenberg, and who had also taught Brendel and Russell Sherman.

Abe combined a dazzling technique with warmth of expression and insatiable musical curiosity. Yet, after reviewing his performance at that concert in highly complimentary terms, I learned that he was far from being able to earn a living through serious performance, and was keeping the wolf from the door by playing in bars (shades of the young Brahms!). I wrote a piece for the paper deploring this state of affairs, and suggesting that any of the several well-established music schools in the city could benefit immeasurably by hiring him. Then one day the phone rang, and Abe, whom I had not yet met, said, "I'd like to take you to lunch." "Well," I said, "that's very kind of you, but what have I done to deserve it?" Chicago Musical College had offered him an assistant professorship, he told me, and had done so as a direct result of reading my article.

Abe and I were in due course to collaborate on a project he dreamed up: to take a piano to a number of inner-city schools in more or less impoverished areas and play lunchtime recitals for their preteen pupils. The main piano dealer in Chicago, Lyon & Healy, agreed to supply the instrument, and the Illinois Arts Council, on whose Music Advisory Panel I served for several years, picked up the transportation costs. It was a small and relatively short-lived initiative, but we were warmly received at several schools, and may well have provided the first experience of "classical" music for many kids, some of whom, I hope, may have gone on to explore it further. The children were all asked to write something about their reactions to the experience, and I remember in particular one little boy who wrote to Abe: "Your hands were like birds flying over the keys."

Looking back on my time with the *CDN* between 1967 and 1973, I have to say that, in contrast with the current prevalence of digital media and the relatively impoverished state of newspapers, it seems to have been a golden age in newspaper history. Certainly the paper's coverage of the Solti appointment, recounted earlier in this chapter, was by no means an isolated example of its liberality with both money and column inches.

I was encouraged to take a reviewing trip abroad generally once a year, which led among other things to repeated reviews of the Edinburgh International Festival, and within the US borders there were few events of note that I was unable to attend and write about. Performances I reviewed on visits to New York included a revelatory recital by Erica Morini, which established her in my mind as one of the greatest violinists of her time, partly but not only because of the perfection of her bowing (which was totally free of the tendency to pull away from a straight line at the end of a down-bow common among lesser performers), and what I think was the US debut appearance of the Dutch early-music ensemble Syntagma Musicum. Kees Otten, the group's director, had recorded with it a fascinating and unusual two-record "Seraphim Guide to Renaissance Music" that featured a superb tenor named Marius van Altena. I was eager to hear these fine musicians live, and I learned some years later, when I finally met Otten after a concert he gave with the group in London's Wigmore Hall, that he was very glad that I had: he told me that my review had been the key that opened for Syntagma Musicum the door to repeated US invitations.

I traveled also to such institutional events as the 1968 opening of Powell Symphony Hall, a beautifully renovated former cinema, as the new home of the St. Louis Symphony, and the completion in 1972 of the University of Cincinnati College-Conservatory of Music's physical facilities with the opening of the Patricia Corbett Pavilion. Even a single concert of importance was enough to justify a trip, and I was back in St. Louis not long after the Powell Hall opening when Michael Tippett stepped in for a concert that Stravinsky had been scheduled to conduct, but from which he had had to withdraw owing to illness. Tippett had received a knighthood in 1966, and rather as in my reaction to the case of Sir Georg Solti narrated above, I asked him, over an *al fresco* snack in the orchestra's executive director's garden a few hours before the concert, whether as an inveterate champion of democracy he was uncomfortable with such royally bestowed honors. His answer—that "Sir Michael" made it easier for people to graduate to addressing him as "Michael" than it was when he had been plain "Mr. Tippett"—may well have been sincere, but I didn't find it quite convincing.

Rather closer to home was Milwaukee, where I went to cover the scheduled premiere of Roy Harris's *Père Marquette* Symphony, commissioned to celebrate the tercentenary of Jacques Marquette's opening up of newly explored territory in Wisconsin in the 1660s and '70s. Guests were treated to a lavish meal, at which the only slightly incongruous touch on the white napery, among the elegant silverware and dishes, was provided by glasses designed not for wine but for beer: the Schlitz brewing company was the sponsor of the event. As it happened, Harris had not completed the symphony in time, so we heard just half of it. In the intermission, a fellow guest, John Edwards, the redoubtable general manager of the Chicago Symphony, sidled up to me and said: "Well, Bernard, it just goes to prove the truth of the old saying—'half a loaf is better than one.'"

John, with whom I enjoyed a cordial relationship, was as passionate in his love of cats as Laura and I are. He had an aged and warmly cosseted one named Gus Mahler, who actually lived in John's office near the top of the Orchestra Hall building, and whom visitors were invited to admire. Guests of an ailurophobic disposition, it was clear, were not welcome.

In Milwaukee I made the acquaintance of Michael Hammond when he invited me to come and hear him conduct what astonishingly seemed to be the Milwaukee premiere of *Verklärte Nacht*, a full half-century after Schoenberg had made his string-orchestra arrangement of the score. The program also included Mozart's *Serenata notturna*, which the conductor rendered more effective than usual by placing one of the two small ensembles it is scored for in a separate room.

But Michael was not only a conductor, exceptional though I found his gifts in that capacity. The director of the Wisconsin Academy of Music, he doubled at the same time as an instructor in physiology and anatomy and a researcher in neuroanatomy at the University of Wisconsin–Madison, also teaching neuroanatomy and physiology at the Marquette Medical School. He had taken a degree in classics and philosophy from Lawrence University in Appleton, Wisconsin, studied Indian music and philosophy at Delhi University, taken sitar lessons from Ravi Shankar, and won a Rhodes Scholarship in 1956 to attend Oxford University, where he studied philosophy, psychology, and physiology (the same elite PPP course that my friend Peter Delin was taking at the same time), then staying on at the university for premedicine studies.

Returning to Wisconsin, Michael lived for a year on the Menominee Indian Reservation, learning to speak Menominee, and wrote a novel drawing on this experience. He moved to New York State in 1968 to be dean of music for the newly created State University of New York at Purchase, and he served from 1977 to 1980 as the college's president. While he held that post he invited me to give a lecture at the college, but it was badly scheduled for a period when almost all the students had other commitments: only two showed up, so I simply took them to the cafeteria and turned it into a two-on-one seminar.

With characteristic tireless versatility, Michael diversified his activities during his time at SUNY by serving as an associate conductor with the American Symphony Orchestra under Leopold Stokowski and as music director and conductor of the Dessoff Choirs. The next stop in his extraordinary career was Houston, where from 1986 to 2001 he was dean of the Shepherd School of Music at Rice University. Nothing seemed to be beyond his powers. On December 20, 2001, having been appointed by President George W. Bush, he was unanimously confirmed by the Senate as the new chairman of the National Endowment for the Arts. He took up the post on January 22, but died just a week later, apparently from cancer, at the age of sixty-nine.

Relatively short journeys took me also to several other universities in the Chicago area. On one such trip, to the University of Illinois's Urbana-Champaign campus, I met John Cage. This was at "Musicircus," a huge musical jamboree he had devised that brought together a great number of resident and visiting composers and performers, including Lejaren Hiller (director of the University's Experimental Music Studio between 1958 and 1968), Ben Johnston, Salvatore Martirano, William Wegman, Ron Nameth, Herbert and Norma Marder, Laetitia Snow, Morgan Powell, and the remarkably original and charismatic Kenneth Gaburo.

I had always felt—and this encounter did nothing to change my mind—that Cage was a more important composer *about* than *of* music: reading about his works, many of which are of philosophical rather than artistic value, is more interesting than hearing them. But there could be no denying, to judge from the time I spent talking with him at Urbana, that he was not only a deeply serious but also an exceptionally kind and generous man. Talking about the recording of *HPSCHD*, the piece for harpsichord and computer generated sounds that he had composed jointly with Hiller in response to a commission from Nonesuch Records, he told me he was especially pleased that Ben Johnston's String Quartet no. 2 was on the other side of the record, "so people will buy the record for our piece, which isn't that important, and Ben's wonderful quartet will be heard by a lot more people than would otherwise have come across it." My own reaction to the record, I have to say, bears out Cage's valuation: *HPSCHD* was really no more than a box of technical and electronic tricks, whereas Johnston's quartet clearly manipulated its microtonal textures for expressive and poetic purposes, to often beautiful effect.

At Northern Illinois University, located in DeKalb, I met another gifted local composer, named—perhaps somewhat problematically—Jan Bach, and my visit there also provided me with the opportunity to get to know the playing of the Vermeer Quartet, which served as resident artist from 1970. I was already acquainted with the group's original violist, Scott Nickrenz, who had been one of the Claremont Quartet's members when I recorded Schoenberg's *Ode to Napoleon Buonaparte* with them in 1968, but the quartet's first violinist, the brilliant virtuoso Shmuel Ashkenasi, was new to me. I felt at once that this was a quartet of the highest artistic stature, on a similar level to that of the Cleveland Quartet. I greatly preferred the Vermeer's richly resonant sonority to what always seemed to me the anemic, even soapy, sound of the Guarneri Quartet, despite the strong contributions that second violinist John Dalley and violist Michael Tree made to that group's performances.

There was also an occasion to visit Western Illinois University, in Macomb, when the Chicago Symphony went out there for several days of a well-planned residency on the campus and with local schools. But I remember that trip more vividly for geographical than for musical reasons. Ever since arriving in the United States in 1964, I had been telling people how much I liked America. This always produced responses to the effect that, "oh, this isn't really America." They said it in New York; they said it in Philadelphia, and in Chicago. But when I drove out to Macomb through the Spoon River country celebrated in verse by Edgar Lee Masters, and saw a huge billboard advertising "Purina Hog Chow," I decided that I had finally found a place where nobody could tell me "this isn't really America."

Another university visit was undertaken not for the paper but in pursuit of a freelance interest. In England in the 1960s I had given several preconcert lectures on the BBC and in concert halls on the music of IANNIS XENAKIS. The publishing firm E. P. Dutton was now proposing to publish a *Dictionary of Contemporary Music*, encyclopedic in scope, edited by John Vinton. Having heard some of my talks, Xenakis asked Mr. Vinton to commission me to write the article on his music. Xenakis was a faculty member at the music school of Indiana University from 1967 to 1972, and had established a studio there for research into computer-assisted composition along the lines of the Équipe de Mathématique et Automatique Musicales (EMAMu) that he had established in Paris. So I went to Bloomington to spend a whole intensely stimulating day talking with him.

The interpenetration of art and science was central to Xenakis's conception of his role as a musician. Despite his background in architecture and engineering and his strongly scientific turn of mind, it was clear from everything he told me that his recourse to those disciplines in his own compositions was essentially no more than a shortcut to results that could otherwise have been reached only through laborious and time-consuming means. Even early in his career, he always kept the vital aesthetic decisions in his own hands, applying what he called the final "sheen" or "embellishment" to a piece on the subjective basis of what would be most "interesting." I was amused, incidentally, by his consistent use of the word "interesting" as a term of musical praise and of the word "beautiful" to characterize scientific formulas.

Back in the city, my typical daily routine was to go into the *CDN* office around lunchtime and sort through the inevitable mountains of mail. My desk was next to that of our television critic Norman Mark, who would sit down to his typewriter every Friday to fill out his expenses report for the week saying, “Right—now for the day’s creative writing.” Norm was a fine critic and a lovely man who, to my sorrow, died in 2012, very soon after we had put years of noncontact right by getting together again in Seattle.

I sympathized with Norm over the routinely abysmal quality of most of the televised pap he had to review, but he had his compensations, usually in the form of interviews with distinguished actors and directors, and one of those provided me also with a *frisson* of pleasure. When I appeared at my desk one afternoon, Norm said, “You’ll never guess who was sitting across from me this morning.” The interviewee in question had been Tony Randall, who, Norm told me, had asked him, “Who sits at that desk next to yours?” On being told “Bernard Jacobson,” Randall, a highly cultivated man with a keen interest in classical music, said, “Oh, please give him my regards: I’ve read a lot of his writing, and I’m a fan of his.” Critics aren’t used to having fans, especially among the ranks of bona fide stars, so I was delighted, years later, to find myself with an opportunity of reciprocating the admiration in a musical context when I reviewed Randall’s recording of Poulenc’s *Babar, the Little Elephant*. His narration is firm, funny and touching as the story dictates, and, unlike the insufferably arch and mannered recording perpetrated by “Dame Edna Everage,” blessedly unpatronizing.

Going through the mail that littered my desk, I would drop any press release that informed me someone was “world famous” in the wastepaper basket, since I felt that if he or she was world famous I would know it, and if he or she wasn’t, it was a lie. Then I would go home to read scores for the evening’s performance, eat dinner, go to the concert or opera, return to the office around 10:30 p.m., and turn my review in to the copy desk in the city room usually by around 2 a.m. (the deadline being 4 a.m.).

The publication schedule was such that my review would first appear midmorning. I started my days by reading first my own review, in case it had acquired any typos that I could call the office and have them correct for the second printing, and then the day’s column by the man who was probably my most famous colleague, Mike Royko. His columns were always stimulating and often hilarious: who could resist a writer who told us that the driver behind him put his flashers on and proved to be a policemen after Mike had stuck his arm out of his car’s window and protested the man’s driving by giving him “half a peace sign”? His book *Boss* must be among the best political biographies ever written. It explains that its subject, Mayor Richard J. Daley, prevailed over his rivals for office by recounting how his chief competitor was interested in power and money, but Daley was interested only in power.

My own single personal encounter with Daley was at a press conference to announce that the city was supporting the Chicago Symphony's first European tour to the tune of a munificent $50,000. I asked the mayor one question, and he demonstrated in response that he was as masterly as a politician as his biographer was as a writer: he made a fluent and articulate speech that went on for a full five minutes and had absolutely nothing to do with the question I had asked.

Royko called me in the office one day. He asked if it was true, as he had been told, that the toilet facilities at the Grant Park concerts were in shockingly bad condition. I explained that I couldn't tell him: I had never used them, preferring always, what with my professional responsibility for unwavering concentration, to arrive at a concert prepared for several hours without such recourse. He wrote a column celebrating, or at least divulging, my eccentricity. I still have the copy of *Boss* that Mike gave me, inscribed to "Tin-Ear," which was his name for the paper's music critic, whoever that might be at any given time.

I rarely wrote my own headlines, since I had discovered very soon that the city-desk men were much better at it than I was. There were occasional exceptions: when Adolph ("Bud") Herseth, the Chicago Symphony's principal trumpet for more than fifty years, had a momentary technical lapse in the performance Martinon conducted of Mahler's Tenth Symphony, I couldn't resist heading my review: "Herseth Plays Wrong Note." I was fairly confident that, in the light of all the rave notices I had written about his playing over the previous years, he would realize that this was purely a compliment. I have always tried to avoid writing hurtful things about performers, and also to avoid comments related to their physical appearance. But a remark I couldn't resist including in my review of a Lyric Opera *Traviata*, again in the context of an overwhelmingly positive review of Montserrat Caballé's Violetta, was that, while she was superb in the role, "she looked more like a victim of conspicuous consumption than the other kind." I hope she either never saw the review or forgave me.

More usually, part of the pleasure of opening the paper in the morning consisted in finding out what pithy locution the editors had prefaced my piece with. Having written a review of a Bach recital by Rosalyn Tureck in which I inveighed against all the coughers in the audience (quoting Bernard Shaw's suggestion that a regiment of sharp-shooters should be posted around the hall to pick off such people), I found it headed "Bach Battles Bronchial Brigade."

The paper had a weekend magazine section that was useful for "think pieces" and for record and book reviews. Lillian Libman, who had been a personal representative for Stravinsky, wrote a book titled *And Music at the Close: Stravinsky's Last Years*, which, as her obituary in the *New York Times* observed, "created a controversy in the music world by challenging previously published portraits of the artist," including those from the pen of Robert Craft. My review of it appeared under the delicious headline: "If You Knew Igor Like I Know Igor!"

Ms. Libman had been in town some time earlier in connection with a set of visiting performances by Sarah Caldwell's Opera Company of Boston. Caldwell's company presented two works, Verdi's *Falstaff* and Berg's *Lulu*, the latter in its long-overdue Chicago premiere. I had breakfast one morning, in a small hotel just off elegant Michigan Avenue, with Lillian, Sarah, and the Australian soprano Marie Collier, who took the title role in the Berg work. There was, to be sure, a good deal of talk about music across the table, but these three formidable ladies were also eager to teach me how to drink a bullshot, an enjoyable if somewhat gross beverage related to the Bloody Mary, but varied by the inclusion of beef bouillon. Marie Collier's Lulu was a devastatingly vivid and brilliant rendering of the part. She was also a charming woman, and I was much grieved to read, a year or two later, that she had fallen from a window to her death, aged only forty-four.

All in all, my six years at the *Chicago Daily News* provided some of the most enjoyable professional and human rewards of my life. One especially positive facet of the job was the freedom that my features editor, Richard Christiansen, gave me in choosing what to review. He was happy for me to follow my instinct even if it led to neglecting the appearance of a big-name performer in order to cover someone much less starry. When the Rotterdam Philharmonic was to give its first concert in the Chicago area at nearby Wheaton College, and I told Dick that I thought the orchestra needed a review much more than Arthur Rubinstein's umpteenth Chicago recital, and that it might be of at least equal interest to readers, he immediately assured me that such decisions rested entirely with me. Under Jean Fournet, its principal conductor at the time, the orchestra played a largely French program beautifully, and I further benefitted from my decision to review it by getting to know its manager, Willem Vos, whose friendship I continued to enjoy years later when I worked in The Hague, and whose death at a too early age was a sad blow to me and many musician friends.

Years later, when I was in Washington, DC, to attend a concert in the Library of Congress, I was invited for a preconcert drink by Joris Vos, Willem's brother, then serving as the Dutch ambassador to the United States. He had promised to drive me to the hall in plenty of time for the concert, but our conversation proved too engrossing to be cut short. In the end, we drove off, but he confessed he didn't know the way. At one point, in a distinctly insalubrious part of town, he jumped out of the car, and I enjoyed the incongruous sight of the elegantly dressed Dutch ambassador asking a group of young men who looked as if they were in the middle of a drug deal how to get to the Library of Congress. They didn't know either, but, through some bold guesswork, we eventually got there just in time.

Dick Christiansen transferred to another position about a year before I left the paper, and for the rest of my time there my editor was the gentle and thoughtful Bill Newman, who was no less pleasant to work for. There were easy contacts also with a group of stringers, whom I could always call on to help out when there were multiple events that had to be covered. One of them in particular, Avrom Joshua Epstein, wrote with remarkable sensitivity about music, and I envisaged a brilliant critical career for him, but he opted instead for one in medicine.

My decision to leave the paper—and the city—in 1973 may in the light of so many satisfactions seem hard to understand. (My old friend Tony Brown had said to me, after a 1971 CSO concert in Edinburgh, "Bernard, it's obvious you can't ever leave Chicago!") In the next chapter I shall try to explain it.

CHAPTER FIVE

EXCHANGING CRITICIZING FOR SUPPORTING

1973–76

By the early months of 1973 I felt ready for a radical change of professional direction. There were both negative and positive reasons for this.

On the negative side, having in nearly six years reviewed probably well over two thousand performances, I had begun to find the job too easy. It was not that I was jaded by the sheer bulk of the activity I was reviewing: I had been able to maintain freshness by setting aside two weeks every year for a vacation on which listening to music was firmly proscribed. Friends I visited on those trips were no doubt puzzled, or even shocked, when they asked what I would like to listen to and I firmly replied, "Nothing!" (I have in any case never been able to talk to people with any degree of concentration when music is on the radio or the record player), and equally puzzled when I no less firmly rejected any suggestion of attendance at a genuinely interesting concert. But the payoff would come when I returned to Chicago and entered Orchestra Hall, and the orchestra began to tune up, and my immediate reaction was: "Oh, that's so beautiful!"

No, I still loved listening to music. But my daily routine had reached a point where I could go to a concert, return to the *Chicago Daily News* offices, and write a review (a perfectly adequate review—I am not indulging here in false modesty) *without actually thinking*, and I had begun to feel that this was bad for the musicians, and for music, and for me.

The more positive reason for such a move was simply a feeling that it was all very well to pontificate about musicians' virtues and vices from a safe seat on the sidelines, but that it would be a healthy and fruitful step to put my own head for once on the chopping block. It's true that I had done this in a small way by my sorties into choral singing and performing as a narrator, as well as by virtue of the text I had written to be performed in Wilfred Josephs's *Death of a Young Man* song cycle. But that was merely part-time stuff—I really felt the need to make a firm commitment in the direction of submitting my own ideas to the scrutiny of others. I was searching for a framework that would align me in a structured way with the constituency of artists and presenters that I had hitherto stood outside.

Then I saw an advertisement for the position of Director of the Southern Arts Association in Winchester, Hampshire. SAA was one of a network of twelve regional arts associations around England that worked in cooperation with the Arts Council of Great Britain (ACGB) and with local government bodies to offer financial support and practical advice to organizations and individuals engaged in arts activities in their respective regions. My immediate impression was that the job could be shaped to emphasize not only assistance to existing arts programs but also pioneering new areas of activity.

SAA's region included the counties of Hampshire, Berkshire, Oxfordshire, Wiltshire, West Sussex, the Isle of Wight, and the city of Bournemouth (part of Dorset after a 1974 reorganization of local government, but remaining with Hampshire for arts administration purposes thanks to a friendly agreement with Ian Watson, the director of Southwest Arts). This was a sizeable and attractive swath of southern England—and I have to confess that, aside from the professional possibilities of the job, I had by then spent long enough in the States to have started to miss my native country. (The telltale sign: I had started reading novels with English settings less for the sake of their literary merits than out of sheer nostalgia.) So I put in an application and was invited to Winchester for an interview, at which I faced a formidable panel of six members of SAA's governing council, led by its chairman, Harold Baldry, a local professor who specialized in the history of ancient Greece.

When I was offered the job, I thought at first that it would be impossible for me to accept it, because it would entail a reduction of salary of more than 50 percent. But after spending a couple of days driving around the region, and reveling in its physical beauty and the sense of old-fashioned

English culture and civility that I had been missing, I changed my mind, called home, and won Bonnie's hesitant but obliging agreement to the move. (I was confident that she too would be able to find rewarding work in England. That did eventually happen, but only after she had gone through a long delay caused by an immigration officer's having put the wrong stamp on her passport; she was not permitted to work until we had laboriously prevailed on the bureaucracy to correct the error.)

My own job was centered on attending anything up to thirty meetings a week, some of them with arts groups, others with government or commercial organizations from whom we were soliciting financial contributions. These were needed because the subsidy from the Arts Council provided less than half of the various regional associations' budgets. The importance of local government financial support subjected my hopes of initiating new activities to a degree of resistance on the part of our own governing General Council: the majority of its members, being drawn from the ranks of elected office holders, were understandably reluctant to appear to be neglecting the interests of those of their constituents who were already involved in arts activities. In addition to that, while I had been hired as a man from outside who could be expected to come up with creative new ideas, by the time I actually started in the job the 1973 Arab-Israeli War, coupled with the squeeze on Western economies exercised by OPEC's oil-pricing policies, meant that subsidy from all sources could no longer be relied on to fund new activities.

Nevertheless, one of the advantages of starting as an outsider is that you don't know what is impossible, so that you try to do all sorts of things that you might not otherwise have even attempted—and one or two of them may after all prove to be possible. I had considered the resources the region possessed: they included several orchestras, with the Bournemouth Symphony and its sister ensemble the Bournemouth Sinfonietta at the top of the pyramid that constitutes a healthy artistic life; a fair number of theaters and cinemas; some excellent museums and multidisciplinary arts centers; and a great number of individuals engaged in writing, some of whom also gave public readings of their poetry and other work.

I thought also about what the region did *not* possess. Very few people, in a largely rural region, had ever seen a composer. I determined that my top priority for a new activity would be the creation of the first composer-in-residence position ever instituted by a regional arts association. I decided to put the project in hand, and promptly made my first big mistake. Working in a hurry, in order to make the post a reality before dwindling subsidies might ruin our chances, I was foolish enough to make my first presentation of the idea to the General Council at the end of a meeting under "Any Other Business."

This was a strategic error, though I didn't feel it deserved quite the lengthy and scornful diatribe that Andrew Murdoch, who was on the Council by virtue of his position as a Hampshire County Councillor, delivered. What hurt more than his words—"The director ought to know," etc., etc.—was the fact that he never once had the gumption to look at me while he was delivering them. (Incidentally, I had initially expected another Hampshire man, Ben Dufton, who was the country treasurer and also served as our treasurer, to take a negative position on some of my hoped-for activities, simply because his job was centered on necessary financial conservatism, but he proved instead to be a positive influence on his colleagues, with a mind that was always open to new ideas.)

The first consequence of my poor strategy, aside from the fact that getting approval for the project would have to wait for a better-prepared proposal to the next Council meeting, was that I learned who one of my strongest supporters was. Denys Hodson, a vice-chairman of SAA who had been a member of the panel that hired me, had been a consistently sensible contributor to previous discussions. Now, saying goodbye to the Council members as they left at the end of that meeting, I became aware that Denys was standing quietly in the corner of the room with a slight smile on his face. When we were the only two people left in the room, he came up, put his hand on my shoulder, and said, "I think you need a drink." He took me off to the bar in the Wessex Hotel next to the cathedral, and though Bloody Marys were not my usual tipple, I think I consumed two or perhaps even three of them.

My friendship with Denys lasted for many years after I had left SAA. With a desk always so full of work to be done that he could never clear it, he once pithily said to me, "You know, Bernard, I could save myself so much time if I had the time." As Swindon's controller of arts and recreation over a span of twenty-two years, as his obituary published in the *Guardian* in 2013 noted, this "inspirational arts administrator" provided Swindon and its people "with vibrant, accessible and forward-looking cultural opportunities, one of the first new-style municipal leisure pools and important heritage initiatives." He served as governor and deputy chairman of the British Film Institute, as a director of the Oxford Stage Company, and as vice-chairman of the Arts Council.

He also became, in due course, my chairman at Southern Arts. As vice-chairman, Denys had been such a tower of strength during my first year or so as the association's director that, when Harold Baldry announced his resignation from the chairmanship, I was eager to have Denys as his successor. Harold, aware of the disparity of status between elected local government members on the Council and paid local government staff, thought it was highly unlikely that I should be able to get the Council to agree to Denys's elevation to the top position. We knew also that Commander Reggie Cooper, a Portsmouth city councillor and owner of the city's King's Theatre, coveted the post.

I felt that Reggie was not a suitable man for the chairmanship, certainly possessing nothing approaching Denys's personal qualifications. So I thought I was being very clever when I phoned Reggie, told him that Denys was going to be nominated, and very politely asked him if he would be kind enough, as a prominent and valued member of the Council, to second the nomination. It would have been too embarrassing for Reggie to refuse. He seconded Denys's nomination, and Denys was duly elected. And from that moment, though we remained on as cordial and collaborative terms as ever, he became a much less useful supporter at Council meetings, for the simple reason that he must have felt, as a paid staff member employed by the Swindon council, that he had to lean over backward not to appear in any way to lord it over elected members.

The position of Southern Arts Association president was altogether free of the contention that affected the choice of chairman. At the time I arrived, the purely honorific post was held by the Duke of Wellington. Bonnie and I were invited to a very pleasant lunch with His Grace at Stratfield Saye, the family's estate near Basingstoke in Hampshire. The manager of the estate at that time was another member of the panel that had offered me the directorship, Christopher Scott, who, as an ex-regular soldier, easily eradicated the thoughtless prejudice I had long harbored against military persons. Christopher, another friend from those days with whom I am still in touch, is what the eighteenth century used to call "a man of parts": a man who writes a book about any subject that takes his fancy, gives his first piano recital a mere few months after his first (adult) lesson on the instrument, switches from estate management to running a museum to working in the travel industry, and from England to the United States, and who makes it all look effortless.

With several other guests, Bonnie and I dined with him and his first wife, Amoret, in their cottage on the Stratfield estate, and the evening was a beguiling combination of ancient and modern elements. Everyone was formally dressed, the men in tuxedos, most of the women in long gowns, and at the end of the meal there was the traditional call for the women to retire upstairs for coffee while the men lit cigars and passed the port—yet there were no servants: Christopher and Amoret themselves did all the cooking and all the serving. More recently, Laura and I spent an evening in Savannah, Georgia, where Christopher now lives with his third wife, June Hopkins. June, professor of history at Armstrong State University, is the granddaughter of President Roosevelt's closest advisor, Harry Hopkins. Laura was on her way to a medical conference, we'd always wanted to see Savannah, which proved to be an exceedingly picturesque and charming town, and Christopher kindly lent us his house to stay in, along with his cat to warm the bed.

When the Duke of Wellington resigned from the presidency and SAA needed to find a successor, it seemed to me that it was time we had an artist rather than a socially distinguished figurehead in that position. One of the greatest English composers of the twentieth century, MICHAEL TIPPETT, lived within our boundaries, in the county of Wiltshire, and I was delighted when he declared himself willing to become our president. I have felt very close to Michael's music ever since my first encounter with it at the Royal Festival Hall in 1951, and had great satisfaction over the years from reviewing the music and interviewing the man several times. He was a gracious host, who introduced me to Muscat de Beaumes-de-Venise at one especially sybaritic lunch, and the possessor of a Jung-influenced intellect so sharp yet elusive that conversation with him often felt like watching him bury a thought deep in the ground and then looking around in protracted puzzlement to see where on earth it might surface again.

Back in my Oxford days, I recorded (on an old open-reel tape machine) the premiere of Tippett's Second Symphony when it was broadcast by the BBC Symphony Orchestra, and was astonished a minute or two after the beginning to hear the music grind slowly to a halt. Then came Sir Adrian Boult's voice saying to the audience, "Entirely my mistake, ladies and gentlemen," after which the performance started again from the beginning. I was assured by a friend who had been in the hall that the fault actually lay very clearly with the concertmaster, Paul Beard, who emphatically gestured for the violins to come in at the wrong moment, but Boult was far too gracious a gentleman to let the blame fall on any shoulders but his own. Despite the momentary confusion, the symphony impressed me as a remarkably beautiful and original work, and I still love it, though I have subsequently come to think of Tippett's First Symphony as the greatest of the four.

Gennady Rozhdestvensky perhaps did Tippett no favors when, as principal conductor of the same orchestra around 1980, he included the First

Symphony in a program that contained something to keep every potential attender away: the concert waltz *München* preceded the Tippett, and the second half of the concert began with Hindemith's Piano Concerto and ended with Waldteufel's waltz *Les Patineurs*. Predictably enough, when I looked around just as the concert was about to start, there appeared to be more people on stage than in the audience.

The composer-in-residence project, reintroduced with a suitably bureaucratic-sounding preliminary proposal at the next council meeting, went well. Harold Baldry summed up a sensible discussion by saying, "I think we can say that we will be happy to consider the director's specific proposals at a future meeting"; and another of my most loyal supporters on the Council, Frank Pickstock, the mayor of Oxford, trumped that summation: "No, Mr. Chairman—I think what we should say is that we have full confidence in the director to put this program in place as soon as he can and in the light of his own professional judgment."

This was a fillip for my spirits, and also a relief, because I had told my staff before the meeting that the composer-in-residence project was so central to my vision of what the association should be doing that if the proposal were rejected, I should have to resign. We interviewed a large number of talented applicants, for a position that would go far beyond actual composing to include close contact with people all over the region through workshops, lectures, and presentations of all kinds in community settings such as working men's clubs and women's institutes. Our first appointee was Dominic Muldowney, who served from 1974 to 1976, went on to succeed his teacher Harrison Birtwistle as music director of the Royal National Theatre in London, and has become well known more recently for the scores he has contributed to the *Wallander* TV series and other such productions. He was succeeded by Judith Weir, who held the post from 1976 to 1979, and was subsequently appointed (in mid-2014) to succeed Peter Maxwell Davies as Master of the Queen's Music—the first female composer to hold that position.

My staff at SAA was about fifteen strong, roughly half of them specialist officers, each looking after one branch of the arts, backed up by an administrator and a few secretaries. My predecessor, Neil Duncan, who had left to become director of the recently established Regional Development Department within the Arts Council, had chaired a weekly meeting of SAA's specialist officers, but I decided to democratize the meetings by opening them up to the entire staff. This proved to be a problematic idea. What I quickly learned was that it is very hard to force people to be free: while about half of my staff—and not only among the group of officers—were delighted to be given more of a voice in the institution's decision-making, the other half clearly just wanted me to tell them what to do. I tried my best to orchestrate some kind of rapprochement between the two disparate attitudes, but the difference remained an area of contention at meetings.

I had more success in reinforcing my officers' self-confidence about the specific decisions they had to make for their various arts constituencies. When there was a difficult decision about advice or subsidy to arts groups to be made, I developed the practice of sitting down with the officer who had to make it. We would discuss the intricacies of the case for perhaps half an hour, after which I would say, "Well, you know my views by now. I want you to go away, think about it a bit more, make your decision, and *don't* tell me what you decide." Although initially those last six words surprised them, I had gleaned some useful lessons from a book about management that the principal bass player of the Chicago Symphony, Joseph Guastafeste, had handed me as a parting gift. It preached the gospel of delegation: I was convinced that the only way you can help people who work for you to grow is by allowing them to make their own mistakes—and that entails refraining from constantly looking over their shoulders.

Delegation, of course, only be done successfully if you have good people working for you, and in that respect I felt blessed. David Altshul for film, Tony Covell for theater, Teresa Gleadowe for visual arts, Graham Fawcett for literature, and CHRISTOPHER KERR for what we called "general arts," which involved working with multidisciplinary arts centers, were all first-rate professionals, and John Murphy was a strongly supportive deputy director. In the nature of the organization, it was with Chris Kerr that I had the closest contact, because his area of operation tended to take the two of us together on journeys to embryonic arts centers, and his always stimulating and at the same time supportive conversation was of considerable benefit to my own state of mind. The result of our collaboration was a warm personal friendship, with him and his wife, Jessa, that despite our subsequent wide geographic separation has lasted nearly forty years. I was especially touched when, on one of our visits back to England from Philadelphia, Laura and I solved the problem of how to see as many of our friends as possible by throwing a party in my daughter's and son-in-law's house—they lived at that time in London—and Christopher traveled two hundred miles down from the north of England to be there.

You may have noticed the absence of music from that list of talented staff members. Every hiring decision I made during my three years running

Southern Arts turned out well, except for the appointment of two music officers in succession who turned into near- or real disasters. The first was of a woman who greatly impressed our music-panel chairman, Peter Evans, and me at her interview by provoking the two of us into heated argument, but the same dynamism went missing when she was actually working in the field. She did not last long in the job, and Peter and I, licking our wounds, tried again, this time with an even worse result. The man we picked from a strong list of candidates turned out to be so introverted that within two or three months he became completely incapable of communicating with me face to face: he took to working at home, and staying in touch exclusively by means of terse handwritten notes.

So I am not proud of my record as a hirer of music officers, and I suppose I must level with readers by disclosing that one of the candidates we did *not* hire went on to become head of the BBC Proms and then managing director of the Barbican Centre in London: Nicholas—now Sir Nicholas—Kenyon. We felt, I think, that Nick was clearly a gifted high-arts figure who belonged in the metropolitan center, rather than in a regional position, and the way his distinguished career subsequently developed has surely justified that view.

I used to drop in on meetings of all the other arts panels from time to time, but I made a point of not doing so with the music panel, for fear that my own specialized music background might inhibit its deliberations. But there was one area where my specific experience and expertise came into play. As director of its local arts association, I became a member *ex officio* of the Bournemouth Symphony Orchestra's board of directors. At the orchestra's board meetings, I again tried an inherently democratic move, this time with more success. The two players' representatives on the board had previously sat by themselves on their own side of the boardroom table. I insisted instead that they should not be isolated in that way, and their resulting integration among the other directors did, I think, improve the atmosphere of the gatherings.

More significant was my membership of the jury at the first John Player International Conducting Competition, which the Bournemouth Symphony Orchestra hosted in 1974. The competition had drawn about two hundred competitors, and a handful of finalists were put through their paces with the orchestra before a panel of six jurors. By the time we came down to our final discussions, several problems had arisen. The biggest one was the position taken by four of the jurors, including (significantly enough if you want to take psychology into account) the two conductors on the panel, Paavo Berglund and George Hurst, to the effect that "we don't want to award a prize—there is no talent in this competition."

One of my colleagues, however, my former boss at EMI, Peter Andry, and I were of a very different opinion. We felt that a field that included Richard Hickox, Geoffrey Simon, Colin Metters, Christopher Lyndon Gee, and Ronald Zollman, all of whom have gone on to make respectable careers, could hardly be called devoid of talent. And there was one other candidate, at nineteen the youngest of the finalists, who had impressed both Peter and me enormously (as Peter recalled in his 2008 memoir *Inside the Recording Studio*), and after long argument we managed to persuade our fellow jurors to give him the first prize. His name was Simon Rattle.

In addition to the second prize, very worthily taken by Geoffrey Simon, there was in the end another one awarded. Before the final jury discussion, representatives of the orchestra came to the jury room and told us that, if we did not include another candidate whom I have not named among the winners, they would be very disappointed. We did not regard Maestro X as a serious contender for a main prize, but we decided there was nothing to prevent us from offering him a special "orchestra prize," which would consist simply of a concert with the orchestra. A few months later, in an amusing validation of the position we had taken as jurors, the orchestra sent to tell us that the concert had revealed the young conductor to be seriously lacking in skill.

When Tony Covell left to take another job, I had to appoint a new theater officer. By far the strongest applicant was an American, ALAN PEARLMAN, who was born in Pittsburgh, studied at Yale and elsewhere, and had been involved with community-theater activities in Holland. In order to hire a foreigner for the job, I had to visit the government-run employment agency in Winchester and make the case that no comparably qualified British candidate had been found. As I sat waiting for my turn to come to the desk, I overheard the conversation the man before me had with the clerk.

He was a man probably in his sixties, dressed a little shabbily, but clearly making an effort to look as respectable as he could. Asked what kind of job he was looking for, he said anything would do—messenger, office boy, tea boy. But then, when the clerk told him that she had something that might suit him in Eastleigh, perhaps ten minutes down the road by bus from Winchester and not much more by bicycle, he said, "Oh, no—it has to be in Winchester." I reflected at that moment how lucky those people are who, in contrast to probably 99 percent of humanity over the ages, are able to look at their surroundings and say, "No, this won't do—I'm going to move somewhere else."

Permission was duly granted to hire Alan Pearlman, and his arrival brought a breath of fresh transatlantic air into our rather cozy English group. A big man in cowboy boots and "granny" glasses, he taught Bonnie and me how to play poker, and communicated superbly with all the groups in the area who needed our help or advice. Alan told us that when he went to open an account at the local Barclays Bank and was asked for references, he replied: "Just a minute—I'm giving you my money to look after, and *you* are asking *me* for references?" It didn't make any practical difference to the arrangements, but I thought it was a very good line.

For many of my post-Southern Arts years, Alan and I fell out of touch, but we have recently reconnected, to my great pleasure. An enormously gifted man, he spent many years teaching drama at the University of Canterbury in Kent. More recently he has been engaged in translating and editing the works of the German left-wing playwright Ernst Toller (1893–1939), whom I had never previously heard of, but who seems, to judge from the volume of plays Alan gave me when Laura and I visited him and his wife, Britta, in Canterbury, to have been a figure at least comparable in importance to Bertolt Brecht.

In some ways, Winchester did prove to be a good place to live. There were amenities ranging from the cathedral and the beauty of the surrounding countryside to the presence of one really fine restaurant and, beyond what the city itself possessed, the possibility of reaching London by train in about an hour. The city itself, however, was not the idyllic place that might be expected by anyone knowing only about its ancient monuments and associations, including Winchester College (a famous public school founded in 1382) and the eleventh-century cathedral where Jane Austen, who lived on College Street in the last weeks of her life, is buried.

When we lived there, Winchester was an amalgam of several social strands that impinged on one another in a decidedly stressful way. There were the people associated with the cathedral; those associated with the College; a strong army presence; a large number of people who commuted to their jobs in London; and the more proletarian ranks of those who worked in service industries and other local enterprises. When these last and the army people finished drinking and the pubs closed down for the night, there were frequent clashes between various groups, and a tendency for some on their way home through the more well-heeled parts of town to encroach on and mildly vandalize the gardens of the more opulent houses.

Nevertheless, the cathedral itself was a place of beauty that was always an obligatory visit for guests from out of town. One of the sights we liked to show them was the memorial stone in the graveyard that carried the inscription:

In Memory of
Thomas Thetcher
a Grenadier in the North Reg. of Hants Militia, who died of a
violent Fever contracted by drinking
Small Beer when hot the 12 May 1764. Aged 26 Years.

Here sleeps in peace a Hampshire Grenadier,
Who caught his death by drinking cold small Beer,
Soldiers be wise from his untimely fall
And when ye're hot drink Strong or none at all.

Not many yards from the cathedral was the studio of the sculptor Heinz Henghes. Born in Germany in 1906, he had by the time we knew him become a British citizen and Head of Fine Art at the Winchester School of Art, but he also had a house perched spectacularly on a hilltop in the Dordogne. One summer Bonnie and I visited him there, and it was fascinating to observe the mutually respectful relationship this brilliant creative artist had established with the local peasantry: he contributed decorative features to the town hall for no fee, and received copious gifts of food in completely noncommercial recompense.

Just beyond Heinz's Winchester studio was the city's one top-class restaurant, the Old Chesil Rectory, which occupied a fine six-hundred-year-old half-timbered former ecclesiastical residence. It featured really superb Italian food prepared by the Ferrarese chef-owner, Mauro Bregoli, whose Glasgow-born wife, Esther, presided graciously over the dining rooms. Mauro was a keen fisherman, who often served salmon trout that he had caught in local rivers like the Itchen, which is widely regarded as one of the world's premier chalk streams for fly fishing. One evening at dinner he said to Bonnie and me, "Don't forget to come to the kitchen before you leave—I have something for you." It was the largest salmon trout we had ever seen, and we had to fold it in half to get it onto our modest grill.

Such pleasures were not to be enjoyed every day, because the salary cut I had sustained left us in far less opulent circumstances than we were used to. In any case, the job itself frequently had me traveling around the region, and I would quite often find myself sharing a quick snack at the end of the day with the people I was advising.

Once or twice a year, staff and some governing members of all twelve regional arts associations got together as the Standing Conference of Regional Arts Associations (SCRAA). Our discussions were about arts administration, but they taught me much more about administration than about the arts. Just as I was later to find in the Boosey & Hawkes Paris office, the meetings gave me the feeling that the women in the no. 2 jobs were consistently outperforming their directors; and it was frustrating that, in general meetings, these competent women hardly ever took it upon themselves to speak.

The chairman of SCRAA was Peter Duncombe, the 6th Lord Feversham, who was known informally as Peter Feversham. Wearing a picturesque beard that make him look like Henry VIII, he was, as his 2009 obituary in *The Telegraph* put it, a man "of sharp mind, ever-present mischievous humour and *bon vivant* tastes," who liked to describe himself as the only Communist peer. If that sounds like an oxymoron, it nevertheless accurately captured the diverse interests he displayed in ambitiously restoring his extensive family estate in the north of England while sedulously improving the living conditions of its tenants.

Peter fulfilled his leadership role in English arts administration circles with a skillful but light hand, and it was always a pleasure to spend relaxed time with him. Soon after I left Southern Arts, he invited me to join him for lunch at the House of Lords. Sitting in the dining room, with its handsome William Morris wallpaper, I said I thought it was a pity that the closed-circuit television screen positioned high up on one wall to warn their Lordships of an impending vote somewhat impaired the classical elegance of the room. "Ah well, Bernard," he replied, "you have to learn to move with the times, as we do here."

Not only within the ranks of regional arts administrators but also in the course of our joint meetings with the Arts Council of Great Britain, one of the topics most frequently occupying minds was the controversial field of community arts—the practice and organization of arts activities supposedly more closely engaged than "fine arts" with the lives and interests of what are rather dismissively referred to as "ordinary people." I say "controversial" because the entirely honorable theories of the field seemed too often to be neglected in practice. On one occasion I received a letter from an arts organizer living in another part of England who wanted to come to the Southern Arts area and set up a community arts program, asking me how he could get an idea of the nature of our community. This seemed a curiously upside-down request, since the whole idea of community arts is that they are not devised by outsiders but arise naturally out of the impulses and interests of the community itself.

On two occasions, there were invitations for parties of some twenty or so representatives from the associations around England to visit other countries and find out how they managed the field of arts subsidy. My first such visit was to the United States, where the subgroup I was in concentrated its studies on the East Coast, and where it was interesting and somewhat alarming to discover how subsidies from public funds such as the National Endowment for the Arts were rapidly being supplanted by the effort to raise support from private sources such as business firms, foundations, and individuals. I had the pleasure a year or two later of receiving three of the American arts administrators we had met on our travels, Clark Mitze, Henry Putsch, and Lara Mulholland, as guests of Southern Arts, where I think they were more impressed by ancient monuments like Arundel Castle than by our administrative set-up.

Our second foreign visit was to West Germany, where we inevitably found ourselves drooling over the lavish level of state support for the arts. At that time, we learned, a typical German Land spent as much on subsidy for a single one of its symphony orchestras as the entire ACGB budget for all of Britain's orchestral life.

At a conference center in the town of Yerres near Paris, I learned an important lesson in the principles and priorities of French living. I had been nominated by the British Council to be the British government representative at a Council of Europe conference on public subsidy for the arts. The discussions went on for two or three days, and on the last day I was elected to the small drafting committee charged with writing the report on our conclusions that would be submitted to the various participating governments. The idea was that we should have a completed document ready by lunchtime for consideration by the full conferring members after lunch. Finding it impossible to complete the assignment before the end of the morning, we were in a time bind: if we were forced to continue the drafting process after lunch, the conference would not be able to end at the scheduled time, and most of the delegates had homeward flights or other transport booked. Lunch, it is hardly necessary to say, was supposed to consist of hors-d'oeuvres, first course, salad, main course, cheese, and dessert. With commendable fortitude, the organizers decided that the meal would have to be substantially reduced in scale. We skipped the cheese.

By 1976, Bonnie and I had decided it was time for another move. We conceived a desire to live a more rurally based life, and found the kind of environment we were looking for in the county of Norfolk in the northern part of East Anglia. I had also come to feel that administration, and more specifically the administration of an organization with more than a dozen members, was not my strongest suit. It was all the more gratifying, therefore, that when I resigned I could look back on a record of more than doubling SAA's annual budget, despite the general tightness of the economic climate. At my last General Council meeting, I was called out of the room to take a phone call from which I learned to my surprise that the next year's grant from ACGB would be several thousand pounds more than I had asked for. The reason, I was told, was that the regional committee found the budget I had submitted more realistic and better worked out than that of any of the other associations. Walking back into the meeting with that news left me with as warm a glow as I had experienced at any committee meeting in my three years at Southern Arts.

CHAPTER SIX

THE PASTORAL DREAM

1976–79

Bonnie and I had been hankering for some time after a move to "the country." Graham Fawcett had left Southern Arts and moved with his wife, Bodie, to live in a farmhouse in Tuscany. We visited them there, found the atmosphere beguiling, and discussed with them the possibility of finding a country house for all four of us, together with our recently born babies, to live in. We suggested France rather than Italy—a suggestion that in retrospect I find incomprehensible—and rented a house near Toulouse to serve as a base for our search.

It was lucky that we had the experience of living in the same house with Graham and Bodie, even if for only a week, because it quickly became apparent that we were incompatible as sharing couples. They would thunder up and down the stairs, whereas we were basically quiet people; and Bodie, having polished off every one of her meals at lightning speed and wanting to clear the table forthwith, would look at me and say, "You do eat very slowly, don't you, Bernard!"

So, having amicably agreed with the Fawcetts to abandon the plan of cohabitation, Bonnie and I started to look northward rather than southward, and we very soon settled on the market town of Wymondham (pronounced "Wind'm") near Norwich in the East Anglian county of Norfolk as our next place of residence. We found a beautiful and spacious house on the edge of the town, and moved into it in the autumn of 1976.

My study was on the third floor ("second" in British usage, where the ground floor doesn't count), and what with my view of a field full of horses and cows, the majestic copper beech in front of the hotel across the street, and the twelfth-century Wymondham Abbey next door to it, concentrating on work was not easy. I buckled down as well as I could, and over the next three years produced many reviews of concerts and opera productions all round East Anglia for *Classical Music Weekly*, liner notes for several record companies, and my first two books: *The Music of Johannes Brahms* and *Conductors on Conducting*.

Much of my live-performance reviewing was centered on the Aldeburgh Festival on the Suffolk coast southeast of Wymondham. The most memorable performance I heard there was of Schubert's Piano Sonata in G Major (D894), which seemed to go on forever at the tempos adopted by Sviatoslav Richter, yet never for an instant lost its sense of magic. There was also a festival in King's Lynn, near Norwich, that featured some impressive choral performances. At the end of one of them, I was standing in front of my aisle seat when Queen Elizabeth, the Queen Mother, the official Patron of the festival, walked ceremonially past; despite my misgivings about royalty in those days, I had to admit that her smile looked absolutely genuine and quite enchanting.

Of the various liner notes I wrote at this time, one in particular, for the booklet accompanying Daniel Barenboim's recording of Mozart's *Le nozze di Figaro*, occasioned an extraordinary coincidence—if it was indeed a coincidence and not evidence of some more mysterious phenomenon. In writing about the character of the page-boy Cherubino, I wanted to illuminate the emotional turmoil of his "Non so più cosa son, cosa faccio" (I no longer know what I am, what I'm doing) by quoting a remark by Keats that I had read in Lord Houghton's *Life and Letters of John Keats* to the effect that "the imagination of a boy is healthy, and the imagination of a man is healthy, but there is a space between." I wanted to check the exact wording, but I had no hope of finding the book, which lay among several hundred books, recently retrieved from my parents' house after my father's death and still piled higgledy-piggledy in the dining room. I wrote the bulk of my note, and left the envelope unsealed on my desk.

The next morning, not having mentioned the matter to anyone, I was sitting at breakfast when my one-year-old daughter, Katharine, came prancing in from the dining room with a big smile on her face and put the book in question on my lap. She had never done anything remotely like this before, and, though of course brilliant, she wasn't yet a dedicated reader. Perhaps it was the pink binding of the Everyman's Library edition that had attracted her. Anyway, I went upstairs with the book, found that my quotation was accurate except for having omitted the word "mature" before "imagination of a man," inserted that into my text, and felt that I really owed Katharine a credit as research assistant.

Witnessing a production conducted by Barenboim subsequently in Paris, I was struck by the consistency of his approach to the score first in the recording, when I eventually heard it, and in live performance. I would subsequently write a second booklet essay on *Figaro*, this time for Riccardo Muti's recording some years later. I was subsequently commissioned to write essays for Muti's *Don Giovanni* and *Così fan tutte* recordings, and all three were gathered together in 2002 for inclusion in Muti's Da Ponte box set on EMI. I still find it hard to arrive at a firm preference between Barenboim's and Muti's *Figaro*s. The presence in Barenboim's cast of such soloists as Heather Harper, Dietrich Fischer-Dieskau, and above all Teresa Berganza, whose mercurial portrayal of Cherubino—even in the eighth month of pregnancy!—was a highlight of the production I had seen years earlier in Amsterdam—tended to swing my vote in favor of that version. But for years I found Erich Kleiber's old recording the wittiest and most insightful version of the work on disc, though even that classic recording must yield place now to René Jacobs's recent CD version, which establishes its supremely theatrical character right from the start. To listen to Patrizia Ciofi as Susanna and Lorenzo Regazzo as Figaro in the duet that follows the overture is not just to hear a soprano and a bass singing their parts: it is to be in the company of two people in love.

The first of my two books, about Brahms, resulted from an invitation to write a book about Liszt for the London-based Tantivy Press. Expressing my interest in the series it was to be part of, I said that I would be prepared to write about Liszt but would much rather write about Brahms. My suggestion was accepted, and work on the book proceeded in a pleasantly relaxed manner with the editor, Derek Elley, who, though himself a specialist in film, proved to be sensitive and skillful in his understanding and treatment of my musical subject.

Just as I have always disliked preconcert talks that proceed on "first-you-hear-this" and "then-you-hear-that" lines, and just as I have always tried to avoid the style of program-note writing based on similar dreary thematic cataloging and invocations of modulations, I decided I wanted my Brahms book to avoid the familiar chronological trawl through the composer's output. It's true that there is more justification for the chronological method in a book devoted to a specific composer's work, because, after all, people do live serially, and composers do create their oeuvre generally along time-related lines. But I thought it would be more illuminating to structure the book around cardinal aspects of Brahms's compositional style, such as his highly original treatment of rhythm and his gift for lyric melody. The result was a series of chapters each devoted to one such topic, followed by a consideration of three works—the First Serenade, the Third Symphony, and the Clarinet Quintet—that endeavored to put the general features thus expounded into a more specific context. The book is no longer in print, but it has had its admirers, including most of the reviewers at the time, and I still occasionally receive comments on it.

The other book, *Conductors on Conducting*, arose out of my proposal to Bernard Rabb of Columbia Publishing Company in New Jersey that we should collaborate on a manual of performing style. I had in mind a kind of counterpart, for the classical and romantic areas of the repertoire, to the fairly copious literature that already existed to help performers in their interpretation of music written before about 1800. Bernard persuaded me to produce something less formal and more personal in tone, and the result was a collection of interviews with eight conductors designed to elicit the views of each about conducting one composer.

For most of the interviews, I was able to meet with my conductors after a performance, usually in their dressing-rooms. I was impressed by the unvarying sense of dedication all eight of them clearly possessed: there was no facile attention-seeking at work here. Each of them had brought closely focused intelligence to bear on the challenge of identifying and meeting the stylistic demands of the composer he was now discussing, and I learned from them a great deal about composers I thought I already knew well. I spoke about Handel with Charles Mackerras, who told me about the preparations for a performance he had once given in Germany at which he congratulated and thanked the one player that had attended every single rehearsal, only to be told that, regretfully, the man would not be able to make it to the performance. (The pattern of rehearsing with people who are not the eventual performers is called, in Britain, "deputizing." Long widespread in certain countries, it is almost unknown in the United States.) Conducting, Charles concluded, was essentially a matter of "Ausstrahlung"—something like "emanation"—and if you could "strahl aus," you could conduct.

For Bach I enlisted the participation of Nikolaus Harnoncourt, who impressed me with his healthy lack of dogmatism: he told me that the way he wanted to conduct Bach was in no way intended to masquerade as a *permanent, universal* method. It was just *the best way for him to conduct Bach now*, and in keeping with that attitude he said he never used the word "authentic." My other chapters emerged from talks about Berlioz with Colin Davis, Verdi with James Levine (whose wide-ranging interview inevitably expanded to include Mozart as well), Brahms with Carlo Maria Giulini, Elgar with Sir Adrian Boult, Mahler with Bernard Haitink, and Ives with José Serebrier. In almost every case, the resulting chapters offered frequent anecdotal evidence to support the view I had espoused in my introductory chapter to the effect that most composers expected their interpreters to bring powerful personal qualities and insights to the performance of their music. Sibelius's mandate to Boult, "If ever your musical instinct seems to contradict the instructions in my score, please follow your instinct," was only the most striking among many such examples, and Stravinsky's injunction to Davis, "My boy, the metronome mark's only the beginning," was another.

Those were days long before the Internet made such collaborations effortless in practical terms, so that much of my work on the book was done in the course of visits I made to the States. Several chapters appeared in the pages of *High Fidelity* before the book's publication, after which it was soon translated into Japanese. In the Japanese edition, the pictures of the participating conductors and of me on the back flap were presented in slightly slanting oval frames, two of which made Carlo Maria Giulini and me look Japanese—a surprising effect, but not unpleasant. A year or two later, in the lobby of the Queen Elizabeth Hall in London, where I was attending a concert, a young Japanese man accosted me, having recognized me from that photograph, and told me that he had been responsible for the translation. It turned out that he was an English teacher in Tokyo and was in London on his honeymoon, and I had the pleasure of taking him and his bride out to lunch the next day.

Wymondham was a pleasant enough place to live in, perhaps rather more so than Winchester had been. There was, again, one good restaurant, while Norwich, just ten miles to the northeast, offered several more, as well as a food cart from which I often brought spicy Korean food back to eat at home. We made a few good friends in the town, including David Brown, a talented furniture-maker who made me a substantial chopping board that I am still using more than thirty years later, and who, after moving to the States a little later, was commissioned to build some elements in the Metropolitan Museum's collection of architectural detail and interior decoration.

Every now and then, I would take half an hour off and go and stand by the gate near our front door, enjoying the peaceful sight of the horses and cows in their meadow. On one such occasion, I got in conversation with a woman who lived nearby. A cousin of the Queen, she shared with her relative a keen interest in animals, and was active in the local work of the society that promoted their welfare. She asked me what I did for a living. I told her I was a music critic. "What kind of music do you listen to?" she asked. "Classical music," I said, quite unprepared for her response, which was "Oh, you poor thing!"

A few miles to the southwest of Wymondham, on the road from London, was the market town of Attleborough, where the English composer Malcolm Arnold lived for the last years of his long life. I drove down to visit him, and found a man who, after periods of alcoholism and depression, as well as intensive treatment in psychiatric institutions, had come out on the other side with a reasonably contented and settled outlook, no doubt thanks in part to the calming influence of Anthony Day, who lived with him and looked after him for many years. A composer whose range encompassed symphonies of darkly serious import as well as many lighter works including tuneful sets of dances, he was well known also for his copious output of film scores.

In 1964 Arnold had been commissioned to write the music for the BBC's ambitious twenty-six-episode television series *The Great War*. I mentioned this to him when we met, because I knew that the music had eventually been written instead by my friend Wilfred Josephs, who had had to produce the score for the first forty-minute episode within the space of two weeks. With disarming generosity, Arnold told me that it had been one of his spells of drunkenness that had precipitated his last-minute withdrawal, and added, "It was a good thing for the series, because Wilf wrote a much better score for it than I could have written."

On a trip to visit friends in Holland around this time, I had a revealing experience in Utrecht's concert hall, the architecturally fascinating Vredenburg, where the steep rake of the seats and the high barriers in front of each row leave the listener feeling almost as if he is being treated to a private concert all on his own. On the evening I was there, Jaime Laredo played Mendelssohn's Violin Concerto in E Minor, op. 64. I had met Jaime first many years before, when, as a violinist in his twenties, he was giving performances that wonderfully combined technical precision with lyrical grace. A little later, after his marriage to the pianist Ruth Laredo, I began to feel that the grace had diminished, and that he was playing in a much more forceful, at times almost brutal, manner. Suddenly, with the Mendelssohn I heard in Utrecht, all the magic I had formerly associated with him was back. Backstage afterward, I told Jaime that the performance was the finest I had heard from him in a long time. Then, in the course of conversation, I asked, "How's Ruth?" "I believe she's fine," he said, "but we split up more than a year ago." I don't want to draw pretentious pop-psychiatric conclusions, or to associate that rough period in Jaime's music-making with my judgment that Ruth was herself a player much more given to forceful, *martellato* effects than to delicacy or grace. So I shall merely say that, not surprisingly, a happy man plays better than an unhappy one. Or at least this one did.

And I tell that story here because it is not unrelated to one of the main reasons Bonnie and I decided to leave Wymondham and move back to London, when the possibility of a suitable job for me should arise. I say "for me" because, our son Sam having recently been born, Bonnie was mostly occupied with looking after our two children, and all efforts to arrange our lives so that she could also look for gainful employment had failed. Quite apart from the financial strain of trying to make a living purely from freelance fees, the tensions in our marriage had reached a serious peak. The pastoral dream, we had discovered, doesn't work for two people who are not happy with each other. I explored one or two job possibilities, which didn't pan out. Then the music-publishing firm of Boosey & Hawkes became the answer.

CHAPTER SEVEN

INSIDE MUSIC PUBLISHING

1979–84

In 1979, having seen a newspaper advertisement offering a position as deputy director of publications at Boosey & Hawkes in London, I called DAVID DREW to ask whether the job was associated with his own. "Well," he said, "I'm director of publications, so the answer is 'yes.'" I had come to admire David greatly both through his contributions as a sleeve-note writer for a contemporary music series when I was working at EMI and for his superb chapter on French music in the book *European Music in the Twentieth Century*, edited by Howard Hartog. So I replied that in that case I hoped he wouldn't mind if I applied for the job. I was duly appointed, and spent a very satisfying five years at Boosey.

Contact with David's brilliant mind was one prime source of satisfaction, even though I discovered fairly quickly that it was also a mind of somewhat Byzantine complexity. When David said to you, "That's a very interesting point of view," what he really meant was, "Oh, come on—you can't possibly be so stupid as to think that!" But if I was bothered by such concerns, David's sheer breadth and depth of knowledge provided ample compensation, and there were, moreover, aspects of his administrative style that were to have a very positive effect on my own subsequent methods. Crucially, he would never countenance the use of such words as "crisis" or "panic"—and indeed, I quickly realized that if instead you call a problem merely a problem, the solution to it becomes much easier to find.

In deciding whether to go and work for a music publishing house, the most important question is: who are the composers it publishes? In 1979, when I joined the staff of B&H at its London head office, another firm such as Universal Edition would not have been for me a viable alternative. UE was before all else the house associated with the Second Viennese School—with the music of Schoenberg and his pupils and followers—and in view of my lack of sympathy for Teutonic expressionism, that was not music of a kind I could happily have worked with. Boosey's extensive catalogue, by contrast, was full of my kind of music. Quite apart from such twentieth-century classics as Strauss, Bartók, Stravinsky, Shostakovich, and Britten, this was the publishing home of Nicholas Maw and Robin Holloway, with both of whom it would be a pleasure to be associated.

Nick Maw and I developed the habit of lunching together almost monthly at a vaguely "continental" restaurant in London's cosmopolitan Swiss Cottage neighborhood—in fact, I think it may even have been called "The Cosmopolitan." We used those occasions not just for plotting future promotional efforts, but for ranging in conversation over the whole world of music. Nick was a warm and sympathetic person, and the only slightly anomalous thing about him was his refusal ever to allow the slightest ghost of a smile to intrude on the poker-faced seriousness of the photographs we took of him. His move to the United States in 1984, like mine two decades earlier, was occasioned initially by personal considerations—he fell in love—but he continued to compose copiously for the remaining twenty-five years of his life.

Robin Holloway I had first met during my time running Southern Arts Association. He had been a candidate for our newly created post of composer-in-residence, and if the criterion for choice had been exclusively a matter of musical talent he would almost certainly have been appointed, for he was clearly among the most prodigally gifted young composers of the day. But the post also called for someone with the ability to relate easily with the diverse groups of people to whom we were intent on communicating the approachability of "classical" music. Robin was and remains a shy and introverted person, who expresses himself preeminently through his music, and we had felt that to appoint him would be tantamount to throwing him into the lions' den.

It had been one of those decisions dictated more by a candidate's personality than by his fitness for the central challenge of a job. In this respect, it resembled our passing over Nicholas Kenyon for Southern Arts music officer, and indeed Riccardo Muti's feeling that I was better suited to the post he and Steve Sell created for me in Philadelphia than I would have been for the general managership of the Philharmonia. In the different context of music publishing, working with and working for Robin was always both personally pleasurable and professionally satisfying.

The same may be said of one of Boosey's composers from the United States who came to live in London for a while. This was Richard Wilson, who is not only a prolific composer but a pianist good enough for Laura, who is no mean judge of such matters, to come into the room once when I was listening to his performance of a Mozart concerto, listen for a minute or so, and ask, "Is that Brendel?" One of the most rewarding aspects of Richard's orchestral music, and particularly of his three symphonies, is the unusual subtlety of his writing for timpani, which he treats essentially in melodic terms rather than merely as agents of punctuation and dynamic emphasis. From the personal point of view, our frequent lunches together at a Spanish restaurant a few yards from the B&H offices—to be followed up, once I had moved to the States, by similar meetings at a Spanish restaurant near Carnegie Hall that has now sadly disappeared—acquainted me with one of those rare composers who do not seem to feel that the world owes them fame and prosperity, and a man of gentle disposition and wide-ranging intellectual curiosity.

Aside from the friendships that soon developed with admired composers like Robert Saxton and Simon Bainbridge, who were with other publishers but with whom Boosey enjoyed cordial contact, our own list was to be the source of close relationships with Nali Gruber and Alberto Ginastera, whose music I only now came to know at all well, and with Andrzej Panufnik, whose name I found the most interesting in the catalogue; the two of us soon were soon enjoying a particularly close rapport, both musical and personal. Jonathan Lloyd, who was signed by the firm during my time there, became another enthusiasm.

The first of these associations to develop was with Igor Markevitch, not just as conductor but as composer and man. I had joined B&H at a crucial moment in his career, for David Drew had unearthed Markevitch's own long-suppressed output of more than two dozen works and was starting on the project of bringing them together for the first time as B&H publications. As was natural, during our early contacts I addressed him in writing as "Cher Maître," and his letters to me began "Cher Jacobson." But when I arranged to go to Madrid early in 1980 as Boosey's representative at performances he was to conduct of his biggest work, the oratorio *Le Paradis perdu* (*Paradise Lost*, after the John Milton poem), he suggested we should stay at the same hotel, "so that we can spend some time together,"

With Frank Martin and his wife, Maria, in the garden of their house in Naarden, the Netherlands, where I interviewed the composer for the *Times* of London in 1960. Photograph by Gaston Richter.

With H. C. Robbins Landon in the Richters' house, Baarn, the Netherlands, 1963. Photograph by Gaston Richter.

With Wilfred Josephs in David Rubin's office at the former Fifty-Seventh Street offices of Steinway & Sons in New York, 1970. Photographer unknown.

Igor Markevitch—a photograph he gave me when I was staying with him in Saint-Cézaire, near Grasse, in December 1981. Photographer unknown.

Andrzej Panufnik with Robert Thompson preparing for a performance of Panufnik's Bassoon Concerto, 1987. Photograph by Camilla Panufnik.

Congratulating Riccardo Muti after a concert was a frequent pleasure for my wife, Laura (seen here lurking in the background), and me, 1988. Photograph by Emilio Gravagno.

With Emanuel Ax, preparing for a concert in the Church of the Holy Trinity, Philadelphia, to benefit the Philadelphia Orchestra's chamber music series, 1989. Photograph by Jean Brubaker. Courtesy of the Philadelphia Orchestra.

With Riccardo Muti and Philip Gossett, general editor of the critical edition of the works of Verdi, in a public discussion after a concert performance of *Nabucco*, 1989. Photograph by Jean Brubaker. Courtesy of the Philadelphia Orchestra.

With Bea and Dick Wernick in the Academy of Music, Philadelphia, 1989. Photograph by Jean Brubaker. Courtesy of the Philadelphia Orchestra.

Working hard on a train segment of the Philadelphia Orchestra's 1991 European tour. Photograph by Diana Burgwyn. Courtesy of the Philadelphia Orchestra.

Chairing a discussion in 1998 at the Curtis Institute of Music, Philadelphia, titled *It's Too Late to Apologize*, about the trials and tribulations of performing under some of the twentieth century's greatest conductors. With me are (*from left to right*) cellist Orlando Cole, bassoonist Frank Ruggieri, and flutist Julius Baker. Photographer unknown.

With Gerard Schwarz in the restaurant in Lansdowne, Pennsylvania, where we were celebrating my seventy-fifth birthday in 2011. The chef—my son, Sam—prepared a spectacular seven-course tasting menu for fifty-three people. Jerry and I are obviously discussing an abstruse musicological point. Photograph by Carol H. Goodfriend.

and when I checked in I was given a hand-written message from him that began "Cher Bernard." That was Step no. 1 in the direction of informality. Step no. 2 came later the same year in Monte Carlo. After a concert there that I attended, we had a breakfast appointment in his hotel. When I said "Bonjour, Maître," he asked me, in the quirky little voice he sometimes affected, "Pourquoi m'appelez-vous toujours 'Maître'? Est-ce que vous ne m'aimez pas?" (Why do you keep calling me "Maître"? Is it that you don't like me?) So, after that, just as in the earlier transition with Giulini from "Maestro" to "Carlo," I obviously had to call him Igor.

That sensitivity was just one strand in an unusually complex personality. Anyone who has spent time with artists in any genre is likely to have made the acquaintance of monsters of self-absorption, and probably we all know people who are deeply receptive to the needs and quirks of others: Igor Markevitch possessed both characteristics at the same time.

One striking example of his thoughtfulness about other people came after I attended a concert he conducted with the Staatskapelle Weimar, at the invitation of the orchestra's chief conductor, his former student Rolf Reuter. A few days after returning to London, I received a letter from Igor saying he wanted to send a thank-you gift to Reuter. Reminding me of the painting by Piero Della Francesca that we had seen in the conductor's office, he asked me to see whether, having access to more bookshops than were to be found near his home, I could look for a good book about the painter and send it to him. There didn't seem to be any good new books on the subject available at the time, but I did find at Hatchard's in Piccadilly a second-hand copy of Kenneth Clark's classic monograph, and Igor was delighted to pass that on to Reuter with his personal greeting and thanks.

There were other such evidences of empathy from time to time. One instance was surely the fact that, despite the move to first-name terms, he never switched from "vous" to "tu" with me—I think because he instinctively felt that, coming from someone twenty-four years my senior, "tu" would have seemed condescending. And yet, on the other side, his self-regard was such that he could make dismissive negative judgments about people for decidedly eccentric, if understandable, reasons. My greatly respected boss, David Drew, was indisputably the "onlie begetter" of Markevitch's resuscitation as a published and performed composer. Nevertheless, on one occasion, when we were strolling together in Montreux, Igor attempted to enlist me in some sort of anti-David cabal, simply because David had apparently had the temerity to suggest, quite reasonably, that Prokofiev and Hindemith might have had some influence on the style of his music. (The French critic Boris de Schloezer once described Markevitch as "un mystique sec"—freely translated, "a buttoned-down mystic"—and the description neatly encapsulates, alongside the predilection for hard-edged textures that he shared with those two senior contemporaries, the vein of introspection and of cosmic search that perhaps aligns him more closely with the spirit of a composer like Honegger.)

Then there was a remark he made one December when, after having had to turn down a couple of previous invitations, I spent a very pleasant week staying with Igor at his Provençal home in Saint-Cézaire, near Grasse. He had an English secretary at the time, with whom I enjoyed a convivial dinner at a local restaurant during my stay. She was a charming and attractive young woman, who so far as I know managed his administrative affairs efficiently. But Igor rated her below the intellectual standard he wanted in a secretary: "Elle a une telle manque de culture," he told me: "Imaginez-vous, Bernard—elle n'a même pas lu *War and Peace*!" (She is so uncultured! Imagine, Bernard—she hasn't even read *War and Peace*!)

During that same visit, Igor remarked one day, "We must go and have coffee with Jacqueline." This was the widow of Picasso, who lived nearby in Mougins; the couple had been friends of Igor's for a long time. Having in due course been invited, we found ourselves sitting with her in a room where we were surrounded by easels bearing portraits of her, with that unmistakable long, straight nose. After about ten minutes, Jacqueline suddenly excused herself, left the room, and came back a moment later carrying a large portfolio. "Donne-ça à ton ami" (Give that to your friend) she said, handing it to Igor. I thought she just wanted me to look at this superb collection of twelve lithographs, *Faunes et flore*, but no, I was being given it. She signed and dated the portfolio, and then when Igor said, "Écris 'pour Bernard'" (Write, "for Bernard"), she duly added those words.

On the way back to his house, I asked Igor whether she was always so generous. "Never," he said—"I don't understand it." My own theory is as follows: when we had arrived at her house, Jacqueline had answered the door barefoot. Igor rebuked her for not wearing shoes, and when she made a sort of apologetic shrug in my direction, I said, "Pas de problème—j'aime bien les pieds" (No problem, I like feet). I think she must have decided at that moment that I was an acceptable person.

Looking at some reference sources back at Igor's house, I found that she and Picasso had married on the same date as my birthday, so I wrote her a thank-you note mentioning that it would therefore always be easy for me to remember her generosity. I saw her only once more after that, at a 1982 concert in Vevey honoring Igor's seventieth birthday. The Swiss tenor Hugues Cuénod sang on that occasion with undiminished vocal artistry; he lived to be 108, having made his Metropolitan Opera debut as the Emperor Altoum in *Turandot* in 1987 at the age of eighty-four.

Jacqueline committed suicide in 1986, depressed, I believe, by the unsavory machinations surrounding the disposition of the Picasso inheritance. By then, Igor himself had been dead for three years. His death left me conscious that it would take me years to come fully to terms with my recollections of so mercurial and ambivalent a person.

My first two years and a half at B&H were spent not only in reorganizing the structure of the promotional effort worldwide but also in direct promotion of our composers' music in ten countries. To the latter end, I spent an average of ten weeks a year on the road in continental Europe—another member of the department looked after contacts in the British Isles—talking with conductors, instrumentalists, singers, and radio station directors. In the thirty years since I left Boosey, I have enjoyed a variety of highly satisfying activities in Europe and the United States. But there was one aspect of my job there of which now, living in the United States, I find myself regretting the loss, and that is the facility I developed for switching languages at the drop of a hat. Whether in my office, or taking a ferry and driving in a single day from France perhaps through Belgium, Holland, Germany, and Denmark, or through Switzerland and Italy, I progressed from carefully saving calls in foreign languages to be made—after taking a deep breath—at the end of the day, to simply picking up the phone and dialing without giving language a thought. That faculty has inevitably withered away, now that I no longer have occasion to use it on a regular basis.

Organizing my travels was in most cases greatly facilitated by the cooperation of the company's agents in various European countries. Lauri Tammivuori in Finland, José Monge Moya in Spain, and Herman Albersen in Holland were especially helpful, and Herman touched me deeply when he welcomed Laura, on a visit to The Hague on which she for once accompanied me, by presenting her with a gigantic bunch of flowers.

In Paris we had our own office. It was run, officially, by Didier Duclos, though I had the feeling that his secretary, Magdeleine Albert, was really the person that had all the reins of management firmly in her grip. Didier's hospitality to me was masterly. For our first lunch together, he took me to a pleasant little bistro; on my next visit, when I said it was my turn to treat him to lunch, he chose a much more expensive restaurant. Sadly, the food there was not nearly as good as the simple and traditional *lapin au moutarde* I had enjoyed so much at the other place.

That first meeting with Didier had come in the course of a visit I paid to Paris with my managing director, Tony Fell, in salute to Leonard Bernstein, whose *Songfest* was having its French premiere. After the performance there was a lavish party at the Plaza Athénée, I think in belated celebration of Bernstein's sixtieth birthday a year or so earlier. Tony and I sat at opposite sides of a long table, and found ourselves looking down a few places to where Bernstein and some Parisian friends of his seemed to be playing somewhat unpleasant word games. By "unpleasant" I do not mean obscene but combatively hostile. Catching sight of our puzzled glances, the maestro said, "You don't know what we're doing down here, do you? You'll be much better off not knowing!" I realized at that moment that Bernstein, who in New York had been an unpretentious, down-home kind of guy, inviting me to his dressing-room during a break in rehearsal for "a cup of Mamma's chicken soup," felt the need to be a different, consciously sophisticated person when he was in the Old World.

Rather than carrying with me a case of samples when I was criss-crossing Europe, I simply tried to get to know the tastes of the musicians and administrators I was meeting. I would then write to each of them, after returning to London, and send them a selection of scores that seemed to fit with their predilections. I also developed the sneaky technique of withholding one highly suitable work, which, if I had had no response within a few weeks, I could then send with another letter to jog their memories.

Promoting composers in this way turned out to be rather like planting seeds, which might or might not bear fruit years later. For example, I gave Henri Vachey, the conductor of the Jeune Orchestre Symphonique de Douai in northern France, a score of the one Honegger work we published, a Nocturne for orchestra; he never replied to my letter—but some dozen years later, browsing through a CD bin in the Albersen music shop in The Hague, I was delighted to find that he had recorded the piece with his orchestra. And when I was working for the Residentie Orchestra in that town, I received a message from Marien van Staalen, then principal cellist of the Rotterdam Philharmonic, inviting me to hear him play—"in your own hall," as he put it—Gerald Finzi's Cello Concerto, of which I had sent him a score all those years earlier.

On one Paris trip, for pure goodwill rather than promotional purposes, I visited the musicologist and Mahler biographer Henry-Louis de La Grange, who lived in an impressive apartment occupying an entire floor just across from the Eiffel Tower. The elevator opened straight into his apartment, where an appropriately elegant butler showed me into the presence of M. de La Grange, who could not possibly have been more affable. The telephone rang, and Henry-Louis, explaining that the caller was Maurice Fleuret, the director of music and dance in the Ministry of Culture headed by Jack Lang, told me he needed to talk to him about one or two serious matters, so would I mind looking at this for a while?—"this" being a collection of reproductions of the work of Klimt, nothing less than a perfect match for the decor and the company.

In view of my somewhat indirect methods of promotion, it was amusing to encounter, on a trip to Copenhagen, the Finnish conductor and composer Leif Segerstam, who happened to be the guest conductor of the week at the Danish Radio Symphony Orchestra. Visiting him during a rehearsal break with the intention of sounding out his possible receptivity to any of Boosey's composers, I found a man contrastingly and unblushingly straightforward about promoting his own music. A case of samples was exactly what he thrust under my nose, and it contained a healthy collection of scores, if only a small fraction of his gigantic series of symphonies: in contrast to the relatively restrained symphonic output of Brahms, whom Segerstam physically somewhat resembles, he has by this time a portfolio containing nearly three hundred of them.

A Danish musician I got to know on that visit to Copenhagen and, within limits, to admire was the radio orchestra's principal violist, Richard Dahl Eriksen. I say "within limits" because some of his colleagues in the orchestra were accustomed to refer to him as "the conductor-killer," and I think his abrasive manner at rehearsals provided justification for that sobriquet. Aside from such considerations Eriksen was a dedicated scholar. He was responsible for important revisions to the published score of Carl Nielsen's Fifth Symphony, and he also showed an interest in learning about composers he wasn't acquainted with, such as those I was representing on behalf of B&H.

My own priority on Boosey & Hawkes trips was naturally with the furthering of our own composers' careers, but, as in the rather extreme case of Segerstam, I also profited from my travels by becoming acquainted with rising as well as established composers in the countries I was visiting. In Denmark, Poul Ruders, Bo Holten, and Hans Abrahamsen constituted a young generation whose works spoke—or sang—with especially persuasive tones, and who seemed to me to be bringing their country's musical stature back toward a level it had not enjoyed since the death of Nielsen in 1931. In Finland, I was particularly impressed with string-orchestral works and a violin concerto by Pehr Henrik Nordgren, whose music moreover had a devoted champion in the person of Juha Kangas, conductor of the

Ostrobothnian Chamber Orchestra, founded in 1972 as a student orchestra and later to become fully professional.

One of my European journeys was partly made together with one of our composers, Jacob Druckman, who in 1982 was Resident-in-Music at the American Academy in Rome. He invited me to join him there for a few days, during which we ate very well, mostly at Jewish restaurants in the Trastevere. I also met several young American composers who were in residence, most notably Nicholas Thorne, who was to be the recipient a few years later of one of the Constitutional Commissions at the Philadelphia Orchestra. Jacob and I then drove together to Milan, where we intended to see and hear the world premiere of Luciano Berio's *La vera storia* at La Scala. Somewhat characteristically, the rehearsals had fallen behind schedule, and on the last day we could still be in Milan the planned premiere had become a dress rehearsal. We duly attended that, and enjoyed this highly original and fascinating work enormously. An amusing aspect of the performance was that the sheer vocal dynamism of Milva, the Italian singer and actress who took the part in the score designed to be sung by a pop artist, came close to making the contributions of all the conventionally operatic voices in the cast sound pompous and even a trifle silly.

David Huntley, who fulfilled some of the same responsibilities in B&H's New York office as I did in London, was a valued colleague, and his untimely death from AIDS a few years later was a grievous blow to the organization. Meanwhile, I had acquired a secretary of unusual talent. I was in David Drew's office one day when the Artists' manager and author Howard Hartog telephoned and put Janis Susskind on the line. A native of Houston, she was the sixth wife and widow of the well-known and much-recorded conductor Walter Susskind. (She and his first wife, the cellist and BBC producer Eleanor Warren, became good friends, and Eleanor used to introduce her to people they met at parties as "my wife-in-law.") Janis was clearly going to be a major asset to the department and the company. We hired her at once, and within two weeks renamed her position from my secretary to my assistant. She later married Tony Fell, and succeeded him as managing director after his retirement.

Besides Markevitch, I soon became busily involved with several B&H composers in ways that combined professional commitment with warm personal friendship. It happened that only a short time before I joined Boosey, Wilfred Josephs had sat me down to listen to a pair of LPs that contained nearly all of Andrzej Panufnik's music that was available at that time on record. One record coupled *Sinfonia Rustica* and *Sinfonia Sacra*, the other *Sinfonia Concertante* and the Violin Concerto. This was music, it seemed to me, that combined utter freshness and originality with intensely dramatic and lyrical expression and with an awe-inspiring strength and clarity of structure.

That judgment has only been confirmed, and more than confirmed, in the forty years that have passed since then. *Sinfonia Sacra* may not be the greatest of the ten symphonies the composer eventually left us—that distinction probably belongs to *Sinfonia di Sfere*, which possesses perhaps the most complex structure of all his works, and could, along with *Autumn Music*, be matched with *Sacra* in terms of sheer emotional power. These would be followed, between 1979 and Andrzej's death in 1991, by such impressive works as *Arbor Cosmica*, the Ninth and Tenth Symphonies, the concertos for bassoon and for cello, the Second and Third String Quartets, and the String Sextet *Trains of Thought*.

The Bassoon Concerto came about in a way that illustrates how an enthusiastic publisher and a sometimes reluctant composer could work together. I had known Robert Thompson, professor of bassoon at the University of Wisconsin-Milwaukee, since my Chicago years. He came to see me at the B&H London office because he wanted to commission a concerto and needed advice on what composer he should approach. I immediately suggested Panufnik. When I broached the subject to Andrzej he was at first unenthusiastic, but I took Bob to meet him, and their rapidly established rapport changed Andrzej's mind. The result, its poignant character inspired by the murder of the priest Jerzy Popiełuszko by agents of the Polish secret police, is one of the rare concertos for bassoon that transcend the instrument's often jocular treatment.

The collaboration and friendship that grew up with Andrzej was to be one of the closest and most rewarding I have ever experienced. The splendid house where he and his wife Camilla lived on the bank of the Thames in Twickenham (just a few yards from the former home of the early eighteenth-century poet Alexander Pope, whose *Universal Prayer* had supplied the text for Andrzej's big choral work of the same title) became a regular meeting-place for us. Bonnie and I were frequent dinner guests—Camilla, besides being a superb professional photographer with many books to her credit under her maiden name, Camilla Jessel, is also a great cook—and, after dinner, I was occasionally offered the chance to look at the latest Panufnik score. The latest *completed* score, I should emphasize. Unlike many composers, Andrzej was careful to keep each work under wraps until—pending revisions that often followed after a first rehearsal or performance—he was satisfied that it really was finished. After the moment of completion, Camilla would be accorded the first opportunity to examine the score, and as we grew ever closer during my five years at Boosey, I was increasingly often allowed the second look.

In keeping with this policy was the fact that Andrzej was formidably well organized in his composing activity. I have never known anyone less like the kind of absent-minded professor many people think a creative artist must be. Consistent also, indeed well beyond necessity, was his reluctance to expose what he thought of as his imperfect command of English by speaking in public about his music. Actually, he spoke the language beautifully. But I became the regular beneficiary of his diffidence, because as time went on, whenever he was asked to come and give a preconcert talk or take part in an interview about his work, he took to saying, "No, ask Bernard Jacobson—he knows my music better than I do."

It was to this that I was to owe him, in 1982, the stroke of fortune that inaugurated my second marriage. I went to Boston to lecture at the Boston University School of Music about the forthcoming premiere of Andrzej's *Sinfonia Votiva*. (In delivering my lecture, I enjoyed encouraging eye-contact with Steven Ledbetter, program annotator at that time for the Boston Symphony Orchestra. When speaking in public, I have always found it helpful to single one member of the audience out and to address him or her directly. Steve, whom I had never previously met, was my man on this occasion. He came up and greeted me warmly when I had finished speaking, and we have enjoyed a mutually supportive professional friendship ever since.) I had also arranged to give talks in several other cities. The next place on my itinerary was Chicago, where I was to talk about Tippett. A few months earlier, when I went backstage at the Royal Albert Hall to greet my old friends from the Chicago Symphony after a Promenade concert they had given there, the orchestra's doctor, Marshall Sparberg, had introduced me to his girlfriend, Laura Belcove, and invited me to stay with them the next time I visited Chicago. After my Panufnik lecture, I called Marshall to ask if I might take up that invitation. Laura and I discussed the possibility of her marrying Marshall, but I quickly realized that such an outcome was not my highest priority. When we had spent just six hours together, I told Laura that she was going to marry me, and the die was cast.

In the subsequent two years and a half that I remained at Boosey, I made a number of other journeys in connection with Andrzej's music. One of them, a visit to Lyon with Andrzej and Camilla for the premiere of the ballet, *Bogurodzica*, that the brilliant New-Zealand-born choreographer (and later opera director) Gray Veredon had created to the score of *Sinfonia Sacra*, was especially memorable. The three of us enjoyed at least one great meal together, at a charming restaurant where the waitress made no difficulty about explaining to us the exact technique they used to make their *confit de canard* so crisp and delicious. Then we drove back north in their venerable Jaguar by way of Paris.

The three of us went together to hear a rehearsal in which Ivry Gitlis was preparing for the performance of a Paganini violin concerto. When I went to talk to Ivry afterward, Andrzej, always shy, was unwilling to join me, preferring to wait for me on the stairs. Ivry, certainly aware that my congratulations after a very poorly conducted performance I had heard him give in London a few years earlier had been a little hollow, first of all put his arm around my shoulders and said, "You see—I'm a not-half-bad violinist after all!" Then, when I asked him whether he was acquainted with Panufnik's Violin Concerto, he said musingly, "Ah, yes—I did know Panufnik. Where is he now?" "Just out on the stairs," I was able to reply, and a warm handshake between the two men followed.

This time, I am not aware that any particular performance blossomed from the seed I had tried to plant. It was merely one of those attempts that needed to be made in the hope that a reasonable proportion might bring concrete results. Even after my time at B&H, I continued to do whatever I can to further the cause of this great composer's music, which I think ranks among the finest created in the second half of the twentieth century.

Incidentally, one seed that produced immediate and copious fruit was sown jointly by Janis and me when, with a very set purpose, we took Gerard Schwarz to lunch at an Italian restaurant next door to the London Coliseum, home of the English National Opera, during the break between two of his rehearsals there. I had first come to admire Jerry when I heard him conduct a concert with the English Chamber Orchestra in which the opening piece, the overture to *Le nozze di Figaro*, not only sounded truly Mozartean, but exuded an almost palpable smell of the theater—a difficult feat to achieve in the more staid surroundings of a concert hall.

Arriving for our lunch, Janis and I put a large score under the table. In due course, after a wide-ranging conversation about musical matters in general, we picked it up, put it in front of Jerry, and asked him to examine it. The score was of *Arbor Cosmica*, one of Panufnik's most important later works: it is a set of "12 Evocations for 12 Strings," based, the composer explains, on "the symbol of the Cosmic Tree which often appears in art and literature upside-down with its roots in heaven and its foliage running into the earth."

Jerry was immediately intrigued by his first quick examination of the score, and after further consideration determined to give the work its world premiere, which happened in New York in 1984. From that time on,

Schwarz established himself as one of Panufnik's most devoted champions, performing his music on numerous occasions in New York and during his conducting tenures in Seattle and Liverpool, and making with the Seattle Symphony an outstanding recording of four of his works that unfortunately fell into limbo when the company it was made for scuttled its JVC Classics label a mere two weeks after the disc was released. This was one of the two "musical marriages" Jerry was to credit me years later with having made for him, the other being with the Czech pianist Ivan Moravec through the invitation I extended to these two previously unacquainted musicians to perform Mozart together with the Residentie Orkest.

Another incidental aspect of the Panufnik-Schwarz connection is a family matter. Just as would be the case with the friendship Laura and I developed with Gerard Schwarz and his family in our later West-Coast period, getting to know Andrzej and Camilla was a process greatly enriched by the pleasure of seeing how beautifully they got on with their children, Jeremy and Roxanna, to whom we also became close.

Roxanna is herself a composer and has made rapid strides in her international career in recent years. Some years ago, when she was visiting us in Philadelphia (a visit during which she paid me the compliment of designating me an "honorary girlie"), I ventured to suggest that her music did not yet possess the kind of indefinable personal "voice" that stamps a composer's identity from the very first notes of a piece—the kind of voice, though of course it would have to be different in her case, that made any one of her father's works instantly identifiable as Panufnik. Her characteristically disarming response was "Oh, I know, and I probably never will." So I found it especially gratifying, in 2013, to encounter a new CD of her music, titled "Love Abide," that made me think she was wrong in that negative prediction. The composer of "Love Abide" is unmistakably Roxanna Panufnik and no one else. Particularly satisfying, and at times intensely moving, is her ability to write close harmonic intervals, especially between notes a mere semitone apart, and make them sound sensual rather than abrasive.

Jeremy, usually called Jem by family and friends, is no less talented, though in a different pair of fields. He is a brilliant graphic artist—his Christmas cards are always gorgeous and often hilarious—and he has worked with great success in the field of popular music and, with his wife, Mischa Gianeovich, in staging public presentation events. In 2009, moreover, he was the central figure in a searching documentary television and DVD program, *My Father, the Iron Curtain, and Me*. Written and directed by Krzysztof Rzą期czyński, it was filmed in Warsaw and London under the auspices of the Adam Mickiewicz Institute, and I felt privileged to fly from Seattle to take part in the London segment of the filming.

Another of my Boosey & Hawkes enthusiasms was for the music of Alberto Ginastera. I had not been greatly impressed by Ginastera's opera *Bomarzo* when I saw and heard it in Washington, DC. But that work, I came to realize once I had the opportunity to become acquainted with a large proportion of his output, belonged to a part of it that too facilely reflected the aesthetic of what I have come over the years to call the *avant-derrière garde*—Modern Music with capital letters, prizing originality over communication. Ginastera's more characteristic music, often strongly informed by folk and other traditional elements, was at once highly personal, emotionally compelling, and often searingly beautiful.

I knew Alberto only for a relatively short time, when he and his wife, the talented cellist Aurora Natola Ginastera, were living in Geneva. My first meeting with them was memorable: welcoming me into their apartment, Alberto, dressed as usual with flawless formality in suit and tie, sat me down with a glass of sherry. Our best shared language was French—his command of it was sufficiently unidiomatic that I could understand him perfectly. "Vous savez," he told me, "c'est très difficile, chez Boosey & Hawkes, pour un compositeur ordinaire comme moi, parce que vous avez tant de *grands* compositeurs, comme Britten, et Bartók, et Stravinsky" (You know, it's very difficult at Boosey & Hawkes for an ordinary composer like me, because you have so many *great* composers, like Britten, and Bartók, and Stravinsky). At this point, Aurora flashed a remark at him in rapid Spanish; he smiled sheepishly, and she said to me in English, "He's fishing, you know!"

Their hospitality was lavish. We became good friends, meeting companionably at several performances of his music, and then, in 1983, I spent an emotional hour or so with him in the hospital just before his death.

Besides my close collaboration with David, I found Tony Fell a most congenial boss to work for. Sometimes after a particularly stressful day he would invite me to join him in the upstairs boardroom, where there was a good piano, and we would decompress for half an hour by going through a few Schubert songs together. There was also an occasion when, in that same room, I was invited to look over and comment on scores by a number of composers that Tony and David were considering adding to our roster. It was a revelation to discover that a relatively rapid glance over the first few pages of a piece could serve at once to separate what I would call "real" composers from the rest. The decision unanimously reached was to offer a contract to Jonathan Lloyd, who went on to write several excellent works for us, among them a violin concerto that I would rank among the very finest works created in the genre in recent years.

A thoroughly sensible young man, Jonathan (known informally as "Jo") came to see me in my office to seek a sense of the way I would want to work for him. I explained that there were a large number of orchestras, in France and elsewhere, that were interested in programming new works, but that did not have enough players to cope with the outsized performing apparatus that many contemporary scores call for. It was only a few weeks later that he came by the office and deposited a score on my desk: it was his Symphony no. 1, which he had composed after our conversation and duly scored for just double woodwinds, two trumpets, timpani, and strings. It is in my opinion a particularly fine piece, but I was by no means successful in every initiative I took in hand, and I was unable to promote a performance of it during my remaining time on the staff. So much for the wisdom of my helpful advice. (The work was eventually premiered in 1989 by Simon Rattle with the City of Birmingham Symphony Orchestra.) Still, my association with Jo remained cordial, and I was touched later on when he came to my office again and handed me the score of a brass quintet—until now, so far as I know, unperformed—that he had dedicated to me.

I was very disappointed when the decision was made, after I had left B&H, to drop Jo from our current roster of composers. Another similar, and I thought similarly regrettable, decision was made in regard to Nicholas Maw, whose gigantic *Odyssey* deserves to be ranked alongside such a work as Mahler's Ninth Symphony among the greatest orchestral masterpieces of the twentieth century. It was, indeed, *Odyssey*'s sheer size—originally commissioned as a work of about thirty minutes' duration, it grew in the course of composition to more than an hour and a half in length—that precipitated Nick's removal from the B&H list: in writing it at such length, he was judged to have been unpractical and even irresponsible. But I find it hard, in the face of the work's sheer sonic splendor and formal cohesion, to imagine how such a wealth of arresting ideas could have been deployed on any smaller scale.

Toward the end of 1982, my colleagues and I decided that the time had come for an administrative restructuring. So, for the second half of the five years I spent with the company, I was promoted to the newly created position, not under David but beside him, of director of promotion. We then split the second-tier responsibility for direct promotion (actually going out to stimulate performances) and publicity (creating printed materials about our composers and their works), with administrative backing supplied by the excellent Jane Burwell.

Janis Susskind took on the first of these tasks, and the second was handled by a new member of staff. Paul Meecham's presence was the result of what was probably the best hiring decision I ever made. Though only twenty-four years old at that time, he immediately demonstrated a poise and balance that established him as the one member of the department I would choose to have lunch with whenever a personnel or policy problem needed talking through. Paul had the gift of asking the crucial question that no one else had thought of. Very soon after he took up his post, David Drew, Tony Fell, and one or two other staff members joined Paul and me at a meeting with a graphic design firm with the idea of establishing a new graphic image for all our publicity materials. After a number of conflicting opinions about various visual proposals had been aired, with no clear priorities emerging, Paul simply said: "Who's it for?" At once, the direction we needed to take became evident.

It has been enormously satisfying to watch Paul's steady ascent through several major administrative posts, with orchestras including the London Sinfonietta, the Liverpool Philharmonic, the San Francisco Symphony, the New York Philharmonic, and the Seattle Symphony, to his present job as president and chief executive officer of the Baltimore Symphony Orchestra. He is at once one of the most competent and one of the nicest people I have ever worked with.

Funny things can happen to titles. Back in my Chicago days, I had heard about the old lady who walked into the Lyon & Healy music shop and said: "I'm looking for a piece I heard on the radio last night. It was by Mozart. I couldn't quite get the title, but it was something like 'I'm inclined to knock music.'" Funny as that was, it was trumped by an order taken over the phone by a staff member in Boosey's sheet music department. It was for "Kodály: 'Buttocks-Pressing Song.'" When I heard he'd written such a piece, my respect for Kodály increased enormously. What a disappointment, then, to find that what the customer had actually wanted was a romance by Leonid Malashkin titled "Oh, could I but express in song"!

Such frivolous pleasures aside, the opportunity, over the course of my five years at B&H, to work closely with a number of outstanding composers ranks among the most satisfying of my career. Along with the other relationships I have mentioned in this chapter, my friendship with HK Gruber has been especially productive professionally and rewarding personally. A leading member of what may be called the Third Viennese

School, Nali—the nickname he is widely known by—is a composer of phenomenal gifts whose music I was happily able to promote with much success around Europe.

Within a few years of its 1978 premiere in Liverpool, his best-known work, *Frankenstein!!*, a "pan-demonium for baritone-chansonnier and orchestra" based on children's rhymes by H. C. Artmann, achieved several hundred performances around the world, including premieres in the United States, in Göteborg, Sweden (in a Swedish translation), in France, and in several Dutch cities. Among the latter, it was in Nijmegen that the piece found itself on the most surprising program: an 11 a.m. Sunday family concert at which an audience composed largely of children delightedly applauded a performance of *Frankenstein!!* sandwiched between two Slavonic dances by Dvořák.

At least two of *Frankenstein!!*'s Dutch performances in that period were brought into being through the cooperation of Hans Hierck, one of the most effective administrators that I met in dealings with the Dutch radio and orchestral worlds. Another highly positive and talented man was Eddy Witters. As artistic advisor of the former Limburg Symphony Orchestra (merged since 2013 with Het Brabants Orkest as a single ensemble with the new name of the philharmonie zuidnederland), Eddy certainly did not fall into the category of self-absorbed artistic directors discussed in chapter 9. Himself a former violinist in the orchestra, he was not obsessed with "putting his stamp" on its programs; rather he was a person with broad intellectual interests—including an enthusiasm for the works of Plato—who was eager to absorb all the creative influences he could from the outside world.

In connection with one of the Dutch performances of *Frankenstein!!*, I enjoyed renewing acquaintance with a conductor I had previously met through my friends the Richters during my time at Philips. This was Jan Stulen, a versatile musician whom I had previously associated with the relatively popular programs of the Promenade Orkest, but who showed himself thoroughly adept in realizing Gruber's technically challenging if stylistically approachable orchestral writing.

After *Frankenstein!!* had its Amsterdam premiere in the Concertgebouw, I threw a small party in a cozy café near the hall. The people I had invited included four who were planning to take trains home afterward: the wife of one of the best-known of Philips's record producers, a keen music lover from a provincial town, and my old Philips friends Gaston and his wife. So it came about that, on my drive to the Central Station, I had taking rides with me together for the first time Mrs. Straus, Mrs. Wagner, and Mr. and Mrs. Richter—quite a carload of celebrity!

Nali was, in the best sense, a trouper. Our hire librarian, the late Malcolm Smith, was an extraordinary resource on the London musical scene, treasured by a vast number of musicians to whom he was always willing to dispense information, whether about our own catalog or about anything else under the musical sun. But on one occasion, when Nali was in Luxembourg for a concert at which he was collaborating with his Viennese colleague Kurt Schwertsik, our usually impeccable hire library had sent the orchestra there an uncorrected set of parts for one of the works on the program, and Nali and Kurt had to sit up for most of a night putting the parts in order. When we spoke on the telephone, and I remarked that I owed Nali a very good dinner next time he was in London to make up for the error, he said, "Oh, you don't owe me anything. Maybe a nice glass of whiskey. It's show business!"

We have maintained a close friendship ever since my B&H days. On one occasion, I was engaged as the speaker for two performances, in Graz and Vienna, of Schoenberg's *Ode to Napoleon Buonaparte* with Klangforum Wien thanks to Nali's recommendation. Exciting as it was to find myself performing in the Mozartsaal of the Vienna Konzerthaus, and with musicians of Klangforum's quality, the experience of working with the conductor of those performances was less enjoyable. Surprisingly for a respected composer, Friedrich Cerha showed himself to be somewhat dismissive of certain details in Schoenberg's score. Most egregiously, when we came to a passage with something like sixteen syllables to be delivered by the speaker within a single expanded measure, he admonished me, "follow my beat very carefully in this bar," though the composer clearly marks the passage to be performed *colla parte*—which means that the conductor is supposed to follow the speaker, not the other way around. Taking their farewells after our second performance together, several of the players declared, "We must do this again with you some time—but without conductor!" I regret that that has never happened.

On that Viennese trip I stayed in Nali's house, and he even proposed to train me up as a possible replacement for him as the soloist for performances of *Frankenstein!!* that he might be too busy to do himself. But discretion prevailed: there was no way I could have rivaled his charm and professionalism in the piece, which he performs with equal mastery whether in the original German or in his succulent rendering of the expert English translation by Harriett Watts.

Later still, we have enjoyed dining together when Nali has given performances in London, Philadelphia, and Seattle. His generosity also manifested itself in a purely financial way in 1994 when Laura and I were planning to move back from The Hague to Philadelphia. We were facing the tough challenge of buying an expensive house that we were afraid might be beyond our resources: he called me and said, "How much can I lend you?" Fortunately, it turned out that we didn't need to take him up on the offer, but it was greatly appreciated.

I cannot pretend to have loved every composer that figured in the B&H catalog, though I tried to do my duty by the ones I was not especially enthusiastic about. The most celebrated among those was Peter Maxwell Davies, about whom I was in the curious position of liking his music but enjoying very few of his works. What caused this oddity was that I liked his general compositional style, and especially its creative incorporation of elements from traditions going back to the Renaissance and even earlier, but the clarinet parts he wrote, in almost every ensemble piece, for Alan Hacker's painful and piercing fortissimo high notes (at least in the first half of his career, which is what I was dealing with) made me fear for my hearing every time I heard them.

There were also personality issues that clouded my feelings about Max (as he is often informally called). On a visit to Kirkwall in the Orkney Islands for the St. Magnus Festival that Max had helped to found there, I heard him give a lecture that left me fervently hoping he would never be my judge. At once attracted to religion and repelled by it, he exhibits on such occasions a distinct touch of the Savonarola, with little tolerance for ordinary human weakness. Such considerations aside, the trip to the Orkneys was thoroughly enjoyable. Together with my fellow-publisher Bálint András Varga, who worked at that time for Editio Musica Budapest, I rented a car and we toured the island together, visiting its great wealth of prehistoric sites. This was not only edifying but rather amusing, because the actress Eleanor Bron, whom I had admired in the Beatles' film *Help!*, and whose brother Tony had been one of my fellow cast members in the production of *Othello* I acted in at the City of London School, was engaged in a similar tour at the same time, and every time Bálint and I arrived at another set of atmospheric ruins she and her companion were just leaving it. Another colleague, Malcolm Rayment, music critic for many years of the Glasgow newspaper the *Herald*, took my education in Scottish matters in hand, introducing me by way of Highland Park and Scapa to single-malt Scotch in general, and thus setting me up for one of the enduring pleasures of my life ever since.

Max was not the only one of the many eminent musicians I met in my time at B&H that I had mixed feelings about, either personally or professionally. I have sometimes had negative reactions to performances conducted by Lorin Maazel, but I generally thought him a musician of exceptional gifts. I had enjoyed an excellent working relationship with him when I was covering his recording sessions of Strauss's *Also sprach Zarathustra* for EMI. In his Sony recording of Brahms's *German Requiem*, I thought his management of the timpani part in the "Denn alles Fleisch" section exceptionally crisp and effective. Then there was a performance of Brahms's First Symphony in the Royal Festival Hall in which he brilliantly avoided the problem that sometimes arises about the tempo of the return of the chorale theme just before the end of the finale: his solution was to take the preceding fast section of the coda at an unusually moderate speed, so that the chorale could follow it in full majesty without an undue application of brakes.

I have heard Maazel described as "a cold musician." On the contrary, my impression was that he was so passionate an interpreter that he felt the need to tamp his intensity down in the interest of balanced performances. It's strange, but one can rarely accurately predict which works a conductor will be best attuned to performing. At an all-English program in London's Royal Festival Hall, I found Maazel's direction of two Elgar works, the Introduction and Allegro for strings and the Cello Concerto, seriously misconceived in their tightlipped and quite un-Elgarian costiveness of manner. After intermission came Vaughan Williams's most ethereal symphony, the Fifth, which you might have expected to be outside Maazel's highly polished and sophisticated range, yet he captured the music's *Pilgrim's-Progress*-derived poetry and magic unerringly. When I happened to meet him a couple of weeks later, I couldn't resist a bit of teasing: I said, "I heard your Vaughan Williams Fifth the other day; I have to tell you that it's a work I feel particularly close to, and it's a work I heard Vaughan Williams himself conduct [by which point he was clearly feeling very nervous], and I have to tell you that your performance of it was probably the greatest I have ever heard."

With Zubin Mehta, meanwhile, I had always had mixed experiences. A highly positive first acquaintance with his work had come in 1964, when he conducted a lyrical and poetic performance of *La traviata* at the Maggio Musicale in Florence. Further encounters were of unpredictable quality. The only really compelling playing at a London concert with the touring New York Philharmonic in 1980 came in the encore, "Nimrod," from Elgar's *Enigma* Variations, offered as a personal greeting to Jacqueline du Pré, who was in the audience. This was preceded, however, by performances that fell far short of the kind of vitality demanded by Stravinsky's

Symphony in Three Movements and Mahler's First Symphony. In strong contrast were superb recordings of Bruckner's Ninth Symphony and Mahler's Sixth with the Vienna Philharmonic and the Brahms Second with the New York Philharmonic. And then, in September 2014, came a performance of *Ein Heldenleben* in the Rudolfinum in Prague—an especially emotional encounter (given the current state of Middle Eastern politics) with the Israel Philharmonic—that stood with the very finest I had ever heard him conduct. What added further significance was the fact that the composer was Richard Strauss, whose music has led at best a half-life on Israeli concert platforms since World War II. Mehta's 1981 appointment as Music Director for Life of the Israel Philharmonic was a no more than just recognition of his courageous devotion to that orchestra through days both of relative peace and of war.

Another conductor I came to admire, in this case largely on account of his performances of Panufnik's music, was Frank Shipway. Something of a maverick, with a distinct talent for alienating orchestral players, he was nevertheless a truly great maestro. I have listened to a recording he made with the São Paulo Symphony of Strauss's *Alpine Symphony* (shortly before his lamented death in a road accident in 2014), and, even through the artificial medium of recording, it achieves perhaps the most utterly gorgeous orchestral sound I have ever heard. His Panufnik was scarcely less remarkable. Conducting the *Sinfonia Sacra* in a London suburb, he asked the composer's permission to add an organ to the scoring, feeling that for him its sonority would be, as it were, the icing on the cake: Panufnik told him to go ahead, and the result was bone-shakingly splendid. Even more impressive was the European premiere of Panufnik's *Sinfonia Votiva*, which he conducted in Copenhagen with the Danish State Radio Orchestra: it began with a pianissimo piccolo solo of almost impossible delicacy, and continued to outshine in every respect the world premiere that Seiji Ozawa had given with the Boston Symphony Orchestra.

One concert I attended at Wigmore Hall in central London in 1984 brought me an unexpected and indeed unimaginable encounter. It was midwinter, and there was ice on the ground. In the Green Room at the end of the evening, where I had gone to greet friends among the performers, an elderly gentleman with a cane asked if I would do him a favor. He said he would be fine once he got to his car, which was parked on Wigmore Street, but would I kindly give him my arm for support on the way there? We walked around three sides of the hall, and by the time we reached his car we had discovered, through a couple of simple questions and answers ("Where were you born?": "Commercial Road, Stepney"; "Which hospital?": "Mother Levy's Maternity Home"; "What year?": "1936") that he was the doctor that had delivered me, forty-eight years earlier.

A year or so later, my cousin Bella, knowing that I was acquainted with the playwright Arnold Wesker, sent me his autobiography. When I read it, I found a passage relating how Arnold came home one evening and was told by his wife that she had had a phone call from a doctor who said he had delivered him. Arnold and I hadn't seen each other for years, but I got back in touch with him. When we talked, and sorted out the details, we discovered that this nice Jewish doctor, delivering babies in the 1930s in the East End of London, was the father of none other than the celebrated neurologist and author Oliver Sacks. I had once met Dr. Sacks briefly, and thought he might like to know about my encounter with his father; he responded warmly to my letter, sending me a signed copy of his autobiographical book *Uncle Tungsten*.

Several promotional trips to Scandinavia and Finland provided results that were satisfying and sometimes surprising. In Norway and Denmark I always had a good time, enjoying my contacts with musicians, managers, and the general public. On a 1983 visit I took the extraordinarily beautiful train ride from Oslo to Bergen to attend a concert given in the Grieg Hall by the Bergen Philharmonic Orchestra, one of the oldest continuously performing orchestras in the world, founded in 1765 and often known by its old name, "*Harmonien*." Karsten Andersen conducted, and the soloist, in the Piano Concerto by the hall's eponymous composer, was Eva Knardahl, a Norwegian pianist who had a distinguished career on both sides of the Atlantic, and whose complete recording of Grieg's *Lyric Pieces* is of unsurpassed quality.

I met both conductor and soloist at a lavish dinner party after the concert, at which the orchestra's general manager told me that Ms. Knardahl was "a national hero." I suspected, given the circumstances, that there might be a touch of hyperbole in that description, but I soon changed my mind. Eva, then in her midfifties and with a delightfully bubbly personality, shared a taxi with me back to our hotel. We were both staying at the luxurious Norge, which offered the most lavish and delicious *smörgåsbord* brunch I had ever eaten. It was a weekend, and when we entered the spacious lobby we passed through a large crowd of teenagers obviously enjoying their regular Saturday-night hop. As we walked from the entrance to the elevators, I heard all around us the name "Eva Knardahl!" pronounced in hushed and awed tones by dozens of these young people.

In Denmark, I had friendly meetings with Lars Grunth, the Tivoli Symphony Orchestra violist who had recently become director of

Copenhagen's Tivoli Gardens, and with several talented people at the Danish Radio Symphony Orchestra. One of them was a young man named Per Erik Veng, whose wife bore a startling resemblance to Marilyn Monroe, and who in recent years has served as the Danish cultural counselor in Berlin. I also spent several busy days in Denmark's second-largest city, Aarhus, where the ISCM (International Society for Contemporary Music) held its annual World Music Days in 1983. Quite aside from the pleasure of hearing a superb performance of Nielsen's Fifth Symphony by Ole Schmidt and the Aarhus Symphony Orchestra, this was a particularly educational visit for several reasons, and it also served to inaugurate another warm new friendship.

The education element emerged from one particular small-scale concert, and it was provided not by the music, which shared the fairly nondescript, *lingua franca* character (or lack of character) common to much contemporary music, but by the length of time we had to sit in the hall before we were able to hear it. The performers included a group from Sweden, who had brought with them electronic equipment needed for some mixed live/electronic pieces; unfortunately, their equipment was incompatible with the hall sound system to which it had to be hooked up. During the delay of about two hours before a technical solution was found, the audience was laudably patient, and very few people left before the concert finally got under way. But I gleaned an important realization from the experience. I don't know how many concerts I have attended in my life: the number must certainly be up in the many thousands. Among them, I have only had to wait for a delayed start perhaps ten or a dozen times—and all of those have been due, not to a musician's late arrival, but to a problem related to electronics. Blessedly, I have concluded, despite whatever huge developments and advances music may experience on the technical front, it is still essentially dependent on the human element.

That, certainly, was a salutary lesson. But more important from the personal point of view was an encounter at another of the festival concerts that brought me a valued new friend. This was another small-ensemble concert, though mercifully free from electronic distractions. There must have been about two hundred people in the audience, and 198 of them were of student age and were wearing sweaters and jeans, so I suppose it was natural that the two older members of the audience—the two wearing suits and ties—should get into conversation.

"Are you a composer?" Nikolaus Zwetnow asked me. "No," I said, "I'm a publisher. What about you?" "Well," he said, "I'm here as a member of the composition class at the Oslo Conservatory, and I *am* a composer, and a balalaika player, but I make my living as a neurosurgeon." He was, I discovered, Polish-born and a professor of experimental neurosurgery at the National Hospital in Oslo, where he was acquainted with another more famous Polish musician, Witold Lutosławski, who spent a considerable amount of time every year in the city. The balalaika was by no means a minor element in Nikolaus's musical life: the Estonian composer Eduard Tubin had written a concerto for him, which he had premiered and recorded with the Stockholm Philharmonic Orchestra. My contact with Nikolaus continued for several years. On a visit to Philadelphia, he came to see Laura and me, and played his balalaika for us. He also tried several times to persuade us to take a vacation in Oslo, but for Laura, who thaws at the same temperature at which I melt and declares that "it's freezing!" when the temperature falls below 70°F, the orientation of choice for a vacation is always southward rather than northward.

I had meanwhile discovered yet another remarkable side to this extraordinarily versatile man's talents. In 1983, after I underwent an operation for the removal of a spinal tumor, I was chatting with the neurosurgeon who had performed the procedure, Alan Crockard, at a follow-up consultation, and asked him whether he had heard of Nikolaus Zwetnow. He certainly had; and when I remarked on how amazing Nikolaus's combination of activities was, embracing as it did composing, playing the balalaika, and playing the piano as well as neurosurgery, he said, "Oh, didn't he tell you about his Olympic career?" Nikolaus had, Mr. Crockard told me, been a member of the Norwegian Olympic pistol-shooting team. With the exception of Michael Hammond (see chapter 4), I don't think I have met anyone else who does so many widely disparate things and does them so well.

Surprise visitors while I was in the hospital recovering from my spinal operation were a pianist friend, Alberto Portugheis, and his wife. They had heard (probably through the B&H office) about the operation, and traveled all the way across London just to spend ten minutes with me. I found this very touching, but it was only characteristic of Alberto, who is a gentle soul. He has also been a champion of Panufnik's music, as well as of his fellow-countryman Ginastera, whose complete piano music and chamber music with piano he has recorded.

It was with the Stockholm Philharmonic that I heard—and more pertinently saw—one of the most creative and entertaining children's concerts in my experience. Conducted by Yuri Ahronovitch, it featured his fluent account of the history of conducting, which he illustrated by changing his position on the podium as appropriate, and by using a variety of batons.

(Happily, when he deployed a massive staff to beat time on the floor *à la* Jean-Baptiste Lully, he escaped the legendary fate of that worthy, who on one stroke missed the floor, hit his foot instead, and died as a result of the gangrene that consequently set in.)

Over dinner one evening in the hotel next door to the Stockholm Konserthuset I had a rather sad conversation with PETER DONOHOE. A pianist of phenomenal gifts who had in his fingers such technique-stretching works as Messiaen's *Vingt regards sur l'enfant-Jésus* and the Busoni Piano Concerto, he once gave a Wigmore Hall recital consisting of the Messiaen work, over one hundred minutes long, followed after intermission by the scarcely less challenging twenty-plus minutes of Ravel's *Gaspard de la nuit*. ("I thought I ought to give them more than just one piece," he said to me afterward.) I had suggested to Andrzej Panufnik that we should invite Peter to be the soloist at the premiere around this time of the newly revised three-movement version of his Piano Concerto. Duly invited, Peter explained to me that, though his career was going through something of a depressed period, the date scheduled for the premiere happened to be the only day of the month when he had an engagement booked.

I tried to help by recommending Peter to Michel Glotz, the well-connected agent in Paris who looked after the career of Alexis Weissenberg, but Michel very politely explained that his list was so full of pianists that he really couldn't see his way to taking another one on. He must very soon have regretted that refusal. It was while I was sitting in a restaurant on Long Acre in London, where I had arrived early for lunch with Colin Davis, that I saw on the bar's television the report of Peter's taking a joint silver medal at the International Tchaikovsky Piano Competition in Moscow, which in no small degree revived his career.

Peter having been unavailable for the Panufnik performance, an already celebrated pianist stepped in. I had first been impressed by JOHN OGDON when I was working for EMI, both by his playing (especially, coincidentally, of the *Vingt regards*) and by the depth of his musical and cultural interests. When we had met for a meal, he was full of insights into such subjects as Mahler's Ninth Symphony, in strong contrast to another pianist I met in those days—it would be uncharitable to name him—who only wanted to talk about money.

One amusing episode in the course of my long friendship with John happened in Chicago. We were having breakfast together on the morning after he had given a recital at the Arts Club. John had an unmistakably individual appearance: he was tall but stockily built, and he had very unusual ears that seemed to be countersunk in his skull. So, when a group of people at another table kept glancing in our direction, I, and even the inveterately modest John, naturally assumed that they had recognized him. But then the waiter came over to our table, and said, looking straight at me, "Pardon me, gentlemen, but the people at that table would like to know if you are Peter Sellers." I didn't have the presence of mind to purr, "Yes, of course: would they like my autograph?"

By 1983, it would hardly have been an exaggeration to say that John Ogdon was a shadow of his former self. He was suffering episodes of mental breakdown that repeatedly landed him in hospital. There have been suggestions that the problem was inherited, since his father had suffered in a similar way. John was by now slovenly in appearance, with cigarette ash often dripping down his shirt-front, somewhat uncertain in gait, and forgetful—he arrived late for a rehearsal because he couldn't remember where he needed to get off a train. He died only six years later, at the age of fifty-two. The wonder is that he was still a supremely great pianist and musician, and he gave an unforgettable performance of Panufnik's concerto.

In theory, Sweden is a country I should have loved. But both on my earlier visit to Stockholm covering the Chicago Symphony's first European tour, and on visits I now made for B&H, I heard racist comments made by orchestra fans who should have known better, and witnessed instances of boorish public behavior (old people pushed off the sidewalk by aggressive youths, as well as other young people urinating and even copulating in plain view), and such encounters altogether soured my impressions.

I had found it hard to communicate with some of the Swedish men and women I met in Stockholm. (A notable exception was the Konserthuset's affable director, Bengt Olof Engström, who was a pleasure to be with, and not only because he took me to dinner at a superb restaurant, the Stallmästaregården.) The reason for my difficulty with many other people may sound paradoxical: it was that Swedes, to generalize wildly, seemed to be so up front, so unambiguous, in their way of communicating that I, being Jewish and thus needing *chiaroscuro*—some degree of complexity and ambivalence in communication—had difficulty in relating to them.

It was a pleasure, by contrast, to arrive at the provincial city of Göteborg and find a less noxious atmosphere prevailing. When a lunch with the executive director of the Göteborg Symphony, Björn Simensen, found the two of us in complete sympathy, I took the liberty of telling him that he was the first Swede with whom I felt I had established total understanding. "Oh,"

Björn replied, "I'm not Swedish. I just live here—I'm actually Norwegian." (Some time later he did indeed return to Norway, spending periods as a journalist and as director of the Norwegian National Opera, from which latter post he resigned in 2009.)

This first visit to Göteborg was a particular pleasure also for musical reasons. The orchestra was excellent, and the concert hall is both beautiful and acoustically superb. The concerts I attended, which included the cabaretier Bo Maniette's sparkling Swedish premiere of *Frankenstein!!*, were conducted by Esa-Pekka Salonen, already in his early twenties a conductor of unmistakable talent. Salonen was and remains the only conductor I have ever taken to lunch at McDonald's. He had just an hour free between morning and afternoon rehearsals, it was the closest eating option to the hall, and he was blessedly free from affectation.

Björn, incidentally, told me a revealing story about the conductor. When he had first got to know Esa-Pekka a couple of years earlier, he recommended to him a book about how to handle positions of authority. Esa-Pekka, just nineteen years old at the time, thought for a moment and then said, "Thank you, but it seems to me that if you have to read a book about it, you've lost the battle already."

In Holland during this period, one of my favorite operas, Strauss's *Arabella*, had a particularly compelling Holland Festival production in Rotterdam during one of my promotional visits to the country. I had had the good fortune to see and hear Lisa Della Casa's enchanting portrayal of the title role at the Metropolitan Opera in the 1960s, but in the Dutch production the young American soprano Ashley Putnam seemed to me fully equal to her great predecessor, and John Bröcheler's Mandryka also matched any realization of the role I had seen, most notably John Reardon's suave portrayal at the Metropolitan Opera in 1965.

Knowing that there were plans to present *Arabella* at the Glyndebourne Festival during a coming season, I called the company's general administrator, Brian Dickie, to ask whether the cast for that production had yet been set. Yes, he said: the Arabella was to be Felicity Lott and the Mandryka Håkan Hagegård. "But why do you ask?" he wanted to know, so I told him how impressed I had been by Putnam and Bröcheler. He thanked me, and I thought no more about the matter until a few months later. It emerged first that Felicity Lott had become pregnant and withdrawn from the upcoming production, and would be replaced by Ashley Putnam. Then Håkan Hagegård had decided he was not yet ready for the role of Mandryka and also withdrawn, to be replaced by John Bröcheler. Of course, Dickie might well have made the same choices without any input from me, but I like to think that our conversation may have had something to do with his decisions.

John Cox's Glyndebourne production, conducted by Bernard Haitink, opened in July 1984, just in time for us to see it before we left for Philadelphia. I had been in touch with Ms. Putnam after the Rotterdam performance, and I naturally wanted to greet and congratulate her on her equally fine Glyndebourne performance (which, by the way, can still be enjoyed on a DVD). I was also looking forward to introducing my wife to her: "Laura . . . Ashley." But I was not familiar with the backstage layout in the old Glyndebourne theater, and we were wandering somewhat confusedly down a corridor when an elegantly dressed lady asked if she could help. "Ms. Putnam's dressing room is the second door on the left down this corridor," she told us. We made the necessary turn, and Laura asked me, "Do you know who that is?" "She did look familiar," I said, whereupon Laura enlightened me: it was Kiri Te Kanawa.

In retrospect, there is a certain touch of irony for me about the encounter. I had once seen Kiri Te Kanawa as Arabella at Covent Garden, in company with a friend who asked me, as we headed for the lobby during the first intermission, what I thought of her performance. "Ah, well," I started to reply, "once you've seen Lisa Della Casa as Arabella . . . ," whereupon the woman walking beside us cut in with an enthusiastic "You can say that again!" The curious thing about Ms. Te Kanawa in my opinion is that, for all the beauty of her voice, she has virtually no stage presence. When, as Arabella, she was on stage alone, I found myself looking at the set. The phenomenon is precisely the opposite of my experience with the German mezzo-soprano Waltraud Meier, whom we once saw as Sieglinde in a wonderful La Scala production of *Die Walküre* that also starred Plácido Domingo as Siegmund: when Meier is one of several persons on stage, it is almost impossible to look at anyone but her.

Glyndebourne had also been the scene of such memorable experiences as Peter Hall's magical production of Britten's *A Midsummer Night's Dream* in 1981 and, a year after that, of the same director's *Orfeo ed Euridice*. I was invited to the latter by a good friend from Chicago days, Hope Abelson, a respected patron of the arts who had served on various supportive committees and boards alongside my former boss, Richard Christiansen. Hope was a fiercely dedicated and outspoken music-lover. She delighted me once, at a Chicago Lyric Opera production of *Così fan tutte* featuring Rachel Yakar as a rather prosaic Fiordiligi, by responding to a friend's intermission remark, "Isn't Rachel Yakar wonderful?" with a simple "No." (On a more personal level, Hope also endeared herself to me by observing, after she met Laura for the first time, "She's beautiful, and she doesn't look like everyone else.") In 1982 she was on vacation in England and we drove down to Sussex together for the *Orfeo* performance, which had a certain archival importance: Janet Baker was appearing in her last operatic role. Thus it was that I had the opportunity to witness two cardinal moments in the English mezzo-soprano's career, for, nearly two decades earlier, I had attended her New York recital debut in Town Hall—an evening when, during intermission, it seemed as if all the assembled local connoisseurs of great singing were whispering the name of Lotte Lehmann as the only singer comparable to Baker that they could think of.

Not all of my travels during my B&H years were concerned with company business. Lloyd Haldeman, who had moved from Cincinnati to become the executive director of the Dallas Symphony, invited me to come to that city to give a series of lectures at a Brahms festival that the orchestra was presenting in partnership with Southern Methodist University. The concerts were conducted by KURT MASUR, whom I already admired as a musician and now came in the course of several long conversations to admire also as a human being. Having read the book on Brahms that I had written during my freelance years in Norfolk, Kurt told me that he wanted me to come to Leipzig to lecture at one of the Gewandhaus's biennial conferences, which in 1983 was to mark the 150th anniversary of Brahms's birth.

That was to be one occasion when, instead of speaking from skeletal notes, I wrote out my entire lecture in advance, because I wanted to deliver it in German. For that purpose, I asked Josef Heinzelmann, a highly literate colleague of mine in B&H's German office and the author of several books and translations, to translate my text. My already pompous English title, "On the Misunderstanding among Composers of the 20th Century of the Compositional Technique of Johannes Brahms," became even more grandiloquent in German: "Über das Mißverständnis der Komponisten des 20. Jahrhunderts gegenüber der Kompositionstechnik Johannes Brahms.'" (I particularly loved that "gegenüber.")

When I came to deliver my lecture, I became aware from stirrings around the lecture room that some of the younger people in the audience—perhaps latter-day devotees of Theodor Wiesengrund Adorno—were clearly offended by my argument, which in essence was a thinly disguised attack, not on twentieth-century composers in general, but on Schoenberg. I was arguing that in the chapter about "Brahms the Progressive" in his book *Stil und Gedanke* (*Style and Idea*), and more specifically in his suggestion that at this late and sophisticated stage in music history the recapitulation of musical materials has become otiose, because "we no longer need to hear the same thing twice," Schoenberg was failing to heed Heraclitus's dictum stating that we cannot step into the same river twice. When a composer offers a seemingly identical repetition of thematic material, it cannot ever *sound* the same, simply by virtue of its arriving at a later stage in the musical continuum. I illustrated this with a recorded excerpt from the instrumental accompaniment to the chorale "Zion hört die Wächter singen" in Bach's Cantata no. 140, *Wachet auf, ruft uns die Stimme*: the opening line of the melody is immediately repeated—but to any sensitive ear the leading-note-to-tonic cadence sounds completely different the second time around. I also played for the audience a doctored version of the recording, in which the repetition of the opening line had been removed—and with that line heard only once, the piece sounded totally ridiculous.

When my lecture was over, a number of youngish Leipzig musicologists came up to the lectern to protest at various things I had said. One of them actually confused the cantata from which I had taken my illustration with Cantata no. 80, *Ein feste Burg*, which I thought provided no very strong proof of the quality of current Leipzig musicology. But I was also greeted by an older gentleman with white hair and horn-rimmed glasses who thanked me for finally saying in public something that, as he put it, "we have all been thinking in private for years." I asked Kurt Masur, when he came to take me off to dinner, who that distinguished gentleman had been. It was Kurt Sanderling. And Masur put his arm around me and said, "You have to understand the others, who criticized you. When you love Brahms as we do, and someone attacks a little bit Brahms, it makes no difference to all the rest that we love. But you see, if you love Schoenberg, and if someone attacks a little bit Schoenberg—well, perhaps there isn't so much left over to love?"

The various lectures were interspersed with concerts, which included fine concerto performances by Viktor Tretyakov and Emil Gilels. I had been amused on arriving in Leipzig to see so many large red pictures of Brahms adorning the exteriors of buildings—until I realized they were not Brahms but Karl Marx. The Gewandhaus auditorium itself was a surprisingly bourgeois-looking hall for a Communist country, but I was much impressed by the signs in the lobby that invited all members of the audience to come and greet the performers after the concert in the Arthur Nikisch Room, a very welcome difference from the tight exclusionary security arrangements that prevail in most American concert halls.

As Gewandhausmusikdirektor, Kurt had his own always-reserved table in the hall's restaurant, and at several meals with him I also met a number of local composers and performers. It was poignant to hear them say how thrilled they were at the chance to spend time with a visitor like me from the West, because, as they put it, "of course we can't visit you." (A vacation abroad for them at that time meant only one thing: a trip to Poland.) One important contact was with the composer Siegfried Matthus. Kurt arranged for Deutscher Verlag für Musik to commission me to translate Matthus's *Holofernes*, for baritone and orchestra, and out of this first association would come my translations of his related opera *Judith*, which Santa Fe Opera was to perform in my English version, and of his compellingly lyrical chamber opera *Die Weise von Liebe und Tod des Cornets Christoph Rilke* (*Cornet Christoph Rilke's Song of Love and Death*), of which I have seen performances in my English version in New York by the opera department of Manhattan School of Music and in Oxford by Glyndebourne Touring Opera.

I never met one of the other leading conductors before the public at that time, Carlos Kleiber, but I had the opportunity to write liner notes for a couple of his recordings, and one of these, on the Brahms Fourth Symphony, was to occasion one of the most touching letters I ever received from a reader. It was handwritten, on two small sheets of notepaper. The writer wanted to know why I described the theme of the finale as the "bass" of the passacaglia: the theme is, as he pointed out, not always in the bass, but can sometimes be found higher up in the orchestral texture. My response was to explain that I was using "bass" purely as a technical term, commonly used to denote the theme of a passacaglia or chaconne, and not ruling out the possibility of the theme's migrating to other parts of the texture. What, however, was touching about the letter was what came to my eyes when I turned to the second page: "You see," I read there, "I love music too"—and the letter was signed "Vladimir Ashkenazy."

My journeys for B&H in Italy and Spain, while intensely enjoyable for the obvious general cultural reasons (not to mention the gastronomic riches they afforded), were less productive in purely musical terms, and they also provided one or two disturbing encounters in the socio-political sphere. In Madrid, a taxi driver, frustrated by traffic delays, complained about the way democracy had robbed the city of the charms it had possessed under Franco. And in Rome, before a concert in the Accademia Nazionale di Santa Cecilia, I was enjoying a conversation with two fairly elderly people—a brother and sister, I guessed—and assuring them of how much I loved Rome, when one of them regretfully demurred, speaking of a deterioration in the social fabric, and nostalgically remarking, "Ah, non era così negli giorni degli Fascisti!" (Ah, it wasn't like this in the days of the Fascists!) I found it impossible to continue chatting with them in the face of that observation, though at the same time I didn't think it meant that they were evil—just people living in a world of the past and blissfully unaware of what had been wrong with it.

In 1982 my first marriage, long in a parlous state, broke up. I spent several months staying in the spare rooms that various friends had in their flats and houses: first in a western London suburb with Miranda Fulleylove, a violinist with a special interest in period-instrument performance; then on Welbeck Street in the Marylebone area with the pianist Geoffrey Saba and his family; and then in the flat in Highgate that my friend Sue Brown had vacated when she moved to Washington to take up a post at the British Embassy. I advertised for someone to share with me in the Highgate flat, and a theater man named Monroe Werthman, but answering preferably to Jeff, moved in. He was excellent company, and taught me the perfect line that you can use when you have to go backstage after a performance because your friend knew you were there but it was terrible: "Oh, my dear, superb isn't the word." Another possibility he offered was "My dear, you couldn't have played better!"

In January 1983 I married Laura, but it was another five months before she could join me in London, as she had first to finish her medical residency in Chicago. She finally arrived just before the end of June, and was instantly pitchforked into my busy B&H life. Not that the initiation was in any way unpleasant: a scant few hours after her arrival we went to Aldeburgh for a concert that featured two works by Boosey composers, *Miss Donnithorne's Maggot* by Peter Maxwell Davies and *A Water Bird Talk* by Dominick Argento. The evening ended with dinner on the Aldeburgh barge, with Argento, Peter Pears, John Shirley-Quirk (soloist in the Argento work), his wife (the oboist Sarah Francis), one or two people from the B&H management, and Laura and me gathered around the table.

With all the rewards, both personal and professional, of my job at Boosey & Hawkes, I might well have stayed with the firm for many more years. But a new opportunity came along which, as I relate in the next chapter, made a drastic change of scene inevitable.

CHAPTER EIGHT

PHILADELPHIA, FIRST INSTALLMENT

1984–91

By 1984, I already had some acquaintance with two men who were to be instrumental in my next big change of course: STEPHEN SELL and RICCARDO MUTI. I first met Stephen around 1970 when he was managing the Saint Paul Chamber Orchestra. The warm rapport we established then was cemented in the mid-1970s: he was working for the National Endowment for the Arts when, as director of Southern Arts Association, I traveled to the United States with a group of my colleagues to study the workings of public arts subsidy in the States, and I spent valuable hours with him in Washington. And in 1976 I had reviewed with great enthusiasm a concert Muti conducted at the Edinburgh Festival, which included dynamic performances of Beethoven's *Christus am Ölberge* and the original version of Schumann's Fourth Symphony.

Despite the successful decade Muti spent as principal conductor of London's Philharmonia Orchestra, his performances in England did not always meet with critical admiration. In 1982, the year he left that post, he conducted the Philadelphia Orchestra in two BBC Promenade Concerts at the Royal Albert Hall. Paul Griffiths, who had recently become chief music critic of the *Times* of London, reviewed the first of them in terms so intemperately scornful and dismissive that one of his deputies, reviewing the second concert a day later, disregarded protocol to the surprising point of more or less explicitly apologizing for what his boss had written.

It was in about 1979 that I finally met Muti face to face. At the Westbury Hotel in London, he interviewed me for a possible appointment as general manager of the Philharmonia Orchestra. We had a very pleasant conversation, and I was then invited to meet the orchestra's player-chairman, the clarinetist Basil Tschaikov. He seemed enthusiastic, and suggested I was likely to receive a positive message very soon. But several weeks passed without further word. I guessed that the orchestra would choose one of Muti's recording producers at EMI, and my hunch proved correct when Christopher Bishop was appointed to the post.

Soon after that, I went to work instead for Boosey & Hawkes. But publishing has never been a well-paid trade, and my divorce in 1982 left me in severe financial straits. So when Stephen Sell, then the recently appointed executive director of the Philadelphia Orchestra, came to London in June 1983, took me out to dinner with my new wife, Laura (who had joined me in England only a week earlier), and asked, "How would you like to come and work for the Philadelphia Orchestra?" I could hardly respond other than positively.

We agreed that he would take his time to design a suitable job. In the following March Steve came to London again, and invited me to lunch with him and Muti. What I was expecting was another preliminary discussion, but after some general conversation they simply asked, "When can you start?" My position was to be titled "Manager, Publications and Educational Programs"—a combination of responsibilities that, Muti remarked, would be much better suited to my particular abilities than the orchestra managership would have been. The central element in my work would be to write the program notes, and I was delighted when Muti emphasized that these ought to be "on a level with the stature of the orchestra." In other words, he wanted highly serious notes, stimulating to the most sophisticated members of the audience, and illustrated whenever I thought it appropriate by music examples.

As director of promotion at Boosey, I was officially required to give six months' notice of intention to leave, but my managing director, Tony Fell, kindly agreed that I should go at the end of July, just four months away. During that time, as a manager-designate on the orchestra's staff, I particularly enjoyed a concert Muti conducted under severely taxing circumstances at the Royal Festival Hall in May 1984. Industrial action at the airport of Verona, where the previous concert of the orchestra's European tour had been given, caused a major delay in its flight to London. In an admirable spirit of cooperation, the musicians voted while in the air to go straight from Heathrow to the hall, instead of stopping first at their hotel. The concert nevertheless began well over an hour behind schedule. I was amused to watch Alan Blyth, seated a row or two in front of me, and another colleague across the aisle lifting their hands up in mounting anxiety as Muti, never one to compromise, observed one rarely taken repeat after another in Schubert's "Great" C Major Symphony, bringing both critics perilously close to their deadline hours.

During the same period, Muti was to conduct a production of Bellini's *I Capuleti e i Montecchi* at the Royal Opera House. Laura and I were invited, and when we went to his dressing-room to collect the tickets he had organized for us, the door was opened by his wife, Cristina, who smiled broadly and exclaimed: "Welcome to Philadelphia!" (To render the tone and accent of that greeting accurately, I should really spell it the Italian way—"Filadelfia.")

This proved a harbinger of the warmth we would experience from both Riccardo and Cristina, as well as from Steve Sell, over the next years. Having on a preparatory visit found an excellent apartment to rent just a block away from my future office, we arrived in Philadelphia in the first week of August, and gratefully accepted Steve's suggestion that we should live in his own nearby apartment for the first few weeks, while he was away with the orchestra at its summer home in Saratoga Springs, NY, and while our furniture and other possessions were being shipped across the Atlantic.

I started work almost immediately. One of the first big projects was an "opera week." Riccardo (as he at once invited me to call him) had decided a year or two earlier that it would be enormously beneficial for the musicians of the orchestra to take on, besides its symphonic repertoire, the different challenge of playing one major opera score each season. In 1984 the work chosen for concert performance was Gluck's *Orfeo ed Euridice*. In the week of the two scheduled performances the orchestra would also present a public discussion featuring Muti and the critic Andrew Porter, two showings for subscribers of the Marcel Camus film *Black Orpheus* to illustrate another treatment of the legend, a lecture by Martin Bookspan on "Orpheus in Music: Monteverdi to Stravinsky," and two public rehearsals.

As it turned out, the first of these ancillary activities was put in peril when, a mere two hours before the discussion was scheduled to start, Porter telephoned from New York to say he couldn't make it: he was suffering from the flu, and had been waiting till the last possible moment in case he might find he felt better. Riccardo immediately asked me to replace Porter—jocularly, we talked about whether I should merely impersonate him, since Porter and I both had British accents, but decided in view of our radically different hairstyles that the deception wouldn't work. There's nothing like being thrown in at the deep end. Riccardo introduced me to the audience in flattering terms, and we were soon launched on what I think was a most illuminating discussion, which revealed how eloquently he could bring music to life for the public, not just as a conductor but also as a speaker, even in a language that was not his own. He ended the session with a virtuoso demonstration at the piano of the way Gluck built up the various textural strands in the aria "Che puro ciel!," adding one line to another as he went on, and eventually demonstrating the affinity between the nature sounds in this piece and those Beethoven created in his *Pastoral* Symphony four decades later.

All this was impressive enough. But when we went out to dinner with other members of the orchestra's administrative staff afterward, I was to discover that Riccardo's sensitivity was as finely tuned in the human as in the musical context. The public relations director of the day, Judith Karp (later Kurnick), outlined to him the plans for the week, mentioning in turn the film, Martin Bookspan's lecture, and the two open rehearsals. Before each of these last, she explained, someone from the management would go on stage and explain to the public—which might well include a number of nonsubscribers—that these were to be full working rehearsals, and that it was therefore important not to have any distracting noise from the house. "Fine, we'll do all those things," Riccardo replied, "except that we won't have the speech from the management about the need for quiet." "Why?" Judith asked. "Well, it sounds to me as if you are saying that there will be many people there who are not used to being in the Academy of Music, and speaking for myself, if I were to go somewhere I was not used to being, and the first thing that happened was that someone told me how to behave, I don't think I should like it very much. So I will go on stage and conduct, and if there is any problem, I'll turn around and deal with it."

This, clearly, was someone it was going to be an enormous pleasure to work with, and everything that happened in the following seven years and a half confirmed the impression. It quickly transpired that the combination of responsibilities I was to carry exceeded what one person could fulfil with any degree of thoroughness, so the educational component was quickly spun off to other staff members, and my job title was changed to "Program Annotator and Musicologist." I balked somewhat at that last word, my experience being that many musicological writings are unreadable and have little to do with music, but in the end I accepted it as realistic. (Riccardo's own suggestion for my new title was "Wordsmith," which I rather liked.)

Along with the program notes, vocal works frequently presented me with the need to supply translations of texts for inclusion in the program.

The only time this really constituted a serious challenge was when several songs of Sibelius with texts in Swedish, and his cantata *Luonnotar*, which has a Finnish text, were programmed. For these two languages that were unknown to me, I had recourse to a method similar to the one I had used for the chapter on Chopin's songs in Alan Walker's book about the composer (discussed in chapter 3). I sat down with the original texts and four or five existing translations in front of me, and deduced from tracing repetitions which words in those translations represented which words in the original. Then I transformed the ungainly English hodgepodge that resulted into something more graceful and readable in style, though still literal in meaning. This time, though, I had no native speaker of either of the languages to help me, and I fully expected to have made many mistakes. By great good luck, two or three days before the program had to go to press, Tuuli Tammivuori, the wife of Lauri Tammivuori, the Boosey & Hawkes agent I had got to know in Finland, happened to visit Philadelphia. I put my translation before her and asked her to tell me, without mercy, everything that was wrong with it. I don't know whether she was just being diplomatic, but after studying my version, she told me that it contained no mistakes at all.

Besides writing the notes, editing the program, starting a series of pre- and postconcert lectures and discussions, and serving as *de facto* musicological and programming advisor to the music director, my job was also to include inaugurating a series of chamber concerts performed by orchestra members. Riccardo was firmly of the opinion that, just as with his opera weeks, the musicians would benefit greatly in technical and artistic terms from participating in such a series. (The contrast with his predecessor, in this as in many other respects, could hardly have been sharper: Eugene Ormandy had actively discouraged chamber music activity, regarding it as an irrelevant distraction for his players.) The series duly began in 1985, at the start of my second season in Philadelphia. Within six years, more than eighty-five members of the orchestra had taken part, and the series attracted an enthusiastic audience for more than twenty years.

Quite aside from the benefit to the players, the series was a step toward remedying the serious dearth of chamber music performances in the city. One year later, however, in 1986, Anthony Checchia founded the Philadelphia Chamber Music Society, which has expanded from small beginnings to a point where its 2014–15-season schedule offered more than sixty performances by visiting artists of the highest caliber.

For the concert that inaugurated the chamber music series, I decided to include on the program a string quartet composed by that great and wonderfully versatile Philadelphian, Benjamin Franklin. Scored not for the familiar quartet but for three violins and cello, the piece is slight but charming, and since it is designed to be played on open strings throughout, its rich overtone sonorities are strongly suggestive of the glass harmonica, an instrument of which Franklin developed a new improved version. My wife, moreover, had the arresting idea of borrowing the four-sided music stand, another Franklin invention, which we had seen on a visit to the Benjamin Franklin Museum, and the city's Parks and Recreation District management kindly agreed to lend it to us for the occasion.

I was amused that none of my American colleagues on the orchestra staff had heard of Benjamin Franklin's activities as a composer. In similar vein, when Muti announced his resignation in 1991, and several members of the senior management team were asked to make a list, each of us naming five possible successors, I was both the only non-American involved, and the only one to name an American conductor—Gerard Schwarz, who had conducted several impressive concerts with the orchestra, and indeed come to the rescue of at least one world premiere after the conductor initially engaged had bowed out.

For one concert, we put the suite from Stravinsky's *L'Histoire du soldat* on the program, to be conducted by the orchestra's associate conductor, William Smith. (The work is usually called *The Soldier's Tale* in English, though *The Story of the Soldier* would be a better translation.) Bill suggested, however, that we should do not just the suite but the complete work, and that I should narrate it. This was a very appealing idea, and I spent the necessary hours preparing my own translation and adapting the several dramatic roles so that they could all be represented by a single speaker. Our performance turned out to be the first of several, because in the succeeding years we offered performances, without fee, as a fund-raiser for the orchestra's various volunteer committees. Rehearsing the piece was always fun: I remember Neil Courtney, who played the double bass in several performances, jocularly remarking as we ended our final rehearsal, "Well, it's been a pleasure working with some of you." On one occasion, we performed the work in a savings bank. I was asked to offer a few words of introduction for the audience, and I couldn't resist saying, "If Stravinsky had known that his work would one day be performed in a bank, he would have been delighted, because he loved money more than anything else."

The way the chamber concerts were programmed sheds a vivid light on the concentration and intensity Riccardo brought to the music director's position. After consultations with players who came to my office with repertoire suggestions, I would put together a draft series program, which I would then take to the music director to discuss over lunch. He would usually approve about 95 percent of the proposals, but a few would draw such comments as, "I don't think a trio is right for such-and-such a player—can you find some bigger ensemble for him to play in?" It was clear that he was completely familiar with the strengths and weaknesses of every single orchestra member, including back-desk string players. When I happened to be sitting with him in his dressing-room before a Carnegie Hall concert, and Cathy Barbash (the orchestra's personnel manager at that time) submitted a list of substitute players to be approved for the following season, he showed equal familiarity with those musicians too, designating some for the "A" list, some for the "B," and consigning others to a "not approved" list.

Muti's leadership was remarkable for the sheer detail of his grasp of what was going on in the orchestra, as well as what needed to happen. On one December evening, Laura and I took associate concertmaster David Arben out to dinner after a concert. In the course of our conversation he declared, "If Muti ever resigns from the orchestra, I will resign the next day: he has given me my dignity, and I couldn't work for another music director." The following February, David was scheduled to be the soloist in Szymanowski's Violin Concerto No. 1, with guest conductor Witold Rowicki. "Of course," David said, "it would be great to have the previous week free to prepare for that, but I don't want to bother Muti about it, when he's in Milan preparing to start the La Scala season." A few days later, I heard that Riccardo had been on the telephone from Milan with his administrative assistant in Philadelphia, Mimi O'Malley, discussing various matters, and that at the end of the conversation he had said, "Oh, by the way, David Arben has a solo date in February. He would probably like to have the previous week free from orchestra duty—please tell him that will be fine." (In the event, Rowicki suffered a fatal heart attack before that planned appearance, and was replaced by Christopher Eschenbach in his Philadelphia Orchestra conducting debut.)

Muti was meticulous too about making sure that the house lights were always set at the correct level. For music with sung texts, it was our practice to set the lights higher so that audience members would be able to read the printed text in the program without difficulty—and whenever I was on concert duty he would always ask me, "Are the lights set correctly for the vocal piece?"

With all this attention to detail, there was never any sense that the purpose of the whole organization revolved around Muti. In the choice of repertoire for each season, for example, his method differed radically from that of most music directors, who in general set their own programs first, leaving prospective guests to choose from whatever may be left over. In Philadelphia, by contrast, we would first send invited guest conductors a list I had prepared of important works that had either never been played by the orchestra or were overdue for a repeat hearing, and ask them to consider these gaps in submitting their own program choices; we would then look at the general picture thus created and make a prospective list for the whole season, harmonizing the suggestions and eliminating duplications; and finally Riccardo (who would only have reserved for himself works that he was scheduled to record) would make his own programs with an eye to correcting any glaring omissions this process had left—no Bartók in the season, for example, or not enough Haydn.

More than anyone else I have known, Riccardo knows what makes people tick. The use he turns this knowledge to might seem manipulative, but I prefer to see it as simply the way a man with a job like conducting makes it work. I was surprised but at the same time impressed when Riccardo said to me, shortly after resigning from his post, "I know you think I've failed in my responsibility by not firing some players who are clearly past their best. But you have to remember that I have to make music, and I have to make it with people who want to make music with me. And if I were to fire X or Y, even though the rest of the players would know that the decision was the right one, they would still close ranks in support of their colleagues. So I realized that I simply have to program around the weaknesses." An example of that came, rather late in one season's programming, when a Rossini string sonata proved beyond the abilities of some members of the second-violin section, and it had to be replaced at short notice by the *Guglielmo Tell* overture. Similarly, after an intensive discussion over lunch about how to steer one particular "past-his-best" violinist away from a highly exposed part to a safer one in a chamber concert, using diplomacy to avoid hurting his feelings, I responded to Muti's ingenious solution by saying "I can see why you're such a successful music director," he replied, "Yes, but it took me forty minutes!"

Riccardo's capacity for human contact was exemplified by his open-door policy before concerts and during intermissions. There was a constant flow of orchestra members and other visitors in his dressing room before a concert, and he would often be busily in conversation until a bare two or three minutes before he was to go on stage. One charming and elegant man who came down frequently from New York and was a welcome participant in these informal get-togethers was Tony Caronia, one of Muti's closest contacts on the staff of Angel Records. In strong contrast, Muti's successor, Wolfgang Sawallisch, would have the dressing room door firmly closed at such times. It's purely a personal question how a conductor finds his way to relax before a performance, and I am far from suggesting that either method is superior to the other.

For Muti, playing the piano was another way of staying loose in the hour or so before he was to conduct. I learned a valuable lesson when I arrived early for concert duty one evening, and found him playing some solo piano music that I couldn't identify. It sounded like Mendelssohn, like Schumann, like Liszt—like any number of early nineteenth-century composers. It turned out to be a series of pieces contained in a large volume of Rossini's *Sins of Old Age*—and, along with hearing Riccardo conduct *Guglielmo Tell* at La Scala, the experience was crucial in teaching me that Rossini was a far greater composer than I had previously realized: not a mere entertainer, but a genuine master of the highest rank.

It was in company with Muti that I enjoyed one of the most humanly rewarding moments I have experienced in my whole career. When George Harpham resigned as the orchestra's associate principal cellist, several members of the cello section, including the assistant principal, Lloyd Smith, auditioned for the chair thus vacated. The choice went, however, to Peter Stumpf, later to become principal cellist of the Los Angeles Philharmonic, but at that time newly graduated from the Curtis Institute and in his first season occupying the Philadelphia cello section's rearmost seat. That evening, Laura and I were to have dinner with Riccardo, and as the three of us left the hall, we were greeted in the shadowy backstage area by Lloyd Smith. "What can I do for you, Mr. Smith?" Riccardo asked. "Maestro," said Lloyd, "I just wanted to tell you that you made the right decision." Riccardo threw his arms around Lloyd and exclaimed "You are a wonderful man, Mr. Smith!" I like to think that virtue had its due reward a few months later, when Lloyd's son Peter, on *his* graduation from Curtis, was appointed to the orchestra's oboe section.

One of our after-concert dinners with Riccardo at Il Gallo Nero, the excellent Italian restaurant that used to be just across the street from the Academy of Music building, occasioned a moment of excitement followed by one of disappointment. When we sat down at our table, we noticed that, just two tables away, Anthony Quinn and his wife were having dinner. We all looked forward to being able, at a suitable juncture, to meet the star actor, who that week was appearing at the city's Forrest Theatre, but perhaps half an hour later we noticed that the Quinns were no longer there. "Boris," Riccardo asked his regular waiter, "where is Mr. Quinn?"

"Maestro," said Boris, "Mr. Quinn left. He very much wanted to meet you, but he was too shy to say 'hello.'"

One of the qualities that made working with Riccardo such a pleasure was his generosity in giving credit to others for ideas he accepted and acted on; another was a degree of self-knowledge rare among those with egos big enough to lead them into the conducting profession in the first place. On one occasion, backstage before a concert, the subject of conducting Mahler came up. I asked myself for a moment whether I knew him well enough to say what I wanted to say. Having decided that I did, I said, "You know, Riccardo, I've realized why it is that you are a very good Mahler conductor but not a great Mahler conductor." "Why," he said, "why? I want to know." "Because it's dawned on me," I said, "that to be a great Mahler conductor, you have to have very deep inner insecurity in order to identify with this composer." His response was amusing: "Oh, I'm very insec- . . . no, no, I think you're probably right." How many conductors could I have said that to and lived to tell the tale? I could to Muti because he is very secure—QED.

Muti conducted Beethoven's *Eroica* Symphony several times during my years at the Philadelphia Orchestra. All of those performances were superb, except one that simply didn't fly—it happens, and it's a matter of the delicate chemistry that governs the very complex process of interpretation and performance. I happened to be on concert duty that evening so I had to go backstage afterward, and I was hoping to find Riccardo's dressing-room full of people. When I got there, however, I found an otherwise empty room with Muti standing, arms folded, in the middle. Unable to think of anything to say, I stood in front of him in the same attitude for perhaps five seconds, after which he unfolded his arms and said, "Thank you—for not telling me how wonderful it was. You knew."

Another "Eroica" episode that impressed me came when the work was being prepared for an imminent European tour. There had been four performances, and in the taxi we took to our regular end-of-season lunch together I ventured to remark that, when Riccardo conducted several performances of a piece within a few days, tempos tended to become gradually more relaxed. He knew at once what I was driving at—"The first movement was too slow last night, wasn't it?" he said. "Well," I replied, "I thought last Thursday was closer to what Beethoven had in mind." "When we get to Europe," he said, "I have to get back to that tempo—but I mustn't tell the musicians in advance: they have to be surprised." In Hamburg, just a few days later, he swept onto the podium, launched without delay into the symphony's first movement, back in that original lithe one-in-a-bar tempo.

The players were immediately sitting on the edge of their seats, and the performance was a thriller.

One of the other Muti-generated pleasures of my time working for the orchestra was the invitation he regularly extended to Laura and me to attend the opening program in the La Scala season. For seven years, we went every December to Milan and one other Italian destination, varying the latter for mainly gastronomic reasons. An especially rewarding visit was in 1987, when, in addition to hearing Riccardo's performance of the Mozart Requiem, we saw *Don Giovanni* conducted by him in a staging by Giorgio Strehler that was one of the supreme opera productions I have ever seen. In addition to its all-pervasive stylistic and expressive rightness, it had the priceless attribute of realizing every important "plot point" without descending into literalism. In one example among several, it was a relief for once not to have to watch Don Giovanni, in "Deh vieni alla finestra," trying to give the impression that he is actually playing the mandolin, usually an embarrassingly awkward moment for the singer. And when, in the closing moments of the drama, Giovanni raised his hand in response to the Commendatore's "Dammi la mano in pegno" (Give me your hand in pledge), the moment of sudden freezing contact was vividly depicted—yet the hand he was raising was still several feet away from that of the huge statue.

On that same visit, we were also able to visit, in the museum next door to La Scala, "La camera dei sortilegi," an enchanting exhibition mounted by Strehler of dioramas showing theatrical set designs of the eighteenth century. The entire room was kept unlit, its pitch black environment pierced only by the shafts of illumination emanating from the recesses in which the exhibits were displayed.

In addition to our December jaunts, Riccardo insisted one summer on my coming to witness the production of Gluck's *Orfeo ed Euridice* that he would be conducting. This proved to be abundantly worth the trip, for the production, by Roberto de Simone, made imaginative use of double casting, Euridice being represented simultaneously by a silent dancer and a relatively motionless singer. The dramatic effect was stunning, and it is matter for keen regret that the production was never recorded for DVD release.

During the same weeks, the La Scala forces were recording Verdi's *Attila*, not in La Scala itself, which was undergoing refurbishment, but in the Teatro Abanella. Riccardo invited me to attend one of his piano rehearsals with the four principals, Samuel Ramey, Giorgio Zancanaro, Cheryl Studer, and Neil Shicoff. The experience was both illuminating and somewhat amusing. The only one of the four whose Italian diction Muti repeatedly criticized was Zancanaro, the only Italian among them, thus demonstrating, perhaps, that singers may relax too much when singing in their native language. And it was amusing to an experienced choral singer for the way the conductor had frequently to instruct his eminent soloists on when exactly a sustained note at the end of a phrase should be cut off, something no good choral singer needs to be told. His meticulousness in such matters was perhaps just one aspect of his inveterate determination to rid performances of the kind of attention-seeking that often manifests itself, with singers, in a habit of prolonging notes beyond their written duration, and a taste for interpolating unwritten high notes. Opera singers tend to like such tweakings of the score, but composers generally don't. Muti always sides with the composer, especially in the case of Verdi, who declared his distaste for such practices vehemently, even if sometimes yielding to them in practice.

After one of our December trips to La Scala, I remarked to Riccardo the next time we saw each other in Philadelphia that he seemed much more relaxed than I had ever seen him away from his own country. "You have to realize," he replied, "we have known each other now for several years. You may not be aware of this, but I'm a shy person, and it takes me a long time to feel really at ease with someone. We've reached that point of closeness now, you and I, where I can be totally relaxed with you, and it has nothing to do with what country we're in."

Muti's resignation from the La Scala artistic directorship in April 2005 gave rise in the press to much ill-founded commentary. A *New York Times* article by Daniel J. Wakin and James R. Oestreich, which appeared in the paper just before news of the resignation came out, was an honorable exception to the tone of Schadenfreude and innuendo that prevailed. The more far-fetched effusions included one by Norman Lebrecht, whom I had regarded as a friend, and who aired the notion that Muti indulges in tantrums. Now, I was not around the parental home when Muti was a baby, but I came to know him rather well from 1984 onward, and feel confident in stating that he has never had a tantrum in his adult life. Riccardo Muti controls himself at least as rigorously as he is alleged, by those who call him arrogant, to want to control everyone else. I have never seen him behave with anything but the most complete courtesy to musicians. Nor, in his Philadelphia days, did his supposed "aloofness" and "arrogance" prevent his dressing-room from being always open to the members of the orchestra: there was a constant coming and going of players wanting to consult him or to make a suggestion, and there was no trace of anything *de haut en bas* in his response to such visitors. I have seen him at work in Milan too, and never witnessed anything that would have justified Lebrecht's headline reference to "the tyrant at La Scala" or another writer's to "the monster of Milan." What was adduced as an alleged tantrum was his withdrawal from a Royal Opera House production of *La forza del destino* when, at short notice, he learned that the sets brought in for it from La Scala were being altered. Lebrecht regarded this as a "maestro huff." From my point of view, it looked more like a characteristic refusal to compromise on matters of artistic principle, and I think the *New York Times* was right in ascribing Muti's withdrawal—on the grounds that the production "no longer met Scala standards"—also to his loyalty to the director, Hugo de Ana.

As brilliant a leader as Muti was in the artistic sphere, STEPHEN SELL demonstrated comparable qualities in his work as executive director. It's surprising, now that I look at old documents, to realize that Steve was only forty-seven when he died: he had accomplished and was still accomplishing so much. In Minnesota, where I had first become acquainted with him, he masterminded a contract that gave him exceptional flexibility in how he could deploy the musical forces of the Saint Paul Chamber Orchestra—dividing it, for example, into smaller ensembles, and even sending small groups of musicians to play perhaps in a prison, or just to sit in a museum and wait for people to ask to hear or even touch their instruments.

In Philadelphia, he showed himself a consummate leader of men and women, and I learned vital lessons from him. Asked to explain to the assembled staff how I intended to handle my responsibilities in the education field, I gave an account of various initiatives I wanted to introduce—realizing only afterward that, as Steve gently suggested, I ought perhaps to have begun by presenting my ideas as a way of building on what my predecessors had achieved. Every now and then, in the regrettably few years we worked together before lung cancer unjustly carried off this long-time nonsmoker, I would answer the telephone in my office to hear him tell me, "Staff meeting in the rehearsal hall in ten minutes." We would gather there, and Steve would explain that his purpose was merely to tell us, for example, that subscription bookings for the next season had reached a new record, and he wanted to thank us all for our part in making that happen. Equally often, he would simply appear at my office, close the door, and tell me some usually very dirty joke.

Another Steve-at-my-office-door moment, and a more serious one, was an invitation to join him in his office with a couple of other senior management members. "The bicentennial of the signing of the US Constitution, here in Philadelphia, is coming up in 1987," he said. "Don't you think that, as the orchestra of Philadelphia, we ought to create a set of commissions to celebrate that event?" Obvious as this sounded once Steve had said it, this was an idea exciting to us all. Steve secured sponsorship for the project from the insurance brokerage firm Johnson & Higgins, which was centered in New York but eager to promote its Philadelphia presence. The contract for funding the commissions was duly signed in Independence Hall—with the very pen that had been used at the Constitutional Convention in 1787—and over the next months and years several of us engaged ourselves enthusiastically in making the Constitutional Commissions a reality.

Altogether Steve knew how to make working for the orchestra as relaxed and satisfying as it was necessarily busy and demanding. It was symptomatic of the results that, when the players reached their latest contract settlement with management a few weeks after I had arrived, several of the musicians remarked to me that they were proud and gratified at the spirit in which the negotiations had taken place. Sadly, three years later, this spirit of collaboration had ebbed away, so far as labor-management relations were concerned. I think the most painful moment in Steve's working life was when the orchestra committee passed a vote of "no confidence" in management, ushering in a period of severe stress in the orchestra's affairs. This new attitude stemmed, I think, from realities that neither Steve nor the board could have had any control over. It illustrated a principle that I codified for myself in the course of my years in orchestra management and arts administration: no matter how intelligent, cultured, and well-intentioned a given group of individuals may be, with every person that you add to a committee or any such group, you divide that group's collective intelligence quotient in half.

It was, meanwhile, in supporting Muti's and Sell's initiatives aimed at promoting the cause of contemporary music that my now thirty-year-old friendship with Richard Wernick came into being. Even before I arrived in Philadelphia in 1984, Riccardo had made it clear that he was fully expecting me to provide him with suggestions on repertoire planning. Dick had been appointed the orchestra's consultant for new music a year earlier, but there was no sense that our respective responsibilities might in some way conflict: we discovered in the course of our first conversation that our priorities were altogether mutually compatible. Dick and his wife, Beatrice, herself a bassoonist who was also beginning to play the cello, and whom he had met when they were both students at Tanglewood in 1956, soon became the center of our social circle in Philadelphia.

My only slight anxiety when I first met Dick stemmed from the fact that, while I remembered reviewing one of his works in Chicago, I couldn't remember what I had said about it. I went home, looked up the review, and found to my relief that I had singled out his piece and one by Ralph Shapey as the two outstanding works on the program. We were soon busily occupied together in devising ways to strengthen the representation of new music on the orchestra's programs.

One initiative arose out of our awareness that, while it may be relatively easy for a composer to have a new work premiered, it is much harder, once the publicity value and prestige involved in the label "world premiere" are no longer in play, to get such a work played again. With this in mind, we devised a program specifically designed to promote such repeat performances. Steve managed to secure funding from AT&T, and the "AT&T American Encore Series" came into being. The works that were chosen for inclusion were played on the orchestra's regular subscription series; we invited conductors from all around Pennsylvania to attend as guests, in the hope that other performances might thus result; and the composers came to town for workshop sessions with local music students at the University of Pennsylvania, Temple University, and other schools.

While that series was running, Steve came up with his idea for a program of Constitutional Commissions, and Dick and I were charged with the administrative task of identifying the six American composers who might be featured in it. We invited two other men to join us for the intensive selection process: associate conductor William Smith, and Sydney Hodkinson, at that time professor of composition at Southern Methodist University in Dallas and a longtime faculty member at the University of Rochester's Eastman School of Music, since he was very well acquainted with the American compositional scene but, as a Canadian citizen, would not himself be eligible to receive a commission. Scores and tapes were solicited from a large number of composers and distributed among the four of us.

After several weeks of intensive listening and score-reading, we met, with Riccardo in attendance, to make our selection. I arrived at the meeting harboring a conviction that everyone would have differing choices, but, as has regularly happened also whenever I have served on a competition jury, it turned out that the four of us were very nearly unanimous. We told Riccardo that we had five clear choices, but that we were not completely sure about who the sixth composer should be. The choice was between composer A, from whom we could certainly expect to receive a thoroughly viable but not necessarily exciting piece, and composer B, with whom, if we chose him, the result would be unfailingly thrilling but completely unpredictable in terms of punctuality and practicability.

Without a moment's hesitation, Riccardo said, "We'll take B." And so it came about that Milton Babbitt received a commission and composed a work for string orchestra, *Transfigured Notes*, that was indeed thrilling in conception, but that also justified our anxiety by proving utterly impossible for an orchestra working within the limits of a three- or four-rehearsal schedule to perform. No fewer than three distinguished conductors in turn—Erich Leinsdorf, Dennis Russell Davies, and Hans Vonk—agreed to lead the premiere, and each in turn was forced to admit defeat. Vonk probably came the closest of the three to achieving an actual performance. (At one of Vonk's sectional rehearsals, a cellist with a sense of humor remarked, when a well-tuned unison prolonged for almost three seconds emerged from the generally splintered texture, "It's going very well!")

In the end, we played another Babbitt work, Composition for Twelve Instruments, in place of the new one. The distinguished composer-conductor Gunther Schuller, meanwhile, poured scorn on the idea that the work was unplayable, and scheduled a performance for February 1991. His comments conveniently overlooked the fact that an orchestra like the Philadelphia, even bending over backward to provide a sizable number of rehearsals beyond its normal tightly packed schedule, could never afford to allot as many hours to the preparation of such a piece as he could with a handpicked ensemble numbering some of Boston's finest players. Legend has it that he spent something like a hundred rehearsals on preparing for his premiere—and though the CD recorded on that occasion seems to be no longer generally available, YouTube provides sufficient evidence that, even then, the performance he secured achieves only a broad approximation of the score.

Muti himself said, in the course of our meeting, "I think I should probably conduct two of the works myself, and we can get guest conductors in the second half of the 1986–87 season and the first half of the 1987–88 season to do the other four." But then he had second thoughts—"No, I should do three of them." And so, within one calendar year, he shouldered the responsibility of learning three complex new scores. It was under his direction that Rouse's *Phaethon*, Stucky's Concerto for Orchestra, and Shapey's *Symphonie Concertante* had their premieres, while William Smith and Erich Leinsdorf, respectively, conducted the first performances of Thorne's *Revelations* and Walden's *Invisible Cities*.

It was perhaps the Shapey premiere that carried the greatest weight of significance for the composer himself. Over the years, Ralph could claim ample justification for his attitude of aggrieved and fiercely aggressive nonconformism (one especially egregious piece of mistreatment he suffered is recounted in chapter 4). As late as 1987 this gifted American composer in his sixties had never had one of his works performed by a major American symphony orchestra conducted by its music director. So when he was handed a Constitutional Commission, with the prospect of having his work premiered by the Philadelphia Orchestra under Riccardo Muti's direction, Ralph's pleasure was understandably mixed with a certain degree of incredulity.

When Ralph came to Philadelphia for the premiere he brought his own baton with him, because he seriously doubted that a conductor of Muti's strong classical and romantic stylistic sympathies would be able to cope with his new work's fiendish textural and rhythmic complexity. When we took our seats in the Academy of Music for the first rehearsal, however, Dick Wernick in the middle with the score on a suitably outsized desk, Ralph to one side of him and I on the other, the first five minutes or so passed without any obvious reaction on the composer's part. Then I heard him whisper something to Dick. "What did he say?" I asked Dick; "He said," Dick replied, "'He's *good*!'"

After that, there was no more danger of Ralph's springing up from his seat and pushing Riccardo off the podium—something he would have been quite capable of doing. He had a rare talent for offending people, and always thoroughly enjoyed throwing the cat among the pigeons. Once, when the pianist Natalie Hinderas was giving a lecture in Chicago and told her predominantly African American audience that Beethoven was black, Ralph piped up from the back of the hall, "Oh, I always thought he was Jewish!"

The premiere of the *Symphonie Concertante* was a considerable success—as much as could be expected for music of an idiom decidedly in advance of the Philadelphia public's conservative tastes—and we also took the work to New York for one of the orchestra's frequent concerts in Carnegie Hall. I shall never forget Ralph's face when he came to greet Riccardo before the performance, and Riccardo said, "Good evening, maestro." Nobody had ever called Ralph "maestro" before.

A few months later, in Milan for a La Scala production of Rossini's *Guglielmo Tell*, Laura and I were accompanied by Dick and Bea Wernick and by Ralph and his wife, the soprano Elsa Charlston. Riccardo accommodated us in a luxurious box, and we headed off after the performance for dinner at one of his favorite local restaurants, which specialized in Sicilian food. "Just give me a few minutes to change my clothes first," he said to us: "If I go in white tie and tails, people will think I'm a waiter."

The regal hospitality we had always been accorded by Riccardo made us all eager to think of some manner beyond mere words to thank him. So, later in the season, when he was scheduled to conduct the Philadelphia Orchestra in concert performances of Verdi's *Nabucco*, Dick went off to a Jewish religious-goods store and bought a very beautiful torah that we would present to Riccardo during an intermission, in the absence of the Shapeys, but on behalf of all six of us. As an ethnic but minimally practicing Jew, I felt duly shamed when Riccardo showed himself fully acquainted with the use of a page pointer in reading the torah, to avoid touching it by hand, something I knew nothing about. We had, incidentally, taken Riccardo to the first Passover Seder he had ever attended, a regular festivity at the Wernicks' house. For the occasion, I made photocopies of the *a cappella* version of "Va, pensiero," the chorus of the Hebrew slaves in *Nabucco*, and we sang it around the Seder table with Riccardo conducting; it remained a standing feature of Wernick Seders in the following years, even in Riccardo's absence.

In 1989, the wonderful mezzo-soprano and champion of contemporary composers Jan DeGaetani died of leukemia. Dick, who had composed a song for her long before, had been planning to write another one for a recording she was to make for Nonesuch. Knowing about the text I had provided for Wilf Josephs's song cycle *Death of a Young Man*, he asked me whether I might have a poem to hand that he could set. I told him that I had very recently written a poem of suitable size—but that there was no way he could use it in a song for Jan because it was written in memory of my friend John Emanuel's first wife, Angela, who had died of cancer, and Jan had already been diagnosed with the disease that killed her.

I told Dick that I had written a short lyric of emotionally innocent character thirty years before, when I was a student at Oxford, and promised to look for it in my files. When I couldn't find it, I sat down at my desk and, to my utter astonishment, had no difficulty in writing the poem, *Ball of Sun*, down from memory. Dick made a simple but beautiful setting of it, and one of Jan's students, Lucy Shelton, gave it its first performance after Jan's death.

Some time later, in 1991, Tracy Sterne organized a series of three concerts in Jan's memory that were given the following year in the McMillan Theater at Columbia University, and Dick was once again asked to contribute a piece. He asked me to write something specifically in honor of

Jan, and I duly wrote a serious, sad poem. But on the very evening of the day I had written it, I heard a performance of Brahms's *German Requiem* by the Philadelphia Orchestra conducted by Kurt Masur, and the movement with soprano solo provoked an immediate impulse to write a companion poem to the first one. This one would be not serious at all. It went like this:

> "Why didn't someone tell me,"
> said Brahms when he heard Jan in heaven,
> "that singing could be like this? If I'd known,
> I'd have written the Requiem for mezzo."
>
> Of course, he also said,
> "Why didn't someone tell me there was heaven?"
> But that's another story.

Dick's setting of the two poems together, under the title *Two for Jan*, took off aptly if obliquely from the orchestral texture of the Brahms movement, using English horn, bass clarinet, and cello in support of one soprano and one mezzo-soprano voice. The singers at the premiere on March 12, 1992, were Karen Holvik and Freda Herseth (daughter of Chicago Symphony principal trumpet Adolph Herseth). Allen Blustine and Christopher Finckel respectively were the bass clarinetist and the cellist, and Jan's widower, Philip West, played the English horn.

Our sequence of memorial pieces did not end there, though we have not gone much further with a series of "Memorials and Celebrations" that we talked about writing. In 2004, Phil West himself died from the same disease, so we wrote *A Song for Phil*. This time the accompanying instrument was a violin, so that Phil's second wife, the violinist Carole Cowan, could play in the first performance, which was sung by the mezzo-soprano Sarah Mesko at the Aspen Music Festival on June 23, 2008.

Dick's position changed in 1989, when the orchestra acquired its first Composer in Residence, BERNARD RANDS. Up until this time, Muti and Wernick had steadfastly resisted urgings to appoint such a person from the Meet the Composer program, founded in 1974 by the composer John Duffy as a project of the New York State Council on the Arts and the American Music Center. The program at that time stipulated that composers appointed under its guidelines would, as a principal responsibility, be required to set up for the orchestras in question festivals devoted exclusively to contemporary music.

In Philadelphia, we preferred to integrate contemporary programming into concerts in the regular subscription series: Muti and Wernick felt—and I fervently agreed with them—that the segregation of contemporary works in so-called ghetto programs was a disservice to the music. But finally, in 1989, we were given to understand that, if we were willing to lend the prestige of the Philadelphia Orchestra to Meet the Composer by making an appointment, we would not be subject to the insistence on separate contemporary festivals.

In 1986, Muti had conducted a work by Rands, *Madrigali*, a sort of combined homage to his teacher Luciano Berio and to Monteverdi. It had impressed us all enormously, and obviously spoke in especially vivid tones to our music director, so, when the moment came to select our composer, Rands was a natural choice. He served as Composer in Residence for seven years and wrote several works for the orchestra, which Muti enthusiastically programmed both for the home audience and on foreign tours. Dick Wernick, meanwhile, of whose counsel Muti was unwilling to be deprived, was appointed to the new position of Special Consultant to the Music Director.

I felt a strong sense of comradeship with Rands, not just because we share our birth date or because we talked frivolously about going on tour as some kind of educational or entertaining duo titled "I Bernardi," but because he is a man of great personal warmth and broad culture, while his past includes some surprising episodes: he played soccer at one time in his native town for Sheffield United, and was apparently good enough to be offered a contract by the famous Tottenham Hotspur.

Music, however, was the stronger draw for him. Bernard is in my opinion one of the finest composers now active, combining highly individual inspiration with an unfailing respect for the legacy of the great classics. His Van Gogh opera, *Vincent*, premiered in 2011 at Indiana University's Jacobs School of Music but still awaiting a professional production, is perhaps the most fascinating, poignant, and downright beautiful work of lyric theater to have been composed in recent decades. And at one of the postconcert Composer Encounters that Muti had encouraged me to set up, Bernard expressed a conception of his role as a composer that I found intensely sympathetic: "My main motive in writing music is to put myself in touch with areas of myself that I might not otherwise discover, and to offer audiences a similar experience."

Stanley Walden is a composer whose acquaintance I first made on the page, when our Constitutional Commissions committee was looking at scores. His chamber symphony *After Auschwitz* was one of the most impressive of the dozens or even hundreds of works we looked at, and made him an unquestioned choice for one of the six commissions. The piece he wrote for us, *Invisible Cities* (its title taken from the novel of that name by Italo Calvino) was everything we hoped it would be. Stan and I then became friends and enjoyed renewing our acquaintance in several places, especially in The Hague when he and his wife, Bobbie, visited us there in the early 1990s.

In turn, I received a commission from Stan: to translate the German text of his *Three Gretchen Songs* (settings of Goethe), which were duly published around 1994 with German and English texts together by the Theodore Presser Company. With all allowances made for the respect due to the original author, translating Goethe posed fewer problems than I experienced with my work on translating operas by Henze and Matthus. Enzenzensberger's libretto *La Cubana*, and Henze's setting of it, featured intricate rhyme-schemes. With Matthus's *Die Weise von Liebe und Tod des Cornets Christoph Rilke*, the difficulty was in preserving at once the sense and the atmosphere of Rilke's complex poetry, in which the last word of a line often trips up the reader—and potentially the listener—by its pithy unexpectedness.

In 2012, after a long illness, Bobbie Walden died. We felt bad about not having seen them for a long time, but eventually Stan paid Laura and me a visit in Bremerton in the late summer of 2013. It was one of those fabled occasions when you feel there has not been the slightest gap in friendship, which in any case should always be measured by fellow-feeling and shared interests rather than by hours spent together. With regard to the latter, we have had too few with Stan, an irresistibly warm-hearted and broadly cultivated man, yet he certainly ranks among the people who have played important parts in my life.

Among the conductors whose acquaintance I made in Philadelphia, a particularly strong ally in our efforts to promote the cause of contemporary music was Dennis Russell Davies, who offered some enterprising programs at the orchestra's home base in Philadelphia, and who in 1984 was appointed the first principal conductor and classical music director at the Saratoga Performing Arts Center in upstate New York, where the orchestra offered several weeks of concerts every summer.

Another regular guest was Erich Leinsdorf. I remember him as a musician who, if he had only been as good at conducting as he was at making programs, would have been one of the greatest of his day. He was also a quirky and endlessly stimulating man. Every now and then, he would write scurrilous letters to the Philadelphia Orchestra management, signing them "Rolf de Henricis," an anagram of his name. His wife also had a good sense of humor, remarking when some visitors came prematurely into the dressing room after a concert, and Erich had taken off all his clothes and was heading for the shower, "Hairy little bugger, isn't he!"

My problems with Leinsdorf's conducting centered around the feeling that he allowed his head to rule his heart rather too comprehensively. There was a tendency in his work to turn emotion into mathematics, exemplified in his book *The Composer's Advocate* by a recommendation about the opening measures of Beethoven's Fifth Symphony that turned what was surely meant to be an unmeasured pause into a calculatedly numerical one. (The point of a fermata is that it should be unmeasured, and that what follows it should not be on a beat corresponding to the one that had preceded it.) The cerebral quality of his interpretations, moreover, was mirrored in the mechanically jerky beat and gestures through which they were communicated. On one occasion, after he had been with us for two or three weeks, the next guest conductor to appear was Charles Dutoit, and the sight of graceful and fluent movement on the podium, along with the luxuriant sonorities it helped to create, came as balm to both the eyes and the ears.

I also felt, in Leinsdorf's performances, that the music, and his leadership of it, often seemed to be straining to get further ahead: there was a pervasive insecurity about the rhythm. I often wondered whether this might have had a purely technical cause. Orchestras in Europe, and particularly in Vienna, Leinsdorf's native city, have a tradition of playing not on the conductor's beat but after it. Sir Thomas Beecham was a rare conductor from outside continental Europe who liked to preserve this tradition, so that seeing and hearing him conduct, say, the opening of Beethoven's *Egmont* overture could be a dizzying, seemingly syncopated experience: a heavy downbeat, greeted by total silence from the orchestra, and then a crisply unanimous attack from the players just before the next downbeat was due, and so on throughout the opening passage. Could it, I wonder, have been that Leinsdorf, finding American orchestras playing precisely *on* his beat, was always trying to restore the tradition by getting ahead of them again, and thereby upsetting the whole applecart of firm rhythmic unanimity?

I have always enjoyed choral singing, and I joined one of the principal choral groups in the city, the Choral Arts Society of Philadelphia, which performed both on its own programs and sometimes with the Philadelphia Orchestra. Choir practices took place in the Academy of Music ballroom every Wednesday evening. By the end of an intensive day's work in my office, I often felt I was too tired to go and sing—but Seán Deibler, the choir's conductor, quite rightly made it clear that if you missed more than one practice for a specific concert you would not be allowed to sing in the concert, and he was in any case so charismatic a choir trainer that, within five minutes of the breathing exercises that started each session, the adrenaline was running powerfully and I would feel ready for anything.

One concert I should certainly have hated to miss singing in was the local premiere Seán conducted of my friend Wilfred Josephs's Requiem. Such was the sense of concentrated tension that he created in this almost unrelievedly slow and quiet music that, just before the end of the work, one of the women in the choir, feeling faint, nevertheless did not want to cause a disturbance by either going off stage or even just sitting down—so, on the tape that was made of the performance, you can hear the thump when she fainted and fell to the platform floor.

It was only when Seán programmed Rachmaninoff's choral symphony *The Bells* that I eventually resigned from the choir: it's a work that, even in my newfound latter-day enthusiasm for the composer, I really dislike, and I couldn't face the thought of rehearsing it every week. Riccardo later persuaded me to return to the bass ranks for one final project: Brahms's Alto Rhapsody, which we sang, with Jessye Norman as soloist, both in Philadelphia and in Carnegie Hall, and also recorded for Philips. Stepping on stage for the Carnegie Hall performance was revelatory after our Academy of Music performance: in the Academy, the proscenium effectively cut off any feeling of connection with the audience, whereas in Carnegie Hall we were all, performers and listeners, in the same room together. Seán's death in 2009 at the age of sixty-two left a big gap on the city's choral scene.

Another conductor with whom my contact at that time was purely social was Leonid Grin, who lived in a Philadelphia suburb with his wife, Marina, a pianist and piano teacher (who died far too young). Born in the Ukraine, trained in Leningrad and Moscow, and resident in the United States since 1981, Leonid is not only a superb musician but a man of intimidatingly strong instinctive perceptions: he knows what you are thinking even if you deny it. This was one instance where personal friendship developed later into a professional collaboration. Leon Botstein, president of Bard College in upstate New York and music director—decades after Stokowski—of the American Symphony Orchestra, had invited me to prepare an English-language narration for Mendelssohn's incidental music for *Antigone*, which he was to perform at the festival he devoted to the composer at Bard in 1991.

For the first performance, my text was delivered by Claire Bloom, whom, with her then husband, Philip Roth, I had the pleasure of joining at a party in Leon's house after the concert. But when Leonid, who had become the music director of the San José Symphony in California, heard a recording of the Bard performance, he immediately decided to program the music with my narration in 1994, and invited me this time to perform the narration myself. Four years after that, he invited me to return as narrator in Stravinsky's *Oedipus Rex*, in which it was a particular satisfaction to be performing alongside the highly talented American tenor Jon Garrison, who sang the title role. I was delighted, several years later, to recommend Jon to Christopher Lyndon-Gee for the tenor part in a recording he was making of Igor Markevitch's *Paradis perdu*, in which Jon's performance fully justified my faith in him.

Not only at his concerto dates with the orchestra, but also in connection with the chamber music series, a pianist who was always a joy to work with was EMANUEL AX, one of the most enthusiastic musicians and generous men I ever met. When we decided that it was time to put on a benefit concert in the Church of the Holy Trinity with the specific purpose of raising funds for the chamber music series, Manny, already the concerto soloist for the week in question, unhesitatingly agreed to join members of the orchestra in an ambitious program including Brahms's Horn Trio and other works that had piano parts. The conductor that week was Wolfgang Sawallisch, who shared piano duties at the concert with Manny. Both of them, like all the orchestra players involved, performed without fee, and Manny wrote me a cordial note afterward thanking me for having given him the opportunity to take part in what he described as one of the most exciting events in his career.

Though he is associated primarily in the public mind with composers like Mozart, Beethoven, and Brahms, Manny has a lively interest in contemporary music. On one occasion, asked what he would like to play at an upcoming engagement with the orchestra, he at once surprised and delighted us by choosing the Tippett Piano Concerto. He gave a richly expressive and technically flawless performance of this luscious work, which was preceded on the program by Haydn's 99th Symphony and followed by Sibelius's Fifth. The conductor was Esa-Pekka Salonen, whose compelling reading of the Sibelius work was unlike any I had heard before: it emphasized the seamless forward sweep of the music in a powerfully abstract way, making mere sound seem almost an irrelevance. Over dinner after the last performance of the program, Manny exhibited the New-York-centeredness widely prevalent among residents of the Big Apple when he asked Esa-Pekka, "Are you going back to the city tonight?" "Manny," I expostulated, "you're in the city *now*!" He had the grace to apologize.

Through the course of many years and many performances, I have continued to find Ax a musician and pianist of remarkable gifts, and one moreover who seems to get better and better with time. He gave one of the greatest performances I have ever heard of Brahms's Second Piano Concerto in the Amsterdam Concertgebouw, and, with characteristic collegiality, chose an encore that paired him with the orchestra's principal cellist, who had figured in a performance of the slow movement that was the purest and most delectable chamber music.

Another regular Philadelphia visitor, who came almost every year to play a concerto with the orchestra, was the American pianist MALCOLM FRAGER. I had met Malcolm first when, working for Boosey and Hawkes around 1981, I heard him give a superb performance of that same Brahms concerto with the Overijssels Philharmonisch Orkest in Holland. The concert was remarkable also for including the local premiere of Prokofiev's Fifth Symphony, nearly forty years after its composition. Malcolm and I established the warmest of personal relationships, which lasted until his untimely death in 1991 at the age of fifty-six. (He was a Christian Scientist, unwilling to seek medical help, and the cause of his death was never divulged.)

During those ten years of friendship, Malcolm and I formed something of a team, campaigning for the observation of repeats in the *da capo* sections of classical minuets. We drew our support from a variety of historical sources, including Daniel Gottlob Türk's *Klavierschule*, which was categorical in declaring that such repeats should always be taken, in the absence of specific instructions to the contrary in the score. The conductor Max Rudolf commented favorably on an article I had written on the subject, and joined forces with us in some of his own writings. On one memorable evening, by skipping out of one concert at intermission and hurrying to the second half of another, I actually had the pleasure of hearing two Mozart symphonies in performances, by Rudolf and Muti respectively, that followed our recommended practice, and that also seized creatively on the potential for fresh nuance that the second hearing of a section created.

Malcolm was a keen opera lover. Whenever he was in town, he would come over to our apartment on a free evening for a pasta dinner, which would be followed by a listening session that was always devoted to vocal music, and in particular to recordings by singers of an earlier era. This interest I found in no way surprising, because Malcolm's playing always breathed and sang. And I shall never forget how, in a performance of Mozart's Concerto no. 25 in C (K. 503) with the Philadelphia Orchestra, his first-movement cadenza mischievously and delightfully segued from the march-like second subject into a reference to the tune of Papageno's "Ein Mädchen oder Weibchen," from *Die Zauberflöte*, which at that moment I realized for the first time it closely resembles.

It was not only Malcolm that gravitated naturally to vocal recordings. I have gradually realized over the years that, though I have probably spent much more time working in the orchestral field than on opera or song, when I want to listen to music at home purely for pleasure, I will more often choose a vocal than an instrumental recording.

Sadly, on the last occasion when Malcolm was scheduled to play a concerto with the orchestra, and I had arranged for him to play three Mozart works with orchestra members in our chamber music series, illness forced him to cancel. But it was in consequence of this that another important friendship came into being for me. Garrick Ohlsson was engaged to replace Malcolm for the concerto date. I had already come to admire Garrick, early in his career, when I heard him play Beethoven's First Piano Concerto at the Grant Park summer concerts during my *Chicago Daily News* tenure—aside from the general excellence of his playing, the dynamic nuance he fashioned in his first statement of the main finale theme, corresponding to a sudden forte when the orchestra plays it, showed that this young pianist was as well acquainted with the orchestral score as with his own solo part.

I wrote to Garrick and told him that, while he was of course under no obligation, it would be an enormous favor if he would be willing to substitute for Malcolm also on the chamber program. He immediately agreed, and when he arrived in Philadelphia, he came to my office and said, "You must need me to practice with a whole bunch of the orchestra players. Just tell me where I have to go, and I'll go there." Over the twenty years and more that have since passed, the ease and flexibility of Garrick's approach to performing and indeed to people have continued undiminished in all our dealings. (One of the most substantial benefits I have derived from our collaboration occurred during a fraught moment in my time with the Residentie Orkest in The Hague, recounted in chapter 9.)

One Sunday, after the chamber music concert, we had a date to drive with the Wernicks to Reading, Pennsylvania, for dinner with Sergio Proserpi and his wife, Penny, who served for many years as the president of the Reading Symphony Orchestra. In that capacity, she led a music-director search that resulted in 2007 in the appointment of Andrew Constantine, a forty-six-year-old British conductor to whose work I had been introduced by a strong proponent of his talent, Valerie Albert. I have still never heard Andrew conduct in the flesh, but some video recordings had convinced me that he is a musician of notable talent. Through Penny, in turn, I became acquainted with Don Thulean, formerly conductor of the Spokane Symphony in eastern Washington State, who assisted her in that search. Don and his wife, Meryl, subsequently became valued members of our circle of friends in Seattle.

Sergio was a plastic surgeon, who had come to the States and had been compelled, as a penniless student, to sell his blood in order to have something to eat. At this late stage in his career, he had become a millionaire—he and Penny, whose hospitality and culinary skills were peerless, donated a million dollars to the campaign for Philadelphia's new Verizon concert hall—and such prosperity could not have happened to a nicer man. He was also a physician of remarkable gifts, which he exercised far beyond the confines of his professional specialty. On the day of that drive to Reading, I had been working particularly hard, and by the time we reached the Proserpis' house, I felt too sick to get out of the car, and continued to sit in it while Laura went in and told him of my plight. Sergio came out and quickly established that I was showing some highly undesirable blood-pressure and pulse numbers. He took me into the house, laid me on a comfortable sofa, and, while a number of other guests took their places for dinner, glanced in my direction every few minutes from his place at the table, to make sure I was all right. In less than a quarter of an hour, thanks to his soothing words and the gentle pressure of hands that he had bestowed on me, I felt able to join the party, and the rest of the evening passed without a moment's discomfort.

I was not the only one to benefit from Sergio's skill. He and Penny were often in Muti's dressing room among the friends gathered before a concert, and on at least one occasion, when Riccardo was feeling too unwell to go on stage to conduct, Sergio cosseted him, with words, touch, and I think also the quick provision of a prescription, to the point where he, too, felt fully recovered. I shall always remember Sergio, who died in 2004, as a great man, and a great doctor.

Still another pianist whose friendship I owe to my Philadelphia Orchestra days is Stephen Hough. Again, I had admired his artistry when we first got to know each other, which happened during one of the orchestra's summer seasons in Saratoga Springs, New York. Though we hadn't yet had much opportunity to talk, he knew my tastes well enough to send me an excited message about a used bookstore he had discovered in the town that had in stock a number of Trollope novels. Very few of Trollope's works were readily available in those days, and Stephen knew I was busily searching for them. Now that the Trollope Society has magnificently rectified the publication gap, I have been able to read all forty-seven of Trollope's novels, many of them several times over, and to reinforce my conviction that he was not merely the greatest of the English Victorian novelists, but arguably the greatest of all English novelists.

I was reminded of Stephen's discovery years later when I read Ernest Hemingway's memoir, *A Moveable Feast*. It was a pleasurable surprise to find Hemingway, a novelist whose style, both of writing and of life, could hardly differ more radically from Trollope's, being similarly excited to find a bookshop somewhere in the Spanish mountain country where he was able to acquire several Trollope novels previously missing from his collection.

My friendship with Stephen has been salutary in demonstrating, like several other such friendships, that it's not necessary for a critic to share all a performing musician's tastes in order to enjoy a warm personal relationship with him. Some years later, when I was back in Philadelphia and working as a freelance critic, I had arranged to take Stephen to dinner after a concert at which he played a concerto by the German pianist and composer Xaver Scharwenka—one of those sprawling and fulsome late-romantic effusions that I strongly dislike but Stephen loves. When he joined me at the restaurant and we sat down to dinner together, he told me that, while he was playing the piece, he had been thinking, "Bernard must be hating this!" He was not wrong—but I loved the way he played it.

Not only do performer-critic friendships in no way depend on unanimity of taste: they can also thrive in situations where a first review had decidedly negative aspects. In reviewing performances by the Fine Arts Quartet during my time at the *CDN*, I had taken Leonard Sorkin, the group's founder and first violinist, mildly to task for occasional lapses in intonation. After he had appeared one evening at my door and asked if we could discuss the subject, we reached a good understanding, especially on the phenomenon of what I would call expressive intonation—and the two of us were firm friends for the rest of his life.

My years with the orchestra were by no means exclusively devoted to music. Outside the job, one remarkable addition to our circle of friends was the result of a fan letter we wrote. We had read HOWARD JACOBSON's first novel, *Coming from Behind*, and we wrote to Howard—who is no relation—to tell him how much we loved it, and to invite him, if he should ever find himself in or near Philadelphia, to visit us. Just a week or so later, he telephoned to say that he would indeed be in the area in a very short time, because Penguin Books was sending him on a extended journey in search of his Lithuanian-Jewish roots wherever they might manifest themselves, as a preparation for writing his book *Roots Schmoots: Journeys Among Jews*.

Naturally, we invited him to dinner. Along with us he also met Dick and Bea Wernick and Jamake Highwater, who was in town directing a Mythos Festival, and we took Howard also to a Philadelphia Orchestra concert, at which, appropriately enough, Zdeněk Mácal conducted Mahler's First Symphony, with its vivid Jewish inflections in the slow movement that harmonized perfectly with Howard's quest. In the book that came out of his research, we and the Wernicks are generously featured in the chapter titled "High Society." (Mr. Highwater fared less well: Howard thought his claims to American Indian ancestry were fake, which is exactly what articles that appeared after his death in 2001 also suggested.)

Together with Dick and Bea, we have continued on terms of warm friendship with Howard. Laura and I were lucky enough in 2005 to attend his marriage at London's Savoy Hotel to his third wife, the radio and TV documentary maker Jenny de Yong, of whom he said "My last wife. I'm home, it's right." The wedding happened to take place on the day of the London Marathon, which made "getting to the hotel on time" something of a problem for the bride and groom. The Chief Rabbi of the United Hebrew Congregations of the Commonwealth, Jonathan Sacks, who was officiating, told us he had had a call from Howard to say that they hoped to arrive very soon. Nevertheless, said the Chief Rabbi, "It reminded me of the quintessential Jewish telegram: 'Start worrying. Details to follow.'"

We have continued to devour every new book by Howard as soon as it appears, and, with the exception of *No More Mister Nice Guy* (which I found just too obscene to finish reading), to love all of them. Assuring readers then as now that Howard and I were not related, I reviewed his *Kalooki Nights* for the *Philadelphia Inquirer*, describing it as "a moral treatise as intellectually challenging as Proust, and an entertainment funnier than Rabelais." I think it is an even greater book than *The Finkler Question*, worthy winner though that was of the 2010 Man Booker Prize. Writing now in early 2015, I cannot let Howard's latest novel, *J*, go unmentioned: set in an unspecified future time and place, it marks a considerable step forward for him, encompassing as it does a love-story of a touching lyricism that he has never previously essayed.

One day in 1990, Riccardo invited me to join him at a rehearsal he was to lead with the orchestra of the Curtis Institute, just three blocks down the street from the Academy of Music. As we walked to Curtis, and then that evening over dinner at our apartment, he told us about the decision that he would be announcing to the musicians at the following day's rehearsal: to leave his Philadelphia Orchestra post at the end of the 1991–92 season.

I was not present at that rehearsal, but the report was that there had been a good many tears shed when the players heard his announcement. As for Laura and me, though it was a sad development from our personal point of view, we could only tell him that he was surely making the right move at that moment in his own life: the demands placed on his time and energy by the combined administrative and artistic responsibility for the Philadelphia Orchestra and La Scala were no longer supportable for him. "People think I have such a glamourous job," he told us: "I spend my time in such wonderful, cultured cities. What they don't realize is that I never have time in those places to see a play, or visit the art museum. Imagine—I haven't read a whole book in two years!"—and that from a man of deep culture who could probably recite a sizeable chunk of the writings of Leopardi, not to mention Dante, from memory.

Clearly Riccardo's schedule left him little opportunity to indulge his broad cultural tastes, but they did lead him to forge, with two Philadelphia luminaries in other fields, relationships that benefitted not only him but some of the orchestra musicians and staff members. Hilary Koprowski (1916–2013) was himself a man whose interests ran both broad and deep. A virologist and immunologist, and the inventor of the world's first effective live polio vaccine, he was also a fellow class-member of Witold Lutosławski at the conservatory in his native Warsaw. He served from 1957 to 1991 as director of Philadelphia's Wistar Institute, a biomedical center with a focus on cancer research and vaccine development, and the Institute's Christmas parties regularly began with a piano recital by the director. Hilary set up a series of dinners at the Institute to which its scientists and various members of the orchestra family were invited. Conversations there between such people as Riccardo and Hilary and their colleagues offered a valuable way for both sides to surmount the barrier of understanding that too often separates artists and scientists.

In those same years, David Grossman was showing films from his vast archive first at the Temple University Cinematheque and then at Film Forum Philadelphia. He organized small private screenings for Riccardo and a few Philadelphia Orchestra film enthusiasts. The most memorable experience he treated us to was a screening of *El nido*, a Spanish film about a prosperous sixty-year-old man, virtually the squire in his village, who is obsessed with music and spends much of his time "conducting" to a recording of Haydn's *The Creation* in his luxurious listening-room. He becomes involved in an emotionally intense though platonic relationship with a precocious thirteen-year-old girl, a relationship that is inevitably misunderstood in the community. It was one of the most wrenchingly sad films I have ever seen.

Some time later Riccardo, who had also loved it, telephoned me in my office: he said he was in a bar in Milan with a group of critics who were attending a film festival there. Did I remember, he asked, the name of the director who had made *El nido*? I didn't—but I asked him to wait ten minutes for me to call him back. I dashed to the film rental store round the corner and provided him with the information that the director's name was Jaime de Armiñán. One of this deeply sensitive artist's earlier films, *Mi querida señorita*, had been nominated for a foreign film Academy Award in 1972, as *El nido* also was in 1980. The little spot of research was a pleasant change of focus from my usual musicological duties.

A few months later, in 1991, I was on Muti's final European tour with the orchestra. In the course of the tour, I had the opportunity to chat for almost an hour with Riccardo's designated successor, Wolfgang Sawallisch, in his office at the Bavarian State Opera. One thing he said in the course of our conversation was astonishing. He had asked me to explain my views, which he had heard something about, on the subject of observing repeats in the classical and romantic repertoire. I said that I thought, for example, that taking the exposition repeat in the first movement of Brahms's First Symphony was vital; if it was disregarded, the beginning of the development section, with its sudden pianissimo, wouldn't make sense, because its effect was essentially the result of breaking with a previously established regularity. "Oh," Sawallisch said, "you're absolutely right, it's essential for the form, but I would never do it."

Hearing a conductor say that something was essential for the form but that he would never do it left me bereft of words. From that moment on, I had the feeling that Sawallisch was at bottom a compromiser. When I came to hear him regularly in Philadelphia a few years later, I felt fully justified in that view, especially when he brought the soloists on for the finale of Beethoven's Ninth Symphony not at the beginning of the work, nor at the reasonable break between scherzo and slow movement where the players always do some retuning, but at the sudden transition from the slow movement to the raucous start of the finale, which really *mustn't* be disrupted by a pause and the inevitable applause. Rather like the way Bruno

Walter's widely admired performances of Mahler's Ninth were in my view weakened by the failure to set an ever-slower tempo at the end, Sawallisch's choice seemed to me a sign that he did not trust his audience, or his own ability to hold its attention.

If Riccardo had not resigned, I do not think I should ever have taken the step of leaving my job in Philadelphia—our working relationship was simply too good to walk away from. But on that last European tour, I suppose I could say that fate took a hand. Through the intervention of an old friend from my Boosey & Hawkes days—Henk Guittart, the brilliant violist of the Schoenberg Quartet—I was interviewed for the post of artistic director of the Residentie Orkest, or Hague Philharmonic as it is called internationally. They offered me the job, perhaps swayed in part by Riccardo's own warm recommendation. And given that he was leaving, I couldn't resist.

CHAPTER NINE

BACK TO HOLLAND

1992–95

Before accepting the Residentie Orkest post, I had asked Carli van Emde Boas, a friend since my time at Philips who lives in Amsterdam, whether moving back to Holland was a good idea. His response, penetratingly, was: "Let me put it this way—Holland is a terrible country, and Holland is the best country in the world." I was to discover that both halves of his divided judgment were accurate. I already knew about the good side of Dutch society—notably the openness to foreigners and foreign cultures, which would be illustrated by a poster we saw on a house door on the street we were soon living on: "Nederland zit te vol mensen—racisten uit!" (Holland is too full of people—racists out!) But the society had changed radically since I had lived there in the early 1960s. Now a people of whom many were highly gifted seemed to have succumbed to a kind of national abdication of responsibility, and against that background what was in many ways a dream job soon took on nightmarish aspects.

What were the dreamier sides of my position? Well, one was the joy of occasionally discovering a notable talent in a performer previously unknown to me. I tried to listen to as many as possible of the unsolicited CDs that arrived on my desk every day. In one case, a disc of Mozart concertos by a gifted young German pianist named Gerrit Zitterbart, I was able to act immediately on the discovery. I had an opening for a soloist in a Mozart concerto and felt that, though I had not heard Zitterbart in the flesh, his live recording gave me sufficient evidence of his quality, so I dug out the letter that had accompanied the CD and called him with an invitation. He duly made an impressive debut appearance with the orchestra, and I have subsequently had the pleasure of encountering him again in recordings of Brahms piano trios and of three sonatas by Johann Christian Bach coupled with the concertos (K. 107) that Mozart arranged them into. (The arrangements offer proof of the keen understanding of form that Mozart possessed even at the age of sixteen, for he prefaced each of the first movements with modest orchestral ritornellos that serve to transform traditional sonata structures into legitimate concerto movements.)

There was much pleasure also in working with a varied and talented assortment of players in the orchestra. Whatever administrative difficulties were to arise over the next couple of years, my personal relations with the musicians were never less than cordial, and were always marked by humor and a conscious sharing of goals.

One unfailing source of humor was an exceptionally bright member of the orchestra's viola section, Wladimir Polak. "Dima," I asked him once, "why are there so many viola jokes?" "That's perfectly simple," he replied: "They're the only jokes violinists are intelligent enough to understand." Then there was our American tuba player, Carl Kleinsteuber, who was determined to persuade me to program Prokofiev's Fifth Symphony: whenever I took my seat in the front row of the balcony for a concert while the players were tuning up on stage, he would immediately launch into the tuba part of that work.

Other players with whom I, and Laura too, enjoyed warm friendships and many convivial meals included our Australian concertmaster John Harding, two of the trombonists, Tim Dowling from Australia and Art Moore from the United States, violinist Janice Morwood, coprincipal violist Esther van Stralen, with whom I used sometimes to eat lunch at a Greek restaurant just across from the concert hall, German-born coprincipal cellist Gregor Horsch, principal double bass Quirijn van Regteren Altena (wonderful name!), and any number of other Dutch and foreign players from front and back desks alike. Quirijn, like several of those others, proved to be a strong artistic collaborator, and since he was not only a virtuoso performer but an exceptionally idiomatic speaker of English, he delighted everyone with his performance of Tom Johnson's hilarious piece for bass and speech, *Failing*, in which the hard-pressed player does exactly what the title suggests.

Another satisfaction was being able to put my own programming ideas into practice, after years in advisory positions. That should be understood in a sense of still restricted freedom: I soon discovered that my opposite numbers in the artistic leadership of other Dutch orchestras seemed principally focused on putting their personal stamp on programming. I certainly had my personal enthusiasms, but my view of the artistic director's role was the very different one of, as it were, midwife to talent, and I took as my motto Falstaff's "I am not only witty in myself, but the cause that wit is in other men."

Thus, for example, my planning sessions with Oliver Knussen, one of the orchestra's two principal guest conductors (the other being Günther Herbig), were exercises in true teamwork. My immediate predecessor as artistic director, Theo Muller, had saddled Olly, with no consultation to speak of, with some extraordinarily complex and demanding programs, tailored purely to suit his own taste. For me, the sessions at which Olly would say, "Why don't we do so-and-so?" and I would counter with "Great—that means we could also do such-and-such," and he would respond, "Hey, that gives us the possibility of [whatever it might be]," were much more fun than foisting indelibly Jacobsonian programs on him would have been.

Still, one of my highest programming priorities was to bring contemporary music into a more mutually supportive relationship with the core classical repertoire. To that end, I instituted a "Composer's Choice" series: the idea was to invite composers who were also performers, asking them to perform one or more of their own works together with their choice from the entire orchestral repertoire.

A natural participant in such a series, I though, would be my friend Andrzej Panufnik, who had enjoyed a distinguished conducting career, having studied with Felix Weingartner and served at various times as chief conductor of orchestras in Kraków, Warsaw, and Birmingham. In the interim period between my appointment in the late autumn of 1991 and starting work in The Hague in January, I called his home from Philadelphia to initiate the plan. When I talked to Camilla about the idea on the telephone, however, she said sadly that it was not going to be possible for Andrzej to take part: he was suffering from cancer, and was already too ill to think of such a commitment. I immediately changed the flight plan I had made for a preliminary consulting trip to The Hague, stopping off instead in London for a few hours, and took a taxi from Heathrow to Twickenham. Andrzej sat with me in the garden, a blanket over his knees, and showed me the score of the Cello Concerto he had just completed for Rostropovich. After about an hour, too tired to continue with our conversation, he went to bed. I flew on to Holland that night. He died a few days later, and I have never ceased to be glad that I made that change of plan and had those precious last minutes with him.

In the event, I was able to realize just three programs in the "Composer's Choice" series. Richard Wernick paired his own Piano Concerto, with its dedicatee Lambert Orkis as soloist, with Copland's *Billy the Kid* and Brahms's Second Symphony. Simon Bainbridge led a program consisting of Debussy's *Prélude à l'Après-midi d'un faune*, his own wonderfully lyrical Double Concerto for oboe, clarinet, and orchestra, Stravinsky's *Orpheus*, and the suite from Janáček's *The Cunning Little Vixen*. The program I devised in collaboration with the American composer and pianist Richard Wilson, to be conducted by Gerard Oskamp, provided an additional benefit. It consisted of Schumann's Overture, Scherzo, and Finale, Wilson's Piano Concerto, and the Mozart Concerto for Two Pianos and Orchestra. Richard did not play his own work, in which the soloist was the superb Colombian pianist Blanca Uribe, his colleague on the music faculty of Vassar College, but joined her instead in the Mozart, thus signaling to the audience that a contemporary composer need not be exclusively focused on his own creations.

One one occasion I received a letter from Gunther Schuller, asserting his inalienable right to an invitation to guest-conduct the orchestra. This was a demand I had neither opportunity nor inclination to accede to. But it was a pleasure to be able to feature Schuller in a different context as part of the orchestra's chamber music series, where I found several occasions to pair contemporary works with classical ones to which they were in some way related. Schuller's Octet was written as an homage to Schubert's, and uses the same scoring of clarinet, bassoon, horn, and string quintet including double bass. The scherzo is a deliciously witty movement, which starts up repeatedly in quasi-Schubert style, breaks down several times, and manages each time—in the manner associated with the fourteenth-century Scottish king Robert the Bruce—to "try, try, try again." The two octets made an excellent program together.

In similar vein I paired Ligeti's Horn Trio with the Brahms work to which it pays tribute, and Richard Wernick's String Quartet no. 4, labeled by the composer "homage to A. D." with the Dvořák Trio in F minor that inspired much of its material. There is also a superb series of three string quartets by Robert Simpson, nos. 4, 5, and 6, which, the composer explained, constitute "a close study of Beethoven's three Rasumovsky quartets, op. 59; that is to say, the attempt to understand those great works resulted in, not a verbal analysis, but music." Simpson's three quartets offer, as he put it, "musical analogies" in his own idiom to the procedures of the three Beethoven works. Again, taking this as my cue, I paired Simpson's no. 6 with Beethoven's corresponding op. 59 no. 3, and several listeners assured me afterward that the experience of hearing them on the same program had deepened their understanding of Beethoven.

Along with the possibility of putting old and new works together in a new way, I also had the opportunity to bring together some outstanding performers previously unacquainted with each other's work. Firmly convinced that a concerto collaboration with Ivan Moravec at the piano and Gerard Schwarz on the podium could be something very special, I invited them for a set of concerts to include Mozart's Concerto no. 25 in C (K. 503). After the performance, Ivan said to me, "You've ruined this concerto for me—how can I ever do it now with another conductor?" Meanwhile, after their first rehearsal together Jerry had gone back to his dressing room, phoned the office of Lincoln Center's Mostly Mozart festival, which he headed at that time, and said: "Find dates! We have to have this man as soon as possible." Ivan and Jerry went on to perform together frequently for several years, and some time later, when I was recommending a pianist to Jerry's attention and remarked that I didn't know how much weight he would place on my opinion, he said, "Bernard, you've made two musical marriages for me [the other had been with the music of Andrzej Panufnik], and they've both been blissfully happy, so of course I'll listen to you about anyone."

In addition to the orchestra's concerts, its hall, the Anton Philipszaal, had its own well-chosen presentations. One particularly exciting evening offered the chance to hear the Drummers of West Africa, a Senegalese ensemble with which our own local percussionists had frequently collaborated. This particular concert, which was purely African in style and personnel, was directed by Doudou N'Diaye Rose, several of whose many sons were taking part. He was a man and musician of outsize charisma and talent. The concert was a sell-out, and the musicians' bar afterward was completely filled with players and audience members. While we were all eagerly waiting for the drummers to arrive, Petra Unger, the manager of the hall, who was sitting at the same table that Laura and I had chosen, asked me whether I knew Doudou personally. I said no, I had never met him—whereupon he suddenly came into the room, looked around, and walked straight up to me with a big smile and a warm handshake.

I have no idea why he did this, unless it's something about my face, something that always, if I am walking down the street with three or four friends, convinces any panhandler to make a bee line for me. However that may be, Doudou certainly remembered me several years later when I took the opportunity of greeting him again after a similarly spectacular performance by the group in Wilmington, Delaware.

During the four years we spent living in The Hague, I had the welcome opportunity to perform a couple of times as narrator or reader on other concert platforms. On one occasion, the Radio Chamber Orchestra came up with the idea of performing the folksily tuneful score Virgil Thomson wrote for Pare Lorenz's searing 1936 documentary *The Plow That Broke the Plains* live in the Amsterdam Concertgebouw while the film was projected. To do this, they had to wipe the soundtrack, so they needed someone to speak the narrative, and I was engaged for that purpose. The conductor was Ingo Metzmacher, who led a thoroughly skillful performance, and I enjoyed finding myself working with a German conductor who would, each time we met for a rehearsal, ask me what the latest cricket scores were.

A more taxing narration was for *De Nachtegaal* (*The Nightingale*), which the Dutch composer Theo Loevendie had written as a companion-piece for Stravinsky's *L'Histoire du soldat*. Loevendie had then made a full orchestral arrangement of the original seven-piece score, and I was invited to give two performances of it with the Radio Philharmonic Orchestra conducted by Edo de Waart. The first performance was to be in the Concertgebouw, in English because it was being presented as part of an international festival; the second, a few weeks later, would be in the Cologne Philharmonie. It was in connection with this assignment that problems of the kind I have hinted at began to intrude.

Working with the management of the Radio Philharmonic proved to be a somewhat cliff-hanging experience. After what I had thought was the final rehearsal, Edo casually remarked, "See you on Saturday." What was this, I wondered? Surely the performance was scheduled for Sunday. It turned out that the management had simply forgotten to put the real dress-rehearsal on my schedule. "Can you make it on Saturday morning?" Edo asked me. "Well, I'll have to, won't I?" I said. Edo then called the orchestra manager into the hall: "I want you to send a taxi to The Hague on Saturday morning to pick Mr. Jacobson up, bring him to Hilversum for the rehearsal, and then wait and take him home afterward." The manager's eyebrows went up, and he accepted these instructions with obvious bad grace. The episode furnished some insight into why De Waart had a somewhat ambiguous reputation in Dutch musical circles: he was a consummate professional.

That there are many consummate professionals, and an ample supply of fine artists, on the Dutch musical scene must surely be beyond dispute; likewise, that the country's music-making can reach remarkable levels of artistry. But my experience suggested that these virtues are frequently undercut by a pervasive atmosphere of casual carelessness, irresponsibility even, in what I am inclined to call the infrastructure of Dutch musical life. Orchestra members' contracts, under the strictures imposed by labor-management agreements, are often framed in impossibly complicated fractional terms: this violinist or that percussionist is often required to perform for 36 percent of the season, or 27 percent, or 45½ percent—I cite the numbers approximately, but the point is inescapable. You can readily imagine how difficult this makes it for management to come up with a workable rehearsal schedule—not to mention one in which a player who attends every rehearsal for a given concert will also be available for the actual concert. The sense of frustration that stems from such problems tends to afflict the attitude of many in management with an inclination to simply let things happen just as they will, and when a conductor like De Waart says, in effect, "No—it's our responsibility to make things happen as they *should*," it's understandable that a degree of resentment can arise among functionaries thus challenged.

Not surprisingly in a society so wedded to the principles of democracy that it resists any tendency to elevate an individual above the mass of humanity, many musicians in the orchestras I worked with were opposed to addressing or speaking of a conductor as "maestro." I was reminded of the story Herodotus tells about Thrasybulus, the tyrant of Miletus in the seventh century BC who, when his ally Periander of Corinth sent a messenger to ask his advice on how to secure his place as ruler, took the messenger out into a field of wheat and, without a word, swung his stick and cut the heads off all the best ears of wheat that stuck out above the rest. Returning to Corinth, the messenger related the story to Periander, who understood it, and proceeded to eliminate any men in his city who might be powerful enough to challenge him. The "Tall Poppy Syndrome" takes its name from this episode.

Further evidence of casual drift surfaced with the Concertgebouw performance. When I arrived and went to my dressing-room, I had to go back to the janitor's desk and ask whether I might perhaps have a coat-hanger, and where I might be able to get a glass of water. ("Aren't you making a fuss about nothing?" Martijn Sanders, the manager of the Concertgebouw, asked me when I mentioned this to him some time later.) More seriously annoying was the fact that, though we did our sound check (to set microphone levels) with a sound engineer in the hall, he wasn't there for the actual performance, so I had to manipulate the volume control while narrating. To cap everything, my music stand partly collapsed while I was delivering my text.

Edo himself was a joy to work with. I had given narrated performances with several other conductors before, but this was the first time a maestro, before facing the audience to accept applause, turned to me and said, "That was wonderful!"

Before that final rehearsal that almost wasn't, he had told me that there was a request from Cologne for our performance there to be spoken in German—was I willing to do that? I reckoned that, if you are a professional, you don't refuse such a request. I speak reasonable German, though my accent is much better than my vocabulary or comprehension, and I took the precaution of a coaching session with Hans Drewanz, the excellent German conductor at the time of the Noord Nederlands Orkest, with which I was then associated as artistic advisor, having by that time left my position at the Residentie Orkest.

The Cologne experience was in the happiest contrast to what had transpired in the Concertgebouw. The Philharmonie is a superb modern hall. There is even a little button you can press in each dressing room to get an "A" to tune to (admittedly more useful to instrumentalists than to me). And whereas it took six months to extract a recording of the Amsterdam performance from the Dutch radio bureaucracy (a tape that then turned out to be defective), in Cologne, I was handed my cassette on the way back to my dressing room two minutes after we had taken our bows.

In addition to those two guest engagements, I also appeared in speaking roles for two Residentie programs. One of them was led by the Swiss composer and conductor Jürg Wyttenbach and included one of Luciano Berio's finest works, *Laborintus II*, for voices, instruments, and tape. In addition to three solo sopranos, there is a speaking part in the score that may be performed in English, but the original Italian is much more beautiful and atmospheric. Wyttenbach asked if I would be willing to do it, and to do it in Italian. I called Muti, to ask whether he thought my Italian accent would be up to the task, and he assured me that it would be fine. The performance was one of the most satisfying I can remember being part of, and it was a particular pleasure to be on the same platform with the British soprano Catherine Bott, a specialist in the contemporary and baroque repertoires, who sang with spectacular beauty of tone and clarity of line and diction.

My other speaking role on the stage of the Anton Philipszaal materialized at the suggestion of the aforementioned OLIVER KNUSSEN. Unbeknowst to me, Olly and I had met, or more accurately passed each other, during my Chicago years when he, a teenager at the time, stepped out of an elevator and I stepped into it in the city's Carl Fischer music shop. "Wasn't that Bernard Jacobson?" I was told he had asked, the next time I was buying scores there. It was during my time at Boosey & Hawkes that we finally met properly, whereupon he became a colleague and collaborator I valued and still value enormously.

Olly knew and admired the Nonesuch recording of Schoenberg's *Ode to Napoleon Buonaparte* that I had made in 1968 with Joanna Nickrenz and the Claremont Quartet, so when Stravinsky's *The Flood* came up for performance during my first Residentie season, he asked me to take the role of Noah. A few years later, I was privileged to make my BBC Promenade Concerts debut in the role when Olly conducted it in the Royal Albert Hall and Simon Callow dropped out of the cast to take a film role; later still we recorded the work together for Deutsche Grammophon. Working with Olly was an undiluted pleasure, both in The Hague and later in other places. As well as being a gifted composer, he is perhaps the most efficient and best prepared conductor of any in my performing experience. He always knew, from the start of each engagement, exactly how many full rehearsals, and what half and sectional rehearsals, he needed for every work, and his use of rehearsal or recording time was unerringly scheduled. Toward the end of our DGG recording, with just about an hour of the session left and none of my lines yet recorded, I might have become nervous—but he brought the recording in with perhaps thirty seconds to spare, and without the slightest sense of stress.

Back at the Residentie, meanwhile, difficulties were piling up. Getting any new administrative methods adopted, not to mention making existing ones actually work, was as hard as pulling teeth, and so was balancing my time between artistic concerns and practical problems. I would be in my office, sketching out program plans for a season or two in advance—and with a knock at the door someone would say, "Bernard, you have to come down to the stage—there's a meter too little room for the fourth desk of violas." Perhaps I should have been flexible enough to switch my attention more readily between one preoccupation and the other. But over dinner together in Amsterdam, at a time when my frustration was reaching a peak, Olly told me: "Bernard, you can be an ideas man, or you can be a nuts-and-bolts man, but you can't be both at the same time and do it properly."

I should have seen the problems coming even before the start, when Bert van den Akker, the orchestra's executive director, hired an assistant for me whom I was not given the opportunity to vet for the job. He turned out to be an intelligent and extremely amiable young man, but very soon he was telling me, "Bernard, you have to realize that I have no memory"—and he was not joking. Another staff member, even younger, and equally bright and well intentioned, was the orchestra librarian—whose rudimentary music-reading skills did not stretch to any conception of the relation between what was on the page and what would happen on stage. When a visiting singer transposed a Mozart aria down a tone, and the librarian had to make violin parts in the new key, the rehearsal was held up repeatedly because violins don't have in their range the F below middle C, to which he had lowered all the bottom Gs.

It was not only administrative appointments that were made without what I should have regarded as adequate consultation. At the time I was engaged, a successor to Hans Vonk as chief conductor was being sought. There were two men who had collaborated successfully with the orchestra, either of whom I thought might be an excellent choice: Iván Fischer and Jiři Bělohlávek. But by the time I actually arrived to take up my post, I was presented with another *fait accompli*: Yevgeny Svetlanov had been appointed. Though the appointment apparently had the enthusiastic support of many of the players, it added considerably to the difficulties of my job (quite aside from what I felt were problems on the purely musical side with a conductor of severely restricted stylistic sympathies). Svetlanov was something of a genius at communicating his musical intentions wordlessly to his orchestra in rehearsal, and some of his performances reached an impressive height of eloquence and power—I remember especially a remarkably noble and expressive account of Bruckner's Eighth Symphony—but words were something I needed in my work with him, and rarely succeeded in prising out of him in a timely manner.

The artistic direction of many European orchestras, including the Residentie, works in a different way from in the United States. American orchestras usually have music directors, who are responsible both for artistic leadership in general, including programming and the choice of guest conductors and soloists, and for conducting a large proportion of the concerts themselves. The frequent European pattern is to have a chief conductor, responsible only for his own programs, and an artistic director—me in this case—who sets artistic policy and, aside from collaborating with the chief conductor on that individual's own programs, is further responsible for selecting guest conductors and soloists and for making all the other programs in consultation with them.

So far as my consultations with guest conductors were concerned, Svetlanov, understandably enough, wanted to make his own programs first. My task was to elicit his suggestions, before proceeding to discuss the remainder of a season's programs with whatever guest conductors had been or were being invited to appear in the other weeks. But in each of the two seasons for which I actually exercised the programming prerogative, despite the best efforts of Svetlanov's highly skilled and collaborative agent, the late Henrik Lodding of Göteborg in Sweden, it took about three months to extract choices from Svetlanov, by which time very little flexibility remained for negotiations about and with projected guests.

Soloist choice usually presented no problems and often had the happiest of results. One pianist I was particularly keen to invite, even before the "Composer's Choice" program with RICHARD WILSON described earlier in this chapter, was Blanca Uribe. I was anxious to do everything I could to help with the development of her career, partly because she herself was so reluctant to engage in the kind of self-promotion that many musicians feel is unavoidable if they are to get ahead in the profession. I knew Blanca to be a superb interpreter of the Viennese classics, and so I invited her to play Mozart's Concerto no. 9 in E-flat (K. 271) with principal guest conductor Günther Herbig, who in that repertoire would certainly provide strong support on the podium. At the concert, I found myself sitting in my seat at the front of the balcony and completely forgetting to breathe: I was too nervous, worrying about how my chosen soloist, up to that point unknown to all my colleagues at the orchestra, would acquit herself.

I need not have worried. Blanca's success was underlined during intermission, when one of our most knowledgeable subscribers came up to me in the lobby and said, "Mr. Jacobson, while Ms. Uribe was playing, I could think of only one name for a suitable comparison: Clara Haskil!"

In only one case did I feel that my choice of soloist worked out badly. I had invited LEONID GRIN as guest conductor for a program in which two works by Shostakovich sandwiched the Tchaikovsky Violin Concerto. As soloist in the concerto, I suggested Lydia Mordkovitch, whom I had originally met when I was working at Boosey & Hawkes. She had always shown herself, in performances and recordings of such works as the Shostakovich concertos, to be a technically accomplished and passionately expressive violinist, and I thought that in the Tchaikovsky she would be a good fit for Leonid. She was also an exceptionally warm and generous person, who had given my daughter violin lessons for which she refused to take a fee, saying that I had helped her greatly with advice and recommendations in the B&H days, and this was something she wanted to do in return.

Her performance in the Tchaikovsky, unfortunately, turned out to be greatly below her accustomed standard. Quite apart from some extremely wayward intonation, it was beset by rhythmic quirks that made it very hard for Leonid to maintain punctuality in his shaping of the orchestra part. This is where my guilt comes in: I made the usual tactful noises after the performance, but I had such a bad feeling about it that I refrained from calling Lydia or writing to her afterward, because I could think of no way to start a dialogue without either sounding totally hypocritical—since I was sure she would have been all too aware of how unsatisfactory the performance had been—or being honest and hurting her feelings. The longer I allowed my noncommunication to go on, the more impossible it became to resume contact. Very recently, I was saddened to read of Lydia's death from cancer—another poignant reminder that one should never wait to get in touch with someone until it is too late.

It was some of the guest conductors who provided my greatest artistic and personal satisfactions in The Hague. Quite aside from the rather monstrous programs he had dumped on Knussen, Mr. Muller had also bequeathed to me two foreign tours that constituted logistical minefields. Yet with Iván Fischer on the podium for one and Franz Welser-Möst leading the other, it was possible to smooth the worst practical difficulties away and enjoy the really fine musical results.

The tour with Fischer was to England, and included two programs. The Mozart/Mahler program was unproblematical, but to perform Beethoven's Ninth in eight towns with four different choral groups posed enormous complications with regard to travel and rehearsal. Fischer himself was one of the first to warn me of the pitfalls of my position when, rather than congratulating me on getting the job, he commiserated with me instead. But he made the tour a notable artistic success, being both sensitive and unflappable. In one of our eight venues—I think it was in Nottingham—the concert hall lights suddenly failed somewhere in the middle of the Beethoven Ninth, and remained out for something like a minute, but the performance went on without a hitch in total darkness.

My other inherited tour was fraught with even more complications, and was similarly rescued from disaster by another artistically and personally admirable conductor. After Muti, I would rate my professional relationship with FRANZ WELSER-MÖST as the next most satisfying. I had met him first when he appeared as a guest conductor in Philadelphia. Now we found ourselves facing an Italian and Austrian tour that had, again, been inadequately planned, and that was to include performances in Turin and Linz of Mahler's Second Symphony, with demands in the matter of choruses and offstage brass groups that in retrospect made the Beethoven Ninth look like child's play.

The tour had been dreamed up by Baron Andreas von Bennigsen (Franz's former manager and adoptive father, whose wife, Angelika, subsequently married Franz) and Theo Muller. Between them, they had simply assumed that the concert hall in Turin would be available for a rehearsal when we arrived in the city. Wrong! The local radio orchestra already had it reserved for its own rehearsals. The players' labor agreement made slotting a rehearsal somewhere else into the travel schedule close to impossible. During our preparatory period in The Hague, Franz and I sat down to lunch together to try and thrash the problem out. After an hour of discussion, he stood up to leave, and said: "Bernard, work out whatever you can that will be acceptable to the players, and I will fit in with it."

Thanks to the relevant committee's generous willingness to bend the rules, a solution did indeed prove possible—but I can think of few conductors that would have been equally flexible. All my dealings with Franz, both as a conductor and as a human being, have been similarly impressive. Musically, his gifts are remarkable enough, and his way of interacting with the orchestra was, it seems to me, consistent with the high moral stance of a man who, when he was chief conductor of the London Philharmonic and the orchestra was undergoing severe financial strains, called his manager and said, "Reduce my fee—I can't go on being paid so much when the players are having to take a salary cut."

That human and humane side of the man was part of what made my collaboration with Franz so enjoyable—but only part. My early championing and long-standing admiration of Simon Rattle notwithstanding, it is Welser-Möst, just five years younger, who I think stands supreme among conductors of his generation as a musical interpreter of profundity and powerful intellectual and emotional insight. I am not being revisionist here. Rattle, I still feel, leaves pretty well all of his contemporaries in the dust as a performer of dazzling brilliance with a gift for electrifying both orchestras and audiences, but in the deepest and most challenging repertoire Welser-Möst goes deeper. As I write these words it occurs to me that the same kind of distinction may be drawn between these two superb conductors as, in my Chicago days, I drew between the electrifying Solti and the penetrating Giulini.

Distinctions of this kind are illustrated by the differences between the repertoire choices and interpretative strengths of the earlier and later pairs of conductors. Solti concentrated his interest and showed his power best in late romantics like Mahler and Strauss, whereas what was most memorable with Giulini was his predilection and profound feeling for earlier masters: Mozart, Rossini, Schubert, Verdi, Bruckner, and, supremely, Brahms. When we come to consider the later pair, what seems to call Welser-Möst's skills most vividly and profoundly into play is music from the high classical and romantic periods, similarly including Schubert and Bruckner, and no less significantly the works of Mozart, to which his light touch and frequent fleetness of pacing bring a rare sense of freshness. He also has an inexhaustible appetite for more out-of-the-way pieces such as Franz Schmidt's Fourth Symphony, Nali Gruber's *Frankenstein!!*, and the music of Gruber's Third Viennese School colleague Kurt Schwertsik, all of which he performs with keen insight. With Rattle, while I know there are good judges who would disagree with my relatively cool estimation of his Beethoven and Brahms, it is more—how can I put it most delicately?—colorful and superficially exciting composers such as Szymanowski, Gershwin, John Adams, and Steve Reich that speak most characteristically in his performances.

I remember a Welser-Möst performance of Mahler's Ninth Symphony in London's Royal Festival Hall—evidence of his breadth of stylistic range—in which the long-drawn pianissimo final pages of the work were played against a background of silence on the part of the audience as complete and intense as any I have experienced. When he conducted Schubert's "Great" C Major Symphony in The Hague, in preparation for our tour, one of Holland's finest twentieth-century composers, Peter Schat, came up to me after the performance and said, "Mr. Jacobson, this is the first time I have totally understood this symphony." The performances Franz led of the work on the tour were no less revelatory.

For Welser-Möst, any performance in Linz have something of the "local boy makes good" quality. He was born there, and the "Welser" element that his stepfather suggested adding to the original plain "Franz Möst" refers to the nearby city of Wels. While we were rehearsing the Mahler Second in Linz Cathedral, Bert van den Akker told me afterward, a lady came in through the open door in the back of the building and asked him what music was being played, and what orchestra was playing. He answered those questions. Then she asked who was conducting, and when he told her, her face softened and she said in warm grandmotherly tones, "Ah, der Franzi!" Franz was rather embarrassed when he heard about this later, but also, I think, quite pleased.

There were further problems at the Residentie, some of which were to surface only later, when I was no longer working for the orchestra. In purely personal respects, our executive director Bert van den Akker was thoroughly pleasant to work with, but my own rather measured approach to solving problems clashed violently with his conviction that they all had to be solved instantly. Thus we would often find ourselves during the intermission of a concert dashing into a meeting at which half-a-dozen people were compelled to deal in ten tense minutes with highly sensitive matters that needed calm consideration on a much more extended time-scale.

Furthermore, I had tried to set up a proper structure for communication between visiting guest artists and conductors on the one hand and the management on the other, but for some reason I had never succeeded in getting it put in place. One consequence became clear soon after my resignation. Before leaving, I had engaged the English soprano-turned-mezzo Felicity Palmer as one of the soloists in a performance of Mahler's *Das Lied von der Erde* that was scheduled to take place after I left. The week in question arrived, and with it an urgent call from Felicity on my home phone, the number of which I had given her purely out of friendship—she already knew that I would no longer be on the staff when her performance was to happen. She had checked into her hotel a day or two earlier, was now suffering from a throat infection, and was desperate to find medical help—but she had been given absolutely no contact information for anyone at the orchestra. Fortunately my wife, who is a pathologist, was able to give Felicity the phone number of a laryngologist colleague, who was able to treat her condition successfully, and her threatened withdrawal from the performance was averted.

Das Lied von der Erde poked its way into my mind at quite another moment during our time in The Hague. I had been commissioned by the Concertgebouw in Amsterdam to write program notes for a concert to be given there by the St. Louis Symphony. It was to include a work by the orchestra's composer-in-residence, Claude Baker, with which I was unacquainted, his *Shadows: Four Dirge-Nocturnes for Orchestra*. I duly requested a perusal copy of the score from the publisher. It arrived one Saturday in the mail, and I took the sizeable envelope upstairs to my study and left it, unopened, on my desk, with the intention of examining it and writing my note on the afternoon of the following day.

That day happened to be Monumentendag, or Heritage Day, the one day of the year when important monuments and sites normally closed to the public are opened up. Laura and I took the opportunity during the morning to visit The Hague's Jewish cemetery, which is a particularly impressive place. While we were walking around it, I suddenly realized that I was humming to myself the gorgeous theme that wells up in the last movement of *Das Lied*, "Der Abschied" (The farewell), at the words

> O sieh! Wie eine Silberbarke schwebt
> Der Mond am blauen Himmelssee herauf.

"Where on earth," I wondered, not having thought about or heard *Das Lied* in a long time, "did that come into my mind from?" Back home after lunch, I opened up the publisher's package, and found, in the composer's words, that "*Shadows* provides nonvocal commentary on four haiku texts of rather macabre imagery," and that his first movement was inspired by a haiku that brought immediately to his mind "the text of 'Der Abschied' . . . and in particular of the passage that reads, in Harold G. Henderson's translation:

> O see, like some tall ship of silver sails
> The moon upon her course, through heaven's blue sea.

So was this, in some mysterious way, the answer to my "where did it come from" question? My wife, and my old friend John Emanuel, both educated in scientific disciplines, are disinclined to attribute the experience to anything more arcane than mere coincidence. I am not so sure. Perhaps the most important single lesson I took from my philosophy studies at Oxford was the conviction that it ill behooves a man to rule out the possibility of anything—a conviction implicit, surely, in my postchildhood conversion from convinced atheist to careful agnostic.

For all the reasons I have outlined, I decided that I had to extricate myself from my position at the orchestra, which was beginning to have a serious effect on my health. When I said to Bert van den Akker, "We have to find a way to end this relationship—it just isn't working," his reaction seemed to prove my point: "It's working fine," he said—he wasn't even aware of the dysfunction that prevailed.

When I made my decision to leave, I remembered something Erich Leinsdorf had said to me in Philadelphia: "Bernard, let me give you a word of advice: never sacrifice yourself for an institution. Number one, it won't work. And number two, they will never thank you." I would have written to thank Leinsdorf for the influence of those wise words, but he had just died.

During our four years in The Hague, it was some new personal friendships, as well as the resumption of two old ones, that made life seem agreeable enough for Laura and me despite my professional frustrations. One new friendship that was to be especially close was with GUIDO SPRUYT, a Belgian who lives in Antwerp and who at the time was mostly busy with the management of an excellent chamber orchestra, Nuove Musiche, and with nurturing the career of its gifted young conductor, Eric Lederhandler. I attended several of Eric's concerts both during and after our time living in The Hague. One of them was particularly illuminating. It was given in a small church in Antwerp, and the effect of hearing Beethoven's Fourth Symphony in a room with perhaps one-eighth the seating capacity of modern concert halls was to reveal just what a stunning impact this supposedly modest and relatively undramatic piece must have made on its first audiences.

Guido and I met originally because of our shared connection with the English conductor Frank Shipway. I had come to admire Frank enormously during my Boosey days, when he gave brilliant performances of several Panufnik works. Guido also knew and admired Frank, and in about 1994 was managing a tour Frank was conducting with the Turku Philharmonic. They were scheduled to play a Sibelius program in the cathedral of the Belgian city Mechelen (Malines in French), and, knowing that I was living in The Hague, Frank suggested to Guido that he should invite me to the concert.

I accordingly drove the fairly short distance to Mechelen, and after we had enjoyed excellent performances of Sibelius's Violin Concerto and Second Symphony, Guido suggested that I should join him and his wife, Marijke, for a late dinner in Antwerp on my way back to The Hague. Our conversation over dinner quickly revealed a sympathy of thought and feeling so striking that when I got home I told Laura that I had just met lifelong friends, and this has indeed—at least until the time of writing!—proved to be completely true.

We try to see the Spruyts as often as possible, and two other couples with whom old contacts were renewed in The Hague have become part of the same close-knit group. The Australian pianist Geoffrey Madge and the American percussionist Jim Gordon have both lived in Holland for years. I first got to know Geoffrey and his Dutch wife, Truus, when visiting The Hague on Boosey & Hawkes business, though we were to discover that we had both participated, without actually meeting, in the same concert in London, he as piano soloist, and I presenting an introductory interview with the composer of the evening, Iannis Xenakis. Geoffrey plays Bach and a large variety of composers wonderfully, but he was also Xenakis's interpreter of choice for such works as *Eonta*, which he has performed more than seventy times, and his broad and adventurous stylistic sympathies made him an obvious choice as someone to whom I would want to introduce the music of the composers I was championing at that time.

Jim Gordon I had known even longer. He was a frequent performer at concerts I reviewed for the *Chicago Daily News* in the late 1960s, and when he told me he was planning to move to Europe, I spent an hour over lunch in the restaurant of Chicago's Art Institute giving him names and addresses of contacts in Europe who might be able to help him in pursuing his career there. It was a total surprise ten or so years later, when I was visiting the North Holland Philharmonic in Haarlem for Boosey & Hawkes, and the manager asked me where I had lived in the States, to be told that the orchestra's percussionist was also from Chicago, and was none other than Jim.

We became close friends, and for the rest of my time at Boosey I was always welcome to use the spare bed in his flat whenever I was visiting Amsterdam. He also took pleasure in introducing me to his many talented Dutch and immigrant musician friends, including Jared Sacks, an American-born horn player long resident in Holland who was an important pioneer in the development of superaudio recording techniques. (Jared was the founder of the Channel Classics record company, where he has produced recordings of superlative technical and musical quality.) Jim and I continued to see each other frequently when Laura and I were living in The Hague, and we were delighted when he introduced us to a new girlfriend, Nanny, who was soon to become his wife.

These very special friendships have been kept current by means of transatlantic visits in both directions. The eight of us spent a few sybaritic days celebrating my seventieth birthday at a chateau-hotel in Belgium, and five years later, for my seventy-fifth, we forgathered again for a no less delicious gastronomic weekend in a Belgian village near the French border.

Someone else with whom existing ties of friendship were strengthened in The Hague was the composer Rudi van Dijk, to whom I had been introduced some time earlier by WILFRED JOSEPHS. Born in 1932 in Holland, Rudi had spent parts of his career living in Canada and in England, and it was in the English village of Peasmarsh, near the Sussex coast, that he and his wife, Jeanne, would spent the last years before his death in 2003. Piet Veenstra, predecessor of my own predecessor Theo Muller, had bequeathed to his successors the plan for a contemporary music series that constituted a sort of "Twentieth-Century Retrospective" celebrating the Residentie Orkest's ninetieth anniversary. It was a rather schematic project, with concert programs that would each be restricted to containing works written within a specific time-period within the overall ninety-year framework.

Although I have never liked the idea of segregating contemporary music in a kind of "special-program" ghetto, Piet's idea did at least leave me room to program more contemporary works than might otherwise have been possible, and in its context I took the opportunity, for a program of music from the years 1947–62, to set Rudi's Four Epigrams for orchestra alongside Strauss's *Metamorphosen*, Ton de Leeuw's *Ombres*, Penderecki's *Threnody for the Victims of Hiroshima*, and Vaughan Williams's Sixth Symphony. This, as anyone acquainted with any of those five works will perceive at once, is not the jolliest assemblage of music that could be imagined. But it offered Rudi what was for him at the time the fairly rare pleasure of a public hearing in a major hall, and under the baton of a very good young Dutch conductor, Jac van Steen, the program went down very well with the audience. It was particularly gratifying to be approached at the end of the evening by several concert-goers intent on persuading me to program more Vaughan Williams. Rudi himself was almost embarrassingly grateful for what he regarded as the service I had done him, though I should certainly not have put his work on the program had I not found it eminently worthy of its place. A year or two later he paid Laura and me the compliment of dedicating his Piano Concerto to us.

The mention of Piet Veenstra calls for a few more words, both to convey my admiration for that talented man and to point out what radically separated my tastes from his. The difference was very perceptively pointed out to me in the course of a conversation I had with a young local music critic whose name I regret being unable to remember. When I said that I respected Piet greatly, and that he knew an enormous amount about music, but that we very rarely agreed about specific works, my lunch companion's penetrating response was, "Well, the difference is obviously that Piet has a taste for nervous music, and you don't." The thought sounds somewhat simplistic expressed like that, but it is true that I tend to accord especially high value to styles of composition that allow instruments or voices—and the notes themselves—time to speak, and I have benefitted considerably from my awareness of this.

Quite aside from his musical expertise, Piet, whom I had first encountered when I was promoting Boosey's composers in the late 1970s, was a brilliant man, and a lateral thinker of some ingenuity. The story goes that when, driving with his wife, he was stopped by a policeman, who told him that he had been driving at seventy kilometers per hour in a thirty-five kph area, Piet responded, "Het spijt mij, mijnheer—ik dacht dat het per persoon was" (I'm sorry, sir—I thought it was per person), which so far disarmed the officer that he sent Piet on his way with a warning instead of a ticket.

Another contemporary composer for whom I was happy to find myself with the opportunity of, again, not so much doing a service as righting a wrong was the Dutch pianist-composer (and also psychiatrist) Hans Henkemans (1913–95). I had first encountered Hans in the early 1960s as a pianist, especially gifted as an exponent of Mozart and Debussy. His own music I only got to know and admire in my Residentie capacity as artistic director. With a view to discussing what music of his I might suitably program with the orchestra, I visited him at his home in Zeist.

I took an instant liking to this modest and sensitive man, but I found him in a state of intense depression. He explained that the cause of this lay in a disappointment he had suffered about one of his most recent works. It seemed that the Polish pianist Krystian Zimerman, congratulating him backstage after a recital he had given, had suggested that Hans should write him a concerto. There was no talk of a formal commission, but Hans's clear understanding was that if he produced such a work, Zimerman would perform it. He duly wrote his Piano Concerto no. 3 and sent the score to Zimerman. A year or so later, not having received any acknowledgment of the score's receipt, he in turn went backstage after a Zimerman recital, and in the course of an otherwise perfectly unremarkable conversation asked the pianist when he was planning to premiere the piece. In reply, Hans told me, Zimerman said, "Oh, you have to understand that I'm on the fast track now—I don't have time to learn a new work like that!"

This seemed to me a quite unconscionable way to behave. Much as I admire Zimerman's playing, I haven't since then felt much inclination to renew my acquaintance with it. But more to the point, I told Henkemans that it would be a pleasure for me to find a suitable pianist and put the world premiere of the piece on the Residentie schedule. Back in The Hague, I called Garrick Ohlsson in San Francisco, explaining the background of my plan, and asking if he might be willing to consider giving the premiere of the concerto. He unhesitatingly agreed to look at Hans's score, which I duly sent him. Just two weeks later, coming home one evening from a concert, I found the most succinct of messages from Garrick on our answering machine: "Why not?" he said.

We accordingly scheduled the premiere for July 9, 1994, taking advantage of another of those contemporary ghetto programs to juxtapose it with works by Dutilleux, Augusta Read Thomas, and Jacob Druckman, conducted again by Jac van Steen. Just a week before the planned performance, however, Hans, who was still in an emotionally vulnerable state after his experience with Zimerman, decided that the concerto did not meet his own self-imposed standard of quality, and wanted to withdraw it from the program. It was only because both the soloist and the conductor involved, Garrick and Jac, were such decent, gentle, and understanding people that, with their help, I was able to salvage the premiere. Of all the events I ever had a hand in as an administrator, this was the one that gave me the deepest satisfaction, and I like to think that it was a bright spot for Hans in the last somewhat somber two years of his life.

Despite such positive experiences, I nevertheless extricated myself from my Residentie post. This was a workable option since Laura was just about to take up a full-time job at a Rotterdam hospital, so that I could scale back my contribution to the household expenses to whatever freelance work would provide. At this point the Hungarian conductor János Fürst took a hand. I knew Jáni not only through some impressive concerts, but also because his manager, New-Zealand-born Joy Mebus, who worked mainly in Holland and lived just across the border in Belgium, had become a good friend. "You would be wonderful at artist management," Jáni said to me: "Joy needs some help. Why don't you join forces with her?"

Given my enthusiastic admiration of so many performers, I found the idea attractive, and Joy was delighted to draw up a plan for me to work with her from my base in The Hague. We did indeed collaborate, I think with pleasure on both sides, for several months. But this proved to be one occasion when self-knowledge had failed me. I soon realized that I was not cut out to be a salesman: I could write much more persuasively about the talent of a given artist when I had no financial stake in the result. I am full of admiration for the way an agent like the London-based Robert Gilder, another new friend I made through his Residentie visits, works for his artists, but it is not a combination of skills that is within my capacity. My association with Joy, therefore, was terminated by mutual agreement, though I couldn't escape a feeling of guilt about one or two fine musicians whom I had brought into the Mebus management and was now leaving behind.

It was a chance encounter at a meeting of orchestra managers in the lobby of my friend Jim Gordon's orchestra in Haarlem that set up the next productive contact. I got into conversation with Ton Verberne, general director of the Noord Nederlands Orkest, which was based in Groningen but also played regularly in Leeuwarden and other regional centers. When I mentioned that I had just left the staff of the Residentie Orkest, he told me that he was looking for an artistic advisor, and asked whether I might be prepared to take on such a role for him. This turned into a highly congenial collaboration that lasted for several years, first from my home in The Hague and then, using modern methods of communication and one or two visits, after we had moved back to Philadelphia.

Both Ton and his deputy, Peter Adema, were a pleasure to work with (though reading the hand-scrawled memos I received from Peter, who used neither a computer nor even a typewriter, was something of a challenge). In addition to working by way of telephone calls and written documents, I frequently attended meetings of the orchestra committee, which included several players who were cultivated and very positive in their attitude to planning. And—the big difference from my Residentie position—I was not responsible for the administration needed to put my ideas and those of my colleagues into practice. My visits to Groningen, moreover, were all the more enjoyable because of the charming hotel I would stay at overnight, and because of the existence of an excellent restaurant that opened late in the day and stayed open until 3 a.m., which made getting together with musicians after a concert unusually easy and relaxed.

In the course of our work together, the committee and I made and carried through a large number of attractive programs. I put several programming principles in place: we started many concerts with Dutch works, mostly from the eighteenth century; and I treated a number of Haydn symphonies as the closing works on their respective programs. I've always found it a pity that those marvelous works are routinely used as concert-openers, just to warm things up (while the latecomers are still arriving) for the serious musical business of the evening. It was gratifying to have regular subscribers come up to me after one of our second-half Haydn performances and say, "Thank you—I never realized Haydn was such a great composer!"

Perhaps the most eccentric, yet satisfying, program I devised included a sort of deconstruction of the waltz. The evening opened with Ravel's *Rapsodie espagnole*, after which Geoffrey Madge and chief conductor Hans Drewanz gave the world premiere of Rudi van Dijk's Piano Concerto. (I had hesitated for a while about programming it, which might have been thought self-serving since the composer had dedicated it to my wife and me, but I finally overcame that scruple, with the full support of the committee, in view of the work's unmistakably high quality.) The second half began with the overture to Johann Strauss Jr.'s *Der Zigeunerbaron*, continued with the concert waltz *München* by Richard Strauss, and completed the circle of composers with Ravel's *La Valse*. Another friend I was able to bring, albeit posthumously, into the companionable Groningen circle was Panufnik, whose Piano Concerto Geoffrey also played with the orchestra.

I had been severely spooked by my traumatic experiences at the Residentie, but the North Netherlands connection was one factor that helped to lift me out of the resulting acedia. Another was my receiving a commission from Norman Lebrecht on behalf of Phaidon Press to write a study of the music of four twentieth-century Polish composers for the press's newly devised series on contemporary music, of which he was general editor. I accepted this proposal happily, and the book, which examined the work of Panufnik, Lutosławski, Penderecki, and Górecki, duly appeared under the title *A Polish Renaissance*. Through no fault of Norman's, the process leading to publication turned out to be arduous. Being at that time a publisher mostly active in the field of art books, Phaidon did not have a staff copyeditor knowledgeable about music. An outside copyeditor was hired, and when the finished manuscript with her revisions came back, I found that a vast number of passages had been changed from correct English to incorrect: "children's chorus" altered to "childrens' chorus" was just one example among literally hundreds. It took two weeks of my life to prepare a reply of more than two hundred pages pleading for the restoration of my original text. Phaidon graciously accepted about 98 percent of my recorrections; but the whole episode was symptomatic of a modern world in which even persons engaged in such pursuits as publishing may frequently be described as illiterate.

Despite my work with the Noord Nederlands Orkest and Laura's medical salary, the workings of the Dutch tax system made us realize by 1995 that, if we stayed in the country much longer, we were likely to end up bankrupt. (A quirk of the Dutch tax laws was that, if you sold a house on January 1, you, and not the buyer, were responsible for the entire year's property tax. Another problem for someone in my line of work, who had frequently to interview musicians and others in the most convenient setting, which was usually over a meal, was that the expense of such meetings, and even of the travel to get to them, was not deductible.) We began to think about ways of returning to the States.

One attractive possibility arose when Gerard Schwarz expressed interest in hiring me as artistic administrator with the Seattle Symphony. I flew to Seattle for some seemingly successful interviews with the management, headed at that time by Deborah Card. I also attended a superb concert in which János Starker played the Dvořák Cello Concerto and Jerry conducted a performance of Shostakovich's Eleventh Symphony so gripping that I realized, about three-quarters of the way through, that I had completely forgotten to breathe. In the event, I was not offered the job. Laura supportively declared that she would never set foot in the city that had turned me down—a decision we looked back on with amusement when we found ourselves living in the area ten years later.

It would in any case have been a move of dubious financial wisdom. If I *had* been offered the job, we might well have found ourselves living in a fairly expensive city on the somewhat meager salary attached to my position while she was in search of a medical job, medical work at all levels being inevitably better paid than a job in the arts. We realized that finding an American job for her, in some place where I could pursue my freelance activities, would be an altogether preferable scenario. So when her former boss in Philadelphia, Dr. Ierachmiel Daskal, in response to a phone call from me simply asking him to keep his eyes open for a possible opening, replied, "Laura should know that, any time she wants a job, she has one with me," we decided to take the plunge and go back to Philadelphia.

CHAPTER TEN

PHILADELPHIA, SECOND INSTALLMENT

1996–2005

There is something especially satisfying about returning to live in a city you have lived in before. Quite aside from all the old friends to connect with again, there is the purely material benefit that, when construction blocks a road, you can find an alternative route by consulting memory rather than a map.

Our domestic circumstances this time around were very different from those of our first Philadelphia period. Then we had lived in Center City, which was very convenient in view of my frequent long days and evenings at the orchestra offices and hall, which were just two blocks' walk from our apartment. This time we were attracted by the charming and characterful neighborhood of Chestnut Hill, on the city's northwest border, which provided Laura with a relatively short commute, while being only about a half-hour's drive, through some beautiful riverside parkland, to a concert or any of the city's gastronomic pleasures.

Our old friend Jonathan Sternberg, a conductor I had reviewed enthusiastically in my time at the *Chicago Daily News*, and his wife, Ursula, lived in Chestnut Hill, and they found us a beautiful house there that was of reasonable size and not too horrendously expensive. After receiving an urgent phone call from Ursula—our dinner guests in The Hague that evening understandingly left before dessert, realizing that we had to start working on this possibility at once—I flew to Philadelphia as soon as I could to look at the house, and I loved it so much that I felt able to agree on the purchase even before Laura had seen it. She said that she trusted Ursula's taste so completely that, if Ursula thought it was right for us, she was sure she would agree, which proved to be the case.

The Sternbergs were to be a central element in our lives for many years. Jonathan and I would get together frequently to talk about many subjects, but mostly about music. Instinctive rather than intellectual as a musician, and a loyal disciple in stylistic terms of Furtwängler, he has over a very long career and life—he recently celebrated his ninety-fifth birthday—met practically every musician (and every artist in other fields) that one would want to meet. Jonathan has concentrated throughout his career more on teaching, both at Temple University and in European master classes, than on performing. But a recorded performance by a South African orchestra of Elgar's *Enigma* Variations that he gave me to listen to without identifying the conductor proved that this has been by no means because of any weakness on the podium: it was his own performance, and one of the finest I had heard of that much-played and much-recorded work.

Ursula, too, was a cultural powerhouse. Born Ursula Hertz in to Jewish parents in Germany and brought up in Cologne, she had survived the Holocaust in Holland and Belgium, and met and married Jonathan in 1957. She was a gifted and versatile artist, of whose works we eventually collected a considerable number, and her many sketches of musicians at work had no doubt come into being as a result of her keen appreciation of music. She was also a very emotional woman. When she was at our house for coffee one morning, I happened to have just acquired a CD of Schubert songs sung by Ian Bostridge. I played her his extraordinary performance of *Erlkönig*, which transforms that song into a veritable opera, and she collapsed in helpless tears.

Another friend in the neighborhood was the violinist Helen Kwalwasser, who also taught at Temple, where her husband, Harvey Wedeen, was professor of piano. When Ursula died in 2000, Helen and I organized a gathering in her memory at the Sternbergs' house. It was attended, I think, by more than fifty people; and again, as with the memorial for Roland Gelatt in New York back in the 1980s, it was to be the source of an important new contact, for it was there that we met a couple who are now among our closest friends.

Gene Abroms told me when we met in the Sternberg's house that day that he had been reading my work for years, and had long wanted to get in touch and disagree about a number of my critical judgments. Such disagreements have continued to arise from time to time, but they have never threatened to damage the bond of friendship I soon felt with this remarkable man, and they have in any case been vastly outnumbered by those occasions when we have been passionately at one in our appreciation of this or that musical, artistic, or simply human experience. Now retired from regular practice, Gene was active as a psychotherapist when we first met. His wife, HARRIET, is an artist and photographer, a keen amateur pianist, and a wonderful cook, and they are both enthusiastic lovers of music and indeed of all the arts.

Dick Wernick and I had already instituted the practice of meeting for breakfast once a week when neither of us was away traveling; with Gene I began a corresponding weekly series of lunches, at which I would sit figuratively at his feet. From his seemingly effortless ability to cut through any kind of intellectual pretentiousness or political hogwash, I learned much that contributed to my understanding of myself, not to mention the rest of the world. He had grown up in Arkansas, where, he told us, the regular greeting among Jews was "Shalom, y'all!" He had not, however, had a bar-mitzvah, and his more recent desire to make some kind of public statement of at least ethnic if not profoundly religious solidarity led to his rectifying the omission on his seventieth birthday, as one of a class that ranged in age from about twenty to about seventy-five. My son, Sam, who had also become close friends with the Abromses and the Wernicks, asked me, "Does Gene really believe all that stuff?" to which I could only reply, "Sam, Gene has a mind of such subtlety and brilliance that, if I answered your question with either 'yes' or 'no,' I should be oversimplifying."

When we first became friends with the Abromses, they were not acquainted with the Wernicks. But when the subject of a possible vacation trip to Rome came up among us, Laura and I had the idea that a six-some consisting of the Abromses, the Wernicks, and the Jacobsons might work well. So it proved. We had a great time together, and by the time we moved away to Washington State in 2005 the Abromses and the Wernicks were firm friends—couples who have gone on to support each other through various health emergencies and who, at the time of writing in 2015, are living just two doors apart from each other in a pleasant retirement community in nearby Haverford.

Having been a regular record reviewer during my first US residency, and now, without an orchestra post, freed from any risk of conflicting interests, I was keen to find a suitable vehicle for CD reviews. The two magazines

I had written for earlier, *High Fidelity* and *Stereo Review*, were no longer going concerns. I had been approached by someone connected with *American Record Guide* with an invitation to join its reviewing panel, but its chief editor, Donald Vroon, had written about Riccardo Muti in such scurrilous terms that I did not feel I could appear in his pages.

Instead, since several critics I admired were writing for *Fanfare* magazine, I sent a message to Joel Flegler, its founder and editor, to ask whether he might be interested in adding me to his reviewing list. Very soon the telephone rang: "Mr. Jacobson, do you have any idea how much we pay our reviewers?" Joel asked me. The sum in question was derisory, but, as I have said before, music criticism is not a profession one adopts in order to make a fortune. We quickly reached agreement, and I began a highly satisfying association with the magazine, as reviewer and contributing editor, that was to last nearly a decade. When I resigned in 2005, it was only because reviewing CDs of the classical repertoire, often with literally dozens of existing versions to compare a new one with, was so time-consuming as to squeeze all other activities into an unacceptably exiguous time-frame.

In the meantime, my association with the magazine had provided the occasion for getting to know several outstanding performers I had not previously encountered, and I enjoyed the opportunity to interview some of them for publication. A prime example is the brilliant Turkish pianist Idil Biret. When Joel sent me her CD set containing all of Brahms's piano works for review, my first reaction was to think, "Well, this is going to have to be very good to match up to Julius Katchen's wonderful LP recordings." But I have always enjoyed opportunities to change my mind, and when I listened to Biret I quickly decided that many of her performances were even finer than Katchen's. The interview I subsequently did with her for *Fanfare* took place, after a typically excellent Belgian lunch, in her apartment on the gracious Avenue Louise in Brussels. It is a place filled with books and pictures. I felt at home as soon as I spotted, just inside the front door, an entire bookcase devoted to studies of Turner, my favorite painter, and an especial enthusiasm of Madame Biret and of her husband, Sefik Yüksel. In the course of that conversation, Idil revealed herself to be a person of restlessly inquiring mind, with tastes that range not only across the gamut of classical and romantic piano literature but as far as such modern composers as Ligeti, Boulez, and Castiglioni, all of whom feature in her extensive discography.

An equally stimulating interview was with Hélène Grimaud. French-born but living at the time of our conversation in upstate New York, she seemed to me to be quite extraordinarily sure of who she was for a person still in her early thirties. Her repertoire is admittedly less inclusive at the contemporary end than Biret's, but our discussion about *her* Brahms recordings showed how deeply she had thought about the Austro-German classics. I confessed to disliking her recording of the First Piano Concerto with Kurt Sanderling on account of the extremely slow tempo of the first movement, though the gnarled intensity of her playing carried a conviction of its own, but she defended her choice of tempo stoutly, declaring, "That's what I've always loved about Brahms—slow is never really slow and fast is never really fast either; there's always a sort of pulsation that's very close to the ideal heartbeat."

Other superb pianists whose quality I first became aware of through my *Fanfare* work, and whom in response I interviewed, were Eric Le Van, an American who reversed Grimaud's trajectory by living for a while in France, and who has made some masterly recordings of Brahms and Liszt; Russell Sherman, whose profoundly humane book of aphorisms, *Piano Pieces*, should be required reading for all aspiring musicians, not only pianists; Sergey Schepkin, who came to the United States to study with Sherman, and whose recordings of Bach in particular seem to me unrivaled for their blend of stylish insight, imagination, and virtuosity; and the Argentine-born Daniel Levy, whose unfailingly sensitive and probing recordings of a wide variety of repertoire make me eager to hear him in live performance, an eagerness thus far unsatisfied on account of his absence from the American concert circuit: concert presenters please note.

As for reviewing live performances in those days, the local newspaper of record, *The Philadelphia Inquirer*, already had two critics on its payroll, so there was no opening for me there (though I did review a few books for the paper). I reviewed occasionally for some local free papers, most notably the *Welcomat*, founded and edited by the talented and industrious Dan Rottenberg, who more recently, in keeping with changing times and technologies, has transformed it into the online *Broad Street Review*. But it was when I noticed that "Seen and Heard," the live-review section of the London-based online MusicWeb International, founded in 1999, ran only occasional reviews of Philadelphia performances that I saw my best avenue opening up. If *Fanfare*'s fees were derisory, MusicWeb's are nonexistent. My fellow-reviewers and I write, you might say, just for the glory. More seriously, it provides an excellent way to keep up with musical life: there is something infinitely satisfying about attending a concert on Thursday and having a review—without any restrictions on length—appear all over the world by the weekend. So I have been contributing frequently to "Seen and Heard," enjoying online collaboration and occasional meetings with excellent editors (Bill Kenny, Bruce Hodges, and Stan Metzger), first in Philadelphia, then in Seattle, and now again in Philadelphia, for fifteen years.

Another association that developed soon after our return to the city was with the ensemble founded by Marc Mostovoy in 1964 as the Concerto Soloists and renamed the Chamber Orchestra of Philadelphia in 2000, when it was also selected as one of the resident companies in the new Kimmel Center for the Performing Arts. My original contact with the organization was as one of the judges at the orchestra's annual young performers' competitions. But our collaboration soon became closer: I wrote the orchestra's program notes from 2001 to 2014, as well as giving preconcert talks until we left town in 2005.

In 2004, Marc magnanimously took a step back from his leadership position, and IGNAT SOLZHENITSYN (son of Aleksandr), who had been nurturing his relationship with the orchestra as, in turn, assistant conductor, associate conductor, and principal conductor, was appointed music director. This I found to be a really exciting development, for Ignat (b. 1972), ranks in my opinion as one of the finest conductors and pianists now before the public.

I had already been profoundly impressed by a performance of Schubert's last piano sonata (D960, in B-flat) that Ignat had given as a student at the Curtis Institute still in his early twenties. There were revelations here that surpassed almost any I had experienced in that masterpiece before, notably the way he made total dramatic sense of the positively frightening first-time measures at the end of the first-movement exposition, and the subsequent lightening of mood when, in the repeat, one fears that the explosion may come again—and it doesn't. (Alfred Brendel once told me that he couldn't observe the repeat in this movement, because he found the first-time measures stylistically incompatible with the rest of the movement—but surely we can trust Schubert to have been aware of the sore-thumb aspect of the passage, and to have written it with the full intention of shocking the listener.)

In nearly two decades since then, Ignat's prowess as a pianist has continued to grow, while he has demonstrated equal gifts as a conductor. He is, indeed, one of the few conductors of whom I can say that, whenever I have questioned one of his interpretative decisions on stylistic grounds, his response always shows that he knows more about the matter in question than I do. Laura and I have cherished our friendship with Ignat and his wife Carolyn, and I have continued to enjoy consulting with him on artistic questions. And in 2003 I had the pleasure of performing Schoenberg's *Ode to Napoleon Buonaparte* with Mikhail Yanovitsky as the fierily exciting pianist, and with Ignat and his players providing perhaps the best orchestral support I had ever received in several performances of the work.

When JoAnn Falletta came to Philadelphia for a guest appearance conducting the Chamber Orchestra, the guest conductor of the Philadelphia Orchestra in the same week happened to be Marin Alsop. I found Falletta to be a highly talented conductor and a delightful person: a few years later she gave a performance of Ravel's *La Valse* with the Seattle Symphony that set both the orchestra and its audience alight with excitement.) With Alsop, sadly, the experience was far less enjoyable. Though she is an expert champion of such contemporary composers as John Adams, I have yet to hear her give a performance of the classical repertoire that really convinces me.

My encounters with the Philadelphia Orchestra, as an outsider this second time around, were mostly much happier. Among the happiest—if that is the right word for so mentally excoriating an experience—was a performance of Shostakovich's Sixth Symphony conducted by Yakov Kreizberg that threw new and glaring light on Russian humor in the face of political insanity.

When I started—not long ago, to my shame—reading Aleksandr Solzhenitsyn's *Gulag Archipelago*, I found myself understanding this extraordinary symphony better than ever before. The first surprise when you start reading *Gulag*, rather as with Proust, is how downright funny it is. Such gallows humor is evidently the Russian way of coping with hell. That is the way the precipitous scherzo and uproariously circussy finale with which Shostakovich balances the weight of his vast opening slow movement must surely be heard, and that is the way Kreizberg and the orchestra presented its violent contrasts and sudden shifts of mood.

I had first encountered Kreizberg (the brother, incidentally, of another well-known Russian conductor, Semyon Bychkov) when Jonathan Sternberg and I traveled to Wilmington in Delaware to hear him give a performance of Rachmaninoff's Second Symphony with the Bournemouth Symphony Orchestra that challenged comparison with anything I had ever heard the Philadelphians—Rachmaninoff's favorite orchestra—achieve with his music. Yakov and I became friends at once: it was always a pleasure to pick up the telephone and hear his gloriously resonant Russian voice ask, "How is my favorite carnivore?" His death in 2011, aged only fifty-one, from a long but not publicly identified illness, was a grievous blow.

On one occasion, when I was giving a preconcert talk for a program Yakov was to conduct with the Philadelphia Orchestra, he told me when I went backstage to greet him that I had missed a remarkable treat. His soloist that evening was a German violinist still in her teens, Julia Fischer, and through the wall between their respective dressing rooms he had heard her preparing for her performance by playing, not the violin, but the piano, on which her exploration of Bach's *Wohltemperierte Klavier* had apparently been of veritable concert standard.

I still haven't heard her play the piano, but Julia Fischer has continued to impress me as ranking with Leonidas Kavakos and James Ehnes among the very finest of today's many gifted violinists. Kavakos's performance of my favorite Mozart violin concerto, no. 3 in G major (K. 216), was another stand-out Philadelphia Orchestra performance, as was Christoph Eschenbach's presentation of the finest new orchestral work I had encountered in several years, Esa-Pekka Salonen's *Insomnia*. Marta Argerich, too, a pianist I had previously found merely brilliant rather than profound, gave a performance of Beethoven's First Piano Concerto with Charles Dutoit that had me rapidly revising that judgment.

But in 2005 at least, the story of the year had to be Riccardo Muti's return, on February 13, to the Philadelphia Orchestra podium. I think of this as an "event" rather than just a "performance" for some weighty reasons. To be sure, the performance itself was vividly rewarding, from the brilliant opening with Rossini's *Guglielmo Tell* overture, by way of Barbara Frittoli's spine-tingling recreation of all the drama and pathos of a group of Verdi and Puccini arias, to Muti's authoritative realization of every facet to be found in the Brahms Second Symphony. But the former music director's return was significant in several ways. It was, to begin with, his first appearance in Verizon Hall, for whose construction his advocacy in the 1980s and '90s had laid much of the groundwork. Then, it marked a moment of healing in his relationship with the orchestra, a relationship that (largely owing to some questionable decision-making by a former member of the administration) had suffered some deterioration in the years after his resignation. It was the players themselves who had extended the invitation for this benefit concert, at which they, as well as the conductor and soloist, performed without fee. With a sizeable segment of the Philadelphia public, Muti's standing had never been in doubt. It was evidenced by the extraordinary warmth of feeling that could be felt throughout that evening, which culminated—after a graceful speech in which Muti proclaimed his affection for the orchestra and the city—in a typically zestful and passionate performance of the *Forza del destino* overture by way of encore.

It is not by accident that the name of Muti's immediate successor cannot be found in the foregoing list of notable performances. Wolfgang Sawallisch was a talented and technically accomplished musician, and he had the potential to thrill. I'll never forget a performance he gave of the Brahms Fourth Symphony at his London debut, well over forty years ago, that had me sitting on the edge of my seat. But he realized that potential somewhat rarely, and I found little evidence of it between my return to Philadelphia in 1996 and his departure from the music directorship seven years later.

For one thing, I do not think I ever heard the orchestra produce a real pianissimo under his baton. (One young composer, Kevin Beavers, who won a competition and consequently had a piece premiered by Sawallisch, replied, when I asked him whether there surely ought to have been some pianissimo moments in the performance, "Oh, the maestro doesn't like that sort of thing.") Then, the very next week, a guest conductor would come in and would secure the most delicate pianissimo without apparent effort.

Sawallisch's most memorable achievements during those years, and even previously, when I had been still on the orchestra's staff, may well have come at the piano rather than on the podium. He took part in a superb performance of Strauss's early Piano Quartet at one of the orchestra's chamber concerts around 1990, and in the early 2000s collaborated with Thomas Hampson in a no less masterly account of Schubert's *Winterreise*. It's strange how often the piano-playing of some eminent conductors seems to have surpassed the quality of their actual conducting. George Szell demonstrated much more sensitivity at the keyboard than was apparent in many of his orchestral performances, and the recordings of Brahms and Beethoven violin sonatas that he made with Georg Kulenkampff back in 1947 similarly rank among his finest artistic achievements.

Aside from the concerts of the Philadelphia Orchestra and the Chamber Orchestra of Philadelphia, there was a fair amount of good opera to be heard and seen. As used to be the case in New York and still is in Chicago, there had been two main opera companies in the city during the 1980s, but the smaller of them, the Pennsylvania Opera Theater, had closed down in 1993.

Though it had made a useful contribution to the city's operatic life by programming some relatively rare works, the Pennsylvania Opera Theater productions I saw of the core repertoire were often artistically disastrous. A *Rigoletto* with a Duke of Mantua dressed in a long bathrobe upset the moral balance of the story—the black tenor in the role looked so amiable and cuddly that you had to root for him; and company founder and conductor Barbara Silverstein's graceless and unidiomatic English translation did not help. Worse still was her *Don Giovanni*, which sent Laura and me fleeing from the theater after the very first scene. While Leporello sang his “Notte e giorno faticar,” we were treated, courtesy of a very translucent scrim, to the plain sight of Giovanni and Donna Anna in vigorous and clearly consensual intercourse, so that the whole ambiguity of a plot in which you are never quite sure whether he had actually brought his sexual pursuit of her to a successful conclusion was destroyed.

This was not to the first time we walked out of an opera production. When Pierre Audi directed *Così fan tutte* at the Netherlands Opera in the early 1990s, the overture was played not before a curtain but before an open stage. This is a far-too-common practice among today’s opera directors, for it removes that wonderful feeling of sitting in a darkened theater before the curtain goes up and thinking about what might happen when it does. In the case of this *Così*, apart from all the other distractions that were going on, the front of the stage was dominated by a chaise longue with a naked woman resting languorously on it. Now, I don’t think anyone likes to look at a naked woman more than I do, but there is a time and place for everything, and this was not it. Again, we fled.

Meanwhile, the Opera Company of Philadelphia continued to offer largely traditional productions of mostly traditional repertoire under the leadership of its then artistic director, Robert B. Driver. For the most part, I found the company’s work enjoyable, though here too there were sidesteps into “innovative stagings” (a phrase to strike fear into the heart of a relative purist like me), such as another regrettable *Così fan tutte*, this one with its action shifted to a seaside café so that the essential intimacy of the action was transformed into an entirely inappropriate public spectacle.

On the whole, I felt that Driver, though he did put on a fetching *Italiana in Algeri* in his own staging, was a rather less creative head of the company than general manager Margaret Anne Everitt had been in the 1980s. Yet again, it is a *Così* production she offered that in retrospect supplies perspective. Directed by Gray Veredon, it was played on Roy Lichtenstein-esque sets in a pop-art vein—perfectly acceptable, since, unlike *Le nozze di Figaro*, with its implication of a *droit du seigneur*, and *Don Giovanni*, with equally indispensable trappings of feudal social organization, *Così* is free from anything much in the way of corresponding social baggage. And I loved the way Veredon solved at a stroke the vexed problem of supertitles—are they distracting, or are they an invaluable aid to communication?—by putting just one sentence per aria on a small screen, thus giving the audience the gist of what was being sung without adding yet another (and inevitably conflicting) tempo to the already complex sound-and-vision combination inseparable from opera. Veredon’s other operatic successes in Philadelphia included a *Rusalka* and a Britten *Death in Venice* that both profited from his experience as a former choreographer by their richly imaginative exploitation of stage movement.

Back in the concert world, the Philadelphia Chamber Music Society was still presenting a cornucopia of high-quality chamber ensembles and soloists from around the world under the artistic leadership of its founder, Anthony Checchia, and the skillful management of Philip Maneval, a gifted composer who was admirably sparing in putting his own works forward for performance. By 2014, with long-time staff member Miles Cohen recently promoted to the post of artistic director, PCMS's steadily expanding season had reached the very healthy schedule of sixty-five performances.

The British tenor IAN BOSTRIDGE's local debut with pianist Julius Drake was perhaps the most deeply moving of all the PCMS performances I attended. His *Erlkönig* in particular—the same Schubert song whose harrowing effect on URSULA Sternberg was noted above—had such an extraordinary emotional intensity that I remarked to Laura during the intermission, "I don't know if I want to meet him—he's terrifying!," even though I had previously been eager to meet this man who had been a doctoral student at Corpus Christi, the same Oxford college I had attended. Fortunately, I plucked up my courage, and we went off to dinner with Ian and Julius, and Anthony and Philip, at a restaurant in nearby Chinatown, where I found Ian to be a very different person off the stage—as sensitive as is his singing, certainly, but also personally warm, responsive, and amazingly intelligent. (I have actually tried to read the doctoral thesis on the subject of witchcraft that he wrote at Oxford, but found that I was not clever enough to understand its philosophical complexities.)

During the intermission at one PCMS concert, I was approached by PARK DILKS, whom I had met in the 1980s when he was the lawyer for the Philadelphia Orchestra in its employment contract negotiations. He told me about his involvement with the Liberty Fund, an organization founded and generously endowed in the will of Pierre Goodrich (an Indianapolis businessman of inquiring mind), that was mounting colloquia on various philosophical and political subjects centering on liberty and had now decided to include opera among its objects of study. Despite George Bernard Shaw's characterization of an operatic duet as a piece in which "the tenor and the soprano repeatedly call attention to the fact that at last they meet again," there are, after all, relatively few operas of any stature that do not raise important questions about human relations, social organization, political oppression, philosophical beliefs, or indeed personal liberty. Would I be interested, he asked me, in taking part in discussions of this kind?

Over the next few years I participated in perhaps a dozen such colloquia, a few of them on nonmusical subjects, and gained enormously from them both in terms of the often brilliant fellow-participants I met and in the development of my own thinking on the works involved. The format of the colloquia was unusual and, I think, designed with great skill. There would normally be about a dozen discussants at each meeting, along with the organizer of the colloquium in question, a representative of the Fund, and a discussion leader. Since there was inevitably a limit to how much we could discuss the music in detail, the focus, as often with interdisciplinary discussions of opera, was heavily on the libretto, with some side-excursions into matters of casting and staging. (At the first colloquium I attended, on Poulenc's *Dialogues des Carmélites*, in Santa Fe, I was delighted to find two fellow-graduates of Corpus Christi College: Todd Breyfogle, who was the Fund representative, and Gareth Moore, who had become the head of the Dominican Order in Belgium.)

Usually, having digested in advance a recording and a specially assembled collection of readings often two hundred pages or more in length, we would assemble on a Wednesday evening, meet for discussion on Thursday, see the opera being studied on Thursday evening, continue discussions on Friday, and disperse on Saturday. We sat around an open square of tables. No public was present, and, aside from a privately circulated report by the colloquium organizer, no proceedings were afterward published—we simply exchanged ideas. The great thing was that the participants were not drawn only from musical and operatic circles but frequently included teachers of various subjects, lawyers, political philosophers, editors, and the like, whose contributions added immeasurably to the breadth of the insights we all gained. I seem to remember that, in addition to expenses, we were each paid $850 for our participation, which amused Laura immensely—"They pay you $850 just to talk!"

Obviously for the success of the enterprise much depended on the skill of the discussion leader. Most of the leaders I encountered were excellent, but my favorite, who officiated at perhaps half of the colloquia I attended, was Stephen Erickson, professor of philosophy and humanities at Pomona College in California. He was at once witty and profound in his marshaling of the discussion, and he had a positively uncanny ability to spot at once when someone wanted to speak. In his introduction to the proceedings, he would say, "If you find that I have said something stupid in the course of discussion, it will have been said simply to stimulate thought. If on the other hand I say something profound and illuminating, then of course I meant it." Steve's Dutch wife, Pauline, also brought a sharply focused mind to bear on the subjects in hand. On one occasion, invited to a colloquium on a nonoperatic musical subject, Bach's Mass in B Minor, I suggested that perhaps as an agnostic I might be an inappropriate participant, but I was assured that Pauline and I would fulfil a very useful function as two nonbelievers by sitting on opposite sides of the table and providing the resolutely secular element in the discussion.

Having attended several colloquia, I was duly acknowledged as qualified to lead one of my own. I chose as my subject "Feudal Power and Social Change in the Opera *Figaro's Wedding*," and we scheduled the colloquium to coincide with a Metropolitan Opera production. The panel I invited to talk about it included singers, a pianist, a psychiatrist, a university teacher, a composer, a critic, and two lawyers (the last three of whom—Michael Steinberg, Joseph Hennessy, and Dilks himself—have since died and are sorely missed). I ended with the consciousness that I now understood much more than I had before about my favorite work of art, which I had thought I knew so well.

I attended a few more colloquia after that, including two in Buenos Aires, one devoted to *Don Giovanni* and the other to the films of John Ford, and fell in love with the city and its people. Unfortunately, the *Don Giovanni* production was delayed through industrial action, so that the only opera we could actually see at the Teatro Colón was *Il trovatore*. Quick work by the organizer brought some more-than-adequate recorded visual resources into the meeting room. With their help, we were able to consider details of staging during our actual discussions. Soon after my second Buenos Aires visit, which coincided with a spectacular collapse of the Argentine economy, worldwide financial problems led to a decrease in the number of colloquia the foundation could present. I miss my connection with the group and its people, but count my years associated with it as vital enrichment of my cultural and intellectual life.

My own activities during this second Philadelphia residence also included serving on the board of the Theodore Presser Company, one of the most serious and prolific music publishing houses in the United States. Arnold Broido, who headed the company for thirty-eight years until his death in 2007 at the age of eighty-seven, was a witty and urbane gentleman who, like me, had worked at an earlier stage of his career for Boosey & Hawkes. His son Tom, who was in charge of composer promotion as I had been at B&H, was also a joy to work with—a bon vivant with a kitchen decorated entirely with wine labels, and possessed of an irrepressibly droll sense of humor.

Arnold had wanted to have me on the board ever since we had come to know each other in the 1980s, but at that time my position on the staff of the Philadelphia Orchestra would have constituted a conflict of interest. In 1996, there was initially another obstacle: the board was restricted by statute to a certain number of members, and that number had already been reached. I was touched when, hearing of the problem, a long-standing board member, the distinguished former Philadelphia Orchestra bassoonist Sol Schoenbach, resigned purely in order to make a place available for me.

Farther afield, I enjoyed one of the most exciting evenings of my life in 1996, performing the role of Noah in Stravinsky's *The Flood*, when Olly Knussen conducted it at the BBC's Promenade Concerts in London. Among the pleasures of the occasion was the extraordinarily talented roster of fellow-soloists I was working with. It featured the late-lamented tenor Robert Tear, a splendid baritone line-up including David Wilson-Johnson, whom I came to know better when he took part in a Chamber Orchestra of Philadelphia performance of Haydn's *Die Schöpfung*, and Sir Lennox Berkeley's son and fellow-composer Michael Berkeley as narrator.

My son, Sam, came to that concert, and so did Camilla Panufnik. As we left the Royal Albert Hall together after the performance and headed for a nearby Indian restaurant, Sam remarked, "I bet someone will recognize you." "Oh, I doubt it," I said. But in fact a young woman passed us on the way, turned around from a few steps in front of us, and did indeed say, "You were Noah!" In the circumstances, we couldn't help bursting out laughing. She must have thought us very rude.

We loved living in Philadelphia, perhaps even more than we had in the 1980s, and if our life in the city had been the only consideration, we should in all probably not have left. One particularly pleasing aspect was that it was a big enough, and lively enough, town for friends from abroad to show up frequently as visitors. Thus we enjoyed dinners with two friends from my Boosey & Hawkes days—Ilkka Kuusisto, former general manager of the Finnish National Opera, and Björn Simensen, director in turn of the Göteborg Symphony Orchestra and the Norwegian National Opera—when they came through Philadelphia.

Laura's job, however, which had started so promisingly, was becoming increasingly taxing in terms of workload, and she began to look for an alternative. It was as a result of this search that we found ourselves moving in 2005 to Bremerton, in Washington State, just across Puget Sound from the very city, Seattle, that she had declared she would never set foot in after the breakdown of my job negotiations with the orchestra there ten years earlier. We thought at the time that this would be our last move.

CHAPTER ELEVEN

WEST COAST YEARS

2005–14

While my previous contacts with Gerard Schwarz have already been described in the contexts of music publishing and orchestra administration, it was when Laura and I moved to the Seattle area in 2005 that he became a very central figure both in my professional activity as a critic and in our circle of friends.

I think it is no exaggeration to say that, as music director of the Seattle Symphony since 1985, Jerry had raised the orchestra from the status of what was widely regarded as a provincial ensemble to one deserving of national and indeed international respect. Certainly the enormous increase in the number of subscribers, and the orchestra's numerous CD recordings on a variety of labels, support that view, as did the reactions of friends of mine, knowledgeable Philadelphia Orchestra subscribers who came to visit and commented, after a Schwarz performance of Mahler's Seventh Symphony, "We had no idea you had such a great orchestra here." So quite apart from my personal admiration for Jerry as man and musician, I thought it regrettable that, by the time we became regular members of the audience, his tenure was mired in controversy, with factions in the orchestra—and also among the public—passionately taking sides for or against him. By December 2007, the *New York Times* was presenting, in an article by Daniel J. Wakin and James R. Oestreich headlined "In Seattle, a Fugue for Orchestra and Rancor," the picture of a Seattle Symphony that had "carried disharmony to new heights, lurching from crisis to crisis."

How far was this near-apocalyptic account justified? Not very far, in my view. It is true that statistics from an arguably slanted survey, made public in contravention of a confidentiality agreement signed by both the board's and the players' representatives, indicated a majority of players in favor of a change in artistic leadership. Given that Schwarz had by then been at the orchestra's helm for twenty-two years, it would be surprising if this had not been so. I have yet to encounter an orchestra, in the United States or Europe, that revealed, after a few years, no rumblings of discontent with "the Maestro."

This particular maestro, I was convinced, had more supporters in the Seattle Symphony than the *Times* article suggested. (It would surely have been a good idea for the writers to have talked to at least one member of the orchestra's board, but the article offered no indication that they did.) My belief, expressed in a published rebuttal, was, and remains, that there was a small number of malcontents, a perhaps equally small number of Schwarz supporters disgusted with that group's methods, and a large majority somewhere in the middle who had no strong feelings about the conflict and simply wanted to get on with their work—which is how it is with most orchestras in the world. This, several members of the orchestra and the board assured me, was an accurate view.

Still, there was clearly enough discontent to make Jerry's and the board's decision not to extend his contract when it expired in 2011 the right one. In the interim, I had the pleasure of attending, almost weekly, some wonderful performances by the orchestra both under Jerry's direction and under that of a mostly distinguished series of guest conductors. His programming, too, was amply stimulating, with its commitment to championing American composers of the present (and indeed of the past century and more), its dedication to performing their works not just once but repeatedly, and its penchant for devising mini-festivals of compelling stylistic illumination, such as a concentrated examination, under the title "Bridging the 48th Parallel," of Central European composers ranging from Bartók, Kodály, Janáček, Martinů, and Enescu to Ligeti, Kurtág, Lutosławski, and Panufnik.

On stage for a panel discussion before one of the concerts I met the celebrated glass artist Dale Chihuly, who has been closely associated with the Seattle Symphony. Two of his spectacular chandeliers hang in the outer lobby of Benaroya Hall, where they can be seen from the street. Chihuly created the designs for Schwarz's performance of *Duke Bluebeard's Castle*. They consisted of a monumental set of glass towers, behind which, on stage, the orchestra played. As the time came for each of the first six doors in Bluebeard's gloomy castle to be opened, these twenty-foot-high towers, blank on their front surfaces, revolved to reveal Chihuly's magically beautiful evocations of the vistas, from torture-chamber to lake of tears, that lay beyond them. Béla Balázs's libretto being a classic symbolist text, it was especially fitting and illuminating that Chihuly's tableaux were themselves symbolic rather than merely literal representations, right down to the seventh door, whose total blankness made manifest the oblivion to which Judith's rash insistence on delving into another person's soul had now doomed her. The full accouterments of a stage setting in the opera house can add a further dimension of theatrical complexity to the work, but in terms of the concert hall, this deeply considered and expertly realized vision seemed to me the last possible word in dramatic vividness and truth.

Another participant in the discussion was Pierre Loebel. Born in Bucharest to musical parents, Pierre had met their friend Enescu as a child. He told me how, one evening, when Enescu was playing for a group of guests, he had been banished upstairs so as not to cause any disturbance—but, sitting on the landing, he amused himself by rolling billiard balls down the stairs, which doubtless had a no less disruptive effect. A psychiatrist and a generous patron of the arts, he was at Oxford when I was, in the 1950s, as was his South-African-born wife, Felice, a teacher of English; it was only now that we first met, but we made up for lost time by spending several convivial evenings together in Seattle and at our house in Bremerton.

Of course, Schwarz wasn't equally convincing in every area of the repertoire: what conductor is? But as an interpreter of Mahler and Shostakovich he has few equals. It was particularly enlightening to compare the performance of Shostakovich's Eleventh Symphony that the visiting Kirov Orchestra gave in 2006 under Valery Gergiev's direction with the home team's performance under Schwarz. Only a critic endowed with a more than ordinary degree of curmudgeonliness could have called Gergiev's performance a bad one. It was a good performance. There were even moments of real excellence, such as a sequence of bloodcurdling orchestral sonorities toward the end of the work's roughly one-hour duration. There was some superbly atmospheric and musically percipient orchestral playing, especially from a contrabass section—all, I think, bowing underhand in the German fashion—that commanded an exceptionally rich and strong sound. For his part, Gergiev left no doubt of his emotional commitment to his late compatriot's searingly impassioned musico-political statement. It was all very thrilling, and some of the quieter moments, too, had real eloquence. But even the fiercest tearaway rhythms in the fast movements emerged without true propulsive vitality. The effect was that of a well-drilled machine, not a genuine breathing organism. By contrast, Schwarz's performances, both back in the 1990s and again in 2013, ranked among the greatest realizations of the work I have ever heard. The throat-catching intensity and depth of his interpretation were on a level far beyond anything to be experienced in Gergiev's.

I spoke of my admiration of Schwarz "as man and musician." Among the factors that contributed to the human side of that pairing were the warmth and shared sympathies that relations among Jerry, his wife, Jody, and their children, Gabriella and Julian, seemed to demonstrate. Julian, still in his early twenties at the time of writing, is also a musician of remarkable gifts. I love going out on critical limbs, as I noted in chapter 4, recalling that I had adduced such comparable talents as Nikisch, Weingartner, and Furtwängler in evaluating the still young Daniel Barenboim's conducting; and when I heard Julian Schwarz, barely past his sixteenth birthday, give his first full concerto performance with orchestra (of Haydn's Cello Concerto in C), I declared that he was "destined to rank among the major cellists of the twenty-first century." Again, as in the case of Barenboim, subsequent experience has in no degree led me to revise my opinion.

Probably because of his close association with Gerard Schwarz (his former colleague in the brass section of the New York Philharmonic, who had been responsible for his 1996 appointment with the Seattle Symphony), the orchestra's principal horn, John Cerminaro, was also a controversial figure among his fellow players. That is not to deny that John, an uncompromising perfectionist, was fully capable of stirring up antagonism on his own account. But as Bruce Bailey, a cellist in the orchestra, put it in explaining to me some of his colleagues' feelings about John in 2011 (the year Cerminaro's contract was allowed to lapse without renewal): "It's quite simple: he's great, and the rest of us aren't."

Long before then, I had become a devoted admirer and friend of John's—but how differently our relationship had begun! My first encounter with him as a concerto soloist had come during my period of CD reviewing for *Fanfare* magazine. I was sent a disc titled "Cerminaro Plays Mozart," in which he was partnered by the Seattle Symphony under Schwarz's direction. I wrote what I thought was a reasonable and balanced review, the essential conclusion of which was that "John Cerminaro may well be a great player . . . but here he sounds like a sensitive and accomplished musician performing at less than his best."

John's vitriolic response, characterizing my review as "scathing," and accusing me of having had some "personal axe to grind" with him, led to one of those ongoing exchanges of correspondence that often enliven *Fanfare*'s pages. In the course of it I assured him that I had not "not previously encountered either his person or, except during his career with the New York Philharmonic, his playing, for which in that orchestral context I had nothing but admiration."

After a couple of further salvos, the controversy, such as it was, quietly dropped out of sight. But then—act 2 of the story—I happened to meet two people from whom I learned more about the obviously gifted but waspish Cerminaro. Robert Elias came to town as executive director of the Chamber Orchestra of Philadelphia, having previously held the corresponding position with the Los Angeles Chamber Orchestra. At my first meeting with him, I discovered that he was married to a horn-player I admired greatly: Robin Graham, who, at the ISCM Festival I had attended in Aarhus, Denmark, in 1983, had played the Ligeti Horn Trio so brilliantly that after the performance the hallway was crowded with composers eager to write works for her. (Bob told me that unfortunately, owing to a lip problem of the kind that can easily afflict a horn-player, she was no longer performing.)

Laura and I invited Bob and Robin to dinner, and, she being a horn-player, the subject came round through various byways to the Cerminaro disc. As I described to them the brouhaha that my review had engendered, our guests exchanged smiling glances; "That's exactly the way John would react," Robin said. "Oh, do you know him?" I asked her. Not only were they indeed acquainted: an ex-pupil of John's, she had also been his second wife.

Act 3 brought, after we had moved to Seattle, a highly satisfactory peripeteia. I found myself reviewing, week by week, performances in which the Seattle Symphony's horn section, led by John, consistently shone. I began to think that it was the best—the most musical, and the most reliable—orchestral horn section in the country, and John's playing, in this orchestral context, was every bit as beautiful as I had found it in New York in the 1970s. He belongs on the poetic end of the gamut of horn-players, deploying a delicacy of tone and a subtlety of line quite different from the instrument's brassier and more extrovert exponents.

I have no patience with those of my colleagues who make up their minds about this or that musician and never alter their views in the light of subsequent experience. One of my greatest pleasures in the craft of criticism is the opportunity it occasionally offers to change my mind in a positive direction about some performer—or some composer—I have previously been unenthusiastic about. It has happened to me with composers, through the advocacy of outstanding interpreters such as Ivan Moravec is of Chopin and Santiago Rodriguez is of Rachmaninoff. Among conductors, the clearest example of such a shift on my part was István Kertész, whom I discovered, after several concerts that I had found mediocre, to be the superb musician everyone else seemed to find him: he finally gave a Beethoven performance that was enthralling, after which I experienced several more that were equally fine, along with a couple that reawakened my earlier lack of response, so I concluded that he was a great but uneven musician and I had simply been unlucky on my first few hearings.

Likewise, in Seattle, I derived pleasure as well as a certain amusement from writing rave notices about this man who hated my guts. Eventually Jerry, observing all this, said to me, "Bernard, you and John really have to meet." We did so, and we have enjoyed a most cordial friendship ever since. When Charlotte, his third wife, sent me a private CD she had assembled of John's live performances, including one of a Mozart horn concerto, I ventured to write him a note pointing out a passage that was beautifully played in this performance, but had included one slightly out-of-tune note on the commercial disc I had originally reviewed. He wrote back and told me I was right.

Incidentally, it was again through Ivan Moravec (albeit indirectly) that I became acquainted with the work of a writer and broadcaster with whom I was to enjoy a most rewarding collaboration. Jim Svejda is the author of two books evaluating and commenting on classical music recordings, and I first felt we were on the same wavelength when I read his exceptionally perceptive estimation of Moravec's Debussy and Chopin as without peer.

We didn't meet for a long time. But then, out of the blue, Jim got in touch with me, having read a note I had written to accompany a newly issued set of Giulini recordings. He told me that he did the evening program on KUSC, the Los Angeles classical radio station, and had long wanted to have me as a guest on the program. The format he described to me was alluring: each program he did consisted of about four hours of music interspersed with an hour of talk.

The prospect opened up for me the possibility of finally bringing to fruition an idea I had discussed years earlier with Norm Pellegrini, but that for some reason had never reached the radio waves: this was for a program along the lines of the BBC's long-running and popular series, *Desert Island Discs*, but greatly expanded. With Jim I now put together a list of perhaps thirty or forty pieces that had in one way or another been important elements in my musical development, beginning with my initial seduction by Haydn's Trumpet Concerto (recounted in chapter 1). "We can obviously play some Moravec," Jim said, but he encouraged me to include as many as I wanted of my own performances as narrator, as well as a recording of the premiere of *Death of a Young Man*, the song-cycle Wilf Josephs and I had written together, saying "keep in mind this is a show about you!" But I was determined to include, besides such things as my discussion with Muti about Gluck's *Orfeo*, a broad selection from all my enthusiasms, including Panufnik, Gruber, Vaughan Williams, Elgar, Strauss, Handel, and other preclassical masters like Byrd, Dowland, and Campion, and performers I particularly admired and learned from such as Furtwängler, Hans Hotter, Jessye Norman, Julius Patzak, and of course the indispensable Moravec.

Reducing the list to a length commensurate with the design of the program, we then arranged with Sean MacLean, the charismatic announcer at KING FM in Seattle, for me to have access to a studio and his technical help, and duly recorded my spoken sections through a direct ISDN link to Los Angeles. It was especially gratifying, after the program was broadcast, to get phone calls from people I had been out of touch with for years who lived in the Los Angeles area, including Jac Holzman's brother Keith, who reappeared from my Nonesuch days.

When we moved to the Seattle area, one of the things Laura and I were looking forward to was being close to my former Boosey & Hawkes colleague Paul Meecham, who was executive director of the Seattle Symphony at the time. Paul and his wife, another Laura, invited us to dinner on the last days of my Laura's job interviews. They put a magnificent piece of wild Yukon salmon on the grill, and having tasted our first mouthful we agreed that we would not be ordering salmon anywhere else in the States after that experience—there would be simply no point.

Paul and his Laura, though, were soon on the move back to the East Coast, where he was offered the post of president and CEO of the Baltimore Symphony Orchestra. In 2011, after a couple of interim appointments, he was succeeded in the top Seattle job by another Englishman, Simon Woods, formerly a record producer for EMI, who had been in charge of artistic planning with the Philadelphia Orchestra when we lived in the city in the 1990s. Meanwhile, whether the interpretation offered above of Gerard Schwarz's situation at the Seattle Symphony was accurate or not, it was clear that his tenure as music director was coming to a natural endpoint. When it came, he had served for twenty-six years, which is as long as any conductor in these days of global mobility can expect to enjoy a successful relationship with an orchestra. He stepped down in 2011, to be succeeded in the 2011–12 season by Ludovic Morlot.

The search for a new music director had taken place against a background of visits by a number of excellent guest conductors. There were several among them whom I considered worthy potential successors to Jerry. Lawrence Renes, who had led the Residentie Orkest in a particularly fine performance of Shostakovich's Tenth Symphony as part of his graduation from the Royal Conservatory in The Hague, made several impressive guest appearances in Seattle. ("Mr. Jacobson! What are you doing here?" he asked me when I went backstage to greet him after the first of them.) Others who seemed to me well qualified for the post included Asher Fisch, a profoundly musical Israeli already closely associated with the Seattle Opera; JoAnn Falletta; Iván Fischer, probably too far advanced in his career to be tempted by the job; Ignat Solzhenitsyn, young but experienced, with several guest engagements in Seattle already under his belt; Yakov Kreizberg, whose 2005 Shostakovich Sixth with the orchestra had been revelatory; and Ingo Metzmacher, whose appetite for new and stimulating repertoire might be an attraction. There was also the gifted Dane Thomas Dausgaard, who begins an appointment with the orchestra not as music director but as principal guest conductor as I write.

The committee's nod, however, went to Morlot. And though the young Frenchman—he celebrated his fortieth birthday this year—seemed a relatively untried figure, never having had the leadership of an orchestra of his own, and though there were aspects of the appointment that seemed to me administratively dubious, I am happy to say that in the three seasons I watched and listened to him at work he more than justified the choice. He is a superb communicator, with orchestra and public alike; he has made some impressive selections of repertoire and of guest conductors, including two eminent composer-conductors in Oliver Knussen and HK "Nali" Gruber, as well as the judicious Dausgaard appointment; and his 2013 performance of the Britten *War Requiem*, whose world premiere in Coventry Cathedral I heard on the radio all of fifty-one years earlier, was not only worthy of that memory, but brought more reader response than anything else I had reviewed during seven years in Seattle. Perhaps Morlot's Beethoven and Brahms both need a little more time to mature, but in every other area of the literature he has demonstrated remarkable strengths.

The Seattle Symphony gives its concerts in the 2,479-seat S. Mark Taper Foundation Auditorium, one of the two performance spaces in Benaroya Hall, which opened in 1998 after a campaign spearheaded by Schwarz and energized by a $15.8 million donation by Jack and Becky Benaroya. The building also houses the 536-seat Illsley Ball Nordstrom Recital Hall, where smaller-scale events are presented.

Among these are concerts by Music of Remembrance, an organization founded in that same year, 1998, "to ensure that the voices of musical witness be heard." Its founder and president, the pianist Mina Miller, carefully combines music by Holocaust-era composers with newly commissioned works that have a thematic connection to the period and its sufferings. I do not share the taste evidenced by some of her commissioning choices—it is after all not necessary that we should always agree—but a series of works commissioned from Jake Heggie and librettist Gene Scheer has been impressive, reaching a peak of eloquence in their third creation for the organization, a song cycle entitled *Farewell, Auschwitz*. Composer and librettist both know what they are doing: Heggie's distinctly individual way with texts could be called "bad word-setting," but if it is bad, there is method in its badness: the frequent midsentence and even midphrase hesitations and pauses force the listener to think about the words, and the recurrent lengthening of seemingly unimportant syllables paradoxically makes the words pregnant with meaning. The hesitations seem in any case appropriate to the subject of these works: if you are supping full with horrors, waiting a moment before taking the next mouthful is understandable, and the texts Scheer has given the composer are perfectly judged to mesh with his method.

Some Music of Remembrance concerts benefitted from the participation as conductors of Jerry Schwarz, and in due course Ludovic Morlot, and as pianist of Craig Sheppard, the prodigally gifted professor of piano at the University of Washington. Sheppard also gave regular cycles at the university's Meany Hall devoted to the music of such composers as Schubert, Brahms, and Debussy, and some of those performances have been released on CD. Meany Hall was also the scene of piano and chamber music series featuring such performers as Garrick Ohlsson and the Juilliard and Emerson Quartets. It was always a pleasure to attend these concerts in the midst of an unusually knowledgeable and dedicated audience. The music school's students, too, excelled in orchestral performances conducted by Jonathan Pasternack: with his young players, he fashioned impressive accounts of such challenging works as Mahler's Second Symphony and Nielsen's Fourth, and his thrilling realization of the Shostakovich Eleventh came close to emulating the Seattle Symphony performance under Gerard Schwarz that so signally outshone the visiting reading by Valery Gergiev and his Kirov forces.

Of no less value to the city's musical life were the concerts of the Seattle Chamber Music Society, founded in 1982 by the cellist Toby Saks, whom—small world again!—I had known back in New York in the 1960s, when she was a friend of my then girlfriend, Marilyn Dubow. In the last few seasons before her death in 2013, Toby had brought in the brilliant Canadian violinist James Ehnes as associate music director, before passing the sole position of music director to him in 2011. SCMS presents just two relatively short festivals a year, in summer and winter, with a variety of guests who are melded into ensembles for the occasion during more or less lengthy residences in the city.

Another chamber-music series in the area, the Olympic Music Festival, is held on a picturesque farm in Quilcene on the Olympic Peninsula, an hour and a half out of Seattle by car and cross-Puget Sound ferry. The festival is the brain-child of Alan Iglitzin, formerly assistant principal violist of the Philadelphia Orchestra and a founder-member of the Philadelphia String Quartet. He started the festival in 1984, after the quartet moved to Seattle as Quartet-in-Residence at the University of Washington. With the cooperation of his wife, Leigh Hearon, the festival's gracious president, and the only private investigator we have ever met (at least knowingly!), the eighty-three-year old Alan continued as executive and artistic director of the festival until 2014, when he passed the artistic leadership to the young American pianist Julio Elizalde, while continuing in his administrative role. Alan also plays in many of the concerts, and along with his fellow-performers provides unpretentious spoken introductions to the music, in addition to running the farm outside the festival season.

The festival currently offers eleven weekends of concerts each summer, with the same program on Saturday and Sunday afternoons, in a rustic barn of impressive proportions, seating about four hundred people on church pews and hay bales. Performers and audience are informally dressed, and the whole atmosphere is convivial and relaxed, with audience members often strolling onto the stage to chat with the musicians during intermission. Though most of them are less far advanced in their careers than the SCMS players, an ambitious roster of performers is on hand, from local luminaries like Seattle Symphony principal second violinist Elisa Barston to established and emerging musicians from farther afield, including pianists Paul Hersh, who teaches at San Francisco Conservatory, and his former pupil Julio Elizalde, and the performances are usually superb.

The musical rewards of OMF made it, over our last seven years in the Pacific Northwest, our favorite performing organization in the area. In particular, I have come to regard Paul Hersh, who plays the piano (and occasionally also the viola) on at least two or three programs each summer, as a toweringly great and absurdly underappreciated musician. He introduces the works he is about to play with a combination of insight and enthusiasm that is irresistible, and then plays them with a pearly and velvety touch rivaled by very few of his contemporaries. We also discovered over dinner after one concert (what did I say about a small world?) that many years ago Paul and I had the same girlfriend, Marilyn Dubow—though serially, I hasten to add, not simultaneously.

Beyond the qualities of the music-making, Leigh and Alan, who retains an undimmed passion for music and good living, and is as sharp as ever in his capacity for detecting falsity in a book or a person, have joined the ranks of our close friends. For almost every one of our last few West-Coast years, they came to Bremerton to share the goose I like to cook at Christmas.

Back in Seattle itself, another notable group is Pacific MusicWorks (at first briefly titled Pacific OperaWorks), founded in 2008 by conductor-lutenist STEPHEN STUBBS, who is also artistic codirector (with Paul O'Dette) of the Boston Early Music Festival. Born in 1951 in Seattle, Stubbs returned there in 2006 after thirty years of prominent involvement in the European early-music scene. He is the conductor of a number of outstanding Monteverdi recordings, including a DVD of *L'Orfeo* with the Netherlands Opera. With his wife, harpist Maxine Eilander, as managing director, Stubbs's organization has developed into as fine a presenter of early music, as well as a sprinkling of later works, as I have encountered anywhere in the world.

My first experience of Stubbs and his company came in 2009, with their inaugural presentation of Monteverdi's penultimate opera, *Il ritorno d'Ulisse*. Originally mounted eleven years earlier at La Monnaie in Brussels, and revived in Seattle for the first time with a new music director and a cast of American singers, this was a production with a difference. The Johannesburg-born artist William Kentridge had the idea of joining forces with his compatriots of the Handspring Puppet Company to create a production of the work that would combine living singers on stage with puppets.

Having read in advance that the weight of the puppets made them hard to hold for extended periods, so that the length of the opera would have to be cut down by something like half to about ninety minutes, I was prepared in advance to be underwhelmed, since this sounded like the tail wagging the dog. But, in the event, what happened on the Moore Theatre stage was so enchanting that the pluses totally outweighed any minuses. One has also to bear in mind that the notion of a "complete" version of this opera is in any case chimerical, given the sketchiness, and possible partial inauthenticity, of the sources.

In 2010, MusicWorks collaborated with the city's Early Music Guild in a presentation of vastly different character but at least equally extraordinary quality: Monteverdi's monumental Vespers of 1610. In accordance with prevailing ideas about the composer's intentions, the singing was entrusted not to choral forces but to a group of nine soloists, supported by correspondingly small instrumental forces. The wonderful acoustics of St. James Cathedral produced a majestic richness of tone that a large chorus could only have muddied. The result was the most inspiring, exalting, and downright ravishing performance of anything that I heard in my eight-plus years in Seattle.

Stravinsky objected to composers who, as he put it, took the opera house into the church. But the effect of such a mixing of genres or atmospheres in music of the romantic period pales in comparison with the shock Claudio Monteverdi must have administered to his contemporaries three centuries earlier with this masterpiece. What he did in the Vespers was to combine traditional techniques inherited from his Italian and Flemish predecessors with elements boldly lifted from secular music, including a prelude and other borrowings from his own opera *L'Orfeo*. By blending Renaissance counterpoint with cutting-edge Baroque theatrical rhetoric, he humanized the texts, making them into an unprecedented amalgam of religious fervor with fun, and the sheer freshness, indeed effrontery, of music and performance alike under Stubbs's direction electrified the audience.

Pacific MusicWorks's performance of Handel's oratorio *Esther*, too, was one of the outstanding events in the American Handel Festival that the dedicated musical animator and producer Marty Ronish succeeded in bringing to Seattle for the first time in 2011. The only trouble about this massive two-week immersion in his music was trying to think what I could do with myself when it was over. Beethoven—not one to gush—described Handel as "the master of us all—the greatest effects with the simplest means," adding, "to him I would bow the knee."

In most of the places I have had the good fortune to live in, musical life has essentially been structured rather like a three-legged stool: orchestra, chamber music, and opera. Seattle was no exception. As if all the rich concert life I have been describing was not enough, there was also an active operatic scene to witness.

First of all, Texas-born Speight Jenkins, who was general manager of Seattle Opera for thirty-one years before his retirement in 2014, had built the company into one with an enthusiastic base of public support, and also one with which singers love to come and perform. With an inexhaustible appetite for opera and indeed for work, Speight was routinely in attendance at every performance. He was almost always to be found before curtain-up greeting arriving audience members at the top of the main staircase leading to Marion Oliver McCaw Hall's auditorium; he was in attendance at every one of the rehearsals I had the opportunity to watch; and he led a discussion session with the audience after every performance. (I have to confess that this last was the only aspect of his work that I could not unreservedly admire: Speight does not suffer fools gladly, and the occasional silly question could sometimes provoke him into an acid response.)

From my personal point of view, the strong emphasis on Wagner that Speight had inherited from company founder Glynn Ross, and that he had enthusiastically reinforced, with regularly recurring *Ring* cycles, productions of all ten of the composer's major works, and the institution of a recurring International Wagner Competition for singers, was not something calculated to arouse my enthusiasm, since I can by no means be described as a Wagner enthusiast. But my appreciation has certainly increased through experiencing the company's work, and especially its last two presentations, in 2009 and 2013, of Stephen Wadsworth's naturalistic and supremely human *Ring* cycle, masterfully conducted in the latter year by Asher Fisch, and with a cast headed by Greer Grimsley as Wotan and Stephanie Blythe as an unusually sympathetic Fricka.

Speight has, moreover, displayed a welcome willingness to pardon my general lack of Wagnerian passion. And I was greatly touched when, on Melinda Bargreen's retirement as the music critic of the *Seattle Times*, he called to ask me whether I would mind his suggesting me to the paper as a possible freelance reviewer. When I said "But I don't always give you favorable reviews," he replied, "I'm not looking for favorable reviews—I'm looking for intelligent reviews." Speight's advocacy did indeed lead to several years of enjoyable writing for the *Seattle Times*. Pleasant as it is to have a world-wide sounding-board like "Seen and Heard" at my disposal, I also found it satisfying, especially when I was covering controversial aspects of Seattle musical politics, to have a local channel through which to project my opinions (and to get paid for doing so).

One activity largely lacking from Speight's tenure in Seattle was the commissioning of new operas. It was exciting, therefore, when he decided to commission a new work, to be premiered in 2010, from Daron Hagen, who, in his forties, already had nearly a dozen operas to his credit. I had known Daron in Philadelphia, but still I was astonished when we met for a preproduction interview and he greeted me by declaring that it was the first time we had met since . . . and he named a precise date in 1990, which I fear I have forgotten but which he never had. "Well, you see," he explained, "it was the day you called me from the Philadelphia Orchestra offices and told me that the orchestra was going to perform my Symphony no. 1. How could I ever forget that?"

Naturally enough, our friendship soon ripened after such a greeting. I found the opera itself, *Amelia*, with its libretto by Gardner McFall based on a story by Stephen Wadsworth and centered on a fictional treatment of the aviator Amelia Earhart, impressive and moving. Daron's music was at the same time approachable in idiom and strongly individual in inspiration. Especially inspired was the incorporation of the hymn known as "For those in peril on the sea," by the delightfully named John Bacchus Dykes, with "on the sea" neatly changed to "in the sky," and a simple shuffling of words in the previous line to restore the rhyme.

We stayed in touch after Daron left town, and not long afterward he invited me to narrate a performance of my old favorite work, Stravinsky's *Soldier's Tale*, in 2012 at the music festival and school he directed in Yakima, in rich wine country on the other side of the Cascade mountain range. The conductor was Lawrence Golan, the son of Joseph Golan, who had been principal second violin of the Chicago Symphony in my years with the *Chicago Daily News*, and violinist Denise Dillenbeck and her six instrumental colleagues made up an ensemble as musically gifted and as pleasant to work with as any in my experience with the piece.

With the charming and gentle Brooke Creswell, Lawrence's predecessor as music director of the Yakima Symphony and the man in administrative charge of the festival, Daron and I discussed the possibility of a return engagement for the following year, when they were keen to have me back for a performance of Walton's *Façade*. Sadly, the festival's funding evaporated, and its 2013 edition never happened.

Among the pleasures of attending Seattle Opera performances was their usually strong and convincing theatrical effect. Chris Alexander, an American director who lives in Germany, demonstrated an extraordinary breadth of style in productions ranging from searingly dramatic accounts of *Fidelio* and *Elektra*, and an imaginative and indeed magic *Flute*, to a delightfully zany *Italiana in Algeri*. One touch in Alexander's English-language production of *Die Fledermaus* brought the house down. The Rosalinde was that superb English dramatic soprano Jane Eaglen. When her maid, played by the svelte young American soprano Sarah Coburn, showed up at the famous party in clothes she had surreptitiously borrowed from her employer, Eaglen, whom it would be misleading to describe as sylph-like, exclaimed "She's wearing half my dress!" I understand she had come up with that line herself. What a trouper!

But the director whose work made at once the most copiously and surprisingly persuasive impact on my perceptions of opera was PETER KAZARAS, who was in artistic charge of Seattle Opera's Young Artists Program, directed several productions with it, and was also responsible for a number of the parent company's main-stage productions. I say "surprisingly" because I tend, pusillanimously, to be put off by advance statements to the effect that such-and-such a production will be rich in "innovative ideas," or that it will transfer the scene of the opera in question to some period and place far distant from what composer and librettist had in mind. You can imagine, then, with what trepidation I went to see a *L'Enfant et les sortilèges* staged on the platform of a subway station, or a *Midsummer Night's Dream* set in a classroom at a twentieth-century British boarding school.

Well, the amazing thing about Peter Kazaras was the way, no matter how shocked I might be in advance by such dislocations, the actual experience of seeing them on the stage almost always won me over. The man is a genius. The Verdi *Falstaff* he put on with the Young Artists Program and later expanded for the main stage, with its gradual gathering of cast members on an open stage in preparation for the beginning of the music, and its absurd yet brilliantly nonliteral representation of Herne's Oak in the final scene by a vertiginously piled-up collection of chairs, was the finest presentation of that great work I have ever seen.

Besides the Olympic Music Festival, our pleasures, musical and otherwise, were not all confined to Seattle itself. In Bremerton, I fulfilled a lifetime's ambition by becoming the restaurant critic for the local paper, the *Kitsap Sun* ("Kitsap" being not, as I first suspected, a corruption of "ketchup" but the name of a chief of the local Suquamish tribe). The proprietors and chefs of several restaurants also became friends, and we made several other excellent friends in the area.

We had read good things about the mayor of Bremerton, Cary Bozeman, so we took the opportunity, at an open auction for a charitable cause, to buy the chance of lunch with him. But when I called his assistant to fix a date, she told me that "the mayor would like to make it dinner." Over that meal, when I asked Cary whether he had made the change as a result of having read a piece I had contributed to the *Sun* about how Laura and I had moved to Bremerton and loved it, he replied, "You got that exactly right." The now ex-mayor and the warm-hearted Kerri, whom he married a few years later, were to be two of our closest friends for the rest of our time in their town, and their frequent invitations to Thanksgiving dinner and to their annual anniversary party are already much missed.

In addition to the Bozemans, the Iglitzins, of whom I have already written, and fellow dedicated eaters Tamara Gordy and Rick Chavez, our inner social circle in Bremerton also included Frank Carsey, a former scientist and now a gifted potter whose works—artistic, not scientific—we collected in some numbers and with whom I used to lunch almost weekly, and his British-born wife, Sue Digby, a geography teacher at the town's Olympic College. It was there, incidentally, that Laura and I compensated in our first year for the culture shock of having moved to an area where there were practically no Jews by attending a community Seder, over which Jeff Bernstein, one of the very few Jewish doctors at the hospital where she worked, presided. The event was catered by the students in the college's Culinary Arts department, and the food, while faithfully following all the dietary dictates inseparable from the tradition of the feast, was at least as good as any we could remember eating at a Seder table.

Only two or three hours to the north of Seattle lay Vancouver. We had heard that it was a fine city, and so, when Laura attended a conference there I went with her, and we stayed for an extra couple of days to do some serious eating. We fell in love with both the city and its people, and on the drive home I said, "We have to think of some way to keep going there." It was not more than a day or two after our return home that I picked up the phone and took a call from John Allison, the editor of *Opera* magazine in London. In addition to having written for the magazine years earlier, and having contributed an essay about Handel's *Theodora* to the program of the Glyndebourne Festival Opera, which he also edited, I had met John at a conference in Kraków in 2001 commemorating the tenth anniversary of Panufnik's death. While we were there, Camilla Panufnik and I, out with John and Andrzej Kosowski of the Polish music-publishing house PWM for a late-evening drink, made the discovery of Bison Brand vodka—the one with the blade of grass in the bottle—at, of all places, an Irish bar.

John was calling now to say, "I hear you're living in the Seattle area. How would you like to be our Pacific Northwest correspondent?" Thus, suddenly, Vancouver, as well as Victoria on Vancouver Island, became part of my reviewing area. We were to make several visits to both cities over the next few years. Surprisingly, for a city whose population numbers less than an eighth of Vancouver's six hundred thousand, I found that Victoria possessed an opera company at least the artistic equal of the one in the larger city. Timothy Vernon, a conductor who I think could have made a major career internationally, had instead dedicated himself unwaveringly to the company he founded as far back as 1979, and his work with it maintained a standard of consistent excellence, rising in a 2014 performance of Strauss's *Ariadne auf Naxos* to a level of orchestral enchantment that challenged comparison with any I have heard. Our visits have established warm friendships with Tim and with Patrick Corrigan, a company staff member since 2000 and its executive director since 2010.

Trips to Victoria have also brought a welcome revival of contact with the great bass-player GARY KARR and his partner and pianist HARMON LEWIS, both men of profound humanity, great charm, and keen humor, who have lived just outside the city for many years. Gary certainly needed his humor at one moment in the past. When the oboist John de Lancie was artistic director of the Curtis Institute of Music in Philadelphia between 1977 and 1985, he suggested to Gary that it was way past time for him to give a master class there. "I don't think the faculty would approve of that," Gary replied, since he plays the bass in German-bow style (bowing underhand), whereas the tradition in Philadelphia, both in the Philadelphia Orchestra and at Curtis, had long been exclusively overhand French-bowing. De Lancie exclaimed that, with someone of Gary's world-wide eminence, that would be no problem. "Well," said Gary, "you're welcome to try, but I have my doubts." A couple of weeks later, de Lancie called Gary and said, "I'm sorry—I'm afraid you were right."

My resumption of contact with Gary had actually come a short time before our move west. After a concert by the New York Philharmonic, Laura and I happened to discuss the fact that the orchestra's principal bass played, like Gary, German-bow. In the course of our drive back to Philadelphia, Laura noticed that I was driving, as usual, "underhand"—with my hands roughly at eight and four on the wheel. "You're driving German-wheel," she said, and I couldn't resist writing to Gary and telling him of this piece of sharp observation by my nonmusician wife.

We tried to have at least one meal with Gary and Harmon whenever we went to Victoria, and we also spent a memorable few hours with them when we took our visiting friends Guido and Marijke from Antwerp to see them, and to enjoy their playing in the private studio where they still make CDs together.

CHAPTER TWELVE

PHILADELPHIA, YET AGAIN

2014–?

When I first started work on this memoir, I fully expected it to conclude with the events recounted in chapter 11, "West Coast Years." Unexpectedly, however, Laura and I found ourselves in 2014 back in Philadelphia—in the same apartment building we had lived in when I was working for the Philadelphia Orchestra in the 1980s, and for a time with the same doorman, Dwight, still on the job, and as courteous and efficient as ever.

The reason for this last move was that, rather as had happened nine years earlier in Philadelphia, Laura's job in Bremerton became insupportable—her fifteen- and sixteen-hour working days were leaving us with scarcely any opportunity of leading a real life together—and she was offered a new job just outside Philadelphia. But also, while we loved the physical beauty of our surroundings in the Pacific Northwest and the remarkably friendly and laid-back attitude of many of its inhabitants, the realization that we really are big-city people made the move even more desirable.

Ironically, now that we have moved from a place where, to go anywhere or do anything, we had to get into a car, to the very heart of a city (with the concert hall, the opera house, and a wealth of excellent restaurants within a mere two blocks' distance), we are walking much more than we did in an area full of people dedicated to open-air pursuits. And though we miss good friends that we made in our eight years and a half in the Northwest, it is good to be renewing older personal and professional friendships on the East Coast, not to mention having my son, Sam, who is chef at a restaurant here, within easy social and gastronomic reach. Sadly, Harvey Wedeen died while I was writing this book, a few days short of his eighty-eighth birthday, but Helen is still a close neighbor, and now I can have my hair cut again by my former barber and valued friend Dino Taormina.

It happened that no one had taken over my Philadelphia berth on the reviewing panel of "Seen and Heard," so I stepped right back into that agreeable activity. I felt that this surely last change of place needed to be signaled as a stage in my career. But at the time of writing there are no major new contacts and no shifts in my relationships with old ones that demand description. So, though I cannot refrain from mentioning the pleasure I have already had in becoming acquainted with the exciting musicianship and winning personality of the Philadelphia Orchestra's current music director, Yannick Nézet-Séguin, I shall otherwise leave this final narrative chapter as a brief and hopefully to be extended "work in progress," and end the book with an Afterword addressing one or two substantial questions that may be of interest to readers.

AFTERWORD

This book is intended to be, above all, about other people, not about me. Nevertheless, the account I have presented of my working life among those other people will inevitably have raised some questions about how I have handled the responsibilities of the critical role. One such question concerns the position I have taken on the thorny issue of directorial methods in opera, adumbrated in chapter 4, with recurring references later in the book. The question of what critical principles I may have followed during more than five decades in the profession is another.

With regard to opera direction, and specifically to the vogue for what is called "Regietheater," the best way to amplify and clarify my views is, I think, to reproduce here two minimally edited reviews originally written for the "Seen and Heard" section of *MusicWeb International* (www.musicweb-international.com). The first, from 2008, takes a tough line on the depradations that one Chicago production inflicted on Mozart's *Don Giovanni*. The second, from 2013, will show, I hope, that I am not so hidebound in my opinions as to be unable to recognize valid directorial creativity when I see it.

* * *

Mozart: *Don Giovanni*. Chicago Opera Theater, soloists, cond. Jane Glover, dir. Diane Paulus, set designer Riccardo Hernandez, costume designer David Woolard, lighting designer Aaron Black. Harris Theater, Chicago, April 30, 2008.

For about the first twenty-four hours after witnessing this deplorable travesty inflicted on a great work of music theater, my head was spinning with recollections of its manifold absurdities. It was one of those productions of the sort justly and cogently lamented by Heather Mac Donald in her article "The Abduction of Opera," published in the summer 2007 issue of New York's *City Journal*, which I urge on your attention. To enumerate some of the more egregious pieces of nonsense:

The setting was a sleazy nightclub; Giovanni—to give him the honorific "Don" would be ridiculous—was represented as its owner; but when Anna called for help in the opening scene (having already been shown to us in enthusiastic sexual congress with her supposed attacker), who should turn out to be in attendance at the same establishment but her father, who emerged from presumably having it off in a back room with one of the many scantily clad females who gyrated around the stage all evening, endlessly drinking, and humping with any available male.

The same Anna, later in the proceedings, demurred from a too hasty tying of the marriage knot with Ottavio, anxious about what the world, as she put it, would say about such a step so soon after her father's death; but she had not taken the trouble to put on mourning for him. Yes, I know—as my wife told me when I came home—people probably don't wear mourning these days; but then the people that don't also don't worry about bourgeois opinion, and it was the combination of the two things that was absurd, and made the character unbelievable. Anna, incidentally, seemed to possess only one dress, and it was, to put it mildly, a garment unbecoming to a person of her bodily habitus.

Elvira, for her part, was sharply got up in high boots, short hair, and what looked like an array of leather gear, which in turn made *her* bourgeois concerns seem pretty fanciful. Giovanni was dressed and made up as an aging and distinctly inelegant roué, for whom even the most desperate Elvira, Anna, or Zerlina would not in a thousand years have raised her knees; in his contemporary rig-out, he nevertheless offered Anna the devoted service of his hand and his sword—score that for one more absurdity. (If you're going to change the period of the drama and the accouterments of the participants, at least you should have the courage to go the whole hog, changing words like "ferro" and substituting something appropriate.)

But these are all details, as was Leporello's description of the deceased Commendatore's marble-like white head, when all we saw was just a chap like the rest of us, recumbent on stage, and still dressed in his everyday (or perhaps I should say everynight) duds. It would be excessive if I were to recount all of the similar idiocies that littered the production. But what I realized after a day's reflection was that the *fundamental* absurdity of Diane Paulus's production was to transfer a drama that is all about morality and law and their flouting to a milieu where no morality or law exists, so that the idea of flouting them becomes meaningless.

Perhaps I shouldn't say that the world of this *Don Giovanni* contained no law. After all, when the surviving principals sang their closing ensemble about what happens to those who do evil, a bunch of personages representing the Chicago Police Department arrived, put up a crime-scene ribbon, and handcuffed everyone left on stage. I suppose the idea was to remind us that we are all guilty of *something*. But the supposed police would have done better to wait a few minutes longer, till the production team came on to take their bows, and arrest them instead.

The only idea that seemed to me a good one was to make the floozies we'd been watching turn, at Giovanni's downfall, into the tormentors who dragged him off to his fate; not a bad notion, but hardly enough to rescue the production from artistic disaster.

I felt deeply sorry for all the good singers and musicians who were being subjected to nothing less than an evening-long obscenity. The singing on the whole was excellent, with Krisztina Szabó's Elvira, Michael Colvin's Ottavio, and Lucas Harbour's Leporello probably the stand-outs, and the orchestra played well under the direction of that fine conductor Jane Glover. If I had been Ms. Glover, or any one of the singers, I should have walked out before sullying my baton or my voice and person with such shameful goings-on. As a member of the audience, I was indeed sorely tempted to walk out. But I have responsibilities as a critic. I had heard reports about the way general director Brian Dickie (formerly of Glyndebourne) had raised the standard of what used to be a respectable small-scale company, mounting traditional productions sung in English, and I wanted to assess progress for myself. In any case I was there also as a participant in a colloquium on the opera, so I had to stay. Call it work. But it felt more like torture. Please read Ms. Mac Donald's article: http://www.city-journal.org/html/17_3_urbanities-regietheater.html.

* * *

Antwerp Turns *Parsifal*'s Moral World Upside Down

Wagner, *Parsifal*. Soloists, Symphony Orchestra, Chorus, and Children's Chorus of the Flemish Opera, cond. Eliahu Inbal, dir. Tatjana Gürbaca. Opera House, Antwerp, April 3, 2013.

The interpretation of *Parsifal* expounded by the director, Tatjana Gürbaca, in the excellent program book of this fascinating Flemish Opera production is a vision not so much of the opera Wagner wrote as of the opera she wishes he had written. If he had indeed written that opera, it would surely have been a greater *Parsifal* than the one he did leave us.

In contradistinction to Wagner's fundamentally Christian conception, Gürbaca sees the knights of the Grail as a profoundly loveless brotherhood, its male dominance in urgent need of an infusion of the female principle that she perceives, rather wishfully, in Klingsor's realm. This, at least, seems to be her theory, and it is a view with considerable appeal to this non-Christian, non-macho, non-Wagnerite critic. But it is not until the third act that what she has actually put on stage gives perceptible reality to such a view. In act 1, the knights are a fairly inoffensive bunch. In act 2, Klingsor's lordship over his female crew hardly suggests even a distant approach to women's liberation. It is only in act 3, with the revoltingly callous and murderous attack on Amfortas that she has invented, that the director finally and decisively paints the knights in what she sees as their true colors.

I should explain that, having first seen *Parsifal* at the 1964 Bayreuth Festival and taken a strong instinctive dislike to the work, I had sedulously avoided any reacquaintance with it until this month, so I am not in a position to compare this Flemish Opera and Grand Theatre of Luxembourg coproduction with other ones. What I *can* say is that to my distinct surprise, while I still found the morbidity of the libretto's Christian symbolism repellent, the music blazingly beautiful only in short stretches, and some elements in Gürbaca's production questionable, I found this presentation in Antwerp's venerable and elegant Opera House a quite enthralling theatrical experience. And what impressed me no less was that the vocal and orchestral impact of the performance conducted by Eliahu Inbal in no way suffered against the remembered background of Hans Knappertsbusch's leadership, and the singing of a cast headed by no less than Jon Vickers, George London, and Christa Ludwig, all those forty-nine years ago.

In a cast without a single weak link, vocal honors should perhaps go first to the Gurnemanz, for that, along with Kundry, is the most demanding role, at least in terms of the requisite stamina. In the first act I thought Georg Zeppenfeld's delivery was a shade too unvaryingly loud, but the voice itself is gorgeous, and it took on subtler nuances as the evening went on, while his psychological identification with the character was unwavering. In his role debut as Parsifal, Zoran Todorovich was no less impressive, affable yet inwardly dignified of stage manner, firm and silver-toned of voice. Werner Van Mechelen made of Amfortas a suitably harrowed—and harrowing—figure, Susan Maclean's Kundry rose to all the varied dramatic and musical demands of the part, from seduction to rage, and Robert Bork sang and acted with style and conviction as Klingsor.

In acts 1 and 3, Gürbaca earned gratitude by allowing long stretches of the preludes to proceed with the curtain down, allowing us to revel in the orchestra's fine playing without distraction from any premature on-stage goings-on. The rise of the curtain revealed a stage (designed by Henrik Ahr) practically bare, with only an assortment of detritus such as plastic mineral-water bottles, and a wheelchair for Gurnemanz's use, in front of a plain, undecorated cyclorama. This was to be the conduit for multiple drippings of blood, a commodity that took a prominent place in the director's view of the work. Congratulations are certainly due to Stefan Bolliger, whose lighting drew all possible dramatic effect from the stark setting.

At least in act 1, the policy of costume designer Barbara Drosihn might well have been interpreted as an instruction to the chorus to "wear whatever you have around the house"—but perhaps that was precisely what Gürbaca's conception demanded, in reducing an assemblage of supposed knights to fallibly ordinary human proportions. And the younger Flower Maidens' striptease-in-reverse was carried out brilliantly in terms of both dress and undress. It was a telling touch, by the way, to represent four of the Flower Maidens as ladies of a certain age.

In conclusion, I should mention that the director's blocking presented one or two problems: some important action took place so far to the side of the stage that it must have been invisible to a fair number of spectators sitting at the edges of the house. More significant, however, than this small technical glitch was Gürbaca's achievement in never once putting a foot wrong in the matter of relations between and among the characters. Thanks to her work, and to Inbal's triumphant direction of the score, while I still don't love *Parsifal*, I thoroughly enjoyed this *Parsifal*.

* * *

As far as critical principles are concerned, it must surely be clear, to anyone who has persevered thus far with my book, that my critical method has been essentially intuitive and spontaneous rather than based in theory. If I say, nevertheless, that one principle I have followed is to try not to give offence or cause pain except out of absolute necessity, you may object that the Chicago review reproduced above gives little evidence of such an effort. I can assure you that reviews as negative as that form only an extremely small proportion of my critical output.

For one thing, unlike some colleagues whom I have seen leaving concerts with the facial expressions of people who have had the most miserable experience of their lives, I like to have a good time. For another, whereas it is sometimes suggested that critics ought to avoid close friendships with performers or composers, the relations of that kind that I have enjoyed have predisposed me to be kind whenever possible: I have seen at close quarters the years of effort and even hardship it takes to become a great artist, and the last thing I want to do is add further misery.

In this regard, readers—and victims—should keep in mind that a lacerating headline is rarely invented by the critic over whose review it appears: much more often, it was devised by someone in the editorial department or on the city desk. I remember a headline in the *Times* of London that dubbed a symphony by Robert Still "Still-born Symphony."

Insofar as I have followed any critical principle of what might be called a philosophical nature, it has been in harmony with the dictum George Bernard Shaw expressed in his days as a music critic, before he took up instead the relatively easy job of playwright: "I never penned an objective criticism in my life, and I trust I never may." The duty of a critic, he explained, is to be passionate in his judgments. As someone once said, a critic is like a piece of litmus paper: you dip him in the music, and watch to see what color he turns. Having come to whatever passionate conclusion he may, the critic should certainly take the next step and provide objective evidence for that subjective conclusion—but the conclusion, the passion, is what matters most, and the evidence plays purely a supporting and persuading role. It can, for example, consist of facts about tempo that explain *why* a performance realized or failed to realize a composer's clearly expressed intentions, which in turn raises the question how far that much-vaunted quality, "fidelity to the score," should be a central element and an unimpeachable virtue in a critic's value system.

In this matter, I found it amusing that my *Sun-Times* colleague in my years working for the *Chicago Daily News*, Robert Marsh, himself also trained as a philosopher, was firmly of the opinion that he was writing objective criticism, yet he very rarely offered factual backup for his often vigorously expressed judgments, while I, who conversely believed myself to be reviewing subjectively, always tried to do so. And for such reasons, I told my students when I was teaching criticism, whenever they found a critic making such a statement as "Eugene Ormandy's performance of the such-and-such symphony was in fact very beautiful"—an example from real life—they might safely disregard that critic's judgments, because the ability to distinguish between factual statement and value judgment must be fundamental to a critic's method.

Such considerations are taken up in the following lightly edited version of a piece of polemic that I wrote for *Fanfare* magazine early in the 2000s. I trust it may serve as an appropriate summation of my views on the proper practice of criticism.

* * *

Since critics are people and therefore not identical, it is perfectly proper for colleagues to disagree with each other's judgment, and very understandable that they should wish to express their feelings on the matter. After all, it is always frustrating to feel that another critic has missed the point of something—has, if I may put it that way, been "snowed" by a work or a performance that one believes one has oneself had the acumen to see through. A colleague of mine in my *Fanfare* magazine reviewing days clearly felt that way when she expressed strenuous disagreement with my praise of Russell Sherman's Beethoven sonata recordings, and specifically advanced the cause of Annie Fischer's recorded performances as their alleged superior,

Such a disagreement, specific though it is, raises general questions that I think are worth examining. What kind of trade is it, after all, that critics engage in? We have the joyful privilege of listening to great musicians performing great music, and of telling readers how we react to the experience. Whatever you or I think, or anyone else may think, about Sherman or Fischer or Schnabel or any other such performer, the magnitude of even a flawed achievement should be constantly in our minds, not precluding this or that negative observation, but prompting respect in the way it is framed, and certainly warning us against assuming that every deviation from our own taste, every conflicting view of what the score means, constitutes a "mannerism," a "distortion," or a lack of "artistic integrity."

Even leaving how we criticize compositions out of account, with most, or at least some, of the performers we write about, the ground of comment ought to be far above the level of simple accuracy or error, so-called "objective" right and wrong. To begin with, critics should always remember, and must continually remind their readers, that to determine even what Beethoven or any other composer "indicated in the score" is a speculative and hazardous business. There are degrees in this, to be sure. When Rachmaninoff, playing the Funeral March in a Chopin sonata, literally reverses the relation of crescendo and diminuendo indicated by the composer, he is plainly subverting a clear creative intention. When George Szell, like many another conductor, conducts the last movement of

Beethoven's Fifth Symphony faster than the scherzo, he is similarly changing the tempo relation indicated mathematically by the composer.

I am not suggesting that metronome markings have absolute validity—their influence must depend on all sorts of factors, not least the acoustical and the climatic—but rather that they tell us something unequivocal about the *relative* speeds of movements. Yet, even with such apparently open-and-shut cases, who is to say that Rachmaninoff and Szell are wrong? If they present a conception of a work at variance with what was demonstrably the composer's own, is that necessarily a bad thing—a "mistake"—or could it be the valid and provocative insight of another generation changing and expanding the scope of the original idea? And given the imprecise nature of musical notation, and the difficulty a composer faces in translating what he hears in his head into marks on paper, is not even the thought that the conception represented by the score was "demonstrably" the composer's own an assumption rather than an ironclad truth?

An important indication of Beethoven's view on matters like tempo modification and phrasing may be found in the following observation, reported by his biographer Anton Schindler: "The poet writes his monologue or dialogue in a certain, continuous rhythm, but the elocutionist, in order to insure an understanding of the sense of the lines, must make pauses and interruptions at places where the poet was not permitted to indicate it by punctuation. The same manner of declamation can be applied to music, and admits of modification only according to the number of performers" (quoted from *Beethoven: The Man and the Artist, as Revealed in His Own Words*, ed. Friedrich Kerst and Henry Edward Krehbiel, reprinted by Dover in 1964 from a 1905 Huebsch original). Schindler may not have been the most meticulous and reliable of Boswells, but there are many other Beethoven statements of incontrovertible authenticity that tend to the same conclusion.

To all such questions there is no easy "yes" or "no" answer, though certainly I have my own view on the examples cited above. Working with Claire Bloom some years ago on the narration I had prepared for a performance at Bard College of Mendelssohn's incidental music to *Antigone*, I came away with a revealing—indeed, a chastening—perception. She changed a fair number of the words, perhaps 10 percent of them, because she was uncomfortable saying some of the specific phrases I had written. In the theater (and the opera house presents a partial parallel) they have a different attitude about these things from the relatively "purist" one that performers and critics in the field of concert music have tended in recent times—though not in all periods—to adopt. Who, again, is to say that they are wrong?

Let us apply these considerations to the Beethoven sonatas, and to my former colleague's suggestions that Russell Sherman is guilty of "fussing with and distorting phrasing, tempo, rhythm, and dynamics," and that Annie Fischer's "musical integrity, artistic vision, and stylistic acumen" lift her recordings of these works to a higher plane. For the purposes of discussion I choose the "Hammerklavier" Sonata, simply because I have had occasion as a reviewer to work on it several times. I fully agree that Annie Fischer was "one of the great pianists of the twentieth century." Nevertheless, it would be child's play for me, just for starters, to give you three examples of distorted rhythm and tempo in her recording of this supremely challenging work.

Firstly, in the opening movement, the upbeat in the bass sounds, at every appearance of the main theme, not like the eighth-note Beethoven wrote, but like a much longer and less taut quarter-note. Secondly, every time she comes to the subordinate theme, she speeds up perceptibly, in a manner not "indicated in the score," contrary to most pianists' relaxation of the tempo at these points (not to mention my own instinct about this theme), and surely subversive of the "cantabile, dolce ed espressivo" character that Beethoven *did* indicate. Thirdly, despite Beethoven's very clearly spelled-out instructions for shaping the rhythm of the introduction to the finale and his meticulous notation at this juncture, she misreads the rhythmic placement of the bass octaves that follow the right-hand chords, thus both distorting the character of the opening phrases, and destroying the contrast when suddenly, in the second measure, Beethoven for the first time writes the figure exactly the way she has been playing it all along.

Now, what are we to say about these "distortions"? Are they deliberate or inadvertent? Are they mistakes? Or are they impositions of a personal view that differs in literal detail from what stands in the score? My own answer would be different in each of the three cases, and categorical in none of them. In the matter of that eighth note, my hunch is that it results from Fischer's determination at any cost to play both the upbeat and the immediately following left-hand chord an octave and a half above it with the same hand. In doing so, she would presumably have been obeying her conviction that Beethoven wanted it that way, but in her manner of doing so she fatally undermines, to my ears, the impulsive character of the theme and thus of the movement as a whole. It is true that making this big skip with one hand reinforces the sense of strain—of struggle—that is, I would certainly agree, integral to late-Beethoven piano music, and is therefore in itself a positive rather than a negative factor; it was precisely the absence of any sense of struggle in the surpassingly smooth and elegant recording of the late sonatas that Maurizio Pollini made back in the 1970s that seemed to me to take the music, in his interpretation, out of the realm of Beethoven and into that of Lisztian studies in transcendental execution.

We are faced with the need to decide between competing priorities: giving due weight to Beethoven's characteristic sense of struggle, for example, and contriving to sound at least in some degree equal to the technical problems that embody the struggle; and what I want to say is that all such questions of interpretative balance are issues to be determined only by personal judgment, not by specious claims to know better than someone else just what Beethoven meant and what he would have cared most about. The speeding up of the subordinate theme may be an interpretative decision, or the result of relief on arriving for once at a passage that is technically less demanding than most of the movement's texture, or a little of both.

Despite all my admiration of Fischer, I have enough experience of what sounds like nervous haste in even her finest performances—some of the Mozart piano concertos, for example—to suspect that the technical point may be the determining one. But if the nuance was deliberate, the question remains, is it a good idea or a bad one? And "good" or "bad" in whose ears? As to the crux in the finale—curiously enough, the same inaccuracy I noted years ago in Eunice Norton's recording of this sonata—I really cannot find any rationale for it other than a simple misreading of the text (unless both pianists were using corrupt editions of the score).

What, moreover, quite aside from these questions of nuance, are we to make of measures 243–46 of the finale, where Fischer seemingly elects not to play the trills Beethoven marked on ten successive beats? Of course, the passage is sufficiently outrageous in its technical demands even without them, and one may sympathize with any pianist who takes the easy way out of yet another problem. But then it does not seem to me proper to criticize a pianist who *does* play these trills, and then to use another one who leaves them out as a stick to beat him with for allegedly departing from "what Beethoven has indicated in the score."

One could doubtless point to instances matching some of these in Russell Sherman's performances of the sonatas, though I should be surprised if they would include any literal misreadings or omissions of notes, as distinct from disputed nuances. For what it is worth, though I judge his set *as a whole* to be the greatest traversal of this music ever put on record, I do not think his the finest "Hammerklavier" on disc. It is a superb performance, and the sheer elan with which he makes the first two phrases sound not as disjunct units but as one irresistible onrush of music is daring and wonderful. But the live recording by Brendel in the Philips "Great Pianists of the 20th Century" series, and a more recent version by Blanca Uribe on the MSR label, seem to me even better as wholes.

Two other among the numerous recorded sets of the sonatas, one by Aldo Ciccolini, the other by André De Groote, offer (or offered—such things tend to disappear from the catalogues almost as rapidly as they appear) further grounds for comparison and discussion. Both of these sets display considerable virtues. Ciccolini demonstrates a remarkable command over all the technical problems Beethoven poses. De Groote is no less proficient. There is much to enjoy in Ciccolini's fluent and intelligent playing, and still more, I think, in De Groote's, which has a most attractive feeling of honesty and directness about it. So far as my sampling suggests, either of their recordings could serve as a magisterial and clear-eyed exposition of what is "indicated in the score." But at the highest level of comparison it might be said that, whereas these fine pianists are playing the notes, a spectacular achievement in all conscience, a Russell Sherman—and, yes, for all my strictures, an Annie Fischer—play the music.

For on any level above that of the mere consumer's guide such details as I have discussed are paltry. They must surely be set in the context and evaluated against the background of an overall artistic vision. My colleague declared that Annie Fischer is a great pianist. I agree. Fischer's view of the Beethoven sonatas convinced her. It engages and often delights but does not entirely convince me. Sherman's view both delights and convinces me. It does not convince my colleague. Is she right? Am I wrong? This is a question that makes little sense to me, and not because I think I am infallible. It is not our job to be right or wrong. It is our job to stimulate and illuminate; to stimulate thought, to illuminate understanding, and hopefully, in the process, to enhance appreciation. That is what I try to do.

INDEX

STAR TURNS are listed thus in CAPITALS; *page numbers for their principal treatment are distinguished by* **bold type**.

Aarhus, Denmark, 168, 251
Aarhus Symphony Orchestra, 168
Abbey Road, 44
Abelson, Hope, 173
Abrahamsen, Hans, 153
ABROMS, GENE, **234–35**
Abroms, Harriet, 235
Academy of Music, Philadelphia, 181, 186, 194, 199, 200
Academy of St Martin in the Fields, 16
Adema, Peter, 230
agnosticism, 8, 225, 245
Ahronovitch, Yuri, 169
Albersen, Herman, 151; Albersen music shop, 152
Albert, Magdeleine, 151
Aldeburgh Festival, 15, 140, 177
Alexander, Chris, 260
Allin, Norman, 1
Allison, John, 262
Alsop, Marin, 239
Altshul, David, 131
American Academy in Rome, 154
American Handel Festival, 2011, Seattle, 258
American Music Center, 196
American Record Guide, 236
American Symphony Orchestra, 57, 117, 200
Amsterdam, 25–28, 30, 162, 210, 227; Municipal Theater, 29
Andersen, Karsten, 167
Andry, Peter, 38, 53; fellow jury member, John Player International Conducting Competition, 133
Andsnes, Leif Ove, 102
Angel Records, 38, 185
Ansermet, Ernest, 56
Anton Philipszaal, The Hague, 214, 217
Antwerp, Belgium, 225–26; Opera House, 269
APRAHAMIAN, FELIX, **67**
Arben, David, 184
Ardoin, John, 65
Argento, Dominick, *A Water Bird Talk,* 177
Argerich, Marta, 240
Arié, Raffaele, 89
Armiñán, Jaime de, *El nido,* 207–8
Arnold, Malcolm, 144
Arrau, Claudio, 103
Arts Council of Great Britain, 125–27, 136; Network for New Music, 112; Regional Development Department, 130

Ashkenasi, Shmuel, 118
Ashkenazy, Vladimir, 67, 102, 176
Aspen Music Festival, 196
AT&T American Encore Series, 192
atheism replaced by agnosticism, 8, 225
Auberjonois, René, 54
Aubort, Marc, 60
Auden, W. H., 23
Audi, Pierre, 242
Ausstrahlung, 142
AX, EMANUEL, **201–2**
Ayo, Felix, 35

Baarn, the Netherlands, 24–25, 27–29, 36–37
Babbitt, Milton, 111, 193; Composition for Twelve Instruments, 193; String Quartet No. 3, 111; *Transfigured Notes,* 193
Bach, Jan, 118
Bach, Johann Christian, 31; influence on Mozart, 31; keyboard sonatas, 211
Bach, Johann Sebastian, 18, 31, 36, 121, 142, 226, 237; Cantata No. 65, *Sie werden aus Saba alle kommen,* 4; Cantata No. 140, *Wachet auf, ruft uns die Stimme,* 175; *Christmas Oratorio,* 14; "Goldberg" Variations, 21, 55; Mass in B Minor, 17, 245; performance practice in choral works, 60; *Das wohltemperierte Klavier,* 240
Badura-Skoda, Paul, 45
Baez, Joan, 100
Bailey, Bruce, 250
Bainbridge, Simon, 148, 213; Double Concerto, 213
Baker, Claude, *Shadows: Four Dirge-Nocturnes for Orchestra,* 224–25
Baker, Janet, 174
Baldry, Harold, 125, 127, 130
Baldwin, Dalton, 34
Baras, Stasys, 108
Barber, Samuel, 83
Barbirolli, Sir John, 11, 38, 49
Bard College, 200, 274
BARENBOIM, DANIEL, 12, 87, **93–96**, 103, 250; Elgar performances, 87; *Le nozze di Figaro,* 140–41
Bargreen, Melinda, 259
Barnes, Clive, 81
Barston, Elisa, 256
Bartók, Béla, 147, 159, 185, 248; *Duke Bluebeard's Castle,* 248; piano concertos, 94; Violin Concerto No. 2, 86–87
Bartoletti, Bruno, 105
Bartoli, Cecilia, 96
Bayeux, 54
Beard, Paul, 129
Beatles, The, 51; *The Baroque Beatles Book,* 59–60; Baroque Beatles Concert, 60; *Help!,* 164
BBC, 1, 49, 104, 119; *Desert Island Discs,* 252; *The Great War,* 144; Henry Wood Promenade Concerts, 10, 49, 132, 178, 218, 246; Music Department, 68, 112; Symphony Orchestra, 5, 16, 129; Third Programme, 11
Beavers, Kevin, 241
Beecham, Sir Thomas, 11–12, 39, 44, 49; playing after the beat, 199
Beethoven, Ludwig van, 8–9, 42, 113, 201, 223, 252, 254; *An die ferne Geliebte,* 110; bicentenary, 93; black or Jewish, 194; cello sonatas, 15, 34; *Christus am Ölberge,* 178; *Egmont* overture, 199; *Fidelio,* 43; on Handel, 258; *Leonore* Overtures Nos. 2 and 3, 113; Missa solemnis in D Major, 14, 90; Piano Concerto No. 1, 203,

240; Piano Concerto No. 3, 102; Piano Concerto No. 4, 12; piano sonatas, 273–77; Sonata in B-flat Major, Op. 106, "Hammerklavier," 275–77; Sonata in C Minor, Op. 111, 8–9, 103; Sonata in F Minor, "Appassionata," 46; Drei Sonaten, 8; string quartets Op. 59, 213–14; Symphony No. 1, 42; Symphony No. 2, 16, 39; Symphony No. 3, *Eroica,* 187–88; Symphony No. 4, 225; Symphony No. 5, 80, 199, 274; Symphony No. 6, *Pastorale,* 181; Symphony No. 7, 102; Symphony No. 9, 22, 42, 208–9, 221; on tempo modification, 274; violin sonatas, 241
Beinum, Eduard van, 29
Belcove, Laura, 156. *See also* Jacobson, Laura
Bellini, Vincenzo, *I Capuleti e i Montecchi,* 180
Bělohlávek, Jiři, 219
Bennigsen, Baron Andreas von, 221
Bentham, Roy, 4
Berg, Alban, *Lulu,* 122
Berganza, Teresa, 141
Bergen Philharmonic Orchestra (Harmonien), 167
Berglund, Paavo, 132
Bergman, Ingmar, *The Seventh Seal,* 22
Berio, Luciano, 197; *La vera storia,* 154; *Laborintus II,* 217
Berkeley, Michael, 246
Berlin, Isaiah, 22–23
Berlioz, Hector, 41–42, 142; *Harold en Italie,* 40
BERNHEIMER, MARTIN, **65**, 70, 78, 107
Bernstein, Leonard, 28, 41, 69, 80, 152; *Songfest,* 152
Berry, Walter, 13
Bhattacharjee, Anne, 9–10, 90
Bhattacharya, Deben, 28
Bing, Rudolph, 41
Biret, Idil, 236–37
Birtwistle, Harrison, 130
Bishop, Christopher, 179
Björling, Jussi, 7–8
Black Dyke Mills Band, 1
Blackstone, Sir William, *Commentaries on the Laws of England,* 64
Blake, Eubie, 22–23
Blech, Harry, 11
Bliss, Sir Arthur, *Morning Heroes,* 92
Blitzstein, Marc, *Triple-Sec,* 65
Blom, Eric, *A Musical Postbag,* 6
Bloom, Claire, 201, 274
Blustine, Allen, 196
Blythe, Stephanie, 259
Boccherini, Luigi, 31
Böhm, Karl, 44
Bolcom, William, 22
Bolliger, Stefan, 271
Bonaventura, Mario di, 73
Bookspan, Martin, 180–81
Boosey & Hawkes (B&H), 61, 135, 145–48, 151–57, 159, 161, 163–64, 171, 174, 176–77, 179; deputy director of publications, 146; director of promotion, 160
Booth, Al, 109
Booth, Webster, 1
Bork, Robert, 271
Boston Symphony Orchestra, 36, 40, 58, 156, 166
Boston University, 156
BOSTRIDGE, IAN, 104–5, 234, **243**
Botstein, Leon, 200–201
Bott, Catherine, 217
Boulanger, Nadia, 50
Boulez, Pierre, 29, 39, 96–98, 236; *Relevés d'apprenti* (*Notes of an Apprenticeship*), 97
Boult, Sir Adrian, 6, 11, 39, 49, 129, 143

Bournemouth, 125; *Bournemouth Herald,* 101
Bournemouth Sinfonietta, 126
Bournemouth Symphony Orchestra, 1, 14, 126, 132, 239
Boyle, Nick, 45, 53
Bozeman, Cary and Kerri, 261
Brabants Orkest, Eindhoven, 87, 162
Brahms, Johannes, 9, 57, 82, 87, 115, 143, 153, 174–75, 201, 222–23, 237, 254–55; Alto Rhapsody, 200; Clarinet Quintet; *A German Requiem,* 17, 91, 165, 196; Horn Trio, 201, 213; Lieder, 18; *The Music of Johannes Brahms,* 75, 140–42; *Nänie,* 109 Piano Concerto No. 1, 237; Piano Concerto No. 2, 110, 202; piano music, 236; piano trios, 211; Serenade No. 1, 57, 75; Sextet No. 1, 37; Symphony No. 1, 85, 165, 208; Symphony No. 2, 86, 166, 213, 240; Symphony No. 3; Symphony No. 4, 6–7, 56, 176, 241; *Tragic Overture,* 78–79; violin sonatas, 241
Braithwaite, Nicholas, 49
Bregoli, Esther, 135
Bregoli, Mauro, 135
Bremerton, Washington, 246, 249, 257, 261–62, 264; *Kitsap Sun,* 261
BRENDEL, ALFRED, 65, 94, 109–10, 114, 148, 238, 277
Breuer, Gustl, 76
Brewer, Bruce, 93
Breyfogle, Todd, 244
British Council, 137
Britten, Benjamin, 15, 21, 30, 147, 159; *Death in Venice,* 242–43; *A Midsummer Night's Dream,* 173; Nocturne, 30; *Peter Grimes,* 46; *War Requiem,* 254
Broad Street Review, 237
Bröcheler, John, 172
Broido, Arnold, 245–46
Broido, Tom, 245
Bron, Eleanor, 164
Brown, David, 143
Brown, Kate, 20
Brown, Sheila, 53
Brown, Sue, 177
BROWN, TONY, **20–21**, 123
Bruckner, Anton, 11, 86, 222; Symphony No. 5, 29; Symphony No. 6, 30; Symphony No. 8, 219; Symphony No. 9, 166
Brusilow, Anshel, 56–57
Buenos Aires, Argentina, 245
Buggiano Castello, 69
Burgwyn, Diana, 50–52
Burton, Richard, 101
Business Executives' Move for Vietnam Peace (BEM), 99
Busoni, Ferruccio, 114; Piano Concerto, 170
Butt, David, 16
Byrd, William, 253

Caballé, Montserrat, 121
Cage, John, 118; *HPSCHD*, 118
Caldwell, Sarah, 122
Callas, Maria, 107
Calvados, 110
Calvino, Italo, *Invisible Cities,* 198
Cameron, Basil, 2
Campion, Thomas, 15, 26, 253; *My sweetest Lesbia,* 55
CANARINA, JOHN, **71**
Canetti, Elias, *The Numbered,* 21
Capecchi, Renato, 37
"Carlyle, Robert," 46
Carné, Marcel, *Drôle de drame,* 23
Carnegie Hall, 32, 57, 72, 78, 83–84, 93, 104, 148, 184, 194, 200; "Perspectives," 96
Caronia, Tony, 185

Carreras, José, 108
Carsey, Frank, 262
Carter, Elliott, 50; Piano Concerto, 75
Casals Festival, 37, 98–99
Casals, Pablo, 98–99
Cassidy, Claudia, 84
Casson, Sir Hugh, 5
Catullus, Gaius Valerius, *Vivamus, mea Lesbia, atque amemus*, 55
Celibidache, Sergiu, 95
Cerha, Friedrich, 163
CERMINARO, JOHN, **250–52**
Chagrin, Francis, 2, 66
Chamber Orchestra of Philadelphia, 238–39, 241, 246, 251
Chamber Symphony of Philadelphia, 56–57
Channel Classics Records, 227
Charlston, Elsa, 194
Checchia, Anthony, 182, 243
Chelsea Opera Group, 39
Cheltenham Festival, 32, 66–67
Cherkassky, Shura, 103
Chestnut Hill, Philadelphia, 233
Ciccolini, Aldo, 277
Chicago; Allied Arts, 109, 111; Auditorium Theater, 99; Carl Fischer music shop, 217; Chicago College of Performing Arts, 64; Chicago Musical College, 82, 97, 100, 113, 115; Chicago Opera Theater, 267–69; *Chicago Sun-Times*, 83, 272; *Chicago Tribune*, 83–84; *Chicago Today*, 83; *Chicago's American*, 83; Civic Orchestra, 85, 95; Dame Myra Hess Memorial Concerts, 109; Drake Hotel, 89; Goethe Street, 109; Goodman Theatre, 111; Lithuanian Opera Company of Chicago, 108; Lyon & Healey, 115, 161; Lyric Opera of Chicago, 105–9, 111–12, 121, 173; Orchestra Hall, 88, 94–95, 99–100, 109, 116, 124; University of Chicago, 106, 111; University of Chicago Contemporary Chamber Players (CCP), 111–12; Schiller Street, 109; Symphony Center, 95
Chicago Daily News, 78–79, 81, 93, 105, 122, 124, 203, 226, 233, 260, 272; Roy Fisher, 79
Chicago Symphony Orchestra, 56, 64, 78–82, 84, 86, 88, 90, 92–96, 101, 105, 109–12, 116, 119, 121, 131, 156, 171, 260
Chihuly, Dale, 248–49
Chopin, Frédéric François, 46, 48, 182, 252; *Frédéric Chopin* (*The Chopin Companion*), 182; Piano Sonata No. 2, Funeral March, 273
Choral Arts Society of Philadelphia, 199–200
Christiansen, Richard, 78, 122–23, 173
Cincinnati, 72; Cincinnati College-Conservatory of Music, 116; Cincinnati Symphony Orchestra, 32
Ciofi, Patrizia, 141
City of Birmingham Symphony Orchestra, 160
City of London School (CLS), 2–3, 5, 11, 15, 17, 38
Claremont Quartet, 60, 118, 218
Clark, Ramsey, 100
Clark, Sedgwick, 103–4
Clark Hall, Justin and Adelaide, 24
Clarke, Jeremiah, 1
Classical Music Weekly, 140
CLS. *See* City of London School
Coburn, Sarah, 260
Collier, Marie, 122
Cologne Philharmonie, 215, 217
Columbia Publishing Company, 53, 142
Colvin, Michael, 269

committees, intelligence of, 191
Concertgebouw, Amsterdam, 46, 72, 202, 215–17, 224
Concertgebouw Orchestra, 27–29, 87, 162
Concerto Soloists of Philadelphia. *See* Chamber Orchestra of Philadelphia
conducting technique, 57–58, 85, 142, 199
Conductors on Conducting, 53, 58, 140, 142
Connoisseur Society, 63
Constantine, Andrew, 204
COOKE, DERYCK, **36**, 68, 70
Copenhagen, 153, 166; Tivoli Gardens, 168
Copland, Aaron, 50; *Billy the Kid*, 213
Corpus Christi College, Oxford, 12–13, 16, 22, 243–44
Corrigan, Patrick, 263
Council of Europe, 137
Courtney, Neil, 183
Covell, Tony, 131, 133
Coveney, John, 38
Covent Garden. *See* Royal Opera House, London
Cowan, Carole, 196
Cox, John, 173
Crawford Seeger, Ruth, 111
Craxton, Janet, 5
Cuénod, Hugues, 150
Curtis Institute of Music, 30, 186, 207, 238, 263
Curzon, Clifford, 12
Cutner, Solomon, 12

Dale, F. R., 2, 5–6
Daley, Mayor Richard J., 120–21
Dallas, 57, 174; Dallas Symphony Orchestra, 57, 174; Southern Methodist University, 174, 192
Dalley, John, 118
Danish Radio Symphony Orchestra, 153, 168
Dart, Thurston, 21
Dartmouth College, Hanover, New Hampshire, Congregation of the Arts, 73–76
Dausgaard, Thomas, 254
Davies, Dennis Russell, 193, 198
DAVIS, COLIN, 4, **39–42**, 71, 142–43, 170; Handel's *Messiah,* 63–64
Daytona Beach, Florida, 71
De Groote, André, 277
de Klijn, Nap, 9
de Lancie, John, 263
de Leeuw, Ton, *Ombres,* 227
de Sabata, Victor, 69, 107
de Simone, Roberto, 188
de Smith, Joan, 49
de Waart, Edo, 215–17
de Yong, Jenny, 206
Debussy, Achille-Claude, 11, 93, 228, 252, 255; piano music, 63; *Prélude à L'Après-midi d'un faune,* 213
Defauw, Désiré, 84
DeGaetani, Jan, 195–96
Deibler, Seán, 200
Del Mar, Norman, 49
DELIN, PETER, **18–19**, 117
Delius, Frederick, 67
Della Casa, Lisa, 66, 172–73
Dermota, Anton, 13
Dettmer, Roger, 83
Deutsche Grammophon Gesellschaft (DGG), 218
di Stefano, Giuseppe, 51, 107
Diamand, Peter, 29
Dickie, Brian, 172, 269
DILKS, PARK, **243**, 245
Dillenbeck, Denise, 260
Doig, Donald, 108
Domingo, Plácido, 108, 173
DONOHOE, PETER, **170**
Doráti, Antal, 69–70

Dossor, Lance, 2
Dowland, John, 15, 26, 253
Dowling, Tim, 211
DREW, DAVID, **146**, 148–49, 154, 159–61
Drewanz, Hans, 217, 231
Driver, Robert B., 242
Drosihn, Barbara, 271
Druckman, Jacob, 154, 229
Drummers of West Africa, 214
du Pré, Jacqueline, 93, 165
DUBOW, MARILYN, **57**, 59, 69, 256–57
Duclos, Didier, 151–52
Dufton, Ben, 127
Duncan, Neil, 130
Duncombe, Peter. *See* Feversham, Peter
Dutilleux, Henri, 229
Dutoit, Charles, 199, 240
Dvořák, Antonîn: Cello Concerto in B Minor, 232; Piano Trio in F Minor, 213; *Rusalka,* 242; Slavonic Dances, 162
Dykes, John Bacchus, "For those in peril on the sea," 260

Eaglen, Jane, 260–61
Early Music Guild, Seattle, 258
Eastman School of Music, University of Rochester, 192
Edinburgh, 18, 20; Caledonian Hotel, 92; Edinburgh International Festival, 90, 92; Usher Hall, 92
Edwards, John, 116
Ehnes, James, 240, 256
Elektra/Nonesuch Records, 59–62, 78, 104, 118, 195, 218, 253
Elgar, Sir Edward, 11, 42, 87, 143, 253; Cello Concerto, 165; *Enigma* Variations, 165, 234; Introduction and Allegro for Strings, 165; music for string orchestra, 38; Symphony No. 1, 42
Elias, Robert, 251
Elisabeth (queen of Belgium), 42
Elizabeth (Queen Mother), 140
Elizalde, Julio, 256
Elley, Derek, 141
Ellingham, Rev. Cecil, 4–5
Ellsberg, Daniel, 100
Emanuel, John, 38, 68, 195, 225
Emerson String Quartet, 255
EMI International, 37–38, 40, 42–47, 53, 59, 105, 133, 141, 146, 165, 170, 179, 253
"Endemic Andante," 66
English Chamber Orchestra, 30, 157
English Music Theatre Company, 74
English Opera Group, 67
Engström, Bengt Olof, 171
Enschedé, Johannes, 45
Enzensberger, Hans Magnus, 74, 198; *Der Untergang der Titanic,* 74
Epstein, Avrom Joshua, 123
Eriksen, Richard Dahl, 153
ERICKSON, STEPHEN AND PAULINE, **244–45**
Eschenbach, Christoph, 83, 184, 240
Evans, Geraint, 106
Evans, Peter, 132
Everitt, Margaret Anne, 242

Fairfax Symphony Orchestra, 102
Falconer, Bonnie. *See* Jacobson, Bonnie
Falla, Manuel de, *The Three-Cornered Hat,* 87
Falletta, JoAnn, 239, 254
Falstaff, Sir John, 212
Fanfare Magazine, 236–37, 250–51, 273
FARLEY, CAROLE, **58**
Fauré, Gabriel, Requiem, 14
Fawcett, Graham, 131, 139
Fell, Tony, 152, 154, 159, 161, 179
Fermata, 97, 199

Festival of Britain, 5
Feversham, Peter, 136
Field, John, 22
Fielding, Henry, *Tom Jones,* 101
Film Forum Philadelphia, 207
Finckel, Christopher, 196
Fine Arts Quartet, 111, 205
Finzi, Gerald, Cello Concerto, 152
Fisch, Asher, 254, 259
Fischer, Annie, Beethoven piano sonatas, 273, 275–77; Mozart concertos, 276
Fischer, Iván, 219, 221, 254
Fischer, Julia, 240
Fischer-Dieskau, Dietrich, 141
Fisher, Norma, 31
Fisher, Sylvia, 10
Flanders, Claudia, 72–73
Flanders, Michael, 72–73; *At the Drop of Another Hat,* 72
Flegler, Joel, 236
Fleischmann, Ernest, 104
Fleming, Shirley, 53
Flemish Opera, Antwerp, 269–71
Fogel, Henry, 64
Fontainebleau, The American School at, 50
Fournet, Jean, 122
Fowler, Edward, 44
Fox, Carol, 105
FRAGER, MALCOLM, **202–3**
Francis, Sarah, 177
Franco Bahamonde, Generalissimo Francisco, 176
Franklin, Benjamin, String Quartet, 183
Frittoli, Barbara, 240
Fromm, Paul, 183; Fromm Music Foundation, 183
Fulleylove, Miranda, 177
Fürst, János, 230
Furtwängler, Wilhelm, 30, 94, 234, 250, 253
Gaburo, Kenneth, 118
Gallo Nero, Il, 186
Ganz, Rudolf, 82
Garrison, Jon, 201
GELATT, ROLAND, 53, **54–56**, 234; Lois Gelatt, 54–55
Gergiev, Valery, 249–50, 255
Germany, West, 137
Gerolemou, Christopher, 93
Gershwin, George, 223
Gewandhaus Orchestra, Leipzig, 174–75; Arthur Nikisch Room, 175
Gieseking, Walter, 11
Gilder, Robert, 230
Gilels, Emil, 175
GINASTERA, ALBERTO, 148, **159**; *Bomarzo,* 159
Ginastera, Aurora Natola, 159
Giraudoux, Jean, *Amphitryon 38,* 21
Gitlis, Ivry, 157
GIULINI, CARLO MARIA, 6, 28–29, 85–87, **87–91**, 94, 101, 112, 143, 149, 222, 252
Giulini, Marcella, 88, 90–91
Gleadowe, Teresa, 131
Glotz, Michel, 170
Glover, Jane, 267, 269
Gluck, Christoph Willibald Ritter von, *Orfeo ed Euridice,* 180–81, 188, 253
Glyndebourne Festival Opera, 172–74, 262, 269; Glyndebourne Touring Opera, 176
Glynne, Howell, 10
Gobbi, Tito, 106–7
Godard, Benjamin, *Concerto romantique,* 12
Godfrey, Sir Dan, 1
Goerne, Matthias, 110
Goethe, Johann Wolfgang von, 109, 198
Golan, Lawrence, 260
Goldberg, Szymon, 30

Golding, William, 14; *Lord of the Flies,* 14
Gomberg, Harold, 62
Goodfriend, Carol, 63
GOODFRIEND, JIM, **62–64**, 77
Goodrich, Pierre, 243
Gordon, Edward, 112
GORDON, JIM, **226–27**, 230
Górecki, Henryk, 231
Göteborg, Sweden, 162, 171–72, 220
Göteborg Symphony Orchestra, 171–72, 246
Gould, Morton, 32, 83
Graham, Robin, 251
Gramophone, 61
Grand Street Settlement, 51
Grant Park concerts, 112, 121, 203; Grant Park Symphony Orchestra, 84, 112
Graz, Austria, 163
Great War, The, 34, 144
Grieg, Edvard, 8; *Lyric Pieces,* 167
Griffith, D. W., *Intolerance,* 21–22
Griffiths, Paul, 178
Grimaud, Hélène, 236–37
Grimsley, Greer, 259
GRIN, LEONID, **200–201**, 220
Groningen, the Netherlands, 230–31
Grossman, David, 207
Groves, Charles, 14
Grove's Dictionary of Music and Musicians, 68; *The New Grove Dictionary of Music and Musicians,* 68
GRUBER, HK, 148, **161–64**, 223; *Frankenstein!!,* 162–63, 172, 223
Grümmer, Elisabeth, 13
Grunth, Lars, 167
Guardian, 46, 49, 67, 79, 127
Guarneri Quartet, 118
Guastafeste, Joseph, 131
Gueden, Hilde, 10
Guest, Douglas, 14
Guittart, Henk, 209
Guldbæk, Ruth, 10
Gürbaca, Tatjana, 269–71

Haarlem, the Netherlands, 45, 226, 230
Hacker, Alan, 164
Hagegård, Håkan, 172
HAGEN, DARON, **259–60**; *Amelia,* 260; Symphony No. 1, 260
HAITINK, BERNARD, 26, **27–28**, 29, 64
Haldeman, Lloyd, 32, 174
Hall, Peter, 173
Hallstein, Ingeborg, 43
Hamburg, Germany, 187
Hamburger, Paul, 33
HAMMOND, MICHAEL, **117**, 169
Hampson, Thomas, 241
Handel, George Frideric, 69, 142, 253, 258; *Esther,* 258; *Giulio Cesare,* 32; *Messiah,* 4, 40; *Solomon,* 44, 63; *Theodora,* 262
Handspring Puppet Company, 257
Harbour, Lucas, 269
Harnoncourt, Nikolaus, 142
Harper, Heather, 141
Harpham, George, 186
Harris, Roy, *Père Marquette* Symphony, 116
Harrogate Festival, 33
Hartog, Howard, 146, 154; *European Music in the Twentieth Century* (ed.), 146
Haskil, Clara, 220
Haydn, Joseph, 29, 30, 31, 42, 70, 185; Cello Concerto in C Major, 250; *Le pescatrici,* 29; *Die Schöpfung,* 208, 246; string quartets, 9, 15, 19; symphonies, 69, 231; Symphony No. 47, 97; Symphony No. 59, 69; Symphony No. 81, 69; Symphony No. 99, 201; Trumpet Concerto, 2, 252

Haydn, Michael, 31
HEARON, LEIGH, **256–57**
Heggie, Jake, 255; *Farewell, Auschwitz,* 255
Heinzelmann, Josef, 174
Hemingway, Ernest, *A Moveable Feast,* 205
Hemsley, Thomas, 33–34
Henahan, Donal, 78
Henghes, Heinz, 135
Henkemans, Hans, 228–29; Piano Concerto No. 3, 229
Henle Urtext edition, 109
Hennessy, Joseph, 245
Henricis, Rolf de, 199
Henry Street Settlement, 51
Henry Wood Promenade Concerts. *See* BBC
HENZE, HANS WERNER, **73–75**, 83, 98; *Barcarola*, 75; *Die Bassariden*, 75; *Being Beauteous*, 74; *La Cubana*, 198; Double Bass Concerto, 74, 82; *Memoirs of an Outsider*, 98; *Moralities*, 74; *Nachtstücke und Arien*, 74; Piano Concerto No. 2, 83; Symphony No. 9, 75; *Voices*, 74
Heraclitus, 175
Herbig, Günther, 212, 220
Hermes, James, 96–97
Herodotus, 216
Herrmann, Bernard, 38; *Wuthering Heights*, 38
Herseth, Adolph ("Bud"), 121, 196
Herseth, Freda, 196
HERSH, PAUL, **256–57**
Hickox, Richard, 133
Hierck, Hans, 162
High Fidelity/Musical America, 15, 53, 54, 56–57, 59, 62–63, 70, 78, 143, 236
Highwater, Jamake, 206
Hiller, Lejaren, 118; *HPSCHD,* 118
Hindemith, Paul, 42, 149; *Ludus Tonalis*, 76; Piano Concerto, 130
Hinderas, Natalie, 194
Hitchcock, Alfred, 38
Hodges, Bruce, 238
Hodkinson, Sydney, 192
HODSON, DENYS, **127–28**
Hoffman, Gary, 85
Hoffman, Irwin, 82, 84–85
Hoffman, Jay, 70
Hoffnung, Annetta, 72
Hoffnung, Gerard, 72; Hoffnung Music Festivals, 72
Holland Festival, 28–29, 72, 87, 172
Holloway, Keith, 13
Holloway, Robin, 147
Holten, Bo, 153
Holvik, Karen, 196
Holzman, Jac, 61, 253
Holzman, Keith, 253
Honegger, Arthur, 150; Nocturne, 152
Hoog Wolde, 25
Hopkins, June, 129
Hordern, Michael, 9
Horsch, Gregor, 211
Hotter, Hans, 52, 253
HOUGH, STEPHEN, **204–5**
Houghton, Lord, *Life and Letters of John Keats,* 140
House of Lords, London, 136
Howes, Frank, 66, 72
Hudson, Frank, 102
Humperdinck, Engelbert, 114
Huntley, David, 154
Hurok, Sol, 109
Hurst, George, 132
Husa, Karel, 111

I Musici, 34–35
IGLITZIN, ALAN, **256–57**, 262
Illinois Arts Council, 115; Music Advisory Panel, 115

Importance of Being Earnest, The, 13–14, 22
Inbal, Eliahu, 269–71
Institut de Recherche et Coordination Acoustique/Musique (IRCAM), 97
intelligence of committees, 191
International Society for Contemporary Music (ISCM), 168; Chicago chapter, 96; World Music Days 1983, 251
International Tchaikovsky Piano Competition, Moscow, 170
Israel Philharmonic Orchestra, 166
Ives, Charles, 143; Violin Sonata No. 2, 57; Symphony No. 4, 58

Jacobs, René, 141
Jacobson, Bonnie, 32, 33, 54, 67, 68, 81, 86, 88–90, 94, 103, 126, 128, 134, 135, 137, 139, 145, 155
Jacobson, Cecil, 6
JACOBSON, HOWARD, **205–6**; *Coming from Behind*, 205; *The Finkler Question*, 206; *J*, 206; *Kalooki Nights*, 206; Man Booker Prize 2010, 206; marriage to Jenny de Yong, 206; *No More Mister Nice Guy*, 206; *Roots Schmoots: Journeys Among Jews*, 206
Jacobson, Katharine, 140–41
Jacobson, Laura, 20, 30, 33, 46, 54, 75, 82, 90–91, 116, 129, 131, 134, 148, 151, 156, 158, 163, 169, 173, 174, 177, 179–80, 184, 186, 188, 194, 198, 204, 206, 207, 211, 214, 224–25, 226–29, 232–35, 238, 241, 243–44, 246, 247, 251, 253, 261–63, 264
Jacobson, Paula, 6–7, 86
Jacobson, Sam, 145, 235, 265
Jaja, Bruno Heinz, *Punkt Contrapunkt*, 72
Janáček, Leoš, 248; *The Cunning Little Vixen* suite, 213; piano music, 102
JENKINS, SPEIGHT, **258–59**
Jeune Orchestre Symphonique de Douai, 152
Jochum, Eugen, 29
John Brown's Body, 83
John Player International Conducting Competition, 132–33
Johnson, Tom, *Failing*, 211
Johnston, Ben, 111, 118; String Quartet No. 2, 118
Joplin, Scott, 60
Josephs, Valerie, 31, 89
JOSEPHS, WILFRED, **31–34**, 66–67, 69, 72, 101–2, 113, 154, 227; Arabesques, 33; Concerto da Camera, 31; *Death of a Young Man*, 125, 195, 253; *The Great War*, 144; *I, Claudius*, 34; *Mortales*, 32; *Nightmusic*, 33; *The Nottingham Captain,* 66; Piano Concerto No. 2, 32; Piano Sonata No. 2, 32; *Rebecca*, 33; *Requiescant*, 69; Requiem, 69, 72, 83, 88–89, 101, 200; String Quintet, 69; symphonies, 32; Symphony No. 2, 32, 66; Symphony No. 3, 32; *Twelve Letters*, 72
Juilliard String Quartet, 255
Jurinac, Sena, 10, 13

Kangas, Juha, 153
Karajan, Herbert von, 79, 86
Karp, Judith, 181
KARR, GARY, 82, **263**
Katchen, Julius, 236
Kavakos, Leonidas, 240; Mozart Violin Concerto No. 3, 240
Kaye, Doris, 48
Kaye, Reuben, 7–8
KAZARAS, PETER, **261**
Keats, John, 140–41

Kenny, Bill, 238
Kentridge, William, 257
Kenyon, Nicholas, 132, 147
KERR, CHRISTOPHER, **131**
Kerst, Friedrich, *Beethoven: The Man and the Artist, as Revealed in His Own Words* (ed.), 274
Kertész, István, 252
Kimmel Center for the Performing Arts, Philadelphia, 238
KING, LLEWELLYN, **52–54**
KING FM, Seattle, 253
King's Lynn Festival, 140
Kirkpatrick, Ralph, 6
Kirkwall, Orkney Islands, 164
Klangforum Wien, 163
Kleiber, Erich, 10, 141
Kleinsteuber, Carl, 176
Klemperer, Otto, 11, 30, 42–43, 49; Symphony No. 2, 30
Knappertsbusch, Hans, 270
Knardahl, Eva, 167; Grieg *Lyric Pieces,* 167
Knüpfer, Sebastian, *Machet die Tore weit,* 36
KNUSSEN, OLIVER, 212, **217–18**, 221, 246, 254
Kodály, Zoltán, 248; Missa brevis, 14
Kolodin, Irving, 32, 65
Kondrashin, Kirill, 35
Koprowski, Hilary, 207
Korsman, Margreet, 37
Kraków, 212, 262
Kraus, Lili, 41, 71
Krehbiel, Edward, *Beethoven: The Man and the Artist, as Revealed in His Own Words* (ed.), 274
Kreisler, Fritz, 94
KREIZBERG, YAKOV, **239**, 254
Krips, Josef, 6, 11, 39
Kubelik, Rafael, 84
Kulenkampff, Georg, 241
Kunz, Erich, 13
Kurnick, Judith. *See* Karp, Judith
Kurtág, György, 248
KUSC, 252
Kuusisto, Ilkka, 246
Kwalwasser, Helen, 234, 265

La Grange, Henry-Louis de, 152–53
La Scala, Milan; First Composition Competition, 69
Lamers, Jacqueline, 37
Landowska, Wanda, 55
Laredo, Jaime, 144–45
Laretei, Käbi, 76
Lawrence, Harold, 76
Le Van, Eric, 237
Lebrecht, Norman, 189–90, 231
Ledbetter, Steven, 156
Lederhandler, Eric, 225
Leeuwarden, the Netherlands, 230
LEGGE, WALTER, 42, **43–44**, 47
Lehár, Franz; *The Merry Widow*, 43
Lehmann, Lotte, 76, 174
Leinsdorf, Erich, 193, 198–99; *The Composer's Advocate,* 199; Rolf de Henricis, 199
Leonhardt, Gustav, 26
LEPPER, FRANK, **16**, 23, 24
Levine, James, 113; Schubert Symphony No. 9, 87, 142–43
Levy, Daniel, 237
LEWIS, HARMON, 82, **263**
Liberty Fund, 243–45
Libman, Lillian, 121–22; *And Music at the Close*, 122
Lichtenstein, Roy, 242
Ligabue, Ilva, 87
Ligeti, György, 236, 248; Horn Trio, 213, 251
Limburg Symphony Orchestra, Maastricht, 162
Linz, Austria, 221; Linz Cathedral, 223
Liszt, Franz, 45, 82, 141, 186, 237, 276; piano concertos, 34

Little, Frank, 107–8
Little Orchestra Society, 70
Liverpool, 158; Royal Liverpool Philharmonic, 161–62
Lloyd, Jonathan, 148, 160; Brass Quintet, 160; Symphony No. 1, 160
Lloyd-Jones, David, 33
Lloyd-Jones, Hugh, 16, 70
Lock, Stephen, 15
Lodding, Henrik, 220
Loebel, Pierre, 249
Loevendie, Theo, *De Nachtegaal*, 215–17
Lombardo, Kathleen, 114
LOMBARDO, ROBERT, **113–14**; *The Dodo*, 114; *Erogenous Zongs*, 114; *Fourplay*, 114; *Songs to Kandinsky*, 114; Threnody, 88
London, George, 13, 270
London Mozart Players, 11, 16
London Philharmonic Orchestra, 2, 58, 222
London Sinfonietta, 74, 161
London Symphony Orchestra, 5, 35, 41, 71, 76, 104
Lorenz, Pare, *The Plow That Broke the Plains*, 215
Los Angeles Philharmonic, 94, 186
Lott, Felicity, 172
Ludwig, Christa, 270
Lutosławski, Witold, 169, 207, 231, 248
Luxembourg, 52, 163; Grand Theatre of Luxembourg, 270
Lyndon-Gee, Christopher, 201

Maastricht, 31
Maazel, Lorin, 165
Mac Donald, Heather, 268, 269
Mackerras, Charles, 40, 110–11, 142
MacLean, Sean, 253
Maclean, Susan, 270
MADGE, GEOFFREY, **226**, 231
Maggio Musicale, Florence, 165
Mahler, Gus, 116
Mahler, Gustav, 11, 28, 86, 87, 143, 152, 187, 221, 249; *Das Lied von der Erde*, 224–25; Symphony No. 1, 71, 113, 166, 206; Symphony No. 2, 43, 221, 223, 255; Symphony No. 5, 29; Symphony No. 6, 166; Symphony No. 7, 247; Symphony No. 8, 91; Symphony No. 9, 11, 160, 170, 209, 223; Symphony No. 10, 36, 121
Major, John, 96
Malashkin, Leonid, *Oh, could I but express in song*, 161
Manchester Guardian. See *Guardian*
Mangeot, André, 3, 8
Manhattan School of Music, 1, 176
Maniette, Bo, 172
Marchal, André, 50, 67
Marcus, Bella, 9, 37, 51–52. *See also* Masters, Bella
MARCUS, BERNARD, **8–9**, 22
Marivaux, Pierre de, *Le Jeu de l'amour et du hasard*, 23
Mark, Norman, 119–20
MARKEVITCH, IGOR, **148–51**; *Le Paradis perdu*, 201
Marlboro, Vermont, 73
Marsh, Robert, 83, 272
Martin, Frank, 26; *Monsieur de Pourceaugnac*, 56
Martinon, Jean, 78–79, 82–84, 111, 121; Cello Concerto, 84
Martinů, Bohuslav, 248
Marx, Karl, 175
Massenet, Jules, *Manon*, 12
Master of the Queen's Music, 130
Masters, Bella, 51–52, 167
Masters, Bill, 51–52
MASUR, KURT, **174–75**
Matačić, Lovro von, 43

Matthus, Siegfried, 176; *Holofernes*, 176; *Judith*, 176; *Die Weise von Liebe und Tod des Cornets Christoph Rilke* (*Cornet Christoph Rilke's Song of Love and Death*), 176, 198
Maw, Nicholas, 147, 160; *Odyssey*, 160
Maxwell Davies, Peter, 130, 164; *Miss Donnithorne's Maggot*, 177
McCulloch, Christopher, 22
McDomnic, Godfrey, 38
McFall, Gardner, 260
McMillan Theater, Columbia University, 195
Mebus, Joy, 230
Mechelen, Belgium, 226
MEECHAM, PAUL, **161**, 253
Meet the Composer program, 196–97
Mehta, Zarin, 64
Mehta, Zubin, 64, 93, 165–66
Meier, Waltraud, 173
Mendelssohn, Felix, 83, 186; incidental music to *Antigone,* 200–201, 274; "Italian" Symphony, 40, 56; Violin Concerto No. 2 in E Minor, 144
Mercury Records, 76
Merry, Eileen, 15
Mesko, Sarah, 196
Metters, Colin, 133
Messiaen, Olivier, 67; *Vingt regards sur l'enfant-Jésus*, 170; *Turangalîla-Symphonie*, 48
Metropolitan Opera, 40–41, 65–66, 151, 172
Metzger, Stan, 238
Metzmacher, Ingo, 215, 254
Mewton-Wood, Noel, 2
Meyer, Leonard B., 112
Miller, Jonathan, 106
Miller, Mina, 255
Milne, Hamish, 15
Milne, John, 15–16
Milton, John, 148; *Comus*, 7
Milva, 154
Milwaukee, Wisconsin, 111, 116–17; University of Wisconsin-Milwaukee, 155
Minnesota, 102, 190; Minnesota Orchestra, 71–72
Mirageas, Evans, 36–37
Mitze, Clark, 137
MOFFAT, JOHN, **18**, 19
Monge Moya, José, 151
Monte Carlo, 149
Monteux, Pierre, 29, 30
Monteverdi, Claudio, 74, 197; *L'incoronazione di Poppea*, 46; *L'Orfeo*, 180, 257; *Il ritorno d'Ulisse*, 257; Vespers of 1610, 258
Moore, Art, 211
Moore, Dennis, 5
Moore, Gareth, 244
Moore, Ronald, 5
MORAVEC, IVAN, 63, **102–3**, 158, 214, 251–53
Mordkovitch, Lydia, 220–21
Moreau, Annette, 112
Morini, Erica, 115
Morlot, Ludovic, 253–55
Morse, Gerry, 55
Morse, Senator Wayne, 100
Morwood, Janice, 211
Mostovoy, Marc, 238
Mozart, Wolfgang Amadé, 12, 15, 29, 41, 42, 45, 71, 87, 143, 148, 157, 201, 219, 221, 222–23, 228; chamber music, 203; concert arias, 30; Concerto for Two Pianos and Orchestra, 213; *Così fan tutte*, 141; *Don Giovanni*, 87, 141, 188, 267–69; horn concertos, 250–52; *Idomeneo*, 40; keyboard concertos, K. 107 (arr. from J. C. Bach sonatas), 211; *Eine kleine Nachtmusik*, 161; *Masonic Funeral Music*, 43; *Le nozze di*

Figaro, 28–29, 140–41, 157; Piano Concerto no. 9, K271, 220; Piano Concerto no. 17, K453, 6; Piano Concerto no. 20, K466, 41; Piano Concerto no. 23, K488, 12; Piano Concerto no. 25, K503, 93, 203, 214; piano concertos, 203, 276; Requiem, 188; *Serenata notturna*, 117; Sinfonia concertante, K364, 12; string quartets, 9; symphonies, 202; Symphony no. 35, "Haffner," 11; Symphony no. 39, 41, 87; Symphony no. 40, 30, 88; Symphony no. 41, "Jupiter," 99; Violin Concerto no. 3, K216, 240; Violin Concerto no. 4, K218, 6; *Die Zauberflöte*, 203
Muldowney, Dominic, 130
Mulholland, Lara, 137
Muller, Theo, 212, 221, 217
Murphy, John, 131
Music and Musicians, 46, 49
Music of Johannes Brahms, The, 75, 140
Music of Remembrance, 255
"Music Showcase," 61, 104
Musical Courier, 70
Musical Newsletter, 65
MusicWeb International, "Seen and Heard International," 237–38, 259, 265, 267
Musorgsky, Modest Petrovich, *Boris Godunov* edited by Rimsky-Korsakov, 46
Muswell Hill, London, 67, 94
Muti, Cristina, 180
MUTI, RICCARDO, 6, 75, 81, 91, 141, 147, **178–90**, 191, 193–94, 196–97, 202, 204, 208, 217, 221, 236, 240, 253
Mythos Festival, 206

National Endowment for the Arts, 117, 137, 178
National Gallery, London, 5
N'Diaye Rose, Doudou, 214
NEGRI, VITTORIO, **35–36**
Netherlands, the, 24; democratic principles, 216; Jewish cemetery, The Hague, 20; Monumentendag, 224; "Tall Poppy Syndrome," 216; The Hague, 20, 36, 46, 58, 122, 151, 152, 164, 198, 203, 212, 215, 218, 221–33, 254
Netherlands Chamber Orchestra, 30
Netherlands Opera, 28, 242, 257
Netherlands Radio Chamber Orchestra, 215
Netherlands Radio Philharmonic Orchestra, 215–17
New Statesman, 24, 50
New York, 1, 32, 33, 38, 40–42, 51–53, 56–57, 63, 65, 69, 70, 72, 76, 77, 78, 83, 104, 109, 115, 119, 152, 154, 157–58, 174, 185, 194; Avery Fisher Hall, 56; *City Journal*, 268–69; City Opera, 108; Mostly Mozart festival, 214; New York Clarion Orchestra, 108; New York Philharmonic, 57, 64, 75, 80, 104, 161, 165–66; *New York Post*, 70; *New York Times*, 73, 78, 81, 104, 122, 189–90; Rutgers Presbyterian Church, 60; State University of New York (SUNY) at Purchase, 117; Town Hall, 174
New York State Council on the Arts, 196
Newman, Danny, *Subscribe Now!*, 107
Newman, M. W., 123
Nézet-Séguin, Yannick, 265
Nicklin, Celia, 16
Nickrenz, Joanna, 60, 218
Nickrenz, Scott, 118
Niedersächsischer Singkreis, 61
Nielsen, Carl, 7, 153; Symphony No. 4, 255; Symphony No. 5, 153, 168

Nijmegen, the Netherlands, 162
Nikisch, Arthur, 94, 250
Nobbs, C. G., 3
Nordgren, Pehr Henrik: Violin Concerto, 153; string orchestra works, 153
Norfolk, East Anglia, 137, 139, 174; Norwich, 139
Norman, Jessye, 200, 253
North Holland Philharmonic Orchestra, 226–27
North Netherlands Orchestra, 230–31
Northwestern University, 92, 107, 113
Nuove Musiche, 225

Oakley, Horace, 17
objectivity versus subjectivity, 272–74
Oestreich, James R., 189, 247
Offenbach, Jacques, *Orpheus in the Underworld*, 1; *Tales of Hoffmann*, 65
OGDON, JOHN, 71, **170–71**
OHLSSON, GARRICK, **203**, 229, 255
Old Vic, 9
Olof, Victor, 44
Olympic Music Festival, Quilcene, 256–67, 261
"Once More with Feeling," 65
Opera Company of Boston, 122
Opera magazine, 65, 83, 262
Opera North, 33
Orchestre de la Suisse Romande, 56
Orkis, Lambert, 213
Ormandy, Eugene, 81, 182, 272
Oskamp, Gerard, 213
Ostrobothnian Chamber Orchestra, 154
Otten, Kees, 115–16
Overijssels Philharmonisch Orkest, the Netherlands, 202
Oxford, 12–13, 16–18, 20–24; Bach Choir, 17; University Film Society, 21; University Opera Club, 21; *Oxford Opinion,* 22; Playhouse, 21; Scala Cinema (later Phoenix Picturehouse), 22
Ozawa, Seiji, 58, 166

Pacific MusicWorks, 257–58
Paganini, Niccolò, 157
Palestrina, Giovanni Pierluigi da, 18
Palmer, Felicity, 224
PANUFNIK, ANDRZEJ, 148, **154–59**, 169, 212, 214, 226, 231, 248, 253, 262; *Arbor Cosmica,* 155, 157; *Autumn Music*, 155; Bassoon Concerto, 155; *Bogurodzica*, ballet by Gray Veredon, 156; Cello Concerto, 155, 212; Piano Concerto, 170–71, 231; *Sinfonia Concertante*, 154; *Sinfonia di Sfere*, 155; *Sinfonia Rustica*, 154; *Sinfonia Sacra*, 154, 156, 166; *Sinfonia Votiva*, 156, 166; String Quartet No. 2, 155; String Quartet No. 3, 155; String Sextet, *Trains of Thought*, 155; Symphony No. 9, 155; Symphony No. 10, 105, 155; *Universal Prayer*, 155; Violin Concerto, 154, 157
Panufnik, Camilla, 155–56, 158, 212, 246, 262
Panufnik, Jeremy, 158; *My Father, the Iron Curtain, and Me,* 158
Panufnik, Roxanna, 158; "Love Abide," 158
Paris, 23, 45, 50, 102, 119, 135, 141, 151, 152, 157, 170; Paris Opera, 23; Plaza Athénée, 152
Parsons, Arrand, 92
Passover Seder, 195, 262
Pasternack, Jonathan, 255
Pasternak, Boris, 22
Patzak, Julius, 253
PAUK, GYÖRGY, **86–87**
Paulus, Diane, 267–69

PEARLMAN, ALAN, **133–34**
Pears, David, 16, 23–24, 70
Pears, Peter, 15, 21, 30, 177
Pelican Record, 19
PELLEGRINI, NORMAN, **104–5**, 252
Penderecki, Krzysztof, 71–72, 231; *Saint Luke Passion*, 71–72; *Threnody for the Victims of Hiroshima*, 72, 84, 227
Pennario, Leonard, 44
Pennsylvania Opera Theater, 241–42
Periander of Corinth, 216
Peterson, Wayne, *The Face of the Night, The Heart of the Dark*, 111
Phaidon Press, 231–32
Philadelphia Chamber Music Society, 182, 243
Philadelphia Lyric Opera, 51
Philadelphia Orchestra, 51, 56–57, 81, 102, 154, 178, 179, 184, 187, 194–97, 199, 203, 204, 206–8, 239–41, 246, 247, 253, 256, 260, 263, 264–65; Composer Encounters, 197; Constitutional Commissions, 154, 190, 192–94, 197–98; Saratoga Springs, New York, 180, 198, 204–5
Philadelphia String Quartet, 256
Philharmonia Orchestra, 42, 43, 148, 178–79
Philharmonic Hall, New York. *See* New York, Avery Fisher Hall
philharmonie zuidnederland, 162
Philips Phonographic Industry, 24, 25; Vivaldi Edition, 35–36
Phoenix Picturehouse, 22
Picasso, Jacqueline, 150–51
Picasso, Pablo, *Faunes et flore*, 150
Pickstock, Frank, 130
Pilavachi, Costa, 36–37
Piston, Walter, Clarinet Concerto, 76
Plaistow, Stephen, 61
Platnick, Ken, 53
Poignant, Axel, 38
Polak, Wladimir, 211
Polish Renaissance, A, 231
Ponsford, Brian, 17, 18, 24
Pope, Alexander, *Universal Prayer*, 155
Popiełuszko, Jerzy, 155
Porter, Andrew, 180
Portugheis, Alberto, 169
Poulenc, Francis, 67; *Babar, the Little Elephant*, 120; *Dialogues des Carmélites*, 244; *Les Mamelles de Tirésias*, 65
Powell Symphony Hall, St. Louis, 116
PPE, 20
PPP, 18, 117
Prey, Hermann, 29–30
Private Eye, 101
Prokofiev, Sergey, 7, 149; Symphony No. 5, 202, 211
PROSERPI, PENNY, **203–4**
PROSERPI, SERGIO, **203–4**
Prosser, William, 19–20
Protti, Aldo, 52
Proust, Marcel, 206, 239
Puccini, Giacomo, arias, 240; *Tosca*, 51–52, 107; *Turandot*, 151
Pulitzer Prize for music, 1992, 111
pulse versus tempo, 85
Purcell, Henry, Trumpet Voluntary, 1
Putnam, Ashley, 172–73
Putsch, Henry, 137
Puyana, Rafael, 76

Queen Elizabeth Hall, London, 143
Quinn, Anthony, 186–87

Rabb, Bernard, 53, 142
Rabelais, François, 206
Rachmaninoff, Sergey, 252, 273–74; *The Bells*, 200; Symphony No. 2, 239
"Radiothons," 64
Ramey, Samuel, 188

Ramuz, Charles-Ferdinand, 54
Randall, Tony, 129
RANDS, BERNARD, **196–97**; *Madrigali*, 197; *Vincent*, 197
Ravel, Maurice, 11, 73, 93; *L'Enfant et les sortilèges*, 21; *Gaspard de la nuit*, 170; piano music, 11; *Rapsodie espagnole*, 231; *La Valse*, 231, 239
Ravinia Festival, 112–13
Ray, Satyajit, 22; *Pather Panchali*, 22
Rayment, Malcolm, 164
RCA Records, 76
Reading, Pennsylvania, 203–4
Reardon, John, 172
Records and Recording, 46, 48
Redgrave, Lynn, 72
Regazzo, Lorenzo, 141
Regietheater, 106, 267–69
Reich, Steve, 223
Reining, Maria, 10
Renes, Lawrence, 254
repeats in *da capo* minuets, 202
Residentie Orkest (Hague Philharmonic Orchestra), 36, 58, 152, 158, 203, 209, 210–25, 227–31, 254; Composer's Choice series, 212–13
Reuter, Rolf, 149
Revueltas, Silvestre, *Redes*, 57–58
Rhys, John Marlow, 13
Richards, Denby, 67
RICHTER, GASTON, **26–27**, 29, 162
Richter, Sviatoslav, 34–35, 45–46, 140
Rifkin, Joshua, 60; *The Baroque Beatles Book*, 60
Rilke, Rainer Maria, 198; *Die Weise von Liebe und Tod des Cornets Christoph Rilke*, 176, 198
Rimsky-Korsakov, Nikolay Andreyevich, *Antar*, 83; edited *Boris Godunov*, 46
Robbins Landon, H. C., 29, 69–70
Robinson, Tim, 13
Rodriguez, Santiago, 252
Rome, 154; Accademia Nazionale di Santa Cecilia, 176; Trastevere, 154; vacation, 235
Ronish, Marty, 258
Roosevelt University, Chicago Musical College (CMC), 64, 80, 100–104
Rorem, Ned, *Songs of Love and the Rain*, 114
Rosbaud, Hans, 29
Rosenblum, Frank, 100
Rosenthal, Harold, 66
Ross, Glynn, 259
Rosseter, Philip, *What then is love but mourning*, 15
Rossini, Gioachino, 186, 222; *The Barber of Seville*, 106; *Guglielmo Tell*, 185, 186, 194, 240; *L'italiana in Algeri*, 242, 260; *La pietra del paragone*, 108; *Sins of Old Age*, 186; Sonata No. 6 in D Major for strings, 185
Rostropovich, Mstislav, 34, 93, 212
Roth, Philip, 101; *Letting Go*, 101
Rothenberger, Anneliese, 38
Rottenberg, Dan, 237
Rotterdam, 29, 87, 172–73, 230; Rotterdam Philharmonic Orchestra, 122, 152
Rouse, Christopher, *Phaethon*, 193
Rowicki, Witold, 184
Royal Air Force, 12–14
Royal Albert Hall, 7, 10–11, 49, 156, 178, 218, 246
Royal Conservatory, The Hague, 254
Royal Festival Hall, 11–13, 39, 41, 42–43, 49, 72, 91, 129, 165, 179, 223
Royal National Theatre, London, 130
Royal Opera House, Covent Garden, London, 7, 10, 90, 173, 180, 190
Royko, Mike, 120–21; *Boss*, 120–21
Rozhdestvensky, Gennady, 129–30

Rubenstein, Bernard, 113
Rubin, Becca, 102
Rubinstein, Arthur, 122
Ruders, Poul, 153
Rudolf, Max, 32, 72, 202
Rudolfinum, Prague, 166
Russell, Bertrand, 41–42, 83
Russian Tea Room, 32
Rzączyński, Krzysztof, 158–59

Saba, Geoffrey, 177
Sacks, Chief Rabbi Jonathan, 205
Sacks, Jared, 227
Sacks, Oliver, 22, 167; Samuel Sacks, father, 167*; Uncle Tungsten*, 167
Sadie, Stanley, 67–68
Sadler's Wells Opera, 9, 40
Sadler's Wells Theatre, 74
Said, Edward, 96
Saint Paul Chamber Orchestra, 102, 178, 190
Saks, Toby, 255–56
Salisbury, 13–16; Cathedral, 14, 15
Salisbury Musical Society, 14
Salonen, Esa-Pekka, 172, 201; *Insomnia*, 240
Salzman, Eric, 78, 104; *Nude Paper Sermon*, *The*, 78, 104
San José Symphony, 201
San Juan, Puerto Rico, 98–99; Hotel El Convento, 98
Sanderling, Kurt, 175, 237
Santa Fe Opera, New Mexico, 176, 244
Sanzogno, Nino, 69
São Paulo Symphony, 166
Saratoga Performing Arts Center, 180, 198, 204
Sargent, Sir Malcolm, 10, 49
Saron, Alex, 35
Saturday Review, 32, 54, 65
Savannah, Georgia, 129
Sawallisch, Wolfgang, 186, 201, 208–9, 240–41; Beethoven Symphony no. 9, 208–9; Brahms Symphony no. 1, 208; Brahms Symphony no. 4, 241; as pianist, 241
Saxton, Robert, 148
Scharwenka, Xaver, 205
Schat, Peter, 223
Scheer, Gene, 255
Schepkin, Sergey, 237
Scherman, Thomas, 70
Schickele, Peter, Bach, P.D.Q., 59
Schiller, Friedrich, *Nänie*, 109
Schindler, Anton, 274
Schlitz, Joseph, Brewing Company, 116
Schloezer, Boris de, 149–50
Schmidt, Franz, Symphony no. 4, 223
Schmidt-Isserstedt, Hans, 11
Schmidt, Ole, 168
Schnabel, Artur, 2, 273
Schneider, Alexander, 99
Schneiderhan, Wolfgang, 11
Schoenbach, Sol, 246
Schoenberg, Arnold, 114, 147; Five Pieces for Orchestra, 113; *Ode to Napoleon Buonaparte*, 60–61, 118, 163, 218, 238–39; *Stil und Gedanke* (*Style and Idea*), 174–75; *Verklärte Nacht*, Milwaukee premiere, 117
Schoenberg Quartet, 209
Schöffler, Paul, 13
Schonberg, Harold C., 104, 107
Schubert, Franz, 9, 12, 83, 102, 222, 255; *An die Musik*, 76; *Erlkönig*, 234, 243; Lieder, 18, 105, 159, 234; *Nacht und Träume*, 21; Octet, 213; *Schwanengesang*, 110; Sonata in A Major, D. 664, 45; Sonata in G Major, D. 894, 109, 140; Sonata in B-flat Major, D. 960, 110, 238; *Die Sterne*, 21; String Quartet in G Major, D. 887, 50;

Schubert, Franz—*(continued)* Symphony no. 5, 36, 85; Symphony no. 6, 58; Symphony no. 9, "Great C Major," 6, 11, 12, 39, 87, 89, 112, 180, 223; "Trout" Quintet, 113; "Wanderer" Fantasy, 45–46; *Winterreise*, 241
Schuller, Gunther, 193, 213; Octet, 213
Schumann, Robert, 186; *Kreisleriana,* 15; Lieder, 18; Overture, Scherzo, and Finale, 213; Symphony no. 4, 178
SCHWARZ, GERARD, 157–58, 183, 214, 232, **247–50**, 250, 253–55
Schwarz, Jody, 250
Schwarz, Julian, 250
Schwarzkopf, Elisabeth, 28–29, 43
Schwertsik, Kurt, 163, 223
Schwiller, Isidore, 10
Schwiller, Ralph, 10
Sciutti, Graziella, 29
Scofield, Paul, 72
SCOTT, CHRISTOPHER, **128–29**
Scott, Howard, 57
Seattle, 82, 158, 163, 204, 238, 246, 247, 256, 257, 258; Benaroya Hall, 254; Illsley Ball Nordstrom Recital Hall, 254; Marion Oliver McCaw Hall, 259; Meany Hall, 255; Moore Theatre, 257; S. Mark Taper Foundation Auditorium, 254; St. James Cathedral, 258; *Seattle Times*, 259
Seattle Chamber Music Society, 255–56
Seattle Opera, 258–61; International Wagner Competition, 259; Young Artists Program, 261
Seattle Symphony, 158, 161, 232, 239, 247–54, 255
Seefried, Irmgard, 11
Segerstam, Leif, 153
SELL, STEPHEN, 102, 147, 178–80, **190–91**
Sellers, Peter, 171
"Seraphim Guide to Renaissance Music," 116–17
SEREBRIER, JOSÉ, **57–59**, 143
Serkin, Rudolf, 73
Shacklock, Constance, 10
Shakespeare, William, 5; *Coriolanus*, 9; *Hamlet*, 9; *King John*, 9; *Macbeth*, 13–14; *Othello*, 6
Shankar, Ravi, 28, 79, 117
SHAPEY, RALPH, **111**, 113, 192; *Concerto Fantastique*, 111; Pulitzer Prize for Music, 1992, 111; *Symphonie Concertante*, 193–95
Shapirra, Elyakum, 19
Shaw, George Bernard, 121, 243, 272
Shelton, Lucy, 195
Shenk, Mary Nic, 33
Sheppard, Craig, 255
Sherman, Russell, 114; Beethoven piano sonatas, 273–77; *Piano Pieces*, 237
Shicoff, Neil, 188–89
Shifrin, Seymour, 111
Shipway, Frank, 166, 226
Shirley-Quirk, John, 4, 177
Shore, Bernard, 5; *Sixteen Symphonies*, 5
Shostakovich, Dmitri, 28, 147, 220, 249; Symphonies nos. 2 and 3, 83; Symphony no. 6, 239, 254; Symphony no. 8, 89; Symphony no. 9, 110–11; Symphony no. 10, 254; Symphony no. 11, 232, 249–50, 255; Symphony no. 14, 89; violin concertos, 220
Sibelius, Jean, 42, 143; *Luonnotar*, 182; songs, 182; Symphony no. 2, 51, 226; Symphony no. 5, 201; Violin Concerto, 226
Sills, Beverly, 32
Silver, Alan, 63
Simensen, Björn, 171–72, 246

Simon, Geoffrey, 133
Simoneau, Léopold, 13
Simpson, John, 4
Simpson, Robert; String Quartets Nos. 4, 5, and 6, 213–14; String Quartet No. 9, 97
Skrowaczewski, Stanisław, 71–72
Smith, Lloyd, 186
Smith, Malcolm, 163
Smith, Patrick, 65; *The Tenth Muse*, 65
Smith, Peter, 186
Smith, William, 183, 192–93
Socratic Club, 22
Soika, Egon, 76
Solari, Luis Alberto, 98–99
Solomon. *See* Cutner, Solomon
Solomon, Seymour, 76
SOLTI, GEORG, 79, 82, **85–87**, 88, 91–92, 93, 105, 115, 116, 222; Brahms Symphony no. 2, 86; magnanimity, 88
Solti, Lady, 86, 92
Solzhenitsyn, Aleksandr, 238; *Gulag Archipelago*, 239
SOLZHENITSYN, IGOR, **238–39**, 254; Schoenberg *Ode to Napoleon Buonaparte*, 238–39; Schubert Piano Sonata in B-flat Major, D. 960, 239
Sophocles, *Antigone*, 6; *Women of Trachis, 14*
Sorkin, Leonard, 205
South Place concerts, 9
Southern Arts Association, 125–38
Southern Methodist University, Dallas, 174, 192
Souzay, Gérard, 23, 34
Sparberg, Marshall, 156
Sperry, Paul, 74
Spock, Dr. Benjamin, 100
Spoon River country, 119
SPRUYT, GUIDO, **225–27**
St. Louis Symphony, 116, 224
St. Magnus International Festival, 164
Staalen, Marien van, 152
Staatskapelle Weimar, 149
Stambul, Diana. *See* Burgwyn, Diana
Standing Conference of Regional Arts Associations (SCRAA), 135–37
Starker, János, 85, 232
State University of New York (SUNY) at Purchase, 117
Steichen, Edward, 72–73; *Family of Man*, 72
Steinberg, Michael, 75, 245
Stereo Review, 15, 62–63, 236
STERNBERG, JONATHAN, **233–34**
STERNBERG, URSULA, **233–34**
Sterne, Teresa (Tracy), 59, 61–62
Steuermann, Eduard, 114
Still, Ray, 84
Still, Robert, 272
Stockhausen, Karlheinz, 39, 98
Stockholm, 90, 171; Konserthuset, 170; Stallmästaregården, 171
Stockholm Philharmonic Orchestra, 169–70
STOKMAN, ABRAHAM, **114–15**
Stokowski, Leopold, 51, 56, 57–58, 117, 200
Stout, Alan, 113
Straus, Volker, 162
Strauss, Johann II; *Die Fledermaus*, 9, 260–61; overture to *Der Zigeunerbaron*, 231
Strauss, Richard, 147, 166, 222, 253; *Alpine Symphony*, 166; *Also sprach Zarathustra*, 165; *Arabella*, 66, 172–73; *Ariadne auf Naxos*, 263; *Elektra*, 260; *Ein Heldenleben*, 11, 166; Lieder, 18; *Metamorphosen*, 227; *München*, 231; Piano Quartet, 241; *Der Rosenkavalier*, 10, 39; *Salome*, 49; *Tod und Verklärung*, 45
Stradivarius, 94

Stravinsky, Igor, 41–42, 54, 74, 116, 122, 143, 147, 159, 183, 258; *Firebird* Suite, 39; *The Flood*, 218, 246; *L'Histoire du soldat*, 54, 183, 215, 260; *Oedipus Rex*, 201; *Orpheus*, 180, 213; *The Rake's Progress*, 75; *Requiem Canticles*, 70–71; *Le Sacre du printemps* (*The Rite of Spring*), 97; Symphony in Three Movements, 165
Strehler, Giorgio, 188; "La camera dei sortilegi," 188
Streich, Rita, 13
String, Amadeus, 68
STUBBS, STEPHEN, **257–58**
Stucky, Steven, Concerto for Orchestra, 193
Studer, Cheryl, 188–89
Studio Players, 13–14
Stulen, Jan, 162
Stumpf, Peter, 186
subdivision of the beat, 85
subjectivity versus objectivity, 272
Susskind, Janis, 154, 161
Susskind, Walter, 1, 154
Svejda, Jim, 252–53
Svetlanov, Yevgeny, 219–20
Swift, Nancy, 76
Syntagma Musicum, 115–16
Szabó, Krisztina, 269
Szell, George, 95, 273–74; Brahms and Beethoven violin sonatas, 241
Szymanowski, Karol, 223; Violin Concerto No. 1, 184

Tagore, Rabindranath, *The Kingdom of Cards*, 28
"Talk a Walk," 55
"Tall Poppy Syndrome," 216
Tammivuori, Lauri, 151
Tammivuori, Tuuli, 182
Tantivy Press, London, 141
Taormina, Dino, 265
Tchaikovsky, Pyotr Il'yich: Piano Concerto no. 1, 71; Symphony no. 2, 80; Symphony no. 4, 2; Symphony no. 5, 95; Symphony no. 6, *Pathétique*, 2, 94; Violin Concerto, 220
Te Kanawa, Kiri, 173
Tear, Robert, 246
Tebaldi, Renata, 51
Temple University, Philadelphia, 192, 234; Cinematheque, 207
tempo versus pulse, 85
Theodore Presser Company, 198, 245
Thiollier, François-Joël, 93
Third Viennese School, 223
Thomas, Augusta Read, 229
Thompson, Robert, 155
Thomson, Virgil, 215; *The Plow That Broke the Plains*, 215
Thorne, Nicholas, 154; *Revelations*, 193
Thrasybulus of Miletus, 216
Thulean, Donald, 204
time, subjectivity of, 95
Times, London, 4, 26, 46, 66, 68, 72, 178, 248, 272
TIPPETT, MICHAEL, 11, 116, **129**, 156; Concerto for Double String Orchestra, 11; Piano Concerto, 201; Symphony no. 1, 129–30; Symphony no. 2, 129; Symphony no. 4, 105
Todorovich, Zoran, 270
Toller, Ernst, 134
Toscanini, Arturo, 6, 95
Tovey, Sir Donald, *Studies in Musical Analysis*, 89, 113
Tree, Michael, 118
Treigle, Norman, 32
Tretyakov, Viktor, 175
Trollope, Anthony, 205
Troup, Malcolm, 70
Troyanos, Tatiana, 75–76

Tubin, Eduard, Balalaika Concerto, 169
Turin, Italy, 221–22
Türk, Daniel Gottlob, *Klavierschule,* 202
Turner, J. M. W., 236
Twickenham, 155, 212
Tyler, Marilyn, 29

Unger, Petra, 214
United States Constitution, 191
Universal Edition (UE), 147
University of Illinois, Champaign-Urbana, 118; Experimental Music Studio, 118; "Musicircus," 118
University of Pennsylvania, 192
University of Rochester, 192
University of Washington, Seattle, 255, 256
Uribe, Blanca, 213, 220, 277
Utrecht, Vredenburg, 144

Vachey, Henri, 152
van Altena, Marius, 116
van den Akker, Bert, 218, 223, 225
van der Lugt, Marijke, 49
van Dijk, Rudi Martinus, 227–28; Four Epigrams for orchestra, 227–28; Piano Concerto, 228, 231
van Emde Boas, Carli, 25, 76, 210
van Gogh, Vincent, 197
Van Mechelen, Werner, 270
van Regteren Altena, Quirijn, 211
van Steen, Jac, 228, 229
van Stralen, Esther, 211
Vancouver, BC, 262
Vanguard Records, 76, 108
Varga, Bálint András, 164
Vaughan Williams, Ralph, 10, 71, 253; *A London Symphony,* 6; Mass in G Minor, 18; music for string orchestra, 38; *A Sea Symphony,* 17; Symphony no. 5, 165; Symphony no. 6, 227–28; Tuba Concerto, 83
Veenstra, Piet, 227–28
Veng, Per Erik, 168
Verberne, Ton, 230
Verdi, Giuseppe, 74, 90, 142, 222; arias, 240; *Attila*, 188–89; *Falstaff*, 106–7, 122, 261; *La forza del destino*, 190, 240; *Nabucco*, 195; Requiem, 17; *Rigoletto*, 241; *La traviata*, 121, 165; *Il trovatore*, 245
Veredon, Gray, 156, 242–43; *Bogurodzica*, 156
Vermeer Quartet, 118
Vernon, Timothy, 263
Vickers, Jon, 270
Victoria, BC, 82–83; Pacific Opera Victoria, 262–63
Vienna, 23, 76, 79, 199; Konzerthaus, 163; Sofiensaal, 91; Vienna Philharmonic, 89, 166
Vinton, John, ed., *Dictionary of Contemporary Music*, 119
Virgil, *Georgics*, 5
Vishnevskaya, Galina, 34
Voketaitis, Arnold, 108
Vonk, Hans, 193, 219
Vos, Joris, 122–23
Vos, Willem, 122

Wadsworth, Stephen, 259, 260
Wagner, Richard, 95, 259; International Wagner Competition, 259; *Parsifal*, 95, 269–71; *Der Ring des Nibelungen*, 259; *Die Walküre*, 52, 173
Wakin, Daniel J., 189, 247
WALDEN, STANLEY, **197**; *After Auschwitz*, 197; *Invisible Cities*, 193, 197; *Three Gretchen Songs*, 197
Waldteufel, Émile, *Les Patineurs*, 130
Walker, Alan, 46; *Frédéric Chopin* (*The Chopin Companion*), 182
Walker, Sarah, 74

War and Peace, 150
Walter, Bruno, 43, 208–9
Walthamstow, 34; Town Hall, *35*
Walton, Sir William, *Façade*, 260
Ward, David, 52
Warner, Derek, 14
Washington, DC, 53, 159; Library of Congress, 122–23
Watts, Harriett, 163
Weber, Ludwig, 10
Wedeen, Harvey, 234, 265
Weingartner, Felix, 94, 212, 250
Weir, Judith, 130
Weiss, Sidney, 94
Weissenberg, Alexis, 76, 170
Welcomat, 237
Wellington, Duke of, 128, 129
WELSER-MÖST, FRANZ, 6, **221–23**; married to Angelika, 221
WERNICK, BEATRICE, **191**, 206, 235
WERNICK, RICHARD, **191–96**, 196–97, 206, 213, 235; *Ball of Sun*, 195; "Memorials and Celebrations," 196; Piano Concerto, 213; *A Song for Phil*, 196; String Quartet no. 4, 213; *Two for Jan*, 195–96
Werthman, Monroe ("Jeff"), 177
Wesker, Arnold, 66, 167
West, Philip, 196
West-Eastern Divan, 96
Western Illinois University, Macomb, 119
Westrup, Professor Sir Jack, 21
WFMT, Chicago, 37, 61, 104–5, 111
Wheaton College, 122
When this day's earth is ended, 19
Wigmore Hall, 13, 28, 82, 116, 166, 170
Willis, Thomas, 83, 84
Wilson, Conrad, 25
WILSON, RICHARD, **148**, 213, 220; Piano Concerto, 213
Wilson-Johnson, David, 246
Wilton, Roger, 13
Winchester, Hampshire, 125, 134–35, 143; Old Chesil Rectory, 135; Wessex Hotel, 127; Winchester Cathedral, 134; Winchester College, 134; Winchester School of Art, 135
Wistar Institute, Philadelphia, 207
Witters, Eddy, 162
Wolf, Hugo, Lieder, 18
women in no. 2 jobs, 135–36, 151
Woods, Simon, 253
Wordsworth, William, Symphonies no. 2 and no. 3, 49–50
Wozzeck, 107
WQXR, New York, 61
Wray, John, 3–5
Wymondham, Norfolk, 139–40; Wymondham Abbey, 140
Wyttenbach, Jürg, 217

XENAKIS, IANNIS, **119**, 226; *Eonta*, 226; Équipe de Mathématique et Automatique Musicales (EMAMu), 119

Yakar, Rachel, 173
Yakima, Washington, 260; Yakima Symphony Orchestra, 260
Yale University, 100, 133
Yanovitsky, Mikhail, 238–39
Yerres, France, 137

Zacharias, Christian, 102
Zalsman, Pim, 24
Zancanaro, Giorgio, 188–89
Zelzer, Harry, 109, 111
Ziegler, Anne, 1
Zimerman, Krystian, 229
Zinman, David, 30
Zitterbart, Gerrit, 210–11
Zollman, Ronald, 133
Zukerman, Pinchas, 96
Zupko, Ramon, 97
Zwetnow, Nikolaus, 168–69

Star Turns and Cameo Appearances is the entertaining and insightful memoir by veteran music critic Bernard Jacobson. Its pages are populated by eminent composers ranging from Hans Werner Henze to Andrzej Panufnik and by renowned performers, including Georg Solti, Daniel Barenboim, Sviatoslav Richter, and Jessye Norman.

As a music critic and orchestra administrator, Jacobson has had the opportunity to observe these outstanding musicians and many of their colleagues at close quarters. Assisting Riccardo Muti at the Philadelphia Orchestra for eight years, he saw sides of that maestro not visible to the music-loving public. Throughout *Star Turns and Cameo Performances*, Jacobson adds his own sensitive and sympathetic view to public perceptions of musical luminaries of yesterday and today, helping to explain and illuminate their artistry.

Bernard Jacobson has worked in the music field for over fifty years, including stints as recording executive, music critic of the *Chicago Daily News*, artistic director and adviser for international orchestras in Holland, and visiting professor at Roosevelt University's Chicago Musical College. He has also performed and recorded as narrator of concert works and opera.

"I have admired and continue to admire the great musical culture of Bernard Jacobson, whom I have known since my time in Philadelphia in the 1980s. His deep understanding of the world of the arts and his wit and elegant writing make *Star Turns* particularly interesting and charming."

—Riccardo Muti, conductor, music director,
Chicago Symphony Orchestra

"Bernard Jacobson's remarkable memoir is a musical journey from the perspective of a writer, music critic, music publisher, and a man who has been intimately involved with the classical music world. His extraordinary life's work, knowledge, and integrity have been a great inspiration to me, and this beautifully written memoir now affords others a window into his lifelong devotion to and love of music on the deepest level."

—Gerard Schwarz, conductor and composer

"An extraordinarily vivid and intriguing glimpse of the humans inside the classical music giants of the last fifty years—an invaluable and rare account from a man who's heard it all."

—Roxanna Panufnik, composer

"Bernard Jacobson delights in telling us of his life with music and musicians. His rich trove of anecdotes will amuse, enlighten, and entertain any reader fascinated by the art and business of classical music."

—Garrick Ohlsson, pianist

"Bernard Jacobson has been one of the most illuminating writers about classical music over the past decades, a critical intelligence to reckon with—the sort of critic (all too rare) with whom performers can engage in fruitful dialogue. His memoirs of a life in music are fascinating stuff."

—Ian Bostridge, tenor

"A fascinating look at the life of this distinguished writer. I was especially touched by Jacobson's description of his youthful enthusiasms, and all the great stories about legendary figures of music in England."

—Emanuel Ax, pianist

"A fascinating tour through the classical music world from the 1960s to today. Jacobson has worked with and has stories to tell about most of the major and minor figures of music in England and America of the last fifty years. His analysis of Riccardo Muti as a man, a conductor, and a leader is worth the whole book. It's an involving book, and I feel privileged to have read it."

—Speight Jenkins, general director, 1983–2014, Seattle Opera

"Bernard Jacobson has given us a stylish memoir of his love affair with music and the legends who fueled it: Curzon, Britten, Haitink, Muti. . . . Boldly opinionated and impeccably witty, this beautifully written opus is a valuable memento of recent cultural history."

—Ignat Solzhenitsyn, pianist and conductor